Southern Labor in Transition, 1940–1995

Southern
Labor in
Transition,
1940–1995
EDITED BY
ROBERT H. ZIEGER
The University of
Tennessee Press
Knoxville

 Manufactured in the United States of America. First Edition.

The paper in this book meets the minimum requirements of the American National Standard for Permanence of Paper for Printed Library Materials. ♾ The binding materials have been chosen for strength and durability. ♻ Printed on recycled paper.

Library of Congress Cataloging-in-Publication Data

Southern labor in transition, 1940–1995 / edited by Robert H. Zieger. — 1st ed.
p. cm.
Includes bibliographical references and index.
ISBN 0-87049-990-4 (cloth: alk. paper)
1. Labor—Southern States—History—20th century. 2. Trade unions—Southern States—History—20th century. 3. Southern States—Race relations. 4. Southern States—Economic conditions—1945- I. Zieger, Robert H.
HD8083.S9S664 1997
331.1'0975'09045—dc21 97-21057

To the memory of my late colleague and friend, George Pozzetta, and to Sandy, Adrienne, and Jim Pozzetta

Contents

Preface

Southern Labor in Transition, 1940–1995, is intended as a complement to an earlier volume, *Organized Labor in the Twentieth-Century South.* Reviewers of that book were generous in assessing its contributions, and their responses reinforced my belief that the history of labor in the South is an unusually rich and rewarding subject. Even the most positive critics, however, rightly pointed to certain gaps in coverage and to certain limitations of focus. Thus, the current book is intended as a companion volume that addresses some of the topics omitted in the first book, responds to ongoing developments in historical discourse, and deepens readers' acquaintance with a particularly intriguing and valuable stream of scholarship.

As was the case with the earlier collection, no preset agenda has driven the compilation of this one. An appreciation of diversity and a desire to bring forward the best work available, regardless of political, historiographical, or methodological stance, guided the editor's quest for contributions. We have been fortunate to recruit distinguished senior scholars in the field of labor history, veteran historians venturing newly into that field, and younger scholars sharing the fruits of their innovative research.

• • •

It is a pleasure to acknowledge those whose help has been instrumental in the production of this book. Gary Fink and Tom Terrill provided insightful critiques of the introduction, as did Patrick Reagan and the University of Tennessee Press's other, unnamed, reader. The guidance and encouragement of Meredith Morris-Babb were crucial. Paige Porter-Brown of the University of Florida's Department of History office provided wise counsel and cool reassurance in all matters relating to word processing, particularly complex in a book of this kind. And, as always, Gay Pitman Zieger gave freely of her generous but always rigorous advice, as well as of her equally generous and always validating friendship.

This book is dedicated to the memory of my late colleague, George E. Pozzetta, who died unexpectedly during the beginning stage of this project. George Pozzetta was a distinguished historian of immigrant life in America and made important contributions to southern labor history in the course of his writings on this theme. His book, co-authored with Gary Mormino, *The Immigrant World of Ybor City,* is one of the finest extant depictions of the lives of working people.

George also was one of the most generous and decent people Gay and I have known. Hardly a day goes by that we do not recall fondly his friendship, good humor, and sweetness of spirit. To the extent that *Southern Labor in Transition* manages to convey sound scholarship, humane concern, and fair-minded discourse, it will be a proper tribute to an admirable man.

Robert H. Zieger
Gainesville, Florida
July 16, 1996

Introduction: Is Southern Labor History Exceptional?

Robert H. Zieger

Implicit in any volume with a regional focus is the theme of ex-ceptionalism. Debates over exceptionalism have been a staple of southern historiography, so the questions naturally arise: Has the recent history of labor in the South been "exceptional"? If so, in what ways? If not, why produce a book entitled *Southern Labor in Transition?*[1]

But the very concept of "exceptionalism," be it American or southern, has taken a beating among historians of late. And rightly so. To be "exceptional" implies divergence from some privileged norm. Participants in a recent labor history conference focusing on the theme of American exceptionalism and class formation almost universally rejected the exceptionalist construct in favor of the theme of distinctiveness as a way of characterizing the contours of labor and social history in the United States. Neville Kirk spoke for many when he discounted the claim that the U.S. stood alone among industrial countries, arguing convincingly that the development of its labor and socialist movements forms a continuum of which all Western societies were parts.[2]

But perhaps the South *is* an exception to the anti-exceptionalist paradigm. It is obvious that many southern statistical, historical, and experiential indicators have departed from the "American" norm. At the same time, however, the more closely I look at the story of workers and unions in the South, the more I am reminded of parallel—or at least similar—developments elsewhere. Moreover, as my immersion in "southern" life, both as a resident and as a historian, has deepened, the more diverse and complex "the South" has seemed. The key challenges have become trying to understand the diverse dynamics of "the South" and juxtaposing what I learn about "the South" with the experiences and patterns in other parts of the country and in the U.S. generally.

The issue of race provides an excellent example of the interplay of themes of distinctiveness and convergence. Clearly, until at least the 1970s, the South differed from the rest of the country in its legal regulation of race relations and in informal and attitudinal aspects of race. Thus, in 1935 a Pulp Workers organizer, seeking to establish a local in a North Carolina mill, reported to his New York–based president that the white workers insisted upon creating a separate local for the handful of black employees. "To you and I," observed George Brooks, "this is one hell of a condition but," he mused, in the South, "the question of color is about as strong . . . as it was at the close of the Civil War." More progressive unionists from northern locales were less tolerant of white southerners' prejudices, but in the classic days of union growth in the 1930s and 1940s, few failed to remark upon the distinctive role race placed in labor relations south of the Mason-Dixon Line.[3]

But even during the period of darkest segregation and repression, the South exhibited diverse patterns of racial interaction, albeit within certain rigid confines. The Mississippi that Neil McMillen so ably describes in *Dark Journey* differed sharply from the North Carolina found in William Chafe's *Civilities and Civil Rights*. Moreover, not all southern workplaces were created equal. To be sure, the region's largest employer, the textile industry, was rigidly segregated through most of the twentieth century. But mining, longshoring, food processing, and transport were not. *Subordination* was ubiquitous, but *segregation* was situational.[4]

Growing awareness of the details of the racial order that prevailed in the South has encouraged investigation of the degree of overlap between "southern" and "northern" racial regimes. True, even now African Americans comprise a greater proportion of the population of the southern states than they do elsewhere. It is also true that, in the former Confederate states, legal segregation barred blacks from significant occupational opportunities with unique relentlessness and ubiquity. But evidence mounts that elsewhere white workers accomplished the same end through less formal but equally effective means. Examining the fierce racial antagonisms that shaped working-class politics in postwar Detroit, for example, Thomas Sugrue declares: "Urban antiliberalism had deep roots in a simmering politics of race and neighborhood defensiveness that divided northern cities well before [George] Wallace began his first speaking tours in the snowbelt." Work by Eric Arnesen, Michael Honey, Bruce Nelson, David Roediger, Michael Goldfield, Kevin Boyle, David Halle, Herbert Hill, and others points to the powerful role race has played in shaping white workers' consciousness and the policies of the unions which they controlled, regardless of sectional concerns.[5]

Resistance to unionization provides another angle of vision on southern distinctiveness. We used to think that the South was exceptional in that it fell outside the New Deal dispensation. In other parts of the country, at least in the core industries, employers accepted strong unions and helped forge a "modern" system of industrial governance. However, the tide of unionism in the New Deal era only lapped at the edges of the southern economy. Industrial modernization, it was expected, inevitably would modernize industrial relations, even in the laggard South. Surveying the Piedmont textile mills in the late 1940s, sociologist John Morland noted the passing of the old order and declared, "It appears safe to say that unionization of Southern textile plants will eventually supplant the prevailing paternalistic system."[6]

As late as 1985, economist and former U.S. Secretary of Labor Ray Marshall compared unionization rates in North and South and concluded that a rapidly modernizing southern economy provided reason for measured optimism with respect to the advance of unionism. Historically, Marshall argued, it was the distinctive patterns of the southern economy, with its high degree of decentralization and its reliance upon agricultural, processing, and extractive industries—difficult to organize anywhere—that primarily explained low rates of southern union participation. "Union growth in the South [has historically been and] will [continue to] be determined primarily by the changing patterns of industry," he believed. Expansion of manufacturing into high value–added commodities would permit the South to follow the national pattern of growing union density as a high-wage, consumer-fueled economy steadily encroached on the South.[7]

Presumably, the "northernization" of the South also would spur political liberalization. Union growth would help to liberate blacks and would encourage white workers to embrace the class interests that generated organized labor's engagement with the Democratic party. As V. O. Key declared in his seminal 1950 study of southern politics, union growth and industrial expansion paved the way for "a significant expansion of labor influence," which he expected "to become formidable."

While most labor organizers and liberal sympathizers in the immediate postwar period urged northern-based unions to go slowly and to avoid inflammatory attacks on segregation and racial injustice, they shared a faith that unionization, class-based biracial political action, and "de-southernization" of the South would go hand in hand.[8]

Of course, none of these expectations has been realized. By the 1980s, it is true, union density in the South had increased in comparison with the rest of the country, but this growth reflected a drastic decline in membership in states such as Michigan and Ohio, and not a great surge in southern membership. Increasingly, international competition, the decline of Fordist methods of production, and weakening governmental protections for organization-seeking workers eroded union strength in the rest of the country. The U.S. industrial relations regime of the mid-1990s more closely resembles the historic southern model of weak unions, intense wage competition, and official indifference or hostility toward worker organization. As I observed in *Organized Labor in the Twentieth-Century South,* "more and more [U.S.] employers embrace the [union-resisting] tactics pioneered by [southern] textile manufacturers." Once thought "exceptional" by virtue of its seemingly atavistic resistance to modern unionism and its commitment to low-wage policies, southern industry "has not been the laggard in the realm of industrial relations. It has been on the cutting edge."[9]

Southern electoral politics likewise seem increasingly normative. In Michigan, Ohio, California, and other northern states that once were union-oriented, white workers are joining their southern counterparts in providing the basis for Republican success.[10] Particularly as whites perceive the Democratic party as the vehicle for the grievances of victims of social, gender, and ethnic injustice, coded appeals to racial fears and resentments are restructuring the erstwhile congressional conservative coalition into a mass-based political and electoral movement. Opposition to affirmative action, gun control, and flag burning brings a commonality to the white working-class political *mentalité,* regardless of regional affiliation. A fitting emblem for post–New Deal working-class politics in America is the ubiquitous display of the stars and bars in huge trucks bearing Ohio and Pennsylvania plates, while the transregional appeal of country-and-western music supplies any number of plausible anthems to celebrate white male definitions of civic culture.[11]

But, as many of the essays in these two volumes indicate, the narrative of southern workers is not a unilinear one. As documented in virtually every industry and in every twentieth-century generation, southern workers, like their counterparts elsewhere, have struggled to find a collective voice. It is true that public authorities and business elites in the South often have been unusually resistant and that racial tensions often have impeded union growth more overtly there. And it is certainly true that, at any given point in the century, levels of organization in southern states have lagged well behind those in the East, Middle West, and Far West (though not, typically, in the Plains states).

Still, recent scholarship bulges with evidence of southern labor struggles. If white southern workers—in common with many white workers elsewhere—often have been lamentably parochial in their understanding of the racial and gender components of class membership, they certainly have compiled a rich record of activism. Charles Martin's observations about the experience of industrial workers in Gadsden, Alabama, in the New Deal era here seem pertinent. An industrial town with important steel, textile, and rubber factories, Gadsden experienced an unusually violent and turbulent period as workers struggled to form effective unions. Racially divided and only weakly supported by the National Labor Relations Board, these southern workers did trail their northern counterparts. Even so, they eventually succeeded. "These southern workers were neither passive nor indifferent," remarks Martin. Not so militant as some northern workers and less prone to breaking the rules, these Alabama workers nonetheless fell well "within the broad parameters of the American labor experience in general" and illustrate "the grass-roots desire for genuine worker organizations" below the Mason-Dixon Line.[12]

The rise of public employee unionism after 1960 likewise illustrates the themes of southern distinctiveness and convergence. On the one hand, southern state and municipal workers clearly have participated in the great expansion of unionism among public workers. Certain episodes in the history of public employee unionism in the South in fact are bellwether events of this phenomenon. The struggles of Memphis's sanitation workers, Florida educators' conduct of the first statewide teachers' strike, the epic Charleston hospital workers' strike in 1969, and the Duke hospital employees' battle for union recognition are among the signal events in the surge of unionization among state and local government (and other not-for-profit) workers. Yet rates of union participation and collective bargaining coverage among southern public workers fall well behind national averages and often trail those of even "right-to-work" Plains states, to say nothing of New York, California, and Michigan. On the other hand, public employees in Florida and Alabama have organized and bargained at near northern-state levels.[13]

What, then, becomes of southern distinctiveness as applied to labor history? On the one hand, "southern" policies and patterns have become the apparent national norm. On the other hand, the degree of unionization in the South remains dramatically lower than in other parts of the country.[14] Is there an anti-union southern essence? Or are southern patterns the products of historical and circumstantial forces?[15]

Such questions take on additional meaning as a beleaguered U.S. labor movement looks southward to attempt to stage a comeback. Newly elected AFL-CIO President John Sweeney, whose Service Employees International Union (SEIU) has enjoyed some success in Dixie, has proposed a "Sunbelt Organizing Fund" to channel resources into southern organizing. Declares one southern union activist, under the new regime "labor in the South is finally going to receive the resources, the programs, the strategy, the planning, to wage successful organizing campaigns." Atlanta labor reporter Richard Greer writes of "changes that could transform the face of the South and the nation." On the other hand, in the past, grandiose plans to bring the union banner to Dixie never have come to fruition.[16]

Of course, historians are not prognosticators. We study the past for its own sake, while hoping that our investigations perhaps also may provide some help in confronting the present and future. The historians writing on southern labor history in these two volumes have avoided the "exceptionalism" trap. Their work contributes rather to an understanding of the diversity of the working-class experience in the southern states. Taken together, the work in these two books can serve as a warning against hasty generalization about labor in the South. Nonetheless, these essays do, at least implicitly, raise the theme of southern distinctiveness and thus invite their readers to join the authors in the ongoing task of connecting southern experience to the experience of workers and worker-related institutions in other parts of the country.

Southern Labor in Transition, 1940–1995, features contributions dealing with areas neglected in the predecessor volume. Thus, Cindy Hahamovitch's examination of agricultural workers and Rick Halpern's essay on Louisiana sugar refinery workers focus attention on workers in sectors crucial to the southern economy yet absent from the earlier volume. Essays on sanitation workers, teachers, and fire fighters, by Michael Honey, James Sullivan, and Mark Wilkens, respectively, highlight public employee unionism, a major national postwar development in which the South has played a critical, and sometimes leading, role.

Other areas absent from the earlier book, notably air transport, pulp and paper, and aircraft, are considered in work by Alex Lichtenstein, Bruce Kaufman, and Jacob Vander Meulen. While the current volume contains no general treatment of gender issues comparable to Mary Frederickson's insightful survey in the earlier book,[17] the work by Sullivan, Wilkens, and James Hodges explores recent episodes in southern labor history rich in implications for gender analysis. The work by Hahamovitch, Sullivan, and Kaufman draws attention to a theme especially significant for the South: organizations among workers outside the realm of the "bona fide" labor movement.

In this volume, no less than in its predecessor, the theme of race looms large. Essays by Joe Trotter, Judith Stein, Rick Halpern, and Michael Honey[18] made significant contributions to the understanding of interactions among class, race, and unionism in the modern South. In the current work, race-class dynamics likewise are featured, although here new venues are added and additional issues examined. Extending the geographical and sector-based coverage of southern racial dynamics are essays on the struggles of migrant black agricultural workers in Florida to gain at least a modicum of control over their working lives and on the efforts of black sugar workers in Louisiana to create progressive biracial unions. Michael Honey returns to Memphis, this time to suggest the legacy of the developments he charted in his earlier contribution and to place the tragic murder of Dr. King squarely in the context of the national race-class matrix. Mark Wilkens and Bruce Nelson explore the tensions that black workers experienced in their white-led unions in two sharply different venues, the fire stations of Tampa and an Atlanta steel mill. Illuminating still another aspect of racial labor engagement, Alex Lichtenstein introduces readers to the distinctive world of postwar Miami, with its booming air transport industry, its multiethnic labor force, and its fascinating juxtaposition of radicalism and arrant red-baiting.

No collection dealing with labor in the modern South could ignore the textile industry. As in the earlier volume,[19] this work features two essays, but here both pieces focus on representations of textile workers. Thus, James Hodges illuminates the "Norma Rae" phenomenon, probing the realities behind the "Hollywoodization" of a classic recent episode in southern labor's struggles. Robert H. Zieger traces the ways in which several generations of commentators, apologists, activists, and other observers have created formulaic templates into which they have attempted to fit the South's mill workers.

Nor is the theme of labor and politics ignored. In the earlier volume, shrewd contributions by Gilbert Gall and Robert J. Norrell[20] examined the political *mentalité* of the southern working class and the complex interaction between white workers and segregation-resisting politicians. In the current volume, Patrick J. Maney brings to light still another dimension of southern labor politics. His suggestive study of the significant role that organized labor played in the career of Hale Boggs, the New Orleans congressman, adds importantly to our understanding of southern influence in national politics in the postwar period.

The aim, then, is to illuminate diverse areas of southern life after 1940. The book's premise, like that of its predecessor volume, is that "organized labor has played an integral role in the history of the twentieth-century South," although a broader definition of "organized" widens the focus of this later book. The hope of bringing something of the richness and diversity of southern workers' experience to the attention of historians, students, labor relations professionals, union activists, and general readers is its motivating force. Perhaps the greatest contribution of these two volumes is the vivid reminder that "the South" is a various place in which, historically, many diverse possibilities have existed.

Notes

Tom Terrill and Gary Fink provided useful commentary on an earlier draft of this introduction.

1. A thoughtful recent treatment of the theme of southern exceptionalism is Larry J. Griffin and Don H. Doyle, eds., *The South as an American Problem* (Athens: Univ. of Georgia Press, 1995). Although this book contains no separate essay on labor in the South, the papers by Larry J. Griffin ("Why Was the South an American Problem?," 10–32), David L. Carlton ("How American Is the American South?" 33–56), Hugh Davis Graham ("Since 1965: The South and Civil Rights," 145–63), Robert A. Margo ("The South as an Economic Problem: Fact or Fiction?," 164–80), and John Egerton ("The End of the South as an American Problem," 259–74) are particularly pertinent to the current book. The extensive citations in these papers provide an up-to-

date guide to the voluminous literature on southern exceptionalism\distinctiveness. Dewey Grantham, *The South in Modern America: A Region at Odds* (New York: Harper Collins, 1994), 259–334, reflects on these themes as well.

2. Neville Kirk, "The Limits of Liberalism: Working-Class Formation in Britain and the USA," in *American Exceptionalism? U.S. Working-Class Formation in an International Context,* ed. Rick Halpern and Jonathan Morris (Basingstoke, England: Macmillan, forthcoming 1997). See also Eric Foner, "Why Is There No Socialism in the United States?," *History Workshop* 17 (Spring 1984): 57–80; Kent Worcester, "Reflections on the 'European Model,'" *Trade Union Politics: American Unions and Economic Change, 1960s–1990s,* ed. Glenn Perusek and Kent Worcester (Atlantic Highlands, N.J.: Humanities Press, 1995), 209–33; Aristide A. Zolberg, "The Roots of American Exceptionalism," *Why Is There No Socialism in the United States?/Pourquoi n'y a-t-il pas de socialisme aux Etats-Unis?* ed. Jean Heffer and Jeanine Rovet (Paris: Editions de L'Ecole des Hautes Etudes en Sciences Sociales, 1988), 101–18; Sean Wilentz, "Against Exceptionalism: Class Consciousness and the American Labor Movement, 1790–1920," *International Labor and Working-Class History* 26 (Fall 1984): 1–24; Nick Salvatore, "Response to Sean Wilentz, 'Against Exceptionalism: Class Consciousness and the American Labor Movement, 1790–1920,'" *International Labor and Working-Class History* 26 (Fall 1984): 25–30; Michael Hanagan, "Response to Sean Wilentz, 'Against Exceptionalism: Class Consciousness and the American Labor Movement, 1790–1920,'" *International Labor and Working-Class History* 26 (Fall 1984): 31–36; Michael Kazin, "A People Not a Class: Rethinking the Political Language of the Modern U.S. Labor Movement," in *Reshaping the U.S. Left: Popular Struggles in the 1980s* [vol. 3 of *The Year Left*], ed. Mike Davis and Michael Sprinker (London, N.Y.: Verso, 1988), 257–86; and Roy J. Adams, *Industrial Relations under Liberal Democracy: North American in Comparative Perspective* (Columbia: Univ. of South Carolina Press, 1995), ch. 3 ("American Exceptionalism," 34–62).

3. Quoted in Robert H. Zieger, *Rebuilding the Pulp and Paper Workers' Union, 1933–1941* (Knoxville: Univ. of Tennessee Press, 1984), 114. See, e.g., Robert Korstad and Nelson Lichtenstein, "Opportunities Found and Lost: Labor, Radicals, and the Early Civil Rights Movement," *Journal of American History* 75, no. 3 (Dec. 1988): 786–811; Larry J. Griffin and Robert R. Korstad, "Class as Race and Gender: Making and Breaking a Labor Union in the Jim Crow South," *Social Science History* 19, no. 4 (Winter 1995): 425–54; Bruce Nelson, "Organized Labor and the Struggle for Black Equality in Mobile during World War II," *Journal of American History* 80, no. 3 (Dec. 1993): 952–88; Bruce Nelson, "Class and Race in the Crescent City: The ILWU, from San Francisco to New Orleans," in *The CIO's Left-Led Unions,* ed. Steven Rosswurm (New Brunswick, N.J.: Rutgers Univ. Press, 1992), 19–46, 210–16; and Michael K. Honey, *Southern Labor and Black Civil Rights: Organizing Memphis Workers* (Urbana: Univ. of Illinois Press, 1993).

4. Neil McMillen, *Dark Journey: Black Mississippians in the Age of Jim Crow* (Urbana: Univ. of Illinois Press, 1989); William H. Chafe, *Civilities and Civil*

Rights: Greensboro, North Carolina, and the Black Struggle for Freedom (New York: Oxford Univ. Press, 1980), 3–41; David Colburn, "Introduction," *The African-American Heritage of Florida,* ed. David R. Colburn and Jane L. Landers (Gainesville: Univ. Press of Florida, 1995), 1–17, along with Maxine Jones, "No Longer Denied: Black Women in Florida, 1920–1950," 240–74; and Raymond Mohl, "The Pattern of Race Relations in Miami Since the 1920s," 326–65, in the same volume. See also Richard P. Young and Jerome S. Burstein, "Federalism and the Demise of Prescriptive Racism in the United States," *Studies in American Political Development* 9 (Spring 1995): 1–54, on differences between the Upper and the Deep South; and Robin D. G. Kelley, "'We Are Not What We Seem': Rethinking Working-Class Opposition in the Jim Crow South," *Journal of American History* 80, no. 1 (June 1993): 75–112, on patterns of black resistance.

On labor, in addition to the works cited in note 3, see Daniel Letwin, "Interracial Unionism, Gender, and 'Social Equality' in the Alabama Coalfields, 1878–1908," *Journal of Southern History* 61, no. 3 (Aug. 1995): 519–54; Eric Arnesen, "'Like Banquo's Ghost, It Will Not Down': The Race Question and the American Railroad Brotherhoods, 1880–1920," *American Historical Review* 99, no. 5 (Dec. 1994): 1601–33; Eric Arnesen, "To Rule or Ruin: New Orleans Dock Workers' Struggle for Control, 1902–1903," *Labor History* 28, no. 2 (Spring 1987): 139–66; Mary Frederickson, "Four Decades of Change: Black Workers in Southern Textiles, 1941–1981," in *Workers' Struggles, Past and Present: A "Radical America" Reader,* ed. James Green (Philadelphia: Temple Univ. Press, 1983), 62–82; and Robin D. G. Kelley, *Hammer and Hoe: Alabama Communists during the Great Depression* (Chapel Hill: Univ. of North Carolina Press, 1990).

5. Thomas J. Sugrue, "Crabgrass-Roots Politics: Race, Rights, and the Reaction against Liberalism in the Urban North, 1940–1964," *Journal of American History* 82, no. 2 (Sept. 1995): 551–78. The now-standard work on race consciousness among the white working class is David Roediger, *The Wages of Whiteness: Race and the Making of the American Working Class* (London: Verso Books, 1991). See also Arnesen, "'Like Banquo's Ghost, It Will Not Down'"; Michael Honey, "The Labor Movement and Racism in the South: A Historical Overview," in *Racism and the Denial of Human Rights: Beyond Ethnicity,* ed. Marvin J. Berlowitz and Ronald S. Edari (Minneapolis: MEP Press, 1984), 77–96; Michael Honey, "Labour Leadership and Civil Rights in the South: A Case Study of the CIO in Memphis, 1935–1955," *Studies in History and Politics* 5 (1986): 97–120; Michael Goldfield, "Race and the CIO: The Possibilities for Racial Egalitarianism During the 1930s and 1940s," *International Labor and Working Class History* 44 (Fall 1993): 1–32; Kevin Boyle, "'There Are No Union Sorrows That the Union Can't Heal': The Struggle for Racial Equality in the United Automobile Workers, 1940–1960," *Labor History* 36, no. 1 (Winter 1995): 5–23; Herbert Hill, "Race, Ethnicity and Organized Labor: The Opposition to Affirmative Action," *New Politics* 1, no. 2, New Series (Winter 1987): 31–82; Herbert Hill, "The Problem of Race in American Labor History," *Reviews in American History* 24, no. 2 (June 1996): 189–208; Nelson, "Organized Labor and the Struggle for Black Equality in Mobile";

and David Halle, *America's Working Man: Work, Home, and Politics among Blue-Collar Property Owners* (Chicago: Univ. of Chicago Press, 1984; paperback ed., 1987), 26–31, 189–90, 247–49, 212–14, 227–27.

6. John Kenneth Morland, *Millways of Kent* (Chapel Hill: Univ. of North Carolina Press, 1958), 258.
7. Ray Marshall, "Southern Unions: History and Prospects," in *Perspectives on the American South: An Annual Review of Society, Politics and Culture,* ed. James C. Cobb and Charles R. Wilson (New York: Gordon and Breach Science Publishers, 1985), 3:163–78.
8. Robert H. Zieger, *The CIO, 1935–1955* (Chapel Hill: Univ. of North Carolina Press, 1995), 227–41, esp. 231–32; V. O. Key, Jr., with the assistance of Alexander Heard, *Southern Politics in State and Nation* (New York: Knopf, 1949), 673–74; Numan V. Bartley, *The New South, 1945–1980* (Baton Rouge: Louisiana State Univ. Press, 1995), 38–73.
9. Robert H. Zieger, "Textile Workers and Historians," in *Organized Labor in the Twentieth-Century South,* ed. Robert H. Zieger (Knoxville: Univ. of Tennessee Press, 1991), 52, 53. See also Mary Lethert Wingerd, "Rethinking Paternalism: Power and Parochialism in a Southern Mill Village," *Journal of American History* 83, no. 3 (Dec. 1996): 874n. 7.
10. David Halle and Frank Romo, "The Blue-Collar Working Class: Change and Continuity," in *America at Century's End,* ed. Alan Wolfe (Berkeley: Univ. of California Press, 1991), 152–84. While noting the heavy inroads among northern workers by the GOP, Halle and Romo stress *nonvoting* on the part of putatively Democratic workers as a key factor in Republican success. On the general theme of the "southernization" of U.S. politics, see Michael Lind, "The Southern Coup: The South, the GOP and America," *New Republic,* June 19, 1995, 20ff.; and Alan Draper, "The Long Shadow of the American South," 1996, unpublished paper in collection of Robert Zieger, cited with the author's permission.
11. For a thoughtful exploration of these themes, see James N. Gregory, "Southernizing the American Working Class: Postwar Episodes of Regional and Class Transformation," *Labor History* (forthcoming, 1997); and Kenneth Durr, "When Southern Politics Came North: The Roots of White Working-Class Conservatism in Baltimore, 1940–1964," *Labor History* 37, no. 3 (Summer 1996): 309–31.
12. Charles H. Martin, "Southern Labor Relations in Transition: Gadsden, Alabama, 1930–1943," *Journal of Southern History* 47, no. 4 (Nov. 1981): 545–68. See also Daniel Nelson, "The Rubber Workers' Southern Strategy: Labor Organizing in the New Deal South, 1933–1943," *The Historian* 46, no. 3 (May 1984): 319–38. On the textile industry, see Zieger, "Textile Workers and Historians"; and Zieger, "From Primordial Folk to Redundant Workers: Southern Textile Workers and Social Observers, 1920–1990," n. 1, in this volume, as well as the essays by Bess Beatty, David L. Carlton, Gary B. Freeze, Bryant Simon, and James Hodges in part 1 (that part is called "Southern Textiles: Toward a New Historiographical Synthesis") of Gary M. Fink and Merl E. Reed, eds., *Race, Class, and Community in Southern Labor History* (Tuscaloosa: Univ. of Alabama

Press, 1994), 3–64. Other recent notable work in 20th-century labor history stressing the high degree of worker activism in the South includes Honey, *Southern Labor and Black Civil Rights*; Eric Arnesen, *Waterfront Workers of New Orleans: Race, Class, and Politics, 1863–1923* (New York: Oxford Univ. Press, 1991); Henry M. McKiven, Jr., *Iron and Steel: Class, Race, and Community in Birmingham, Alabama, 1875–1920* (Chapel Hill: Univ. of North Carolina Press, 1995); Emilio Zamora, *The World of the Mexican Worker in Texas* (College Station: Texas A&M Univ. Press, 1993); Letwin, "Interracial Unionism, Gender, and 'Social Equality'"; Kelley, "We Are Not What We Seem"; Nelson, "Class and Race in the Crescent City"; Gary R. Mormino and George E. Pozzetta, "The Reader Lights the Candle: Cuban and Florida Cigar Workers' Oral Tradition," *Labor's Heritage* 5, no. 1 (Spring 1993): 4–27. A perspective that reminds historians of the limits of militancy and of the crucial role of federal intervention in building southern unionism is found in Alan Draper, "The New Southern Labor History Revisited: The Success of the Mine, Mill and Smelter Workers Union in Birmingham, 1934–1938," *Journal of Southern History* 62, no. 1 (Feb. 1996): 87–108.

13. See the essays by Michael Honey and James Sullivan in this volume, as well as Leon Fink and Brian Greenberg, *Upheaval in the Quiet Zone: A History of Hospital Workers' Union, Local 1199* (Urbana: Univ. of Illinois Press, 1989), 129–58; and Karen Sacks, *Caring by the Hour: Women, Work, and Organizing at Duke Medical Center* (Urbana: Univ. of Illinois Press, 1988). Current figures on union membership by state are found in Barry C. Hirsch and David A. Macpherson, *Union Membership and Earnings Data Book 1994: Compilation from the Current Population Survey* (Washington: Bureau of National Affairs, 1995).
14. Steven Greenhouse, "New York Again the Most Unionized State," *New York Times,* Oct. 22, 1995; Richard Greer, "Insurgent AFL-CIO Candidates Propose Big Organizing Drive, Especially in South," *Atlanta Journal,* June 29, 1995.
15. See, e.g., the debate between historian Michael Honey and veteran labor intellectual Solomon Barkin. "'Operation Dixie': Two Views," *Labor History* 31, no. 3 (Summer 1990): 373–85, presents contrasting reviews of Barbara S. Griffith, *The Crisis of American Labor: Operation Dixie and the Defeat of the CIO* (Philadelphia: Temple Univ. Press, 1988), by Honey (373–78) and Barkin (378–85). See also Gilbert J. Gall, "Southern Industrial Workers and Anti-Union Sentiment: Arkansas and Florida in 1944," in Zieger, *Organized Labor in the Twentieth-Century South,* 223–49.
16. Greer, "Insurgent AFL-CIO Candidates."
17. Mary E. Frederickson, "Heroines and Girl Strikers: Gender Issues and Organized Labor in the Twentieth-Century American South," in Zieger, *Organized Labor in the Twentieth-Century South,* 84–112.
18. Joe W. Trotter, Jr., "Class and Racial Inequality: The Southern West Virginia Black Coal Miners' Response, 1915–1932," in Zieger, *Organized Labor in the Twentieth-Century South,* 60–83; Judith Stein, "Southern Workers in National Unions: Birmingham Steelworkers, 1936–1951," in Zieger, *Organized Labor in the Twentieth-Century South,* 183–222; Rick Halpern, "Interracial Unionism in the Southwest: Fort Worth's Packinghouse Workers, 1937–1954," in

Zieger, *Organized Labor in the Twentieth-Century South,* 158–82; Michael Honey, "Industrial Unionism and Racial Justice in Memphis," in Zieger, *Organized Labor in the Twentieth-Century South,* 135–57.

19. Gary M. Fink, "Efficiency and Control: Labor Espionage in Southern Textiles," in Zieger, *Organized Labor in the Twentieth-Century South,* 13–34; Robert H. Zieger, "Textile Workers and Historians," in Zieger, *Organized Labor in the Twentieth-Century South,* 35–59.
20. Gall, "Southern Industrial Workers and Anti-Union Sentiment," in Zieger, *Organized Labor in the Twentieth-Century South,* 223–49; Robert J. Norrell, "Labor Trouble: George Wallace and Union Politics in Alabama," in Zieger, *Organized Labor in the Twentieth-Century South,* 250–72.

Standing Idly By: "Organized" Farmworkers in South Florida during the Depression and World War II

Cindy Hahamovitch

If "organized labor" were defined as trade union activity, the story of organizing among African-American migrant workers would be short indeed. They would appear to be the most powerless and marginalized of American workers. Denied the right of collective bargaining, disfranchised by both race and residency requirements, ignored by all but the most philanthropic labor unions, Atlantic Coast migrants would seem to epitomize the unorganized, if not the disorganized.[1] Certainly the experience of black farm laborers in South Florida during the Great Depression bears out such a characterization. Yet migrant farmworkers have power that industrial workers would envy: not only can they hurt a growers' profits by withholding their labor, but they can ruin a year's investment in a matter of days. The Second World War gave farmworkers the opportunity to wield this power. To farmers, the war brought the prospect of boom prices and the specter of spiraling wages. To farmworkers, it brought federal migrant labor camps, home bases to which they could retreat while they waited for crops to ripen and wages to rise. A tight labor market and guaranteed food and housing allowed black fieldworkers in South Florida to act militantly, bargain collectively, and organize successfully, without a union, a strike fund, a picket line, or a pamphlet.

Farmworkers living in Florida's migrant camps raised their wages, but in doing so they raised Leviathan. Accustomed to workers disciplined by the starvation wages of the Depression years, growers were outraged to find black workers uncooperative and organized. They demanded the importation of foreign workers who could be deported for refusing to work, and their demands were heeded. In 1945 alone, the War Food Administration put 178,000 importees and POWs to work in the nation's fields, while domestic migrants remained frozen in their home counties, denied the right to leave without the permission of county officials.

Thus the story told here can be broken down into three discrete phases. In the 1930s, a "factories in the fields" condition prevailed, as South Florida's truck farmers drove down farm wages by enlisting a reserve army of unemployed and displaced people. The construction of federal migrant labor camps beginning in 1940 inaugurated what might be called the "settlement house" stage. New Deal reformers designed these labor camps both to provide shelter and to convey to the nation's most down-and-out people the virtues of stability, thrift, and self-discipline. This stage ended in 1942, when growers demanded federal relief from what they called labor shortages, insisting in particular on their right to import foreign workers. The third stage we might call "the militarization of agriculture," as federal officials recruited, imported, housed, and moved a new reserve army of foreign workers. In doing so, they destroyed the embryonic organizing effort achieved during the "settlement house" stage.

Federal officials weighed in on growers' side after 1942 because southern farm employers claimed that labor scarcity was widespread and would prevent them from meeting war production goals. However, the question of whether a shortage of labor existed was inherently political. Florida's truck farmers were accustomed to an abundance of farmworkers; to growers, this abundance and the low wages it guaranteed seemed normal, natural, and necessary. Any change in the supply or price of labor could only be a change for the worse. Thus the growers defined as a dearth of labor any circumstance in which farmworkers were powerful enough to make demands upon employers.

Farmworkers, too, had a great deal riding on the price of picking a hamper of beans. As some black southerners joined the military or migrated north or west in search of higher pay and greater opportunities, those who remained behind depended upon rising wartime wages to help them do battle with Jim Crow and pull themselves out of the mire of the Depression. Higher wages for fieldwork meant that black families might be able to keep their children in school and out of the fields; black women might escape the drudgery of cooking and cleaning for white women; black men might enjoy the luxury of choosing one job over another.

Thus the struggle over labor supply during the war came to represent everything that farmworkers hoped for and growers feared. Farmworkers lost this contest, but the story of their defeat defies simple notions of migrants' powerlessness and passivity, challenging us to rethink the meaning of organized labor.

By the 1920s, vegetables, or "truck crops," as they were called, were Florida's most valuable products, despite the greater renown of the state's citrus fruit.[2] Land speculators made fortunes by buying newly drained tracts from the state for two dollars an acre and reselling them for ten times as much to distant buyers, many of whom did not know if they were getting arable land or alligator-ridden swamp. In 1926, a devastating hurricane flattened Miami and burst the land bubble, but a hardy few remained and prospered by putting their money in beans and sugarcane. Although the rest of the nation sank into the depths of the Depression in the 1930s, South Florida's truck-farming industry boomed, and the value of green beans, the state's principal crop, continued to climb.

What made South Florida's agriculture unique in the 1930s was that both its farmers and its labor force often were migrants. While Central Florida's citrus orchards required years of patient tending before the fruit would bring a return, the brevity of the growing season for vegetables attracted suitcase farmers, who would rent land from absentee owners or large operators and gamble on quick returns from a bean crop, much as the nation's rich were gambling at South Florida's race tracks. J. D. Abbin, a self-proclaimed "Florida cracker," smuggled bootlegged liquor and illegal Asian immigrants and then worked at a Ford plant near Detroit before trying his hand at truck farming in Lee City, Florida. In 1936, he heard there was "big money raisin truck," so he went "down there an rented me a piece-a land an putt in a crop uv tomatoers an beans." In a few short months, he had made "a killin. Cleaned up $2,000 cash money."[3]

By the time J. D. Abbin was gambling on truck crops in Lee City, the vegetable growers of South Florida were largely divided into two groups: very substantial operators, who cut costs by doing their own packing and marketing; and tenants, who planted a crop on borrowed land, sold it to a packer, took the money, and moved on.[4] The small landowners in between were gradually squeezed out by the costs of draining, irrigating, and fertilizing land that flooded when wet and caught fire when dry.[5] Both large-scale growers and small-scale tenant farmers, however, were dependent on migrant farmworkers for harvest and packing labor. Neither had much incentive to form personal relationships with such transient employees, because the season was too short, the workforce too large, and the pressure to cut labor costs too great. Since growers hired by the day and paid by the crate or hamper, it mattered little to them how many farmworkers labored in their fields. "[If the tenant farmer] has a thousand hampers of beans to pick," a federal investigator noted in 1939, "he'd as soon that they be picked by two hundred workers as a hundred." The important thing was to get the matured beans picked "as quickly as possible and without regard for a full day's work for a specific number of laborers."[6]

Indeed, South Florida truck farming paid as well as it did in the 1930s because more and more poor people entered the state as the Depression wore on, driving the price of labor down. As Depression prices forced southeastern farmers to take millions of acres out of cotton production and as the boll weevil ate its way through neighboring Georgia, debt-ridden sharecroppers headed for South Florida's "Bean Deal," where there was work in winter and cash wages for day labor, however long the day and low the wage. Jacob McMillan, a white sharecropper from Georgia, came to Florida from Georgia "like a lot of them. I went broke, everything went to the bottom and I had to get away."[7] By the end of the decade, perhaps forty to sixty thousand entered the state annually in search of farm work, half crowding into Belle Glade and the nearby towns that hugged the south shore of Lake Okeechobee, while the other half fanned out into smaller truck farming communities along the Atlantic and Gulf coasts of the state.

Like other white migrants, McMillan found work in a packing house. Black migrants had a virtual monopoly on stoop labor in the fields.[8] The influx drove wages down until they were "the sorriest" in the country, according to one veteran of harvests in thirty-three states.[9] So many people migrated to Florida seeking work and warmth in the 1930s that the state police set up a border patrol along the main highways, turning back "undesirables" who might flood relief rolls, while taking care not to offend tourists "in better automobiles."[10]

The press of unemployed and displaced sharecroppers into Florida meant that black fieldworkers competed for backbreaking stoop labor and the most primitive housing. In Belle Glade, where thousands of black workers gathered before dawn to board the trucks that would take them to the fields, the only guarantee of a day's work was to hurry onto one of the idling vehicles before they all filled up and pulled away. On some mornings, when the weight of the men and women packed upright in a truck was so great that the flatbed pressed down on the wheels and kept them from turning, the local police would oblige the driver by circling the vehicle and beating off workers who clung to the hood and boards, until the wheels could turn and the truck could pull out onto the fields.[11]

The same workers competed for places in Belle Glade's crowded flophouses and rented shacks. As one observer noted, they slept "packed together in sordid rooms, hallways, tar-paper shacks, filthy barracks with one central faucet and toilet, sheds, lean-tos, old garages, condemned and shaky buildings."[12] The development of the vegetable industry had so outstripped the pace of housing construction that one truck farmer remarked that, when he arrived in Belle Glade in 1936, "colored people were paying 25 cents a night to sleep on a truck body, just an ordinary stake truck with bean bags on the platform and a tarpaulin over it, simply because there was no place for them to live."[13]

Farther south, farmworkers would live in housing provided by growers, but this meant they were less able to choose among employers; they worked for the farmer whose shack they occupied. When Mary Jenkins left Georgia for South Florida in 1935, she hoped for more excitement and independence than her parents' cotton farm could afford her. Arriving at Butts Farm in Broward County, however, she found nothing but a sea of beans, a thousand other poor black people like her, and a long row of pickers' shacks. It was the worst she "had ever seen," but with fifty cents to her name, there was no going back until the end of the season.[14] "We just got to live in the house where they people let you stay," Mrs. Johnnie Belle Taylor told a congressional committee in 1940. "Some have to sleep in cars and some few of them have a little tent along with them. . . . We just have to take it as we find it. . . . We just put up with most anyway, just to [be] working, trying to live."[15]

Local relief agencies were little help during the Depression, as residency requirements excluded most farmworkers from receiving aid. "These people have learned not to ask us for anything," one county employee said of black pickers in Belle Glade. Later in the decade, surplus commodities from the federal government became available, but state and county relief officials allotted them in such a way that they provided a subsidy to growers. When farm employers feared large outmigrations of workers due to freezes or floods, for example, they could bring workers to the local relief office and "certify" their need. Once harvests began, relief agencies up and down the Florida coast would cut African Americans off the rolls, because, according to officials, they "wouldn't work as long as they could get relief." Thus federal relief, as doled out on the local level, benefited growers as much as it did pickers.[16]

New Deal relief measures began on a massive scale in 1933 but made no immediate difference in the lives of migrant farmworkers. In 1933, the Federal Emergency Relief Administration (FERA) set up a Federal Transient Program but explicitly excluded migrant farmworkers from its provisions, ostensibly so as not to subsidize industries "that existed and benefited in some degree because of the cheap labor supply furnished by migratory-casual workers." FERA was for "bona fide transients," not migrant farmworkers.[17]

Likewise, although the National Industrial Recovery Act (NIRA), enacted in June 1933, did not explicitly exclude agricultural labor when it granted workers collective-bargaining rights, three weeks later Franklin Delano Roosevelt cut out farmworkers by presidential decree. Cannery and packinghouse workers, who were usually white, were deemed industrial workers with collective-bargaining rights, but field workers, who were far more likely to be people of color, were not.[18]

Despite their exclusion, or perhaps not knowing that they had been left out of the NIRA, farmworkers around the nation launched a wave of strikes the following summer, to which growers in many places responded with massive force. While Central Florida's more sedentary citrus workers joined this organizational wave, bringing the membership of the newly formed United Citrus Workers to a peak of thirty thousand members by the end of 1933, black workers in the vegetable region remained unorganized. Passage of the Wagner Act in 1935 did nothing to improve their organizational prospects, as agricultural workers were excluded, this time explicitly, from its provisions.[19]

Over the next few years, Florida's black farmworkers struggled among themselves for the best picking, the fairest growers, the least brutal row bosses. Then, in the winter of 1936–37, when growers slashed the piece rate for beans from 25 to 15 cents a hamper, thousands of bean pickers refused to board the trucks at Belle Glade's loading area. "We been living up and down the East coast for years," one worker explained, and this "is the first time we have ever seen beans down to 15 cents. We go out and make maybe 30–40 cents a day, and again we might make $1.50 if we had real good picking. . . . We wouldn't go to the fields at the low prices."

The outcome of this conflict starkly revealed the risks of an illegal strike in a glutted labor market, where the employers were far better organized than their workers. While growers in New Jersey and California countered farmworkers' harvest strikes by waging small wars with armed thugs, tear gas, and guns, South Florida's truck farmers had only to open the floodgates to the Southeast's displaced sharecroppers and unemployed. After four days without labor, the growers got the bean pickers to return to the fields by promising to raise the hamper rate to 20 cents. Meanwhile, they alerted the state's border patrol to their "labor shortage." The border patrol settled the issue by flooding the area with labor, simply by "letting Negro hitch hikers through." Once there were enough destitute workers in the area to replace the strikers, the growers reneged on their promise. With exorbitant rents to pay, no strike fund, and no other means to survive in a region miles from urban soup kitchens and hundreds of miles from family members who might lend support, South Florida's bean pickers went back to work.[20]

Excluded from industrial labor law and beyond the reach of federal relief efforts, farmworkers could only appeal to Washington as supplicants who hoped to be treated as workers. Thus James Cheseburough, who had migrated to Florida from New Hampshire, wrote to President Roosevelt in 1942 to ask him to set a nine-hour day and a minimum wage of two dollars a day for farmworkers; to announce his decision by radio; and to "Please think a lot."[21] While Cheseburough ended his letter with a warning, reminding the president that he was still a voter in New Hampshire, his threat was an empty one, for most migrant farmworkers were disfranchised by residency requirements if not by race.

When New Dealers finally began to "think a lot" about the plight of migrant farmworkers, they did so not to cultivate working-class votes, but to prevent mass starvation on the nation's most productive farms. Moreover, their actions were triggered not by the migrants' power to wage harvest strikes, but by documentary photographers' exposés of migrants' poverty. The new policy, formulated by the Resettlement Administration in 1935 and implemented, beginning in 1936, by its successor, the Farm Security Administration (FSA), created a Migratory Camp Program to serve the American families who "were wandering from state to state in a desperate effort to earn a living as migrant farm laborers." In the eyes of the liberal reformers who created the camp program, migrant farmworkers were not workers at all, but wards of the state. They would be sheltered and rehabilitated, not organized or empowered.[22]

The FSA migrant program built both permanent camps in commercial farming centers and mobile camps that provided trailers and tents for migrating farmworkers. By 1936, twenty-six permanent camps that could shelter seven thousand families were in operation or under construction on the Pacific Coast. And, in the spring of 1940, the first camps on the East Coast were finally opened in Belle Glade, with Eleanor Roosevelt in attendance. The Osceola Camp sheltered white packinghouse workers and the larger Okeechobee Camp black field labor. By summer, there were three more camps in Florida; in 1941, union construction workers built two more, as well as an FSA hospital.

The camp program's creators believed that migrant farmworkers were poor because they spent so much of their time and resources moving about, and that they moved about because they were unwilling or unable to save enough to sustain themselves in the off-seasons. The purpose of the program, then, was not merely to provide shelter, but also to teach farmworkers thrift and self-discipline, so that they might escape the migrant life altogether. Therefore, in addition to showers, kitchens, laundries, and medical clinics, the camps offered nurseries and schools for the migrants' children, lessons in personal hygiene, canning facilities where residents could preserve vegetables for the summer months, and sewing classes where women learned to make mattresses and pillows. Those who used the canning facilities had to set aside one in six cans to be sold in the camps' cooperative stores, and proceeds from the stores helped to fund the camps' nurseries. Thus the camps' managers sought to teach residents to be self-sufficient and to manage their affairs.

To convey the skills of self-government in a migrant population that camp managers sometimes found to be a "real test," each site included an assembly building meant to be the "seat of democracy in the camp." Residents elected a camp council that set the rules of behavior for all members and had the power to evict residents who disrupted camp life. The councils fined residents who dirtied the latrines, chastised couples who fought in public, and evicted residents caught selling alcohol.[23]

Some black farmworkers remained suspicious of the camps, choosing independence over the scrutiny of the camp councils; they preferred the cultural freedom of Belle Glade's juke joints over the FSA's "wholesome" Easter egg hunts and table-tennis tournaments. But many others, particularly parents with children, found the camps a welcome alternative to the squalor of most migrant housing. While they praised the facilities, schools, recreational activities, and free lunches for children, they noted that the camps' greatest advantage was the sense of security they afforded by guaranteeing a place to sleep at little cost. Families had to pay just one dollar a week or, in lieu of rent, work a two-hour period maintaining the grounds of the camp. When summer came and it was hot enough in South Florida to bake even the heartiest plants, Mrs. Johnnie Belle Taylor would migrate north to pick truck crops in Georgia, but she would keep paying the low rent on her unit in the Okeechobee Camp, so that she would be guaranteed a space upon her return. James Solomon, who lost his housing at U.S. Sugar Corporation on a day when he was too ill to work and spent the next three months in an overpriced Belle Glade boarding house, moved permanently into an FSA camp thereafter. When he injured his back cutting sugar cane after returning to work at U.S. Sugar, he simply found lighter work; injury or illness did not result in eviction from an FSA shelter.[24]

For over a year after the first camps opened in Florida, growers seemed to dismiss them as a harmless experiment in uplift that served only a small fraction of the migrant population. Some clearly accepted the camps as a sort of growers' subsidy, like the occasional relief provided by county and state agencies in the 1930s during freezes or floods. One noted that the camps seemed to produce "a much more reliable type of laborer." Luther Jones, realtor, farmer, and owner of the *Belle Glade Herald,* commented, "The idea is good and everybody is in favor of it," although he ridiculed camp managers for addressing black residents as equals. Growers in Frostproof, Sanford, Hollywood, and South Broward, Florida, all requested FSA mobile camps in 1941.[25]

In the context of a glutted labor market, local growers seemed largely supportive of the camp program, but by the winter of 1941–42, when the draft and the expanding war economy increased the demand on the nation's labor supply, the camps took on a very different and far more significant meaning. Because truck farmers hired migrants only for the harvest season, they had no way to know how much labor would be available until the harvest was upon them. Thus they panicked early and loudly. And the more growers worried about real or imagined labor shortages, the more camp residents took advantage of their fears to bargain wages upward.

The camps provided farmworkers with all they needed to organize and wait out growers while crops ripened in the fields: a steady source of cheap food and housing from which they would not be evicted so long as they obeyed camp rules. Even the camps' assembly halls could be put to new uses. And, although the FSA staffers were not permitted to advocate or encourage unionization in the camps, nothing said they had to discourage it or evict residents who were on strike.[26] Thus farmworkers did not have to picket, protest, or even affiliate with a labor union to force up wages. They only had to decide among themselves what they considered a reasonable rate of pay, and then wait while the highly perishable truck crops ripened under Florida's glaring sun. This they did, and growers responded immediately and vehemently.

In February 1942, L. L. Stuckey, chair of the Florida Farm Bureau's Vegetable Committee, complained to the U.S. secretary of agriculture on behalf of South Florida's largest growers that "50 percent of the crops are wasting in the fields on approximately 30,000 acres of winter vegetables and 25,000 acres of sugar cane[,] with 1,000 farm laborers idle in the communities and a majority of those working effectively employing delaying tactics."[27] The manager of the Everglades Farm Labor Supply Center noted that, when growers dropped the piece rate for beans, the bulk of the camp's 872 workers refused to leave for the fields. Another grower sent a telegram to Washington, insisting furiously that, while she had "not struck nor sat down," her labor force had done so several times. A Pahokee farmer declared in the *Miami Herald,* "We just don't have the labor. The people we do have, both white and Negro, simply will not work for us. Tons of beans are rotting in the fields." Mrs. Ruth Edgeworth of Belle Glade noted, "We've tried everything but holding a gun to their heads, and still they won't work."[28]

Accustomed to workers disciplined by the starvation wages of the Depression years, growers were outraged to find black workers collectively uncooperative. Farmworkers had not vanished into the armed forces, nor had they all been swept up into the industrial war machine; but they were not behaving in the manner to which growers had become accustomed. Growers blamed the camps as much as the farmworkers' themselves, for, in their minds, the camps coddled the workers, relieving them of the need to work. James Beardsley of Clewiston reported rumors that farmworkers could stay in the camps and pay their rent by "pushing a lawnmower along on the grass." Officials of the U.S. Sugar Corporation protested to camp managers that their employees had "stopped all work and were loafing while housed in the camps." The sugar executives could hardly have been placated when camp managers replied that it was "not within [their] power to require individuals to work at any specified point." In a sense, the growers were right: while the camps did not relieve farmworkers of their need to work (the camps provided only the most basic subsistence, after all), they did allow farmworkers to refuse work at a price set unilaterally by growers. The camps allowed their residents time to stall, and in truck farming a few days could mean the difference between a crop that made its way to market or to the armed forces, and one that rotted or dried on the vine.[29]

Florida's truck farmers' protests found a receptive audience among conservatives in the wartime Congress. As soon as the U.S. entered the war, Republicans and conservative Democrats—dubbed the "economy bloc"—had begun demanding drastic cutbacks in spending not related to defense and an end to New Deal "experimentation." Long the object of conservative attacks on the New Deal, the FSA found its head on the budgetary chopping block early in 1942. Its efforts to resettle farm families living on spent soil, create farm cooperatives, and offer low-interest loans to small farmers all were doomed. What saved the agency, at least temporarily, was the importance of its migrant camp program to the labor needs of the nation's truck farmers. The FSA's advocates fought for the agency on the grounds that the camp program contributed to the war effort and that only an expansion of the program's mobile camps would facilitate the efficient movement of "Migrant Soldiers on the Food Production Front."[30]

As a result, the FSA was saved but transformed. Congress authorized the expansion of the Migratory Camp Program and extended the life of the FSA for another six months so that it could continue to run the program, even as all other FSA programs died a swift death by defunding.[31] The camp program had been designed to provide farmworkers with the means and motivation to stop migrating, but in the winter of 1941–42 FSA officials began to facilitate migrancy in the name of the war effort.[32] In January, the FSA and the U.S. Employment Service (USES) signed a joint policy statement to coordinate farm labor supply activities. The USES would identify labor needs and areas of surplus and recruit farmworkers willing to move from one region to another. The FSA would get them there and provide food and shelter along the way. Both agencies advertised the plan widely, in the hope that growers would not restrict planting the following spring in anticipation of labor shortages. By the summer of 1942, 46 permanent and 43 mobile camps were in operation, six more mobile units were under construction, and 140 more sites to be used by 90 additional mobile units had been proposed.

This plan seems to have placated growers in small truck-farming regions along the Atlantic Coast. When asked by the FSA to provide "good testimonial stories which show the need of our migrant camps," many were happy to oblige. The mayor of Elizabeth City, North Carolina, noted, for example, that he had heard "nothing but universal praise" for the camps and that all the farmers with whom he talked "were most gratefully pleased in that they eliminated the necessity of frequent trips into Elizabeth City in an endeavor to recruit labor."[33] Isolated from each other and too small to hire their own recruiters, these growers depended upon the arrival of migrant workers in time for very short harvest seasons. With defense industries drawing away workers and tire and gas shortages impeding the mobility of those who remained, operators of small truck farms along the coast were glad to have the federal government take charge of domestic farmworkers and organize their travels into efficient troop movements. They could only nod their approval when FSA workers arrived to assemble a mobile camp in advance of an impending harvest.

South Florida's growers, however, were not placated in the least, although USES officials continued to insist that they could meet all growers' labor needs. The presence of year-round, permanent FSA camps had already undermined the power growers had wielded over Belle Glade's bean pickers during the strike of 1936–37. The last thing these growers wanted was for the FSA to take a direct hand in the supply and *removal* of their accustomed workforce. When, in October 1942, FSA officials in Florida arranged for the outmigration of several hundred farmworkers to the Campbell Soup cannery in Camden, New Jersey, growers were outraged, calling it the "most high-handed act of labor piracy ever perpetrated in this state."[34]

Some growers determined to maintain control of their labor supply by resorting to time-honored labor recruitment methods. U.S. Sugar Corporation managers kidnapped, imprisoned, and shot at workers, for example; and the sheriff of Glades County took prisoners from the county jail and put them to work without pay on his farm.[35] However, although some growers were not above the use of force, most chose to wage their war against migrant farm labor and the FSA's camp program in Washington under the auspices of the American Farm Bureau Federation. At their behest, the Farm Bureau fought not to dismantle the camp program, but to turn it over to local control and to use camp facilities to house foreign workers who could be deported for striking.

By the winter of 1942–43, South Florida growers and the Farm Bureau had devised an alternative both to shooting at farmworkers to keep them in the fields and to accepting farmworkers provided by the FSA under contracts that required growers to pay a minimum wage. The growers by then had heard that the FSA was supplying California and Arizona growers with Mexican nationals, and they demanded the same treatment.[36] South Florida's growers demanded foreign workers who could be deported for refusing to work. They began to insist that the government allow them to hire West Indians, who had worked in limited numbers in South Florida since the 1880s. After January 29, 1943, when truck farmers met in Homestead, Florida, near Miami, to discuss ways to stabilize wages, Secretary of Agriculture Claude Wickard received over fifty telegrams from South Florida potato, bean, and tomato growers, demanding imported farm labor. One woman insisted that she wanted "6 Bahama Laborers and need them now. Bahamians are far better help than riffraff now walking our roads and shooting craps in our fields."[37] L. L. Chandler of Dade County's Farm Bureau called the FSA program impractical, bound by red tape, and "dripping" with social reform. "Yet . . . just 48 miles across the Gulf Stream," he continued, "are some 18,000 men, willing laborers who want to come to Florida . . . and despite the fact that Mexican labor is permitted to enter this country . . . we haven't yet had one Bahaman laborer offered to us." He insisted that Florida's farmers had planted every possible plant and seed needed for the war effort, "despite the fact that labor has struck on him," endlessly putting the farmer "across the barrel," and the government, "who could control it," did nothing.[38]

The growers' persistent agitation was effective. In April 1943, the Farm Bureau won passage of a bill designed to remove the Migrant Labor Program from the hands of New Deal liberals and eliminate the program's minimum wage, maximum hours, and housing standards. Public Law 45 permitted the retention and expansion of the farm labor recruitment program, so long as its managers did *not* use it to improve farmworkers' working and living conditions. The new law turned over the renamed Farm Labor Supply Program to the War Food Administration (the wartime version of the grower-dominated Department of

Agriculture) and committed it to the importation, transportation, and housing of foreign workers. No one, not even federal officials, could transport domestic farmworkers out of a county without a release signed by a local county agricultural extension agent.[39]

In 1943, the Farm Labor Supply Program delivered 8,828 Jamaicans to East Coast growers. In the first six months of 1944, it imported over 15,000 more. In the last year of the war, the Labor Supply Program moved only 11,000 domestic farmworkers nationwide, while it supplied growers with 56,000 foreign workers and 122,000 prisoners of war.[40]

The camp managers' reports reveal clearly that the foreign workers brought to South Florida did not simply compensate for labor shortages created when American workers were drafted or departed for industrial jobs. Rather, foreign workers displaced domestic laborers, forcing them out of the camps that had been such a boon to their organizational efforts. In the fall of 1943, managers at the Okeechobee Camp for black labor reported that Bahamians were imported despite an adequate domestic labor supply the previous year. "[T]he farmer had more than necessary labor" in 1942, one staff member noted; with the addition of the Bahamians, "many farm laborers were without day work." In 1944, another Okeechobee Camp official reported that the camp was "filled to capacity" for the bean harvest; "daily we turn down hundreds of applicants who are so anxious to call this their home."[41]

Some camp managers lamented the exclusion of domestic workers, and even some growers protested "regulations which prevented American citizens being housed in Federal farm labor supply centers." But such sentiments were rare. As the manager of the Pahokee Camp pointed out, reserving the camps for foreign workers allowed for more efficient use of space, since domestic workers' children took up room without providing labor. The imported foreign workers were all adults. In 1942, he noted, the Pahokee Camp, while full, had housed only 213 residents old enough to work. In 1943, if the camp were to be used for Bahamians only, it could house at least 800 "easily."[42]

Barred from many of the federal labor camps that had been their winter homes for three years, African-American workers also found that, on many farms, they were hired only as a last resort. Growers in the Fort Pierce area preferred Bahamians, citing their attendance, tractability, adaptability, productivity, and conduct. The local camp manager reported that most employers "considered Bahamians, all things considered, as superior to native American workers," adding that "most of the

Bahamians were quite contented and happy. It is said that they are that way by nature anyway."[43]

Even where African Americans kept their billets in federal camps, they lost their monopoly on field work and therefore their ability to control wages by agreeing among themselves to stay out of the fields. In Belle Glade, Caribbean and African-American workers lived in separate camps about a mile apart. Growers depressed wages by driving from one camp to the other, telling one group that the other had promised to work for less. There was no labor shortage, recalled Rev. David Burgess, the Southern Tenant Farmers Union's "minister to the migrants"; the Farm Labor Supply Program, as he saw it, was merely a bald effort to break strikes and lower wages.[44]

Imported farmworkers also struck, but, when they did, growers merely had to summon War Food Administration officials to have them "repatriated" and replaced. Thus, in 1944, the Pahokee Camp manager reported that "approximately 75 workers held a strike against the 50 cents an hour paid them which was the prevailing wage at that time." After a hearing, the three leaders "were turned over to the Border Patrol for deportation." No other trouble occurred after that, he noted.[45] Camp managers were baffled when the supposedly pliant West Indians refused to work at the proffered wages; some concluded that they were simply picking up bad habits from African Americans. Reports for the week ending June 10, 1944, revealed that, on average, 23 percent of the West Indian workers refused to work for various reasons.[46] All were repatriated.

As a weapon against farmworkers' militancy, the Labor Supply Program was an unmitigated success. In 1945, the Fort Pierce Camp manager reassessed the value of African-American labor, reporting that the "domestic colored did a swell job in harvesting the vegetable crop." "They never once asked for higher prices than prevailed in that area," he noted.[47] In some ways, the war experience was a reprise of the 1936–37 bean pickers' strike, but on a much grander scale. This time, however, when growers complained of a labor-supply problem, the state highway patrol could not simply open the border and let job-seekers flood the state. Instead, federal officials opened the nation's borders to Latin American and Caribbean job-seekers and then enforced labor discipline through the deportation process.

Denied the right of collective bargaining, farmworker movements were easily defeated. Thus the workers were unable to oppose an immigration policy tailored to growers' needs. At the end of the war, Congress ordered the Farm Labor Supply Program's temporary camps dismantled and its permanent camps sold to growers' associations for a dollar each. At the same time, Congress extended the life of the importation program in the East and the much larger *bracero* program in the West. Although public outcry during the 1953–54 recession resulted in the deportation of over a million Mexican workers from the West Coast, Congress continued to sanction the use of foreign workers *in agriculture,* reinventing the World War II Labor Importation Program as the H2 Program (the name refers to section H2 of the 1952 Immigration and Nationality Act).

In the 1950s, African Americans continued to dominate the ranks of farm laborers in Florida, but foreign workers willing to toil for lower wages gradually displaced them. One by one, H2 workers from Jamaica, refugees from Haiti, and, since the 1970s, often undocumented Mexicans and other Latin Americans pushed African Americans out of the farm labor market.

With undocumented workers laboring alongside legal immigrants and H2 workers subject to deportation if they protested their rate of pay or living conditions, opportunities for organization were few. Proof that private power and public policy combined to squelch black farmworkers' militancy came in a 1978 labor dispute near Tampa. In a stark reversal of earlier struggles, 136 Mexican tomato pickers walked off the job to protest wages and conditions, and growers quickly recruited several hundred African Americans to break the strike.[48]

African-American farmworkers' wartime struggle did not fail for lack of organization. It was the growers' ability to enlist the aid of federal authorities that crushed their promising but short-lived initiative. Yet the consequences of African-American farmworkers' wartime defeat were profound—and not just for them, but for all farmworkers on the East Coast of the United States. Because farmworkers were unsuccessful in their organizing efforts, their living and working conditions remained desperate. Belle Glade won infamy in the 1980s as the nation's poorest city and as the capital of the AIDS epidemic in the U.S. Moreover, a recent study found that African-American migrants along the East Coast were three hundred times more likely to have active tuberculosis than the average American.

Sporadic reform campaigns led to state laws regulating crew leaders and housing and, finally, to the inclusion of farmworkers in federal minimum wage, unemployment insurance, and workplace safety legislation. These provisions were rarely enforced, however, and even if appropriations committees had been generous with funding for enforcement (and they were not), there still would not have been enough inspectors to check for housing, labor, and pesticide violations on every farm in the state. If farmworkers had enjoyed the right of collective bargaining, and if they had been successful in organizing, they might have been able to take advantage of such protective legislation. But so long as they feared displacement and deportation, they could not afford to protest inadequate conditions or report employers' violations of health and safety laws to state authorities. To make matters worse, farmworkers still lack political leverage. Now dominated by an immigrant workforce, Florida's farmworkers remain a disfranchised population.[49]

The story of Florida's farmworkers is not a sort of throwback to nineteenth-century labor relations, with labor unorganized and federal officials determined not to intervene in an unequal struggle between capital and labor. Farmworkers did organize, and federal officials did intervene in farm labor relations on a massive scale—first by feeding, housing, and attempting to uplift them; and then by setting wage ceilings, shuttling farmworkers from field to field, prohibiting American farm laborers from moving to better-paying jobs, and replacing militant migrants with farmworkers recruited under no-strike contracts. Leaving growers with permanent access to foreign workers in the postwar period, Congress made it unlikely that Florida farmworkers will organize effectively in the future.

Notes

1. Labor historians have largely ignored migrant farmworkers on the East Coast of the United States, doubtless because they produced no tradition of trade unionism, no Cesar Chavez, no national boycotts. Florida's citrus workers flirted with the American Federation of Labor several times during this century, and some black field workers joined the Southern Tenant Farmers Union in the 1940s, but the former movement spurned all but the most sedentary white workers, while the latter was a fleeting phenomenon. A few exceptions to the neglect of this topic: Louis Persh, "An Analysis of the Agricultural Migratory Movements on the Atlantic Seaboard and the Socio-Economic Implications for the Community and the Migrants, 1930–1950" (Ph.D. diss., American Univ., 1953); Jerrell H. Shofner, "The Legacy of Racial Slavery: Free Enterprise and Forced Labor in Florida in the 1940s," *Journal of Southern History* 47, no. 3 (1981): 411–26; Donald E. Grubbs, "The Story of Florida's Migrant Farm Workers," *Florida Historical Quarterly* 40, no. 2 (Oct.

1961): 103–22; and Sandra M. Mohl, "Migrant Farmworkers in America: A Florida Case Study" (M.A. thesis, Florida Atlantic Univ., 1981).

2. U.S. Census Bureau, *14th Census,* 1920, vol. 6, pt. 2, p. 375; U.S. Census Bureau, *16th Census,* 1940, *Agriculture,* vol. 1, pt. 3, South Atlantic, p. 682; and Joan Pascal and Harold G. Tipton, "Vegetable Production in South Florida," U.S. House of Representatives, Select Committee Investigating National Defense Migration, *Hearings . . . ,* 77th Cong., 1st Sess. (1941) (hereafter cited as NDMH), pt. 33, p. 12893.
3. J. D. Abbin, quoted in *Federal Writers' Project Life Histories,* reel 1, Southern Historical Collection, Univ. of North Carolina at Chapel Hill.
4. South Florida tenancy rates fell during the 1930s, but they were still extremely high. In Broward County, the tenancy rate was 70.9 percent in 1930, 68.9 percent in 1935, and 59.5 percent in 1940. In Palm Beach County, the tenancy rate was 54.6 percent in 1930, 50.3 percent in 1935, and 34.9 percent in 1940. At the same time, harvests on farms of over 500 acres increased in Broward County from 15.7 percent to 41.1 percent, and in Dade County from 18.9 percent to 38.3 percent between 1929 and 1939. Census Bureau, *16th Census,* 1940, *Agriculture,* vol. 1, pt. 3, South Atlantic, County Table 2, Farm Tenure.
5. One of Belle Glade's more successful truck farmers estimated in 1942 that it would take 640 acres and $35,000 in equipment to start a profitable farm in the Everglades. The larger enterprises cut costs by packing and shipping their own crops. Those who had to pay packers gradually went bust and became tenants. Pascal and Tipton, "Vegetable Production in South Florida," 12911.
6. In March 1940, approximately 2 percent of Florida farms hired almost 50 percent of all the seasonal labor employed, according to Harry Schwartz, *Seasonal Farm Labor in the United States* (New York: Columbia Univ. Press, 1945), 9. See also Terrell Cline to John Beecher, May 14, 1939, National Archives and Records Administration (NARA), Record Group (RG) 96, Box 20, File RP-M-85-183-01; and Pascal and Tipton, "Vegetable Production in South Florida," 12911.
7. Cotton prices dropped 50 percent in the three years after World War I, and then the boll weevil arrived to finish the job. Georgia lost two-thirds of its cotton crop to the boll weevil in 1922 and 1923. By 1925, Georgia cotton planters had taken nearly 3.5 million acres out of production, decreasing by that amount the acres requiring sharecroppers to farm them and day laborers to work the harvests on them. Resettlement Administration staffers surveyed 690 workers in winter of 1936–37 and reported that 79.3 percent were from southern states, 39.7 percent were from Georgia, and 10.4 percent were from Alabama. NDMH, pt. 33, Belle Glade, Apr. 25, 1942, pp. 12651–53; Aubrey Clyde Robinson and Glenore Fisk Horne, "Florida Migratory Workers," June 1937, NARA, RG 96, Box 9, AD-124, Region 5, Migratory Labor 1940.
8. Testimony of A. Frederick Smith of the Florida Industrial Commission in U.S. Congress, House of Representatives, Select Committee to Investigate the Interstate Migration of Destitute Citizens, *Hearings . . . ,* 76th Cong., 3d

Sess. (Washington, D.C.: USGPO, 1941), pt. 2, pp. 483 and 583 (hereafter cited as *Tolan Hearings*). See also Memorandum, John Beecher, Research Supervisor, Resettlement Division, Region 5, USDA, to Max A. Egloff, Chief of Research and Investigations, Labor Relations Division, May 15, 1939, NARA, RG 96, Box 20, File RP-M-85-183-01, Monthly Reports.

9. NDMH, pt. 33, pp. 12739–42.
10. Robinson and Horne, "Florida Migratory Workers," 45–46; and Charlton W. Tebeau, *A History of Florida* (Coral Gables, Fla.: Univ. of Miami Press, 1971), 403.
11. Lawrence Will, *Swamp to Sugar Bowl: Pioneer Days in Belle Glade* (St. Petersburg, Fla.: Great Outdoors, 1968), 189–93. See also Robinson and Horne, "Florida Migratory Workers."
12. The observer was Marjory Stoneman Douglas, *The Everglades: River of Grass* (New York: Rinehart and Co., 1947), 356–57. See also Grubbs, "Story of Florida's Migrant Farm Workers," 106–7; and testimony of Howard Haney, NDMH, pt. 33, p. 12604.
13. Testimony of Howard Haney, NDMH, pt. 33, p. 12604. See also Douglas, *River of Grass,* 356–57; and Grubbs, "Story of Florida's Migrant Farm Workers," 106–7.
14. Mary Jenkins, interview by Arthur S. Evans, Jr., and David Lee, in Pearl City Oral History Project, Boca Raton Historical Society Library, Boca Raton, Fla., 1984–85.
15. NDMH, pt. 33, pp. 12625–28.
16. Robinson and Horne, "Florida Migratory Workers," 45–46; *Tolan Hearings,* pt. 2, pp. 483–88; Testimony of Dorothea Brower, District Welfare Supervisor, West Palm Beach, Fla., Apr. 29, 1942, NDMH, pt. 33, pp. 12792–95.
17. John N. Webb, *The Migratory and Casual Worker,* WPA Research Monograph 7 (Washington, D.C.: USGPO, 1937), ix–x; John N. Webb, *The Transient Unemployed,* WPA Research Monograph 3 (Washington, D.C.: USGPO, 1935), 48; Philip Elwood Ryan, *Migration and Social Welfare* (New York: Russell Sage Foundation, 1940), 8–10; Ellen C. Potter, "After Five Years—The Unsolved Problem of the Transient Unemployed, 1932–37," included in the testimony of Bertha McCall, General Director, National Travelers Aid Association, *Tolan Hearings,* pt. 1, New York City Hearings, 54; Doris Carothers, *Chronology of the Federal Emergency Relief Administration, May 12, 1933, to Dec. 31, 1935,* WPA Research Monograph 6 (Washington, D.C: USGPO, 1937), 25 and 81.
18. FDR's decree excluded agricultural workers generally, but later scuffles between the National Recovery Administration and the Department of Agriculture resulting in a distinction between those who worked outside the "area of production" (i.e., processing workers) and those who worked within the area of production (fieldworkers). Austin P. Morris, "Agricultural Labor and National Labor Legislation," *California Law Review* 54 (1966): 1939–89.
19. See Cletus Daniel, *Bitter Harvest: A History of California Farmworkers, 1870–1941* (Ithaca, N.Y.: Cornell Univ. Press, 1981); Stuart Jamieson, *Labor Unionism in*

American Agriculture, Bulletin No. 836, U.S. Department of Labor, Bureau of Labor Statistics (Washington, D.C.: USGPO, 1945; reprint, Arno Press, 1976); and Cindy Hahamovitch, "In the Valley of the Giant: The Politics of Migrant Farm Labor, 1865–1945" (Ph.D. diss., Univ. of North Carolina at Chapel Hill, 1992), 240–61.

20. Robinson and Horne, "Florida Migratory Workers," 40.
21. Jan. 20, 1942, RG 16, Office for Agricultural War Relations, General Correspondence, 1942, NARA, Box 145, File Employment 3 Wages (Jan. 1–July 31).
22. "History of Farm Labor Activities of the Farm Security Administration," U.S. Department of Agriculture, War Food Administration, NARA, RG 287, FSA Publication 132; Memo to Paul H. Appleby, Asst. to the Secretary, from John Fischer, Director of Information, FSA, Dec. 9, 1939, RG 16, Secretary of Agriculture, E17 General Correspondence, Camps, Migratory Labor, 1939.
23. C. B. Baldwin to Sen. Claude Pepper, July 29, 1941, NARA, RG 96, Box 9, AD-124, Region 5; "Community and Family Services Bulletin," Feb. 28, 1941, RG 96, FSA, Migrant Labor Camps Correspondence 1935–43, Box 16, File RP-M-169, Publications; John F. O'Malley, Elba, N.Y., Narrative Report for Period Ending Oct. 4, 1942, RG 96, Migrant Labor Camps Correspondence, 1935–43, Box 19, File RP-M-183, Migratory Reg.
24. NDMH, pt. 33, pp. 12574–77, 12625–38.
25. Ibid., 12603, 12672–74; and NARA, RG 96, Correspondence Concerning Migratory Labor Camps, 1935–43, Box 2, Region 5, File RP-85 M-060, Projects 1941.
26. The acting director had noted as early as 1938 that the FSA "does not attempt either to encourage or to impede the formation of labor organizations. It is true, however, that residents of the FSA camps enjoy certain protection of their civil liberties which often is not available to migrant workers living on private property or in the numerous 'ditch bank camps.'" Memo for Paul H. Appleby, Acting Administrator, June 10, 1938, NARA, RG 16, Sec. of Agriculture, E17 General Correspondence, Camps, Migratory Labor.
27. NARA, RG 224, Box 51, File C2-R36, Narrative Reports Farm Labor Supply Centers, Florida, May–Dec. 1944; and L. L. Stuckey, Chairman, Vegetable Committee, Florida Farm Bureau Federation, Pahokee, Fla., to Claude R. Wickard, Feb. 10, 1942, NARA, RG 96, Correspondence Concerning Migratory Labor Camps, 1935–43, Box 7.
28. NARA, RG 224, FSA Correspondence, 1943–44, Box 75, File 4-FLT-R57; David Burgess, quoted in "The Joads—Still Out of Luck," *New Republic* 110 (1944): 46.
29. Testimony of James E. Beardsley, Clewiston, Fla., Apr. 26, 1942, NDMH, pt. 33, pp. 12565–66; Paul Vander Schouw, Supervisor, Florida Migratory Labor Camps, Jan. 1942, NARA, RG 96, Migratory Labor Camps Correspondence, 1935–43, Box 20, File RP-M-85-183.
30. NARA, RG 16, Office for Agricultural War Relations, General Correspondence, 1942, Box 188.
31. Sidney Baldwin, *Poverty and Politics: The Rise and Decline of the Farm Security Administration* (Chapel Hill: Univ. of North Carolina Press, 1968).

32. Ibid., 329–31; N. Gregory Silvermaster, Director, Labor Division, FSA, to C. B. Baldwin re Proposed Expansion of FSA Camp Program to Meet Agricultural Defense Production Needs (undated), NARA, RG 96, Correspondence Concerning Migratory Labor Camps, 1935–43, Box 2, Region 5, File RP-85 M-060, Projects 1941.
33. Jerome B. Flora to Howard H. Gordon, Regional Director, FSA, Raleigh, N.C., Aug. 31, 1942, NARA, RG 96, Migratory Labor Camps Correspondence, 1935–43, Box 16, File Migratory—84-160.
34. Harry L. Askew, Chairman, Joint Industry Committee, to Hon. Marvin Jones, War Food Administration, Aug. 9, 1943, NARA, RG 224, General Correspondence, 1943–44, Box 61, File 6-R15-Florida, July–Dec. 1943.
35. *Tampa Tribune,* Nov. 5, 1942.
36. In early 1942, Secretary Wickard had traveled secretly to Mexico to negotiate the terms of a labor importation agreement with the Mexican government. According to the agreement, transportation would be provided when growers signed a contract that they would pay prevailing wage rates (but not less than 30 cents an hour), that they would guarantee employment for 75 percent of the contract period, and that certain minimum standards of housing and sanitation would be available. Workers accepting such a contract would be guaranteed their transportation costs; would be furnished food, medical care, and living facilities during the trip; and if the employer failed to pay the agreed wage rate, the government would provide subsistence. NARA, RG 96, Correspondence Concerning Migratory Labor Camps, 1935–43, Box 7, File Migratory-120—A Thru G. See Kitty Calavita, *Inside the State: The Bracero Program, Immigration, and the INS* (New York: Routledge, 1992).
37. NARA, RG 224, FSA Correspondence, 1943–44, Box 75, File 4-FLT-R57.
38. U.S. Congress, Senate, Committee on Agriculture and Forestry, *Hearings Before a Subcommittee on the Food Supply of the United States,* 78th Cong., 1st Sess., pt. 1, pp. 237 and 241.
39. U.S. Congress, House, Committee on Appropriations, *Hearings . . . Farm Labor Program . . . 1943–1944,* cited in Wayne D. Rasmussen, *A History of the Emergency Farm Labor Supply Program, 1943–1947,* Bureau of Agricultural Economics Monograph 13 (Washington, D.C.: USGPO, 1951), 42, 58, and 62–63. See also Baldwin, *Poverty and Politics,* 394. The major opposition to the bill came from the NAACP and the Southern Tenant Farmers Union; neither organization was in a particularly good position to influence Congress. See, e.g., *Atlanta Daily World,* May 4, 1943; and H. L. Mitchell to Frank P. Fenton, June 13, 1944, Southern Tenant Farmers Union Papers, Southern Historical Collection, Univ. of North Carolina at Chapel Hill.
40. Rasmussen, *Emergency Farm Labor Supply Program*; RG 224, General Correspondence, 1943–44, Box 61, File 6-R15, Jamaicans, 1944.
41. Reports by Sadye E. Pryor, Home Management Supervisor, Okeechobee Center, Sept. 1943; and Henry O. Earwood, Okeechobee Camp Manager, Oct. 1944, RG 224, General Correspondence, 1943–44, Box 51, File C2-R36—Florida.

42. Paul Vander Schouw, Monthly Narrative Report, Aug. 1943, RG 224, Box 51, File C2-R36, Florida.
43. S. C. Merritt, Manager, Fort Pierce, Farm Labor Supply Center (FLSC) Report for Oct., Nov. 5, 1945, RG 224, General Correspondence, 1945, Box 78, File Camps 11-1, Florida FLSC, 1945; and John V. Wright, Manager, Fort Pierce FLSC, Jan. 1944, Box 51, File C2-R36—Florida.
44. Rev. David Burgess, interview by Cindy Hahamovitch, May 1990, Newark, N.J., audiotape recording in author's possession.
45. George E. Winston, Pahokee FLSC, *Report,* Apr. 1944, RG 224, General Correspondence, 1943–44, Box 51, File C2-R36-Florida.
46. RG 224, Box 59, File 6-A19, Agreements, Jan. 1944; and Box 78, File: Camps 11-1.
47. Sherwood Brantley, Ft. Pierce FLSC Manager, Jan. 31, 1945, RG 224, General Correspondence, 1945, Box 78, File: Camps 11-1, Florida FLSC, 1945.
48. Fifty-one Latino protesters picketing the entrance of Fulwood Farms were arrested by 40 sheriff's deputies, some armed with riot sticks. Ronnie Fulwood evicted 20 families who participated in the strike. J. P. Schuck, director of the Florida Mediation and Conciliation Service, urged Fulwood to meet with the strike leader, arguing, "We don't want this thing to rage into a wildfire that will spread across the state." *New York Times,* Apr. 20, 1978, p. 13.
49. On farmworkers and tuberculosis, see *New York Times,* Apr. 3, 1991; on AIDS in Belle Glade, see *Los Angeles Times,* Jan. 28, 1993, A5; and on exposure to pesticides, see *New York Times,* Aug. 19, 1990, p. 12. See also "Migrant Workers Straining the South's Health Safety Net," *Raleigh (N.C.) News and Observer,* Oct. 29, 1989.

Warplanes, Labor, and the International Association of Machinists in Nashville, 1939–1945

Jacob Vander Meulen

Youth and industrial inexperience, low wages, stubborn employers, weak and indifferent unions—all presented formidable obstacles and disincentives for American aircraft workers during World War II. Nevertheless, millions of them in factories across the land overcame such hardships and brought about a "production miracle," building swarms of warplanes that projected American military power around the globe. Few succeeded as strikingly as the thousands of Tennessee women and men who made up the workforce at the AVCO-Vultee plant in Nashville, even though most were encountering wage-earning and factory life for the first time.

AVCO-Nashville workers overcame their inexperience and the unique challenges of aircraft manufacture. They proved particularly adept at developing the flexible work attitudes, habits, and skills that warplane production required. They succeeded even though their managers, led by the notoriously anti-labor Tom Girdler, seemed more concerned with thwarting effective unionism and retaining rigid controls over the work process that hindered flexible work habits. Workers also surmounted such obstacles as indifferent and unsympathetic wartime government agencies and a union, the International Association of Machinists (IAM), still so bound up in its old craft and racist traditions that it neglected its responsibilities to its members and even acceded in the company's effort to maintain low wages, work control, and "labor peace." The workers adapted and persevered, however, turning out warplanes, including one of the

Army Air Forces' most complicated and most important fighters, the Lockheed P-38 Lightning.

Each of the hundreds of wartime aircraft plants offers a study in rapid industrial development within a common national and regional framework, but within separate local contexts and traditions. With a workforce peaking in 1943 at the relatively small figure of 6,500, the Nashville-AVCO plant presents a comparatively minor episode in the rise of the southern aircraft industry. But that local history neatly captures national patterns in aircraft industry planning and labor relations. These patterns too often reflected the thinly coordinated nature of the wartime aircraft program, with its considerable waste, mismanagement, and failed programs, as well as the distractions of political, regional, corporate, and bureaucratic friction. The labor story at the Nashville plant illuminates the many weaknesses of the overall approach Americans took toward arming themselves for air warfare. It also highlights what, in the end, made the aircraft program work—the willingness of so many American women and men to accept the challenges and frustrations of the factory in order to manufacture hundreds of thousands of warplanes.

Nashville secured the first of the many warplane factories that sprouted everywhere in the South during the war. Before AVCO Corporation moved its Detroit aircraft business to Nashville's Berry field in 1939, the only other aircraft plants operating below the Mason-Dixon Line were the Glenn L. Martin facility near Baltimore and Bellanca Aircraft at New Castle, Delaware. In 1929, Martin had moved south from Cleveland, Ohio, drawn by the same considerations that later attracted AVCO to Tennessee's capital—low labor costs and the reputed tractability of southern workers, as compared with their wage- and union-conscious counterparts in Cleveland and Detroit.

During the inter-war years, low wages and managerial sway on the shop floor were critical for business success in this skill- and labor-intensive, high-technology industry. Rigorous wage containment and work-control strategies seem inconsistent with such industry dynamics but nevertheless were mandated by members of Congress's naval and military affairs committees, who insisted that army and navy contracting officers observe competitive fixed-price rules in the deals they made with warplane manufacturers. These legislators harbored a populist suspicion that "trusts," Big Business, and Wall Street would control the aircraft industry unless they used the government's dominance over the aircraft market to keep it competitive. They also feared the emergence of what many Americans later called "the military-industrial complex," a dangerous alliance between industrialists and military men that would lead to corruption and militarism.

During the Defense Period of 1940–41, however, such ideological pressures figured less centrally in the aircraft industry's structural and locational development and in the industry's rapid rise in the South. Congress now deferred direct oversight of aircraft contracts to the military and provided billions in cost-plus public money to build an industrial base for an enormous projected air force. Military men, not entrepreneurs, now decided aircraft industry locations. Their prime concern was "strategic," finding those sites least exposed to air attack. Thus, during the Battle of Britain in the summer of 1940, construction of giant bomber and fighter assembly plants began in America's heartland, at Dallas–Fort Worth, Tulsa, Oklahoma City, Wichita, Omaha, and Kansas City, all financed by the government but operated by businessmen on a fee basis. Large numbers of unorganized workers and high levels of unemployment in these regions counted as bonuses in the location calculus, even more so since planners initially imagined a workforce reaching hundreds of thousands of employees in each plant.[1]

By 1942, the South's low wages and politically dormant labor force again figured as the region's main attractions for even further expansion in aircraft manufacture. Pools of unemployed and underutilized southern workers represented the nation's last wartime manpower reserves. Demand had cleared labor markets in Buffalo, Chicago, Connecticut–Long Island, Detroit, Los Angeles, New Jersey, Seattle, and Wichita-Omaha, the main areas of aircraft production. Congestion and dislocation in these areas and efforts to overcome the industry's low wage structure led to unionization and surges of militancy, especially on the West Coast. Until the mid-1930s, organized labor had made little progress among aircraft workers. The Wagner Act of 1935 helped spur organization, although rivalry between the craft-based Machinists (IAM), affiliated with the American Federation of Labor (AFL), and the new United Auto Workers (UAW) of the Congress of Industrial Organizations (CIO) continued to fragment labor's influence into the war years.

As military production shifted into high gear, President Franklin Roosevelt's military and civilian planners generally agreed that unions and collective bargaining ought to be confined to peripheral roles in aircraft. The stakes were high, as the industry quickly was evolving into the nation's largest manufacturer and the leading consumer of the munitions dollar. Indeed, by 1944, it employed 2.3 million workers. Even minor wage improvements threatened inflation, and the idea of negotiating factory-floor conditions with strong unions seemed impractical and ideologically distasteful to the military leaders and corporate executives who during the war dominated Washington's production and procurement apparatus.

The burgeoning aircraft industry, like the overall war economy, offered new ground for a decade-long struggle to find political solutions for the Great Depression's riddle. The industry suddenly emerged as a key area for public investment in a stagnant national economy and seemed likely to continue as such for as long as American global interests needed protection. In the wake of late New Deal failures and a tightening political deadlock, FDR's Wall Street appointees to key oversight posts rode a wave of resurgent business confidence. Aided by the labor-intensive stimulus of massive military spending, they worked effectively to maintain America's regime of free enterprise and limited regulation. They saw little need to include discredited New Deal agencies and perspectives in guiding the war's industrial effort and many reasons to curb the unions that had grown powerful earlier in the New Deal.[2]

In the early war years, such broad political and ideological concerns dovetailed with the South's attractiveness as a repository of low-wage labor. Planners overcame strategic caution and even tagged the Gulf and Atlantic coasts for new plants. Major aircraft works went up at New Orleans; Miami; and Elizabeth City, North Carolina; as well as at points inland: Memphis; Birmingham; Burlington, North Carolina; Marietta, Georgia; Hagerstown, Maryland; and elsewhere. By mid-1944, nearly two hundred thousand men and women, about 20 percent of the national total, worked in southern airframe assembly plants. These new plants and their networks of "feeder" plants were the latest sites for the widening encounter of mostly young and industrially inexperienced southern workers with factory life, advanced technologies, the labor movement, and the military-industry jobs that powered the "southern takeoff."[3]

The Nashville plant was unique among the new southern "war baby" aircraft plants, in that its origins predated the war period. AVCO began the plant in 1939, when Depression-era rules and free-enterprise "bottom-line" business tactics still defined the aircraft industry. Shop-floor supervisors and skilled workers drawn from Stinson Aircraft in Detroit provided the expertise around which Nashville's 145,000-square-foot plant was built and staffed in 1939–40. Stinson figured as one of the few promising lights for its owners at AVCO, a weak and unprofitable combine of aircraft, engine, parts, and air transport subsidiaries, as well as many other interests. Formed by Averell Harriman in 1929 and controlled after 1936 by New York financier Victor Emanuel, AVCO generated steady losses for investors. The company was poorly managed in an overproducing industry. Moreover, strict congressional regulation of army and navy warplane contracts meant fixed-price competition in this high-technology business. The government did not tolerate cost overruns, nor did it allow sufficiently for research and development costs.[4]

AVCO owned stock in Republic Steel, the lead company within "Little Steel," a group of bitterly anti-union producers in the Midwest. In 1937, Thomas Mercer Girdler, president of Republic, joined the board of directors at AVCO. In the 1920s, this obstinate foe of organized labor had operated "the perfect company town" for Jones & Laughlin Steel at Aliquippa, Pennsylvania—known among workers as the "Siberia of the steel industry"—and then, in 1929, organized Republic in Cleveland. Girdler hated unions and the New Deal. He led Little Steel's bloody fight against the Steel Workers Organizing Committee. He was complicit in the 1937 Memorial Day Massacre at Republic's steel mill on Chicago's South Side, where police killed ten workers and injured scores more. This record apparently helped make him attractive to Victor Emanuel.

Girdler's hand in the labor policies at AVCO's aircraft divisions soon became apparent. Both his politics and his personnel methods meshed ideally with the low-wage, open-shop cultures that prevailed in AVCO's aircraft and engine plants in Los Angeles, Detroit, and Williamsport, Pennsylvania. But by the late thirties, AVCO was still losing money and found itself poorly positioned in the rapidly expanding military aircraft business. Its only entries in this market were Stinson's Vigilant O-49, a light four-seat reconnaissance and trainer plane built in Detroit, and the A-35 Vengeance attack planes built by unprofitable Vultee Aircraft in Los Angeles.

In 1939, Stinson-Detroit won a fixed-price Army order for one hundred Vigilants. Seeking a bigger piece of the military market, AVCO planned Stinson's expansion. But Detroit's auto and defense boom complicated hiring and the addition of new capacity. The independent-mindedness of Stinson's employees posed a more immediate problem. They were among the most experienced and best paid workers in this young industry and were proud of their roots in aircraft, which went back to building the big three-motor metal air transports designed by Charles Stinson and financed by Henry Ford in the twenties. They resisted the dilution of their unique skills which volume production of Vigilants entailed. At the same time, they rejected national labor organizations. In 1938, both the UAW and the IAM failed in their efforts to gain bargaining rights. For representation, the workers preferred informal consultation with engineers and supervisors. And to confront the company's efforts to cut wages, the Stinson workers preferred a militant local chapter of the Mechanics Educational Society of America (MESA).[5]

AVCO elected to abandon Detroit and MESA and follow the lead of other anti-labor manufacturers, such as Remington Rand, by accepting Nashville's promises of ideal conditions for industrial relocation and expansion. Mayor Tom Cummings, Tennessee's Governor Prentice Cooper, Ira Parker of the Nashville Chamber of Commerce, and other boosters offered "plenty of cheap labor." They boasted of their success in defying the Wagner Act and maintaining the open shop in the city's tiny but expanding manufacturing base. By fall 1939, construction at the Stinson-Nashville plant was well under way, and city officials helped the firm organize an "Aircraft School"—the Hume-Fogg Technical School. There, noted IAM organizer Fred Laudemann, "farmer boys and high school students" received training in the semiskilled and unskilled jobs to which Stinson managers hoped to reduce aircraft work in anticipation of volume production.[6]

The Nashville move meant significant savings on AVCO's wage bill. On April 1, 1940, when the plant began hiring, some eighteen thousand people applied for Stinson's initial one thousand jobs. Teenage boys and young men filled these positions, along with a few young women. The idea of building aircraft, reinforced by free airplane rides provided by the company, thrilled these new recruits. The new Stinson plant generated much local excitement, patriotism, and anticipation. The press hailed what appeared to be the city's step toward a bold new future in aviation. AVCO's president, Harry Woodhead, a former Trusco-Republic Steel executive in Ohio and a protégé of Girdler, was only trying to fuel this boosterism, but nevertheless predicted accurately what indeed would make the new plant a success. To him, Nashville's labor force seemed not to be "highly skilled in our type of work, but it makes up for that in spirit, disposition, and enthusiasm."[7]

Eager workers even tapped their savings for "tuition" at the Hume-Fogg Aircraft School, in effect paying to go to work. Stinson offered thirty-five to fifty cents an hour, nearly half the rate for beginners in Detroit and well below minimum wage recommendations laid out for the military aircraft industry under the Walsh-Healey public contracts law of 1936. The company also deceived Detroit workers into moving their skills south. Mechanics and electricians making $1.25 an hour in Detroit found their wages trimmed to 60 cents, most of their shop privileges ended, and the company reneging on promises to cover their moving costs. "We were promised more money here and we got HELL!" fumed one angry machinist.[8]

Early in 1940, local Machinists targeted the Stinson works for organization. But the IAM and AFL were weak in Nashville and seemed mainly concerned with helping local employers thwart the CIO. AVCO quickly built a warm relationship with old-line organized labor in the state capital. William Cherry, a local lawyer and former judge, signed on as Stinson's attorney. He had connections with Gerald Foley, president of the conservative Tennessee Labor Federation, whom local business leaders and the mayor, according to one IAM organizer, "always called in . . . and in that way always avoided trouble," such as CIO initiatives in Nashville. Cherry worked for company recognition of the IAM, in anticipation of a CIO effort at AVCO. Indeed, following their usual practice, the Machinists pushed for recognition, an IAM officer admitted, by "first organizing the Boss." Their key man in the plant assured company executives that "I am not in any way radical" and informed them of the IAM Grand Lodge's decision to abandon its rigid craft and apprenticeship rules, which made little sense in mass-production of military aircraft.[9]

But Stinson workers showed little interest in the IAM. In the summer of 1940, the IAM had just sixteen members in the plant. The migrants from Detroit came with a strong sense of solidarity, born of their experiences with MESA, but most left the city in disgust for better-paying jobs elsewhere. So Stinson managers preserved all their options by ignoring the IAM, establishing an illegal "dummy union," and unilaterally imposing their wage and job scheme. They paid wage increases to key workers to distract them from IAM pamphleteers.

Soon, however, the IAM's chance came, when the UAW announced a national drive in aircraft. In Los Angeles, UAW locals made strong inroads among AVCO's Vultee workers and in November 1940 waged a bitter but successful strike there. These developments caused much apprehension in Nashville, particularly since AVCO had collapsed its

Vultee and Stinson holdings into one corporate entity and renamed the Stinson plant Vultee-Nashville. Mayor Cummings, worried about the CIO coming to town, pleaded with Vultee managers to recognize the Machinists' new Aero Lodge #735 so as to preclude a possible UAW challenge. IAM organizers darkly warned of "the possibilities of these people coming in here any minute" and persuaded the company to hold a consent election between Lodge #735 and the company union. That way, the IAM men argued, the company might "avoid the NLRB route" and "public hearings and CIO participation." The IAM's resort to such tactics, its critics charged, smacked of undemocratic organizing and "sweetheart" bargaining, practices they claimed were typical of the union's approach to organizing the aircraft industry. Nonetheless, in a non-NLRB election held on September 10, 1940, the IAM squeaked through with a two-vote victory over the company union, winning 294 of the 586 ballots cast.[10]

Vultee executives accepted the results, but through the remainder of 1940 they ignored the lodge's efforts to negotiate a contract. Finally, on January 22, 1941, when company officials had imposed work and wage patterns in the plant and production had begun, they signed an eighteen-month deal that included some of the industry's worst rates for the unskilled and semiskilled, who made up three-quarters of the production workforce. The contract pegged wages of nonproduction workers such as clerks, janitors, and stock runners at 40 cents an hour. Unskilled workers and Aircraft School graduates got a starting wage of 50 cents, which rose to 62 cents, with time-and-a-half for overtime, after eight months on the job. Salaried managers, accountants, and supervisors did relatively well, as did skilled workers. Wages for the latter ranged from $1.10 to $1.20 per hour. Relatively high wages for skilled employees reflected the IAM's traditional craft consciousness, but more important was the company's need to compete in a rapidly tightening market for skilled metal workers. Lodge #735 agents crowed that Vultee "officials and their lawyer have been as congenial as anyone could possibly ask."[11]

The local lodgemen's acquiescent stance generated some concern at the IAM Grand Lodge in Washington, D.C. There, early in 1941, following the retirement of President Arthur Wharton, industrial unionists at Boeing Aircraft in Seattle, who won control of what quickly had become the IAM's biggest lodge, challenged the union's old-guard leadership. These militants denounced the Grand Lodge's passive and unimaginative approach to organizing and bargaining for workers on the expanding payrolls of West Coast aircraft factories. The conservative Harvey Brown won out in the fray, but only because he used every Red-baiting tactic and received every possible assistance from the FBI, War Department, and White House to defeat the Boeing activists and purge them from the union. During this struggle, Grand Lodge members found it politic to criticize the Vultee-Nashville deal as "only another speed up proposition" and to denounce its substandard wage levels for new workers. Locally, however, IAM agents continued to privilege the union's traditional constituents, the minority of skilled workers, whose rates, they feared, would suffer if the unskilled did better.[12]

Through the summer of 1941, Lodge #735 leaders continued to enjoy their warm relationship with Vultee executives. It "sure is a nice setup," reported the lodge's business agent, even though the firm stalled on scheduled wage hikes for production workers, whose numbers grew to twenty-six hundred by mid-August. Vultee was under much pressure. Production of O-49 Vigilants had fallen well behind schedule, thanks to the many usual complications and mistakes attendant upon rapid tooling up, building jigs, and arranging aircraft assembly so that inexperienced workers could do the job. Meanwhile, the company complicated matters even further by expanding the factory from 170,000 to 720,000 square feet to fill contracts for an entirely new line of aircraft, the A-35 Vengeance attack plane.[13]

In 1940, the Vultee-Nashville plant turned out but one Vigilant. Only in late summer of 1941 did it approach planned output levels. Managers achieved even this level only after heeding the advice of production engineers, who urged them to abandon unrealistic work-flow schemes based on mass-production concepts. Vultee-Nashville found that the widely admired model of Ford's Willow Run bomber plant, which sought to apply auto-industry techniques to aircraft, was misguided, because warplanes were far more complex than automobiles and needed flexible manufacturing techniques. Warplanes underwent constant design changes and modifications during production, in an ongoing effort to improve their military performance. And the military frequently turned upside down such plants as Vultee-Nashville, ordering them to build entirely new aircraft models.

Indeed, whatever success Vultee-Nashville had in producing badly needed O-49 light trainers (171 in 1941) was owed mainly to the adaptability of Nashville workers, who quickly developed the necessary skills and showed great initiative in finding ways to be useful in the plant.

What planners referred to as "manpower methods" proved a better approach to volume production of warplanes than the Fordist model. Rather than gearing production and training toward rigid, mechanized assembly lines that left workers with minimal autonomy, the "manpower" approach relied on team units guided by informal direction and consultation. In this way, managers and supervisors encouraged the skill development, commitment, and shop-floor initiative that quality aircraft production needed. At Vultee-Nashville—and, indeed, wherever large-scale production of warplanes succeeded in plants across the U.S.—engaged and self-starting workers were the key ingredients.[14]

Despite its production gains, however, in 1941 AVCO-Vultee lost nearly one million dollars on its Vigilant army contracts, negotiated on a fixed-price basis before Congress approved cost-plus arrangements. In summer 1941, the company rejected the lodge's calls for wage hikes to give Vultee workers parity with aircraft workers in California. The latter, after the big June strike at North American Aviation in Los Angeles, had gained across-the-board increases. The Nashville company also tried to staunch its financial hemorrhaging by recruiting low-cost female workers—mostly teenagers—from surrounding rural areas. By late 1941, it was hiring three women for every man to fill production jobs. Women got only 50 cents an hour, with increases at the company's discretion. By late 1943, they made up 38 per cent of the total workforce and more than half of direct workers.[15]

For Vultee, the IAM posed little in the way of a challenge on workers' behalf. The workers themselves seemed not to care, despite the well-publicized inferiority of their pay scale. Most workers seemed content with their situations. They seemed to value the regular work, the experience of being involved with the new aircraft industry, and, especially after Pearl Harbor, the opportunity to contribute to the war effort. Throughout the war years, wage drag continued. Discontent mounted, but either a sense of bearing one's patriotic burden contained it or workers moved on to other, better-paying war jobs. Even here, the Nashville workers were unusually restrained. At Nashville, absentee and turnover rates were among the lowest in the industry. The workers achieved these despite the relatively high levels at which male employees left work to join the armed forces. Elsewhere, their counterparts far more often used defense work as a means of avoiding the draft. And since wartime dislocation and congestion in Nashville were hardly on a scale comparable to much larger centers of defense mobilization, there were far fewer of the daily hardships and aggravations for workers that drove up absenteeism and turnover rates. Nashville workers, too, were unusually motivated and dedicated to the war effort; their safety and Victory Bond–buying records were among the nation's best.[16]

Workers showed little interest in the union. They paid dues but only because the company deducted them from their wages through the check-off. Few workers came to meetings. The Machinists' business agent complained that they "have never been educated on the ways of Unionism. You can't tell them they can't do this or they can't do that . . . they politely tell you to go to hell."[17]

Meanwhile, the company continued to benefit from having the IAM as bargaining agent for its workers. Lodge #735 deterred the CIO and helped Vultee deflect the attentions of the Fair Employment Practice Committee (FEPC), which in the spring of 1941 launched an investigation. This presidentially appointed body, along with the Nashville chapter of the National Association for the Advancement of Colored People, targeted the lily-white plant. The handful of African-American sweepers, latrine workers, and young women handling files in the offices comprised .5 percent of Vultee's workforce. And, as part of Nashville's segregated public school system, the Fogg-Hume Aircraft School barred blacks from training and access to production jobs. But Vultee officials argued that expanding opportunities for blacks would create racial tensions and disrupt a production schedule already well behind its targeted pace.

White unionists agreed. During the war, the IAM continued its longstanding discriminatory posture. Its ancient "initiation ritual" harked back to the group's nineteenth-century roots in the Jim Crow South and existed mainly to bar blacks. The IAM's wartime policy, in the words of one frank IAM officer, was: "No colored unless they are present before the IAM gets an organization." In Nashville, Lodge #735 agents vowed "to keep from hiring the negroes to work with our *Southern Gentlemen*."[18]

The company's attorney hoped that the union would bear the onus for the effort to resist the FEPC and black applicants. IAM President Harvey Brown was only too happy to accommodate, and he energetically took up Vultee's race case in Washington, D.C. To him, the matter seemed "a nigger in the woodpile." He thought the FEPC investigation was a smokescreen behind which CIO, FEPC, and Office of Production Management officials plotted to help the UAW organize the plant. He determined to fight back and helped to stall the investigation. When the FEPC proceedings finally began in Birmingham on June 18, 1942, IAM spokesmen defended Vultee. "Management does hire negroes as janitors and in like occupations," the Machinists argued. "Obviously negroes are adapted for that kind of work. Most anyone familiar with factory work, especially where aircraft are being built, can understand why management believes that white workers are the most qualified and competent."[19]

Even under the most favorable circumstances, the FEPC could do little more than expose and catalogue racist hiring and personnel practices. Its efforts on behalf of black workers in a hardened center of racial discrimination such as Nashville were largely futile. An IAM closed shop would have given the FEPC a stronger hand at Vultee, but the union-management deal was only for a "preferential hiring agreement." And Lodge #735 shrewdly set up a Jim Crow "sub-Lodge," the Vultee Colored Employees Association, that in late 1943 had only forty-four members, out of a total Vultee workforce of about sixty-five hundred. The minimal presence of blacks at Vultee was enough to keep the plant within the technical bounds of FDR's Executive Order #8802 which in June 1941 had established the FEPC.[20]

The Machinists successfully defended the discriminatory practices and attitudes of the company, the workers, and white Nashvillians. The IAM proved far less successful in advancing the economic interests of white aircraft workers. On December 8, 1941, the still unprofitable Vultee offered slight increases to production workers in a bid for goodwill, solidarity, and greater effort in the wake of the Japanese attack. But the new rates remained well behind the rates then standard in California and increasingly so among northern aircraft plants. Harvey Brown's criticism of these minimal improvements focused on problems of union rivalry, not equity for Nashville workers. Vultee's wages, he complained, "will allow the CIO to make capital out of such a situation in our future organizing activities." He threatened to launch a review at the National Defense Mediation Board. But Vultee workers and local IAM agents accepted the offer, the latter again pointing to the relatively favorable rates for the small minority of skilled workers.[21]

By late 1941, however, relations between Vultee-Nashville and Lodge #735 took a sharp turn for the worse. It was then that Tom Girdler assumed direct control of the company and led it into a giant new military corporate combine, the Consolidated-Vultee Aircraft Corporation (CVAC). Girdler's aggressive management style increasingly had found admirers in the Washington, D.C., offices of the warplane industry's key administrators. From their top positions at the War and Navy Departments and at the Defense Plant Corporation, these recent corporate recruits, many of them on loan from Wall Street firms, oversaw contracting, production, priority scheduling, and the politics of the nation's immense new supply base for airpower. Aided by the Office of Price Administration and the Office of Economic Stabilization, they hewed to the anti-inflationary line and kept labor union officials on the sidelines for the duration.

Nor did other government agencies, such as the War Manpower Commission, the War Production Board, Congress, or even the White House more than partly offset their dominance over wartime aircraft policy. True, the National War Labor Board (NWLB) frequently defended unions and collective bargaining against the assaults of the corporate "dollar-a-year men." In July 1942, it strengthened unions institutionally by granting "maintenance of membership" status. But the NWLB's increasingly aggressive wage-restraint rulings and its unwillingness to confront wage drag in aircraft made maintenance of membership of limited benefit to aircraft workers and their unions.[22]

Girdler's extensive industrial experience boosted his appeal for planners as an anti-union, low-wage employer, especially since the planners projected an eventual wartime labor force of some five million workers. In autumn of 1941, word of FDR's secret "Victory Program," with its astonishing call for yearly output of 125,000 planes, circulated at high levels in Washington. War Department leaders resolved to gain better control over Consolidated Aircraft, one of the industry's weakest corporate links. In late 1941, Robert A. Lovett, Secretary of War Henry Stimson's assistant secretary for air and his former Wall Street associate, led the push for Girdler to become chairman and chief executive of a new company that would combine AVCO's aircraft holdings in Los Angeles and Nashville with those of Consolidated. The new combine, Lovett hoped, would revitalize Consolidated's vast B-24 bomber and navy seaplane works on San Diego Bay and at its new complex rising on the plains near Fort Worth, Texas.

Lovett planned the ouster of Reuben Fleet, who had run Consolidated since well before its 1935 move from Buffalo in pursuit of Southern California's low wages and open-shop environment. He no longer could manage his mushrooming aircraft works, which had grown from a shoestring employer of a few hundred to a giant defense contractor with nearly fifty thousand workers. Fleet consistently had missed production quotas and bickered with Washington, always demanding draft deferrals and approval of better wages to stem high turnover at his plants. Thus, in December 1941, the War and Navy departments arranged AVCO-Vultee's buyout of the tired and overwhelmed Reuben Fleet. Girdler quickly opened bottlenecks and arranged for new management and equipment and for CVAC's rapid expansion into cities across the East.[23]

The IAM represented workers at CVAC plants, but only nominally. At Nashville, in the summer of 1942, the company continued to ignore the union and stalled negotiations for a new contract, pending the NWLB's decisions on union security rights in the landmark "Little Steel" case. Unreconstructed open-shoppers like Girdler hoped that the board might suspend these rights, at least for the war's duration, but the July maintenance-of-membership decision in the Little Steel case dashed these hopes. Still, at plants such as CVAC's, "union security" meant little beyond the institutional survival of union locals, forcing the company to accept a formal but easily contained presence for organized labor. Otherwise the union had no effective claim on CVAC's managers. In Nashville, in August 1942, CVAC signed a new contract, but only because it contained no improvements and because managers knew that ongoing NWLB consideration of wage stabilization for the entire aircraft industry would delay its implementation.

Increasingly functioning as an inflation-fighting agency, the NWLB dragged its feet. The board, complained IAM leaders, proved "very successful in injecting the issue of price control" into its monitoring of aircraft labor relations. Month after month, it steadfastly avoided efforts to standardize and stabilize the national aircraft labor market and to enable the industry to overcome its long prewar history of wage drag. The NWLB failed to respond, even when high officials in the War and Navy departments and manufacturers such as CVAC urged relief to help them recruit and retain increasingly scarce workers. As a result, turmoil characterized the national aircraft labor market, especially on the West Coast, where wages lagged some 30 per cent behind those paid in other defense sectors. While there were few strikes, heavy turnover, absenteeism, and unmet production schedules plagued contractors. Still, the NWLB stalled, deferring decisions and ordering one study of the problems after another until mid-1944, when a sense of impending Allied victory and the sheer scale and momentum of U.S. aircraft production overwhelmed various local labor crises and rendered systematic national intervention into aircraft labor relations superfluous.

In March 1943, the NWLB approved 15 percent increases in aircraft on the basis of its July 1942 "Little Steel Formula." But this award applied only to West Coast plants. Elsewhere, the board followed FDR's "hold the line" order on wages. Henceforth, the NWLB would consider relief for the nation's other aircraft plants only on a case-by-case basis and only when top military men insisted that low wage rates threatened critical projects. NWLB policies frustrated even the Nashville-CVAC managers. In the fall of 1942, they turned to Lodge #735 for help in attracting and retaining enough trained workers to maintain production. The company accelerated job promotions beyond the contract's terms, "trying to inject wage increases," in the words of a union representative, only to have the board's Atlanta regional office reject this maneuver.[24]

Turnover at the plant increased, as experienced workers saw opportunities elsewhere and quit. Even so, Nashville's turnover rates remained among the lowest in the nation's aircraft factories. In 1943, those workers who remained, along with those newly hired, turned out a remarkable 766 A-35 Vengeances. The accomplishment was real, even if output was half the schedule, and even if the Vengeance, a casualty of the rapidly evolving technology of air war, proved too slow and ungainly for combat use. Indeed, early that year, the Army Air Forces (AAF) had told Vultee that it had "no tactical use for the A-35." But the company was to build them anyway for Lend-Lease export to British forces in the Far East, thus keeping the productive Nashville workers occupied and in position to produce a better warplane.[25]

Frustrating losses of experienced workers continued. In early 1943, CVAC's managers failed to win NWLB approval of lump-sum bonuses for skilled workers, many of whom had tired of delays in these promised payments and were moving on. In Washington, CVAC, AFL, and IAM lobbyists worked together, appealing to the board to make Nashville a test-case for wage relief in southern, northeastern, and midwestern aircraft. In response, in May 1943, the NWLB created a new committee, the National Airframe Panel, under Benjamin Aaron, a young industrial relations lawyer. Soon the panel approved national wage patterns along the lines of the Southern California Aircraft Industry Plan (SCAIP), an allegedly "scientific" program devised by the Los Angeles area aircraft trade association to "rationalize" workplace conditions through detailed job classifications and performance evaluations. In fact, SCAIP reflected its originators' determination to marginalize unions and impose greater control over the workforce and over factory floors, even though this approach ran counter to the flexible work patterns that aircraft manufacture required.[26]

In August 1943, the Office of Economic Stabilization at last concurred with the Airframe Panel's decision. CVAC then promptly lost interest in the IAM. Its managers quickly implemented the SCAIP in all its plants, hoping to contain wages, curb the union, extend factory-floor control, and "rationalize" production. At Nashville, the new system disrupted the flexible "manpower" work relationships and patterns that had become familiar to the workers and that were so essential to the plant's success.

Timing could not have been worse, nor could management's search for greater control have been more counterproductive. In the summer of 1943, Army Air Forces officers, impressed by how Nashville workers could turn out A-35s, pegged them to convert to build center and tail sections for two thousand P-38 fighter planes for final assembly at Lockheed's plant in Burbank, California. CVAC accepted this high-priority work on a fixed-price basis, which, given renewed downward pressure on wages and upward pressure for workplace control by management, again had become the norm in warplane contracts, replacing most cost-plus deals.[27]

The twin-boom Lockheed Lightning was a spectacular and lethal warplane, but of an unusual design and a particularly complex manufacturing process. To be chosen for this program was an honor for Nashville's patriotic workers, who felt even greater pride in the spring of 1944, when the AAF called on them to produce *complete* P-38s. But as they confronted the daunting challenge of converting to P-38s, the workers found themselves confused, irritated, and distracted by management's imposition of the California Plan's rigid job schemes. As a result, Lightning output suffered badly. Lodge #735, its leaders blaming "that Tom Girdler, notorious Labor Hater," could not even get classification and pay lists from management. The union could only complain about the "high-handedness of supervisors" and swamp the NLRB and NWLB with hundreds of grievances, all to little avail. The company reassigned IAM activists and refused to defend their draft deferments.

Toward the end of November 1944, a time when many predicted the end of the war in Europe by Christmas, CVAC's Nashville officials began implementing a plan just developed at a Chicago meeting of CVAC's top executives and managers. Along with other aircraft industry executives, they had gathered to coordinate plans to reestablish the open shop for what seemed an imminent postwar period. "Plant protection" men—armed guards roaming the factories—now replaced industrial relations experts. The pattern of intimidation, designed to highlight the union's weakness in worker's eyes, included regular "downgrading" of workers through reshuffling the job lists of the California Plan.[28]

The performance of Nashville workers suffered because of management's combined confusion and hostility. In all of 1944, they turned out only 235 obsolete A-35s. Despite beginning to convert for P-38s in August 1943, they still had not built a single Lightning by the end of 1944. At last, in January 1945, four P-38s rolled out the factory doors. By April 1945, CVAC, now employing five thousand workers, had raised output to 25 per month, a stellar achievement given the aircraft's unusual complexity and the troubled shop-floor environment.

But almost as soon as CVAC had managed this feat, Germany surrendered. The AAF promptly announced drastic cutbacks in aircraft production, including an end to Nashville's P-38 program. IAM's President Brown could only report the decision to "wash out" P-38 work at Nashville and plead with the AAF and Navy to consider the plant for other military projects. In May, twenty-five hundred workers were laid off. By year's end, only five hundred remained, mostly demoted, nonunion, and male supervisory personnel who occupied themselves by completing navy work transferred to Nashville from other CVAC plants. After the Japanese surrender, military aircraft orders were cut across the board. In November 1945, CVAC announced plans to convert the plant to the manufacture of home appliances under the Crosley brand name.[29]

Throughout the planning, operation, and demobilization of the Nashville plant, company and government officials successfully avoided real collective bargaining or any other *formal* recognition of industrial democracy, even though aircraft production ultimately depended on the workers' *informal* methods of industrial democracy on the factory floor. These patterns, and the belligerent anti-unionism of the postwar period, were similar to those evident in most other U.S. warplane factories. In early 1946, the company unilaterally suspended maintenance of membership, dues check-off, vacation pay, and seniority rights and imposed upon passive IAM negotiators a new contract that even reduced wages to rates prevailing before the Little Steel increases of 1943.

The workers' indifference and conservatism on union matters during the war years certainly facilitated Consolidated-Vultee's anti-labor efforts, as did the stale and hidebound IAM. During the postwar years, the IAM continued to play a dysfunctional role on behalf of the workers, even when they became more militant. In late 1946, the company's executives again turned to Lodge #735, much as they had in 1940–41, for aid in thwarting another drive by the Congress of Industrial Organizations. At first it seemed that the CIO would be victorious. In an August 1947 NLRB election, eighteen hundred CVAC workers, tired of low wages and IAM lethargy and collusion, overwhelmingly voted for the United Steelworkers–CIO. But IAM lawyers convinced the NLRB to void the results, on the grounds that the Steelworkers' leaders had not signed the non-Communist affidavit required by the Taft-Hartley Act for access to NLRB services. That decision sparked a long, violent, inter-union strike that amounted to yet another defeat for the CIO's Operation Dixie and another victory for arbitrary management at CVAC and for low-wage manufacturing in the postwar New South.[30]

Notes

The author is grateful to Bill Berman, Fred Koke, Mark Tamminga, and Larry Stokes for their encouragement and criticism. Financial aid from the National Air and Space Museum, Smithsonian Institution, and the Social Sciences and Humanities Research Council of Canada made this essay possible.

1. On the aircraft industry's formative years, see Irving Brinton Holley, Jr., *Buying Aircraft: Materiel Procurement for the Army Air Forces* (Washington, D.C.: USGPO, 1962); and Jacob Vander Meulen, *The Politics of Aircraft: Building an American Military Industry* (Lawrence: Univ. Press of Kansas, 1991).
2. Melvyn Dubofsky, *The State and Labor in Modern America* (Chapel Hill: Univ. of North Carolina Press, 1994), 171–77; Howell John Harris, *The Right to Manage: Industrial Relations Policies of American Business in the 1940s* (Madison: Univ. of Wisconsin Press, 1982), 41– 89; Steve Fraser, *Labor Will Rule: Sidney Hillman and the Rise of American Labor* (New York: Basic Books, 1991), 441–94; Alan Brinkley, *The End to Reform: New Deal Liberalism in Recession and War* (New York: Knopf, 1995), 137–200; Nelson Lichtenstein, *Labor's War at Home: The CIO in World War II* (New York: Cambridge Univ. Press, 1982), 26–46, 82–83; Nelson Lichentstein, *The Most Dangerous Man in Detroit: Walter Reuther and the Fate of American Labor* (New York: Basic Books, 1995), 154–74.
3. "U.S. Military Aircraft Acceptances 1940–1945, Aircraft, Engine and Propeller Production," U.S. Civil Aeronautics Administration, Dept. of Commerce, 1946, 193–97. Copy in the Library of the National Air and Space Museum. Figures do not include workers in parts subcontracting, engines, props, gliders, ordnance, instruments, and modification. On the "southern takeoff," see Gavin Wright, *Old South, New South: Revolutions in the Southern Economy Since the Civil War* (New York: Basic Books, 1986), 239–74; Robert J. Newman, *Growth in the American South: Changing Regional Employment and Wage Patterns in the 1960s and 1970s* (New York: New York Univ. Press, 1984); Charles P. Roland, *The Improbable Era: The South Since World War II* (Lexington: Univ. Press of

Kentucky, 1975); James C. Cobb, *Industrialization and Southern Society, 1877–1984* (Lexington: Univ. Press of Kentucky, 1984); Bruce Schulman, *From Cotton Belt to Sunbelt: Federal Policy, Economic Development, and the Transformation of the South, 1938–1980* (New York: Oxford Univ. Press, 1991).

4. "Report on Vultee Aircraft, Inc.," Nov. 30, 1940, and Nov. 31, 1941, Arthur Young and Co., in Records of the Senate National Defense Committee (Truman Committee), National Archives and Records Administration (NARA), RG 46, Box 698.
5. Earl Melton, IAM Grand Lodge Representative, to Fred D. Laudemann, IAM General Vice President, Mar. 6, 1940, Reel 343, IAM International President's Records, State Historical Society of Wisconsin, Madison.
6. Laudemann to O. H. Dye, IAM–Grand Lodge Representative, Jan. 29, 1940, IAM Reel 343. Tennessee was one of organized labor's strongest footholds in the South, mainly because of its presence in Memphis, Knoxville, and Chattanooga. But Nashville, a government, commercial, and financial center, offered few opportunities for unionists. See Robert G. Spinney, "On the Homefront: Nashville, Tennessee, and the Early Years of Mobilization in the Second World War" (Ph.D. diss., Vanderbilt Univ., 1995).
7. *Nashville Tennessean,* Jan. 26 and Apr. 3, 1940.
8. *Nashville Tennessean,* Feb. 29, 1940; H. C. Summers, IAM–Grand Lodge Representative, to Laudemann, Mar. 28, Apr. 18, and May 4, 1940, IAM Reel 343.
9. Summers to J. G. Little, IAM Business Representative, May 5, 1940; Summers to Laudemann, May 14, 1940, and Laudemann to Summers, May 15, 1940, IAM Reel 343.
10. Summers to Laudemann, July 25 and 26, and Sept. 10, 1940, IAM Reel 343. See also Spinney, "On the Homefront."
11. Wage patterns in untitled documents dated Jan. 1941, IAM Reel 343.
12. Mark Perlman, *The Machinists: A New Study in American Trade Unionism* (Cambridge, Mass.: Harvard Univ. Press, 1961), 98–128.
13. Summers to Laudemann, July 26, 1940, IAM Reel 343. On Nashville's production delays and successes, see Capt. E. Laughlin to Wright Field, Dayton, Ohio, Dec. 11, 1940, NARA, Army Adjutant General (AAG) files, 1942–44, RG 18, Box 23, .004, classified; Gen. Oliver P. Echols to Gen. Henry H. Arnold, Mar. 29, 1941, NARA, AAG 1939–42, Box 60, entry 293, classified; Gen. Kenneth B. Wolfe to Gen. B. Meyers, Nov. 13, 1942, NARA, AAG 1942–44, Box 25, .004, unclassified. For data on plant layout, see NARA, Records of the Defense Plant Corporation, Plancor 1314, RG 234, Box 490, entry 146.
14. See A. B. Berghell, *Production Engineering in the Aircraft Industry* (New York: McGraw-Hill, 1944); Tom Lilley et al., *Problems of Accelerating Aircraft Production During World War II* (Cambridge, Mass.: Harvard Graduate School of Business Administration, 1947); Jonathan Zeitlin, "Flexibility and Mass Production at War: Aircraft Manufacture in Britain, the United States, and Germany, 1939–1945," *Technology and Culture* 36 (Jan. 1995): 46–49; and Jacob Vander Meulen, *Building the B-29* (Washington, D.C.: Smithsonian Institution Press, 1995). For discussions of "flexible specialization" in production systems, see Michael J.

Piore and Charles F. Sabel, *The Second Industrial Divide: Possibilities for Prosperity* (New York: Basic Books, 1984); Charles F. Sabel and Jonathan Zeitlin, "Historical Alternatives to Mass Production: Politics, Markets and Technology in Nineteenth Century Industrialization," *Past and Present,* no. 108 (Aug. 1985): 133–76; Philip Scranton, "Diversity in Diversity: Flexible Production and American Industrialization, 1880–1930," *Business History Review* 65 (Spring 1991): 27–90.

15. Eric Peterson, IAM–General Vice President, to Summers, Nov. 1, 1941; J. M. Shelton, #735 Business Representative, to Peterson, Nov. 20, 1941, IAM Reel 343; "Labor Statistics for the Aeronautical Industry," Mar. 31, 1944, p. 8, NARA, Box 31, AAG 1942–44, 004.02, unclassified.
16. "Labor Statistics for the Aeronautical Industry," 16.
17. Shelton to Peterson, Sept. 16, 1941, IAM Reel 343.
18. S. Doerner, IAM–Grand Lodge Representative to Peterson, July 31, 1941; Summers to Peterson, n.d. [1941], IAM Reel 343. See Spinney, "On the Homefront." On IAM race policies, see Perlman, *The Machinists,* 276–81; Herbert Hill, "The Racial Practices of Organized Labor," in *Employment, Race, and Poverty,* ed. Herbert Hill and Arthur M. Ross (New York: Harcourt, Brace and World, 1967), 395.
19. Brown to Peterson, Aug. 11, 1941; Brown to Shelton, June 11, 1942; P. Allen, #735 Business Representative, to Brown, Dec. 3, 1943, IAM Reel 343.
20. See Merl E. Reed, *Seedtime for the Modern Civil Rights Movement: The President's Committee on Fair Employment Practices* (Baton Rouge: Louisiana State Univ. Press, 1991). On the minuscule presence of African Americans in aircraft-aerospace into the 1960s, see Herbert R. Northrup, *The Negro in the Aerospace Industry* (Philadelphia: Industrial Research Unit, Wharton School of finance and Commerce, 1968).
21. Brown to Shelton, Dec. 8, 1941, IAM Reel 343.
22. For organized labor's marginal role in aircraft planning and oversight, see R. J. Purcell, "Labor Policies of the NDAC and the OPM," Special Study no. 23, pamphlet, Washington, D.C.: U.S. Civilian Production Administration, 1946. Copy in the Library of the National Air and Space Museum. For labor's weakness in wartime mobilization planning generally, see George Q. Flynn, *The Mess in Washington: Manpower Mobilization in World War II* (Westport, Conn.: Greenwood, 1979); Byron Fairchild and Jonathan Grossman, *The Army and Industrial Manpower* (Washington, D.C.: USGPO, 1959). On the NWLB, see Timothy A. Willard, "Labor and the National War Labor Board, 1942–1945: An Experiment in Corporate Wage Stabilization" (Ph.D. diss., Univ. of Toledo, 1984); Robert H. Zieger, *The CIO, 1935–1955* (Chapel Hill: Univ. of North Carolina Press, 1995), esp. 145–47.
23. "Survey of Consolidated Aircraft, Inc.," Nov. 1941, and telephone typescripts in Records of Artemus L. Gates, Assistant Secretary of the Navy, NARA, RG 72, Box 47, entry 131; *New York Times,* Nov. 26, 1941. See data on AVCO in Records of the Office of the Secretary of War, Henry Stimson, NARA, RG 107, Box 3C, Secret; and in Robert Patterson (Undersecretary of War) Papers, Library of Congress, Box 108–9.

24. Summers to Laudemann, Dec. 12, 1942, IAM Reel 343. On the NWLB's anti-inflationary policies, see "Prospects Under Present Conditions," Aug. 11, 1943, Patterson Papers, Box 141; Dubofsky, *The State and Labor,* 185–86; Joel Seidman, *American Labor from Defense to Reconversion* (Chicago: Univ. of Chicago Press, 1953), 109–30; Lester V. Chandler and Donald H. Wallace, eds., *Economic Mobilization and Stabilization: Selected Materials on the Economics of War and Defense* (New York: Holt, 1951).
25. Minutes of the Aircraft Production Board (APB), Box 334, classified, bulk, 334., AAG 1942–44, RG 18 [hereafter referred to as APB Minutes], Mar. 22 and 29, 1943.
26. F. Coonley, IAM Grand Lodge Representative, to Summers, Apr. 15, 1943; Coonley to Shelton, Aug. 2, 1943, IAM Reel 344.
27. In 1944, CVAC-Nashville ranked first in manpower utilization among the eight U.S. plants building single-engine AAF attack and Navy reconnaissance craft. "Indices of Airplane Production Efficiency," June 26, 1944, K201-45, Simpson Research Center, Maxwell Air Force Base, Montgomery, Ala. Nashville aircraft workers in another, smaller plant nearby also were highly regarded. About 900 of them at the nonunion Tennessee Aircraft Corporation ran "a good busy shop" turning out tail components for the P-47 Thunderbolt, the venerable workhorse fighter built by Republic Aircraft at Evansville, Ind.; APB Minutes, May 15, 1944.
28. APB Minutes, May 23 and Oct. 4, 1943; H. Schrader, IAM Research Director, to the National Aircraft Panel, Oct. 29, 1943; G. Hastings, Chief of Industrial Relations at CVAC-Nashville, to Allen, Dec. 24, 1943; Summers to Laudemann, Nov. 28, 1943; P. Chipman, Grand Lodge Representative, to Schrader, Apr. 29, 1944; C. Lindsey, Grand Lodge Representative, to Chipman, Jan. 16, 1945; Lindsey to Schrader, Apr. 24, 1945, IAM Reel 344. On industrywide planning for a postwar offensive in labor relations, see the records of the aircraft industry trade association, the Aeronautical Chamber of Commerce, "Annual Meeting," Dec. 7, 1944, Reel 50.27.7; and "Committee—Industrial Relations," 1944, Reel 60.21.9; both in the Library of the National Air and Space Museum.
29. Brown to J. Lallemand, Business Representative #735, Apr. 28, 1945. "Airplane Acceptances," 54; "Terminations on the Aircraft Working Schedule," Apr.–May 1945, NARA, AAG 1945, RG 18, Box 321, classified; *New York Times,* Nov. 2, 1945.
30. See correspondence in IAM Reel 344; *New York Times,* Nov. 21 and 27, 1947, and Apr. 18, 1948.

"Scientific Unionism" and the "Negro Question": Communists and the Transport Workers Union in Miami, 1944–1949

Alex Lichtenstein

In May 1945, Charles Smolikoff, director of the Florida Industrial Union Council, described to Lucy Mason the mixed record on race compiled by the state's Congress of Industrial Organizations (CIO) affiliates over the previous two years. He proudly noted that, in Miami's Local 59 of the Industrial Union of Marine and Shipbuilding Workers of America (IUMSWA), the ten white and four black officers of the executive board met together; still, he admitted, the union continued to hold "separate membership meetings" for blacks and whites. In Jacksonville, however, IUMSWA's Local 32 had "finally instituted full mixed membership meetings." Even so, social segregation still proved the rule in both cities; it was "impossible in this state and at this time to have any mixed social affairs sponsored by CIO," Smolikoff confessed. Even so, the union organizer emphasized, "CIO POLICY IN FLORIDA [IS] STRICTLY ORGANIZING ALL WORKERS INTO ONE UNION . . . NO AUXILIARIES."[1]

In 1945, the most recent CIO success in Florida was the organization of Local 500 of the Transport Workers Union (TWU), which in March 1945 won representation for over two thousand workers at Pan American Airways, Miami's largest employer. Two black workers served on Local 500's integrated executive board, even though whites comprised 90 percent of the new union's members. Nevertheless, Smolikoff informed Mason that "opposition by white workers to mixed meetings [is] still bitter" and that he had to combat "extreme Negro nationalism" among the isolated and outnumbered black workers as well.[2] The hostility of their white union brothers in the skilled mechanical divisions must have been a bitter pill for Pan Am's black porters, janitors, and cafeteria workers to swallow, for, despite their small numbers, they had been instrumental in bringing the TWU to Miami's rapidly expanding airline industry.

Located at the heart of the most significant sector of Miami's expanding wartime and postwar economy, Local 500 stood out in Florida as the CIO's Achilles heel, as well as its most important organizational success. Not only did the union's challenges to racial discrimination prove a lightning rod for local white hostility, but also Smolikoff's Communist affiliation and politics eventually brought Local 500 under attack from Miami's press, the House Un-American Activities Committee (HUAC), union dissidents, the TWU's national leadership, the United Auto Workers (UAW), the CIO's Southern Organizing Committee, and even the black workers who had helped build the union in the first place. Communist organizers for Miami's TWU initially found a solid base for the CIO among the airport's small group of black workers and injected into the local a commitment to interracial unionism, racial equality in the workplace, and civil rights activism in the community. Yet, at key junctures, the expediency of retaining power in a white-majority union weakened the Communists' challenge to segregationism, undermining African-American workers' faith in their leadership. Moreover, Smolikoff's promotion of Communist Party causes made the union vulnerable to a broad anti-Communist coalition that represented far more than a mask for racism. By the end of the decade, the combination of internal factionalism and external anti-Communist attacks drove Party members from power in Local 500, extinguishing altogether the union's nascent postwar commitment to racial equality.

The conflict over the presence of Communists in TWU Local 500 both mirrored and influenced the larger paroxysms that shook the CIO during the years 1946–50. This era of trade-union history has become a twice-told tale: first, as the story of the freeing of genuine trade unionism from the pernicious influence (or grip) of a movement loyal only to a foreign power; and, more recently, as the chronicle of a cynical abandonment of the radical social vision of industrial unionism associated with the 1930s. Much of the best recent literature in the field focuses on the South and emphasizes a contrast between a CIO leadership unwilling to aggressively press for African-American members' rights, and a leftist opposition, primarily associated with the Communist Party, that represented "opportunities found and lost" in building a viable labor–civil rights coalition.[3] Each of these accounts resembles a morality play, tailored to the assumptions and programs of anti-Communist liberals or social democrats on the one hand, and post–New Left radicals on the other. The rise and fall of Communist trade unionism in postwar Miami, a rapidly growing southern city with no prewar experience of industrial unionism, reveals a far grayer picture however, with few angels on either side. In a battle for control of an important and militant local CIO union in an expanding economic sector and region, both Communists and anti-Communists frequently placed the struggle for power ahead of the needs of rank-and-file workers in general and of the small group of Pan Am's black workers in particular.

In the 1940s, wherever and whenever the CIO attempted to crack the union-resistant South, organizers found themselves on the horns of a profound racial dilemma. In industry after industry, plant after plant, black workers proved the CIO's most ardent partisans; but interracial unionism appeared deeply threatening to their white counterparts and coworkers. For unions constantly under employer assault, each step forward on racial issues carried with it the danger of two steps backward for the interracial unity so necessary for industrial unionism in biracial workplaces. But building a solid union foundation might mean subordinating the particular interests of black workers, even with regard to their central demands for nondiscriminatory hiring, promotion, and job categorization. In general, southern industries and plants with a preponderant number of black workers proved most amenable to the CIO's wartime and postwar organizing drives. But these same unions also tended to have Communists in their leadership and thus, with the advent of the Cold War, found themselves vulnerable to raiding and anti-Communist purges. Where blacks remained a minority, southern CIO unions often failed to overcome their white members' commitment to racial privilege.[4] As the leading CIO and Communist Party (CP) figure in the Miami area throughout the 1940s, Charles Smolikoff recognized this dilemma and attempted to confront it with a blend of militancy and pragmatism tailored to the minority status of the black workers in the unions he helped to organize.

Born and raised in Brooklyn, Smolikoff moved to Miami in 1937 for his health, even though he was only twenty-one years old, having suffered from rheumatic fever. Upon his arrival in Florida, he immediately helped to organize a movement to support the Spanish Republic's fight against Franco. Subsequently, he organized a South Florida chapter of the American Peace Movement, a CP front that soon outlived its usefulness, when the Nazis invaded the Soviet Union in June 1941.[5] Then, in 1942, at the behest of Florida CP leader Alex Trainor, Smolikoff began trade-union agitation among Miami's shipyard workers. Working as a volunteer, he distributed leaflets and the IUMSWA's *Shipyard Worker,* met (separately) with black and white workers, and even prepared an NLRB case for the union, all the while keeping his political affiliation clandestine. At the end of 1942, a visiting IUMSWA organizer praised his work, especially commending his understanding of the "Southern approach, Negro problem and white workers angle." Smolikoff, this organizer claimed, "is respected by the negroes and whites alike in Miami."[6]

By June 1943, Smolikoff had helped the newly chartered IUMSWA Local 59, the first CIO union in Miami, win a contract for one thousand workers at the Miami Shipbuilding Corporation. Soon unsuspecting IUMSWA officials appointed the Communist organizer Florida regional director, and with Smolikoff's help the shipbuilders union gained a foothold in several yards in Jacksonville and Miami. In 1943, because IUMSWA had more than one-half of Florida's CIO members concentrated in its Miami and Jacksonville locals, CIO officials named Smolikoff director of the state's newly formed Industrial Union Council. In this position he was ideally poised to help spearhead the effort to organize Pan Am, the next logical target for the CIO, especially as shipyard workers began to face the prospect of postwar layoffs.[7]

Despite Smolikoff's wartime success in building IUMSWA in Miami's shipyards, the postwar prospects of industrial unionism in what one economic forecaster called "the least industrialized metropolitan district in the United States," looked bleak. Even though the war had brought a temporary boom, Miami's growth remained constrained by a profoundly constricted manufacturing sector. In 1945, less than 5 percent of the city's total income derived from manufacturing, and only two plants employed more than a thousand workers. The city's economic future appeared limited to tourism.[8] Moreover, Miami's rapidly increasing population consisted largely of transients and newcomers, depriving the CIO of the stable working-class community base it tapped so effectively in older industrial areas. Finally, Florida had the dubious distinction of being the first right-to-work state, having passed in 1944 a constitutional amendment outlawing closed and union shops.[9]

In addition to economic, demographic, and political constraints,

Miami's "southern" character also proved a potential barrier to further CIO organizing. With the exception of the handful of newcomers affiliated with the socialist or communist Left, most of Miami's northern migrants adjusted their mores to the presence of Jim Crow in housing, public facilities, and the labor market, rather than seeking to challenge it. A publicly active and violent Klan chapter, and closely related rampant police brutality against African Americans, completed the picture.[10]

Not only did Miami's African Americans suffer the same discrimination as their counterparts across the urban South, but they also found themselves increasingly outnumbered and isolated. In 1920, blacks constituted a third of Dade County's residents, but by 1940 they accounted for only 18.7 percent of the population, and that proportion continued to decline. For economic forecasters and employers, this meant "a shortage of domestic help and of manual labor"; for Miami's African Americans, it meant that, at a decisive moment in the struggle for civil rights, their political clout and economic significance began to recede, both in the larger community and within the newly organized CIO unions they joined so enthusiastically.[11]

The dependence of Miami's economic future on tourism and Latin American trade meant, however, that the air transport industry might provide fertile ground for the expansion of the CIO. At the close of the war, Miami boasted one of the world's largest airports, with ten thousand employees on the payroll, including those in "new occupations with higher wage . . . levels than those which were customary" in South Florida, according to one study. Between 1947 and 1950, the number of passengers passing through Miami's airport increased 38 percent, while the air freight total more than doubled.[12] Clearly, if the CIO was to succeed in postwar Miami, organizing the mechanics, flight stewards, porters, janitors, guards, cafeteria workers, and clerical staff who made up the large labor force at Miami's airport was imperative.

As early as the fall of 1943, Smolikoff and another Communist TWU organizer named Jerry Lee (who also had worked for IUMSWA) began distributing a union paper, *Contact,* to Pan Am workers, organizing social events, and collecting enough authorization cards from workers enrolled in the company union to petition the National Mediation Board (NMB) for an election.[13] In September 1944, recognizing the importance of breaking into the expanding field of air transport and engaged in stiff jurisdictional competition with the UAW and the AFL's International Association of Machinists (IAM), the TWU launched a national drive to bring Pan Am employees into its fold. As the largest base in the system of the nation's largest airline, with 40 percent of the company's employees, Pan Am's Miami unit was crucial to the success of this drive.[14]

TWU organizers faced significant obstacles to building an industrial union in the airlines. Workers in air transport were covered by the Railway Labor Act (RLA) of 1926 rather than the Wagner Act, and thus fell under the jurisdiction of the NMB and not the National Labor Relations Board. The RLA mandated bargaining units by ill-defined divisions of "craft or class," jurisdictions which the NMB tended to equate with the craft unions that held sway in the railroad industry. In an unorganized sector such as the airlines, this inevitably led to sharp jurisdictional conflict among several unions, most notably the IAM, the TWU, and the UAW. This legal structure also impeded the organization of industrial unions, as representation elections had to be won in as many as nine different NMB units of "craft or class."[15]

The obstacles posed to industrial unionism by the RLA had profound implications for the TWU's approach to Pan Am's black workers. Confined by racial custom to baggage handling (porters), janitorial service (cleaners), and cafeteria serving, blacks in the airline industry were barred from the higher-paying "craft or class" of "mechanics and helpers."[16] At the same time, the high concentration of African Americans serving as porters, and the discrimination they faced, made this homogeneous "craft or class" of airline employees especially ripe for unionization. In Miami, according to a postwar survey done by the Brotherhood of Sleeping Car Porters (BSCP), the "air fields offer the main industrial area of employment for Negroes." BSCP leaders saw this group of black workers as a potential base from which to "carry on its program in behalf of the socio-economic problems affecting all Negro workers" in South Florida; the TWU saw them as their most promising recruits as well and got there first.[17]

With the help of a local black International Laundry Workers organizer and Communist named James Nimmo, white TWU activists turned the racial division of the labor force and the NMB's craft structure to their advantage by gaining an initial foothold among Pan Am's 176 black porters and cleaners. In addition to lending the weight and resources of the Industrial Union Council and IUMSWA to the initial TWU drive, Smolikoff played a crucial role in recruiting Nimmo, a Bahamian immigrant, to the cause. During the war, Smolikoff had won

Nimmo's confidence by proving to the War Labor Board that Miami laundry workers indeed were engaged in war work, and thus helping them win an important contract. He also recruited Nimmo into the Communist Party's Miami activities, although Nimmo later claimed never to have formally joined the Party.[18] In February 1944, with Nimmo providing an opening to Pan Am's porters and cleaners, these workers voted unanimously for TWU representation. Success among African-American workers came a full year before the union won over the far greater numbers of white mechanics and maintenance personnel, most of whom remained in Pan Am's company union until the spring of 1945.[19]

The porters' and cleaners' enthusiasm for a CIO union was natural. TWU's chief rival for the loyalty of airline ground personnel was the IAM, which in the 1940s still barred blacks from membership in many of its locals.[20] With the acquiescence of this core of black unionists, however, TWU leaders declined to charter a local based solely in the porters and cleaners section and set their sights on Pan Am's white mechanics and maintenance personnel, who at Pan Am outnumbered blacks ten to one. Over the next year, TWU fought bitterly against both the IAM and the company union to win representation in this crucial "craft and class." In exchange, in the event of a TWU victory, black workers expected the union to establish a program designed to give them an opportunity to learn semi-skilled trades, a major step in breaking the barriers of segregated work in Miami. Individual porters and cleaners consequently worked hard to extend the union to a "craft and class" to which, because of their race, they had always been denied entry.[21]

Throughout 1944, TWU and IAM hammered away at one another in the battle for the allegiance of members of the Pan American Employees Association, the company union. CIO organizers accused the IAM of acting as a stalking horse for company unionism, offering poor pay scales in its existing airlines contracts, failing to secure premium pay for dangerous work, and using "'Red'-baiting [and] Negro scares." For its part, the AFL union published a newspaper article demonstrating the "communistic leanings" of TWU President Michael J. Quill and the rest of the TWU international leadership, and ran a picture of Quill sharing a platform with Earl Browder, national leader of the Communist Party. The article bluntly asked: Do "Pan Am workers want American unionism or communism?" One federal mediator remarked that "each party has slugged the other with all the adjectives in the dictionary and when they got tired of that the two of them would start slugging [Pan Am]."[22]

In December 1944, fearing a CIO victory, Pan Am unilaterally recognized the IAM throughout its entire system, before the mediation board had the opportunity to conduct a new election. Two months later, the board proclaimed this IAM agreement "of doubtful validity" and called for a new election in Miami only. This unusual ruling—the NMB normally sought to oversee systemwide representation elections—in effect secured a CIO victory among Miami's Pan Am workers. Banking on a systemwide election, the IAM had not even submitted any Miami authorization cards, while the TWU had argued successfully that its organization of the black porters and cleaners the year before should govern this case as well. The result, in March 1945, three weeks after the NMB ruling, was a resounding CIO victory among the 1,800 mechanics in the largest CIO election ever held in Florida: TWU 791, IAM 191, company union 162. According to TWU organizer Elisabeth Whitman, "The election has caused quite a stir in the town."[23]

The victory marked only the beginning of constant turmoil generated by this large and militant CIO union. Workers embraced their new union with such "terrific enthusiasm" that "almost the entire IAM leadership has come over to [TWU] . . . and are getting a taste of a real union for the first time," exulted organizer Roy Whitman. Local 500 quickly began to consider organizing Pan Am's white-collar force (yet another "craft or class" under NMB definitions) and also hoped to dislodge the IAM from Eastern Airlines, which employed eight hundred workers in Miami. Breaking into the rapidly growing air transport industry represented a significant expansion for the TWU, whose members were concentrated in urban mass transit, the vast majority of them in the New York City subway system. The victory in Miami opened up both a vast new transport field and the possibility of national scope for this relatively small but influential CIO union; if TWU won a good contract from Pan Am, Whitman informed the leadership back in New York, their main CIO rivals in this area, the UAW, "will have one hell of a time organizing anyone in air."[24]

Local 500's success in Miami did indeed place the union in the vanguard of CIO unionism in airlines. Within six months, TWU had won a systemwide election and contract representing four thousand Pan Am mechanics and unskilled workers at bases in New York, Brownsville, San Francisco, and Seattle, in addition to Miami. Notably, the Pan Am contract contained an equal-treatment clause. It also granted forty-eight hours' pay for forty hours of work, a demand pressed by militant TWU workers in Miami, who in September 1945 resisted proposed layoffs with a threatened walkout. In that showdown, black cafeteria workers and porters agreed to strike, even though the proposed layoffs only affected the maintenance division. That October, Miami's Pan Am workers also enforced the wage provisions of the new contract with a two-day sit-down strike, a work stoppage backed by Miami organizer Roy Whitman but opposed by a more conciliatory TWU leadership in New York.[25]

Amid these victories, Whitman also felt it necessary to address the "special needs" of the black workers who had shown such patient loyalty to the TWU. With the aid of white TWU mechanics, who served as teachers, Local 500 established the promised trade school for the porters and cleaners in a black church. Whitman also secured back pay retroactive to April 1944, when blacks first enrolled in the union. Local 500 won for Miami's black airport cafeteria workers "wage rates among the highest in the country for their type of work" and extended to them "all the major features of the national contract for mechanics," according to the union's newspaper. The presence of three black women representing cafeteria workers on the union's Negotiating Committee represented an unprecedented expression of respect from both the company and the union. Discriminatory pay scales on the airfield proved more difficult to combat, however. In early 1946, Whitman reported to Maurice Forge, the leftist director of TWU's newly created Air Transport Division (ATD), that "the Negro workers are especially smarting over the refusal of Management to reclassify their members" doing "jobs also done by white workers at considerably higher pay," such as driving trucks or buffing aircraft exteriors.[26]

Whitman's obvious solicitude for the interests of the small section of black workers is important, because, when internal conflict appeared in the union in the spring of 1946, he and Smolikoff accused one another of weakness and hypocrisy on the "Negro question," which Communist-led unions such as the TWU took very seriously. Since 1943, Smolikoff had worked closely with TWU organizers, even though he was still on the IUMSWA payroll. In the aftermath of its January 1946 convention, however, IUMSWA had "rid itself of the communistic . . . elements which had entered this union during the war," boasted President John Green. Despite one trusted organizer's opinion that Smolikoff was "loved by the rank and file" and was "one of the top organizers in the labor movement," in March 1946 IUMSWA dismissed him as its Florida regional director for being "more interested in following [the] party line than IUMSWA-CIO policies." The TWU national leadership, in which the Communist-oriented Left remained strong, did not hesitate to hire a skilled organizer of Smolikoff's caliber to serve as Local 500's director of "education and consolidation" to help build its most important local outside of New York City.[27]

Joining Local 500 in May 1946, Smolikoff almost immediately placed himself at odds with Roy and Elisabeth Whitman. Within one month, with the connivance of the TWU's Secretary-Treasurer Douglas MacMahon, also a Party member, he had maneuvered the Whitmans out of the local with a variety of underhanded tactics. Roy Whitman believed that, under his own leadership, the rank and file of Local 500 was ahead of the international in militantly demanding enforcement of the letter of the contract. Nevertheless, Smolikoff set about undermining Whitman's position by billing himself as the militant, democratic unionist willing to mobilize the rank and file against a cautious and autocratic local leadership.[28]

Smolikoff pressed especially hard on Whitman's supposed weakness on the "Negro question," although it appears that Whitman in effect had followed closely the CP's dictum that "militant trade unionists raise the special demands of the Negro workers, such as seniority readjustments as well as other provisions, to permit equal opportunity for advancement."[29] Nevertheless, Smolikoff charged that "there is not a single Negro on any Committee" and claimed that Whitman, his wife, and their cronies had "deliberately fostered vicious anti-negro anti-Progressive thinking . . . in order to minimize their problems and work." In one of his frequent letters to MacMahon, Smolikoff concluded that "it's going to take a lot longer than we anticipated to straighten out the Negro and related questions."[30]

At least one Whitman ally on the local's Executive Board, Howard Page, complained to MacMahon about Smolikoff's new role, defending Whitman's approach to the "race issue." In January 1946, Page, a Pan Am mechanic described by Whitman as "a very good guy, politically," had been put in charge of efforts to extend the union to Pan Am's white-collar employees. In Page's view, the grievances of Pan Am's black workers posed "a long range problem, which will require many months and possibly years to solve, with careful handling, especially if new organization is continually carried on." Page thus implied that an overt defense of the rights of black workers might alienate the large number of whites at Pan Am, as well as at other airlines the union still hoped to organize. By the spring of 1946, his ultimately unsuccessful efforts to bring Pan Am's white-collar clerks into the union gave Page some basis for this judgment.[31]

Page perceptively regarded Smolikoff's appointment as another example of the international's failure to consult local unionists on key matters. In fact, he likened it to the TWU's ill-informed efforts to check local militancy during the October sit-down strike. But Smolikoff, aided by MacMahon, won over the membership of Local 500 by championing rank-and-file democracy against the local's leadership at every turn. Shrewdly, Smolikoff attended meetings of virtually every committee, met with workers on the field, strengthened the steward system, weakened the Executive Board, settled grievances quickly, and sought to "find militant, faster action techniques that will mobilize the rank-and-file" to win grievances. He urged that the local strive to develop rank-and-file leaders who eventually could run the union's affairs.[32] At the end of May 1946, with Roy Whitman on vacation and his wife Elisabeth on maternity leave, Smolikoff urged MacMahon to transfer or fire his rival. Smolikoff claimed that "the *overwhelming* number of workers on the fields sense . . . that there is more activity than ever before of the kind they need," adding that "the Shop Stewards . . . indicated support for [my] program." He also declared that the black cafeteria workers, porters, and cleaners were "*fully* won to position I take on basis of achievement for them and increasing democratization in all Union affairs."[33]

In black majority local unions—most notably in southern units of the Industrial Union of Mine, Mill and Smelter Workers and the Food, Tobacco, Agricultural and Allied Workers—Communist organizers often found that democratization and the correct line on the "Negro question" reinforced one another. In the Miami TWU, however, one unintended consequence of Smolikoff's approach to winning over the membership was to weaken the position of the union's severely outnumbered black members. In a last-ditch effort to defend himself against removal, Whitman accused Smolikoff of doing "irreparable harm [to] the Negro members of our Union." In order to strengthen his position against Whitman among the mechanics, Smolikoff had "completely retrogressed on the question of their rights in the Union," even proclaiming that "we have no intention of holding joint [interracial] meetings," Whitman claimed. Whitman challenged MacMahon's *bona fides* on the "Negro question" as well, pointing to what he regarded as the secretary-treasurer's reluctance to combat discriminatory pay scales and below-par wages for black workers. In the bitter, behind-the-scenes battle for control of Local 500, both sides readily used the racial issue to their advantage whenever possible, each proclaiming itself the true champion of racial equality. Revealingly, however, in the same letter that boasted of the local's new commitment to democratization, Smolikoff admitted that, when the maintenance section sought to end mixed meetings, he agreed that "if majority votes it there will be whatever kind of meeting majority votes for," effectively capitulating to segregation, just as Whitman had charged.[34]

By June, the hapless Whitman, who had done more than anyone to build TWU Local 500, found himself ordered by MacMahon to Fort Worth to conduct an American Airlines organizing drive. The conflict between Smolikoff and the Whitmans puzzled even the FBI. According to an FBI informant, the Whitmans, who had been sent by the TWU international to Miami in November 1944 to direct the Pan Am organizing campaign, were also associated with the union's Communist faction and should be considered "agitators." Similarly, the NMB mediator who oversaw the union election described Elisabeth Whitman as "a fellow-traveller from way over on the left side of the road."[35] Perhaps the Whitmans had drifted from the Party after moving to Miami, as one informant suggested. More likely, the conflict between Smolikoff and the Whitmans derived from the internal upheaval in the American CP that followed the Comintern's April 1945 repudiation of the "class peace" associated with Earl Browder's leadership of the Party. Smolikoff's efforts to drive the Whitmans out of Local 500 may have reflected both his embrace of the Party's sudden swerve to the "left" with the purge of Browder and the Whitmans' adherence to Browder's suddenly discredited line. Whatever the Whitmans' political affinities, Smolikoff appears to have been far more willing and eager than they were to interject Party business into his day-to-day organizational role as a "trade-union Communist" and to reach into Local 500 to build a trade union section of Miami's Communist Party.[36]

Over the next two years, in his dual position as an international representative for Miami's (and Florida's) largest CIO union and director of the State Industrial Union Council, Smolikoff worked tirelessly to bring Local 500 into alignment with his political role as a Communist. Inside the union itself, Smolikoff sought to recruit new members (especially leadership), create what he called a "Shop Club of Progressives," sell subscriptions to the CP's weekly Sunday paper, the *Worker,* and distribute other Left-leaning literature, such as George Seldes's *In Fact* and the Southern Conference for Human Welfare's *Southern Patriot.* By late July 1946, Smolikoff already was able to boast to MacMahon and Forge that the "basis already exists for good shop club since we have two leading white Southerners ready and some 5 Negro workers to go in this very week."[37]

These activities united Party goals and effective trade unionism. Certainly they reflected the CP's postwar efforts to reconstitute its "proletarian" character and to reach out to southern African-American workers. At the same time, however, they appeared compatible with Smolikoff's militant trade unionism. His small interracial core of Communist recruits "are the people who will ultimately be the real Union builders," he told Forge, adding that, with their leadership, "the local will emerge with a much stronger and [more] progressive board and officers." Indeed, Smolikoff always saw his ongoing Party work as fundamentally bound up with his (and ATD Director Forge's) trade-union philosophy. This was based on what Smolikoff called a "solid programmatic approach," as distinguished from Whitman's "phony . . . basis of impossible promises and commitants [*sic*]"—a "bingo game vs. way-of-life" distinction, in Forge's terms. Even a disillusioned James Nimmo, who later testified before HUAC as a "friendly" witness, insisted to the Committee that Smolikoff was "all interested in building the Communist Party, but I think he was just as much interested in the union."[38]

On more than one occasion, in fact, Forge chided his disciple, Smolikoff, for departing from the principles of "scientific unionism" preached by the Party and practicing "unionism of the moment" by focusing on immediate gains. In one lengthy letter of admonition, Forge urged Smolikoff to move "from agitation to real struggle." Agitation, he instructed, served to build a local, win an election, and consolidate the ranks; real struggle meant a "long-range approach of conducting negotiations and struggling . . . REGARDLESS OF WHETHER A SPECIFIC FIGHT IS WON." This advice conveyed a clear statement of Communist trade unionism as a genuine and indigenous long-range political commitment which regarded rank-and-file gains as a means to an end. Yet Forge's lesson in "scientific" trade union practice sharply departed from the very rank-and-file expectations that Party cadres had encouraged in order to secure the confidence of workers in the first place.

When applied to the "Negro question," "scientific unionism" proved equally contradictory. On the one hand, Miami's Communist trade unionists demonstrated a clear commitment to organizing the small section of black airlines workers and defending their rights both on and off the job. Yet "agitation" on the civil-rights front gave way to the compromises of "struggle" when Smolikoff and his comrades accommodated segregationist sensibilities to win whites to the union or to protect the Party's position within the local. Party trade unionists also promoted Party-backed civil-rights causes without sufficiently consulting black workers.

Trade-union Communists typically focused on the problems of African-American workers; and Smolikoff, perhaps seeking to recoup some of the ground he may have lost in his clash with Whitman, was no exception. On the one hand, this meant including porters and cleaners in unionwide committees, such as the Joint Executive Committee, an ad hoc organizing committee, and the TWU national convention delegation.[39] But it also entailed taking more decisive action directly to address black grievances, action that required a further commitment of solidarity from the airfield's white workers.

Several incidents during the summer of 1946 illustrate Smolikoff's willingness to take risks genuinely to advance on the "Negro question" within the union and at Pan Am. In June, a black navy veteran named Lou Popps stood up at a porters' meeting to point out that Pan Am's black workers had to eat in the kitchen, while whites enjoyed an air-conditioned cafeteria. Smolikoff responded quickly and helped them win the right to "eat in [a] corner of [the] cafeteria instead of on garbage cans in the kitchen," as he told MacMahon. Popps, who had had bitter experience with segregation in the navy, proved ripe for recruitment into the Party. In another challenge to workplace discrimination, Smolikoff got Pan Am's first-aid clinic to treat workers on a first-come, first-served basis. No longer would whites be moved to the head of the line. Not surprisingly, these overt challenges to deeply ingrained southern workplace habits of racial inequality stimulated "Negro membership and payments" in Local 500, according to Smolikoff.[40]

Even more dramatically, in July 1946, one hundred black porters led an interracial job action that resulted in what Smolikoff called a "smashing victory for TWU-CIO on the Negro question." When seven porters were summarily fired for refusing the extra assignment of unloading sandbags from an airplane, Pan Am's white mechanics backed them up, threatening to shut down work in all of the airline's hangars and shops.

Faced by seventeen white and four black union officers who stopped work and directly confronted management, Pan Am backed down on the extra assignment and reinstated the fired porters with pay for hours lost. This was "the first time this kind of white mobilization had ever been done" on behalf of black workers, Smolikoff boasted; he went on to claim that Local 500 was "moving hard and fast on integration."[41]

This sort of militancy on the part of black workers and their white allies drew a direct response from Miami's well-organized Ku Klux Klan. Not only did Smolikoff receive telephone death threats, but three "hooded gangsters" personally threatened Roosevelt Winfield, chair of the Porters and Cleaners Section, with drowning if he "continued taking up grievances" for the airport's black workers, Smolikoff reported. Winfield courageously faced down the Klansmen and reported the threat to Local 500's entire white leadership, the police, the FBI, and the local newspapers. "If they'll come at me one at time we'll all drink out of the bay together," he publicly stated. Southern white union officers met the challenge as well, proclaiming that "there's nobody . . . who's going to split us white workers away from our Negro co-workers" and that "when it comes to color, race or politics, Local 500, TWU-CIO has no weak links." For the handful of Party members in the local, this incident proved an excellent means of educating white workers to the dangers of racism; but blacks, sensing their community's vulnerability, responded less enthusiastically to Smolikoff's exploitation of the Klan threat. Indeed, Smolikoff reluctantly reported that Winfield's wife and others in the black community, fearful of further antagonizing the Klan, were "putting pressure on him not to process grievances."[42]

If such bold action did not necessarily win the full approval of Miami's African Americans, Smolikoff certainly made points with the TWU leadership back in New York. Quill himself wrote to an erstwhile ally of Whitman's that Smolikoff had "done a lot more on the Negro question" than Whitman and had even "turned a spotlight on the activities of the Klan." Not incidentally, Quill also pointed out that "dues payments have almost doubled" in the six months since Smolikoff became Local 500's international representative, a significant achievement in an open-shop state.[43]

Of course, the local's membership—most of whom were ignorant of or indifferent to the issue of Communist influence in their union—measured Smolikoff's leadership by the far more prosaic question of day-to-day trade-union practice. Smolikoff won both blacks and whites to

TWU because he developed what he called a "fighting spirit" in the union and actively pressed grievances against the company.[44] He defended the right to Saturday overtime pay, regardless of number of days worked during the previous week. He helped the flight stewards renegotiate their pay structure and seniority lists. He won reclassification grievances with back pay for forty-one workers in Local 500's small unit in TACA Airways, threatening to take this same group of workers out on strike to block layoffs without proper notice. And he took on the difficult but essential task of strengthening Local 500's auxiliaries at "down the line" Pan Am bases in Puerto Rico and the Canal Zone. Here he pressed to bring wage rates into line with those of the company's U.S. workforce, claiming that the existing differentials allowed Pan Am to "more and more shift [maintenance] work from Miami to these L[atin]-A[merican] bases where . . . cheaper work can be performed."[45]

Most importantly, when TWU's contract was up for renegotiation at the end of 1946, Smolikoff helped push the membership's demands for a twenty-five-cent wage increase, despite what he admitted was a generally "unfavorable situation" for labor. "The workers in Miami are almost unanimously all-out inclined for a struggle" to enforce their basic wage demands, he informed MacMahon two weeks before the 1946 contract expired. Much to the New York leadership's consternation, Smolikoff reported that rank-and-file workers at Pan Am would prefer to strike rather than accept arbitration. When the dispute wound up in arbitration, as the New Yorkers had recommended, ATD Director Maurice Forge scolded Smolikoff for promising more than the International could deliver.[46]

Meanwhile, beyond the airfield and union hall, Smolikoff sought to bring Local 500's growing clout to bear on local, national, and even international political issues of concern to the Communist Party. In Miami he attempted to forge an alliance with AFL unions to use consumer boycotts and picket lines spearheaded by the TWU to protest the rising cost of living that chipped away at workers' wages. In 1947, the TWU backed a labor candidate, Edwin Waller, in a city commission primary election. Waller—who had worked with Smolikoff in the IUMSWA, followed him to the TWU, and briefly joined the CP at his behest—lost the election but did win more than six thousand votes. And, as opposition to the impending Taft-Hartley Act grew that same year, Smolikoff and the TWU helped sponsor a mass meeting which drew an interracial gathering of nine thousand to Miami's normally whites-only Bayfront Park.[47]

Smolikoff also repeatedly brought controversial civil rights and civil liberties matters before Local 500's membership. In August 1946, Local 500's Executive Board passed a resolution in favor of a Puerto Rican independence referendum. Then, in November 1946, at MacMahon's behest but in violation of national CIO policy, Smolikoff circulated a National Negro Congress petition to present to the United Nations. The following year he distributed Civil Rights Congress (CRC) flyers among the membership, and in 1948 he helped organize a Miami chapter of this Communist-supported civil rights organization. Finally, in early 1948, Smolikoff sought to raise money to defend John Santo, a national TWU leader who faced deportation proceedings because of his Communist Party membership.[48]

The Communist labor organizer also envisioned the TWU playing a hemispheric role. He urged support for the struggle for Puerto Rican independence, and encouraged Local 500's Balboa auxiliary to forge a close alliance with the Communist-led United Public Workers (UPW) in the Canal Zone. In August 1946, the UPW and TWU Local 500 formed a CIO Council of Panama and then led a march and rally to protest the "vicious labor practices" in the Canal Zone. UPW leaders subsequently directed Smolikoff's attention to the four thousand unorganized ship and fruit company workers in the Canal Zone who might fall under TWU jurisdiction.[49]

Smolikoff consistently believed that his initial agitational approach had won him "virtually 100 percent confidence of the rank and file." But his increasingly open activities as a Communist began to draw unwanted attention in both the union and Miami at large. By early 1948, anti-Communists were engaged in an open assault on the leadership of Local 500.[50] Miami's anti-labor press and the House Un-American Activities Committee initiated these attacks, but additional pressure soon followed from within the local union itself and from a national CIO leadership increasingly anxious to dissociate the industrial union movement from the taint of Communism.

In the first few months of 1948, three related developments brought Smolikoff's Communist affiliation to center stage in Miami. In early 1948, at Smolikoff's urging and in concert with the Miami chapter of the Southern Conference for Human Welfare, Local 500 endorsed Henry Wallace's Progressive Party presidential campaign. This venture into national politics aligned Miami's TWU with the CPUSA against the CIO and even the TWU's President Michael Quill.[51] At the same time, the

Miami Daily News stirred up a communitywide Red Scare, culminating in a March 1948 HUAC investigation of Communism in Miami, the fingering of Smolikoff as a Party member, and Local 500's temporary rejection of his leadership. Finally, with the help of a cadre of Catholic workers who had built a dissident anti-Communist faction within Local 500, UAW organizers prosecuted a jurisdictional raid on Miami's TWU in the spring of 1948.

Since April 1947, a small cell of Catholic anti-Communist union dissidents had been meeting with a local priest in a "study club." They were led by Robert McNally, a thirty-seven-year-old maintenance worker and shop steward who described himself as an "ardent CIO-er." McNally had helped organize Local 500, and Smolikoff even appointed him to the interracial organizing committee he created in 1946. But, suspecting that Smolikoff was a Communist, McNally had begun a correspondence with the anti-Communist labor priest, Father Charles Rice, who worked closely both with the CIO leadership and the Association of Catholic Trade Unionists (ACTU) to cleanse the new industrial unions of Communist influence. Following Rice's advice, McNally's cadre of thirty-five workers hoped to wield enough influence democratically to swing a union election away from Smolikoff's main allies on the Executive Board, President M. L. Edwards and Chief Steward Phil Scheffsky. McNally's group from the rank and file formed a key constituency for the UAW when the anti-Communist CIO affiliate sought to win over Pan Am workers in March and April 1948.[52]

Maurice Forge characterized the growing internal opposition to Smolikoff as "former Whitman followers, Kluxers, ACTUers, [and] well-meaning-but-not-too-advanced rank and file workers."[53] But UAW organizers also were able to tap growing dissatisfaction with Local 500 among Pan Am's black workers. UAW activists found the black porters receptive to the UAW drive for what one of them later called "good trade union reasons." Led by Smolikoff's erstwhile ally, Roosevelt Winfield, the porters and cleaners decided that the Communists were cloaking themselves in the mantle of the "Negro question" without really representing black interests at the airfield. Indeed, according to UAW partisan Milton Zatinsky, TWU's black members felt that Smolikoff "was not taking on their broader fight in the community, as a black community."[54]

Predictably, Smolikoff struck back by accusing the UAW of sowing "ethnic and racial discord." Indeed, the UAW airline division sent a

Tennessee organizer, William Etheridge, who subtly made "special appeals on an ethnic or racial basis" to Pan Am's southern white workers, according to Zatinsky, who complained to the union's Fair Practices and Anti-Discrimination Department about Etheridge's "personal lack of sympathy with UAW's strong civil rights policies."[55]

Together with the Wallace campaign and the Miami Red Scare, the ultimately unsuccessful UAW raid marked the beginning of the end for Communist influence in TWU Local 500. By 1948, Quill's allegiance to the Party had weakened, and the Wallace campaign proved the last straw. The Party's insistence that its CIO "influentials" back Wallace, Quill felt sure, would "play into the hands of the reactionary forces within the CIO." Seeing in Miami just such a scenario unfold, Quill broke publicly and dramatically with the CP in April 1948. At the TWU's December 1948 convention, Quill drove the remaining Party members from the TWU leadership, effectively isolating the Communist leadership of Local 500.[56]

Six months later, facing accusations that Local 500 was the key link in a Latin American Communist courier network, threats by McNally to take his faction of Pan Am workers into the IAM, and pressure from the Southern Organizing Committee to purge the Communists from Florida's largest CIO affiliate, Quill placed Local 500 under the control of Forge's ATD replacement, William Grogan, and expelled Smolikoff's allies from the union. Grogan called a new election for Local 500 officers in October 1949; "none of these new officers . . . have any connection with the Communist Party," assured one of the FBI's informants.[57]

Ultimately, the anti-Communist attack on Local 500 weakened the union's ability to defend its members' interests and maintain local autonomy, invited jurisdictional raiding, and eroded the rank and file's commitment to the CIO and the social program it once had championed. Despite Maurice Forge's scorn for what he called a "grocery counter type of union," only when Communist trade unionists were able to produce tangible results had most Pan Am workers acquiesced in their leadership.[58] In point of fact, the "scientific unionism" preached by Forge differed little from that practiced by other CIO factions, in that its practitioners constantly balanced seeking immediate gains for union members against the expediency of remaining in power in order to carry out their program. By 1949, in the context of the rising tide of Cold War anti-Communism, this balancing act had become impossible for Party members to maintain.

For Pan Am's small minority of black workers, the conflict over Communism in the CIO had further ramifications. The porters, cleaners, and cafeteria workers had embraced the TWU as a vehicle for their aspirations as African-American workers; some even had been drawn to the Communist Party by its militant defense of their civil rights. But by 1949, one of the remaining Communist activists and Forge allies in Local 500 admitted that "the worst spot [for the Party] is the porters. Grogan [the new ATD director] has them by default. Their stewards have been neglected and their members kept uninformed." Indeed, in a desperate effort to protect the Party's position in Local 500 against Quill's purge, Smolikoff had urged cooperation with workers who "are backward and will never be progressive and [are] even anti-Negro" but opposed Quill on the question of local autonomy.[59]

If the CP no longer was in a position to advance on the "Negro question" or attract black support, the new anti-Communist leadership of Local 500 had little reason to pay attention to the grievances of the small section of black workers either. By the mid-1950s, the struggle for civil rights in working-class Miami passed from the CRC, the SCHW, and the CIO to the NAACP, which worked closely with courageous blacks in the city's building trades to challenge the long tradition of Jim Crow in Miami's AFL unions.[60] Inside Miami's TWU, the membership remained cautious on racial progress. When the union "officially" supported the campaign of state representative John Orr, one of the few Florida politicians who in the late 1950s backed school integration, individual TWU officers and shop stewards nevertheless openly condemned him.[61]

Notes

This essay could not have been written without the assistance of Ray Boryczka, Greg Bush, Josh Freeman, Gail Malmgreen, Miranda Lichtenstein, Steve Rosswurm, Milton Zatinsky, and a National Endowment for the Humanities Fellowship. As always, heartfelt thanks go to Sybil Lipschultz.

1. Charles Smolikoff to Lucy Mason, May 31, 1945, Lucy Mason Papers, Box 4, Special Collections Dept., Perkins Library, Duke Univ., Durham, N.C.
2. Ibid.
3. For two dramatically opposed views, see Max Kampelman, *The Communist Party vs. the CIO: A Study in Power Politics* (New York: Praeger, 1957); and Harvey Levenstein, *Communism, Anticommunism, and the CIO* (Westport, Conn.: Greenwood, 1981). On the South, see esp. Michael K. Honey, *Southern Labor and Black Civil Rights: Organizing Memphis Workers* (Urbana: Univ. of Illinois Press, 1993); Robert Korstad and Nelson Lichtenstein, "Opportunities Found

and Lost: Labor, Radicals, and the Early Civil Rights Movement," *Journal of American History* 75 (Dec. 1988): 786–811; Robin D. G. Kelley, *Hammer and Hoe: Alabama Communists During the Great Depression* (Chapel Hill: Univ. of North Carolina Press, 1990). For critiques of the romanticization of the Communist Party's trade union role, see Eric Arnesen, "Class Matters, Race Matters," *Radical History Review* 60 (Fall 1994): 230–35; Alex Lichtenstein, review of Michael Honey, *Southern Labor and Black Civil Rights,* in *International Labor and Working-Class History* 47 (Winter 1995): 157–59.

4. The literature on this is growing rapidly. Prominent examples include: Honey, *Southern Labor and Black Civil Rights*; Robert Korstad, "Daybreak of Freedom: Tobacco Workers and the CIO, Winston-Salem, North Carolina, 1943–1950" (Ph.D. diss., Univ. of North Carolina, 1987); Rick Halpern, "Interracial Unionism in the Southwest: Fort Worth's Packinghouse Workers," in *Organized Labor in the Twentieth-Century South,* ed. Robert H. Zieger (Knoxville: Univ. of Tennessee Press, 1991), 158–82; Robert J. Norrell, "Caste in Steel: Jim Crow Careers in Birmingham, Alabama," *Journal of American History* 73 (Dec. 1986): 669–701; Bruce Nelson, "Organized Labor and the Struggle for Black Equality in Mobile during World War II," *Journal of American History* 80 (Dec. 1993): 952–88.
5. Smolikoff's background is pieced together from the *Miami Herald,* Dec. 26, 1944, 8B; John Steedman, ed., *Who's Who in Labor* (New York: Dryden Press, 1946), 334; "Smolikoff Identified as a Key Man for Reds," *Miami Daily News,* Mar. 1, 1948, p. 1; Berthe Small (Smolikoff), tape-recorded interview by Alex Lichtenstein, Dec. 8, 1995, New York City, tape in author's possession; "Survey Report of Miami Florida," n.d. (ca. Dec. 1942), Series 6, Subseries 3, Box 6, IUMSWA Papers, Archives and Manuscripts Dept., Univ. of Maryland Library, College Park, Md.
6. Alexander Trainor to Charles Smolikoff, June 8, 1942, reprinted in the *Miami Daily News,* Feb. 25, 1948 (probably acquired by the FBI, which had a "highly confidential source" with access to Trainor's correspondence, "Communist Infiltration of Transport Workers Union of America," Miami Report no. 100-7319-241, Dec. 31, 1943, Federal Bureau of Investigation reports, acquired through a Freedom of Information Act request, in author's possession [hereafter cited as FBI-FOIA]); "Survey Report of Miami Florida," IUMSWA Papers. Many thanks to Josh Freeman for providing the FBI material cited throughout.
7. *Shipyard Worker,* June 4, 1943, p. 6; *Shipyard Worker,* Nov. 19, 1943, p. 6; Charles Smolikoff to Allan Haywood, May 20, 1944, Series 2, Subseries 4, Box 12, IUMSWA Papers; *Miami Herald,* Dec. 26, 1944, 8B; Smolikoff to Tom Gallagher, May 29, 1944, Series 2, Subseries 4, Box 18, IUMSWA Papers; Smolikoff to Tom Gallagher, July 31, 1945, Series 2, Subseries 4, Box 12, IUMSWA Papers.
8. Reinhold Paul Woolf, *Miami: Economic Pattern of a Resort Area* (Coral Gables, Fla.: Univ. of Miami, 1945), 85, 86, 129; Public Administration Service, *The Government of Metropolitan Miami* (Chicago: PAS, 1954), 20–21. In this essay, the term *Miami* refers to metropolitan Dade County.

9. Woolf, *Economic Pattern of a Resort Area,* 117; Public Administration Service, *Government of Metropolitan Miami,* 16; Gilbert J. Gall, "Southern Industrial Workers and Anti-Union Sentiment: Arkansas and Florida in 1944," in Zieger, ed. *Organized Labor in the Twentieth-Century South,* 223–49; *Miami Daily News,* Mar. 21, 1945, 10B.
10. Woolf, *Economic Pattern of a Resort Area,* 119; Raymond A. Mohl, "Blacks, Jews, and the Civil Rights Movement in Miami, 1945–1960," unpublished paper presented at the Southern Historical Association, Nov. 1992, Atlanta, in author's possession; Matilda "Bobbi" Graff, "The Historic Continuity of the Civil Rights Movement," unpublished manuscript; Matilda "Bobbi" Graff, personal interview by Alex Lichtenstein, May 18, 1992, Miami, Fla., notes in author's possession; Milton Zatinsky, tape-recorded interview by Alex Lichtenstein, Dec. 20, 1994, Miami, tape in author's possession; Gerald Horne, *Communist Front? The Civil Rights Congress, 1946–1956* (Rutherford, N.J.: Fairleigh Dickinson Press, 1988), 192–93; Deborah Dash Moore, *To the Golden Cities: Pursuing the American Jewish Dream in Miami and Los Angeles* (New York: Free Press, 1994), 153; Alejandro Portes and Alex Stepick, *City on the Edge: The Transformation of Miami* (Berkeley: Univ. of California Press, 1993), 76–80; British Vice-Consul to A. E. Fuller, Oct. 13, 1938, John E. Culmer Collection, Black Archives and Historical Research Foundation, Miami, Fla.; John E. Culmer to Earl Brown, Aug. 18, 1938, Culmer Collection.
11. Woolf, *Economic Pattern of a Resort Area,* 15, 132; Public Administration Service, *Government of Metropolitan Miami,* 17.
12. Woolf, *Economic Pattern of a Resort Area,* 76, 95, 140–41; Public Administration Service, *Government of Metropolitan Miami,* 20. By 1946, Miami led the nation in air exports; *Miami Daily News,* July 25, 1946, 4A.
13. "Communist Infiltration of Transport Workers Union of America," Miami Report no. 100-7319-241, Dec. 31, 1943, FBI-FOIA.
14. Michael Quill to all Pan American employees, Sept. 1, 1944, TWU Local 500 Papers, Transport Workers Union Collection, Robert F. Wagner Labor Archives, New York Univ., New York, New York (hereafter cited as TWU-500 Papers); Paul Miley to Walter Reuther, June 18, 1946, and Walter Reuther to Philip Murray, June 21, 1946, both in Box 61, Folder 1, Walter Reuther Papers, Archives of Labor and Urban Affairs, Wayne State Univ., Detroit, Mich. (hereafter cited as ALUA-WSU); *TWU Bulletin,* Apr. 1945, p. 7; Smolikoff to Tom Gallagher, July 31, 1945, Series 2, Subseries 4, Box 12, IUMSWA Papers; Joshua B. Freeman, *In Transit: The Transport Workers Union in New York City, 1933–1966* (New York: Oxford Univ. Press, 1989), 261–63.
15. Frank Heisler, "Inconsistencies of the National Mediation Board in its Interpretation and Definition of the Terms Craft or Class," *Journal of Air Law and Commerce* 35 (Winter 1969): 408–13; A. J. Harper II, "Major Disputes Under the Railway Labor Act," *Journal of Air Law and Commerce* 35 (Winter 1969): 3–39; Glen Harlan, "Developments Past and Future in the NMB's Determinations of Craft or Class," *Journal of Air Law and Commerce* 35 (Winter 1969): 393–407; Herbert Northrup et al., *Negro Employment in Land and*

Air Transport, pt. 2: *The Negro in the Air Transport Industry* (Philadelphia: Univ. of Pennsylvania, 1971), 62–65; James B. Frankel, "Airline Labor Policy: The Stepchild of the Railway Labor Act," *Journal of Air Law and Commerce* 18 (Autumn 1951): 461–85.

16. Northrup et al., *Negro in the Air Transport Industry,* 1, 13, 28–33, 62.
17. "Survey of Air Field Porters," July 28, 1949, Subject File: BSCP History 1928–78, Reel 9, A. Philip Randolph Papers, microfilm ed. I thank Eric Arnesen for bringing this document to my attention.
18. "Communist Infiltration of Transport Workers Union of America," Miami Report, Dec. 31, 1943; Apr. 4, 1944; and Oct. 22, 1945, FBI-FOIA; Elisabeth Whitman to Aaron Spiegel, Jan. 8, 1945; Aaron Spiegel to Elisabeth Whitman, Mar. 31, 1945, TWU-500 Papers; U.S. Congress, House of Representatives, Committee on Un-American Activities (HUAC), *Investigation of Communist Activities in the State of Florida,* pt. 2, 83rd Cong., 2d Sess. (Washington: USGPO, 1955), testimony of James Nimmo, 7430–31. At one point, the FBI Special Agent in Charge in Miami recommended closing the investigation of Communist infiltration of Local 500 because it "would merely be repetition of the information contained in the file of CHARLES SMOLIKOFF." J. Edgar Hoover demurred "in view of the relatively large size of this Local in Miami, and the potential importance of it." SAC, Miami to J. Edgar Hoover, May 16, 1945, no. 100-7319-299; and Hoover to SAC, Aug. 29, 1945, no. 100-7319-300, FBI-FOIA.
19. "Communist Infiltration of Transport Workers Union of America," Miami Report no. 100-7319-251, Apr. 4, 1944, FBI-FOIA, p. 3; U.S. Congress, House, HUAC, *Investigation of Communist Activities in the State of Florida,* pt. 2, pp. 7430 and 7436; "Findings Upon Investigation in the Matter of Representation of Employees of the Pan American Airways, Inc.," NMB Case R-1311, Mar. 1, 1945, TWU-500 Papers, p. 5; Elisabeth Whitman to Aaron Spiegel, Mar. 3, 1945, TWU-500 Papers; *TWU Bulletin,* June 1945, p. 4. For a graphic depiction of the racial segmentation at Pan Am, see photos of the Maintenance and Porters Sections in the *TWU Bulletin,* June 1946, p. 9.
20. Northrup et al., *The Negro in the Air Transport Industry,* 23, 67; Clarence Mitchell to Walter White, Jan. 22, 1947, National Association for the Advancement of Colored People (NAACP) Papers on microfilm, "The NAACP and Labor, 1940–1955: Subject Files on Labor Conditions and Employment Discrimination," Part 13, Series A, Reel 15, frames 688–92. The IAM did not even appear on the NMB ballot when porters and cleaners voted for representation; see sample ballot, Case Files, Case R-1210, National Mediation Board Records, NARA II, RG 13, College Park, Md.
21. Roy Whitman to Douglas MacMahon, Apr. 24, 1945, TWU-500 Papers; Elisabeth Whitman to MacMahon, Mar. 24, 1945, TWU-500 Papers.
22. "Can You Figure This Out[?]," TWU leaflet, ca. Sept. 1944, TWU-500 Papers; *TWU Bulletin,* Mar.–Apr. 1944, p. 12; Phillip Whitehead, "Let's Face It," *Wings over the World,* Feb. 21, 1944, reprinted in "Communist Infiltration of Transport Workers Union of America," Miami Report no. 100-7319-266, July 29, 1944, FBI-FOIA; International Association of Machinists, *Air Fax,* No. 5A, June

1945; "Mediator's report on Case R-1311," Case Files, Box 205, National Mediation Board Records, NARA II, RG 13, College Park, Md., p. 36.

23. "Findings Upon Investigation in the Matter of Representation of Employees of the Pan American Airways, Inc.," NMB Case R-1311, Mar. 1, 1945, TWU-500 Papers; *TWU Bulletin,* Apr. 1945, p. 6; *Miami Herald,* Mar. 20, 1945, p. 11A; Elisabeth Whitman to Douglas MacMahon, Mar. 24, 1945, TWU-500 Papers.
24. Roy Whitman to Douglas MacMahon, Apr. 24, 1945; MacMahon to Whitman, Apr. 26, 1945; Whitman to MacMahon, Sept. 13, 1945, TWU-500 Papers. On the TWU's effort to expand into air transport, see Freeman, *In Transit,* 261–63.
25. *TWU Bulletin,* Oct. 1945, p. 5, and Dec. 1945, p. 5. *Miami Herald,* Sept. 23, 1945, 8B; Sept. 24, 1945, 1A; Sept. 25, 1945, 1A; Sept. 26, 1945, 1A; Sept. 27, 1945, 1A; "Communist Infiltration of Transport Workers Union of America," Miami Report no. 100-7319-339, June 10, 1946, FBI-FOIA, p. 2; Howard Page to Douglas MacMahon, May 11, 1946, TWU-500 Papers.
26. "Communist Infiltration of Transport Workers Union of America," Miami Report no. 100-7319-339, June 10, 1946, FBI-FOIA, p. 3; Roy Whitman to Douglas MacMahon, Apr. 24, 1945, TWU-500 Papers; Whitman to MacMahon, Aug. 28, 1945, TWU-500 Papers; *TWU Bulletin,* June 1945, p. 4, and Dec. 1945, p. 6; Elisabeth Whitman to Aaron Spiegel, Mar. 3, 1945, TWU-500 Papers; Roy Whitman to Maurice Forge, Jan. 24, 1946, TWU-500 Papers, p. 2.
27. Telegram from Ross Blood to Jack Livingstone [*sic*], Mar. 19, 1948; and telegram from John Green to Hoke Welch, Feb. 24, 1948; both in Series 2, Subseries 4, Box 12, IUMSWA Papers; William Smith to Thomas Gallagher, "Report and Recommendations of Survey of Florida Area," Jan. 28, 1946, Series 2, Subseries 4, Box 18, IUMSWA Papers; Charles Smolikoff to Douglas MacMahon, May 8, 1946, TWU-500 Papers.
28. Roy Whitman to Douglas MacMahon, Jan. 24, 1946; Charles Smolikoff to Douglas MacMahon, May 23, 1946, TWU-500 Papers.
29. "Resolution on the Question of Negro Rights and Self-Determination," in *The Communist Position on the Negro Question* (New York: New Century, 1947), 13.
30. Smolikoff to Douglas MacMahon, May 9, 1946, TWU-500 Papers.
31. Roy Whitman to Douglas MacMahon, Jan. 9, 1946; and Howard Page to Douglas MacMahon, May 11, 1946; both in TWU-500 Papers.
32. Charles Smolikoff to Douglas MacMahon, May 9, 1946; May 23, 1946; and May 26, 1946; and Smolikoff to Maurice Forge, June 4, 1946; all in TWU-500 Papers.
33. Smolikoff to MacMahon, May 30, 1946; and Roy Whitman to MacMahon, June 4, 1946, and June 10, 1946, all in TWU-500 Papers.
34. Roy Whitman to MacMahon, June 10, 1946; and Charles Smolikoff to MacMahon, June 9, 1946; both in TWU-500 Papers.
35. Aaron Spiegel to Richard Downes, Nov. 13, 1944, TWU-500 Papers; "Communist Infiltration of Transport Workers Union of America," Miami Report,

Dec. 31, 1943; Apr. 4, 1944; and Oct. 22, 1945, all in FBI-FOIA; "Mediator's Report on Case R-1311," Case Files, Box 205, National Mediation Board Records, NARA II, RG 13, College Park, Md., p. 29.

36. On changes in Communist Party policy in 1945–46, see Maurice Isserman, *Which Side Were You On? The American Communist Party During the Second World War,* 2d ed. (Urbana: Univ. of Illinois Press, 1993), 214–43; Joseph R. Starobin, *American Communism in Crisis, 1943–1957* (Cambridge, Mass.: Harvard Univ. Press, 1972), 71–120; and Edward P. Johanningsmeier, *Forging American Communism: The Life of William Z. Foster* (Princeton, N.J.: Princeton Univ. Press, 1994), 293–313.
37. Charles Smolikoff to Maurice Forge, June 4, 1946; Smolikoff to Douglas MacMahon, June 24, 1946; Smolikoff to MacMahon, June 29, 1946; Smolikoff to Forge, July 16, 1946; and Smolikoff to Douglas MacMahon, July 29, 1946; all in TWU-500 Papers.
38. Charles Smolikoff to Maurice Forge, July 25, 1946; Smolikoff to Forge, Aug. 25, 1946; and Smolikoff to MacMahon, Sept. 1, 1946; all in TWU-500 Papers. Smolikoff to MacMahon, Jan. 8, 1947, in Local 257 Papers, TWU Collection, Robert F. Wagner Labor Archives, New York Univ., New York City; Smolikoff to Forge, Sept. 6, 1946, TWU-500 Papers; U.S. Congress, House, HUAC, *Investigation of Communist Activities in the State of Florida,* pt. 1, pp. 7376 and 7398, and pt. 2, p. 7437; Robert McNally to Father Charles Rice, Apr. 7, 1947, Box 22, TWU Folder, Charles Owen Rice Papers, Archives of Labor and Industrial Society, Univ. of Pittsburgh (hereafter cited as Rice Papers).
39. Charles Smolikoff to Douglas MacMahon, June 29, 1946; Charles Smolikoff to M. L. Edwards et al., July 2, 1946; and Charles Smolikoff to Maurice Forge, Aug. 22, 1946; all in TWU-500 Papers.
40. U.S. Congress, House, HUAC, *Investigation of Communist Activities in the State of Florida,* pt. 1, p. 7398; Louis J. Popps, tape-recorded interview by Alex Lichtenstein, Feb. 10, 1996, Miami, Fla., tape in author's possession; Charles Smolikoff to Douglas MacMahon, June 29, 1946, TWU-500 Papers.
41. Charles Smolikoff to Maurice Forge, July 25, 1946; and Smolikoff to Art Shields, Aug. 7, 1946; both in TWU-500 Papers.
42. Charles Smolikoff to Art Shields, Aug. 7, 1946, with *Contact,* n.d., attached; Charles Smolikoff to Maurice Forge, Aug. 7, 1946; and Charles Smolikoff to Douglas MacMahon, Aug. 10, 1946, all in TWU-500 Papers. *Miami Herald,* Aug. 8, 1946, 1B; *Daily Worker,* Aug. 7, 1946, p. 2, and Aug. 8, 1946, p. 3. The *Daily Worker* correspondent used Smolikoff and Local 500 President M. L. Edwards as his "sources" on this story, suggesting the close connection between the Party and the union's leadership. Edwards spoke with the correspondent from the Canal Zone, where he was engaged in an organizing drive.
43. Mike Quill to Carl Simpson, Aug. 26, 1946, TWU-500 Papers.
44. Charles Smolikoff to Douglas MacMahon, June 29, 1946; Smolikoff to Maurice Forge, Nov. 2, 1946; and "Extra," flyer, ca. Sept. 13, 1946; all in TWU-500 Papers.
45. Charles Smolikoff to Maurice Forge, July 2, 1946, and "TACA Grievances

Settled to Date by CIO—July 10" [1946], both in TWU-500 Papers. *Miami Herald,* Aug. 2, 1946, 1B, and Aug. 3, 1946, 1B. "Union Plans Ultimatum Against PAA," news clipping, n.d.; Charles Smolikoff to Maurice Forge, Aug. 14, 1946, and Smolikoff to Forge, Oct. 21, 1946, all in TWU-500 Papers.

46. Smolikoff to Forge, Oct. 21, 1946, and Smolikoff to MacMahon, Dec. 13, 1946, both in TWU-500 Papers. "Communist Infiltration of Transport Workers Union of America," Miami Report no. 100-7319-353, Mar. 5, 1947, FBI-FOIA, p. 4; Forge to Smolikoff, Dec. 27, 1946; Forge to Smolikoff, Feb. 18, 1947, TWU-500 Papers.
47. Charles Smolikoff to Miami Central Labor Union and Railroad Brotherhoods of Miami, July 1946, TWU-500 Papers; *Miami Daily News,* July 24, 1946, p. 1, and July 25, 1946, 4B; Charles Smolikoff to Mike Quill, Apr. 15, 1947, TWU-500 Papers; *TWU Bulletin,* June 19, 1948, p. 6; *TWU Bulletin,* Nov. 1947, p. 7; U.S. Congress, House, HUAC, *Investigation of Communist Activities in the State of Florida,* pt. 1, pp. 7292–98; Transcript of Hearing, *Leah Adler Benemovsky vs. Jimmy Sullivan, Sheriff of Dade County,* Apr. 27, 1948, Dade County Circuit Court, Box 31, Folder 38, John M. Coe Papers, Special Collections, Emory Univ., Atlanta, 20–26; Robert McNally to Father Charles Rice, Aug. 11, 1947, Box 25, Rice Papers.
48. Douglas MacMahon to Charles Smolikoff, Oct. 31, 1946, TWU-500 Papers; John Brophy to all Industrial Union Councils, Nov. 26, 1946, NAACP Papers on microfilm, pt. 13, Series A, Reel 14, frame 303; "Communist Infiltration of Transport Workers Union of America," Miami Report no. 100-7319-491, Oct. 27, 1949, FBI-FOIA, p. 4; Resolution Passed by Local 500, Aug. 12, 1946, TWU-500 Papers; *TWU Bulletin,* Aug. 1946, p. 12; Charles Smolikoff to Aaron Spiegel, Feb. 2, 1948, Folder 26, Maurice Forge Papers, Robert F. Wagner Labor Archives, New York Univ. (hereafter cited as Forge Papers).
49. Charles Smolikoff to Maurice Forge, July 14, 1946; Aug. 14, 1946; Ed Cheresh to Charles Smolikoff, Sept. 2, 1946; Charles Smolikoff to Ed Cheresh, Sept. 4, 1946, TWU-500 Papers.
50. Charles Smolikoff to Douglas MacMahon, July 25, 1946, TWU-500 Papers.
51. Robert McNally to Charles Rice, Mar. 16, 1948, Box 22, Rice Papers; *TWU Bulletin,* Jan. 3, 1948, p. 3. *Miami Daily News,* Jan. 11, 1948, 11A, Jan. 26, 1948, 8B; and Feb. 20, 1948, 1A. Maurice Forge to Michael Quill, Feb. 1948, Folder 22, Forge Papers. Clark Foreman to Leo Sheiner, June 10, 1947, Box 18, Folder 3; and SCHW Board of Representatives, Minutes, Oct. 16, 1947, Box 18, Folder 6, p. 4, both in Carl and Anne Braden Papers, State Historical Society of Wisconsin, Madison, Wisc.
52. Robert McNally to Charles Rice, Apr. 7, 1947, and Aug. 11, 1947; and newspaper clipping on McNally, n.d., Box 22, Rice Papers. Charles Smolikoff to M. L. Edwards et al., July 2, 1946, TWU-500 Papers; "Program of the TWU Committee for Democratic Action," n.d., provided to author by Milton Zatinsky; UAW Temporary Steering Committee, "Fellow PAA Employees," n.d., provided to author by Milton Zatinsky; *Airline Facts,* Mar. 29, 1948, provided to author by Milton Zatinsky; Thomas Starling to Emil Mazey, Apr. 12, 1948, Emil Mazey Papers, Box 21, Folder 1, ALUA-WSU. On the impact

on the CIO of Rice's Catholic anti-Communism, see Steve Rosswurm, "The Catholic Church and the Left-Led Unions," in *The CIO's Left-Led Unions,* ed. Steve Rosswurm (New Brunswick: Rutgers Univ. Press, 1992), 130–33; Msgr. Charles Owen Rice, "Confessions of an Anticommunist," *Labor History* 30 (Summer 1989): 449–62. On the UAW's anti-Communism, see Martin Halpern, *UAW Politics in the Cold War Era* (Albany, N.Y.: SUNY Press, 1988); and Bert Cochran, *Labor and Communism: The Conflict that Shaped American Unions* (Princeton, N.J.: Princeton Univ. Press, 1977), 272–96.

53. Maurice Forge to Michael Quill, Feb. 1948, Folder 22, Forge Papers.

54. Milton Zatinsky, interview by Alex Lichtenstein, Dec. 19, 1994, Miami, Fla., tape in author's possession; TWU Local 500, "Bulletin," Aug. 1948, TWU-500 Papers.

55. Zatinsky, interview by Lichtenstein, Dec. 19, 1994; Milton Zatinsky to author, Dec. 28, 1994; William Oliver to Milton Zatinsky, June 15, 1948, provided to author by Milton Zatinsky; Milton Zatinsky to author, Oct. 10, 1994; Milton Zatinsky, telephone conversation with author, Nov. 1, 1994.

56. There exists a wide range of material on the internal CIO fight over Communism; the most useful (and pertinent to Quill's role) are Starobin, *American Communism in Crisis,* 144–48, 166–77, 293n35, 293n36; Johanningsmeier, *Forging American Communism,* 314–32; Freeman, *In Transit,* 286–317; Levenstein, *Communism, Anticommunism, and the CIO,* 208–9, 227, 253, 270; Shirley Quill, *Mike Quill—Himself: A Memoir* (Greenwich, Conn.: Devin-Adair, 1985), 194–207; L. H. Whittemore, *The Man Who Ran the Subways: The Story of Mike Quill* (New York: Holt, Rinehart, and Winston, 1968), 143; Curtis D. MacDougall, *Gideon's Army* (New York: Marzani and Munsell, 1965), 1:259–63; Robert H. Zieger, *The CIO, 1935–1955* (Chapel Hill: Univ. of North Carolina Press, 1995), 253–93; Rosswurm, *CIO's Left-Led Unions,* 1–16. For Quill's discussion of his reasons, see Michael J. Quill to Dear Friend [Luigi Longo], Apr. 16, 1948, reprinted in Philip Jaffe, *The Rise and Fall of American Communism* (New York: Horizon Press, 1975), 144–51. Thanks to Ed Johanningsmeier for bringing this remarkable document to my attention. Despite the TWU's relatively small size (100,000 members), its break with the Communist Party was significant because of Quill's prestige within the CIO and his union's political power in New York City, the East Coast Mecca of the American Left.

57. *Miami Daily News,* May 10, 1949, and May 11, 1949; U.S. Congress, House of Representatives, Committee on Un-American Activities, *Testimony of Paul Crouch,* May 6, 1949, 81st Cong., 1st Sess. (Washington: USGPO, 1949), 215–16; U.S. Congress, Senate, Committee on the Judiciary, Subcommittee on Immigration and Naturalization, *Communist Activities among Aliens and National Groups,* 81st Cong., 1st Sess. (Washington: USGPO, 1950), 142–43, 150–52; Charles Cowl to Gustav Faber, May 2, 1949, TWU-500 Papers; Robert McNally to Mike Quill, May 4, 1949, and Gustav Faber to Allan Haywood, May 23, 1949, both in TWU-500 Papers; Mike Quill to William Grogan, July 2, 1949; Mike Quill to All members of Local 500, July 6, 1949; "Report to the ATD Membership and Other Members of TWU," n.d., TWU-500 Papers.; *TWU Express,* Oct. 1949, p. 10; "Communist Infiltration of Transport Work-

ers Union of America," Miami Report no. 100-7319-491, Oct. 27, 1949, FBI-FOIA, p. 3.

58. Smolikoff to Forge, Oct. 21, 1946, and Smolikoff to MacMahon, Dec. 13, 1946, both in TWU-500 Papers; "Communist Infiltration of Transport Workers Union of America," Miami Report no. 100-7319-353, Mar. 5, 1947, FBI-FOIA, p. 4; Forge to Smolikoff, Dec. 27, 1946, and Forge to Smolikoff, Feb. 18, 1947, both in TWU-500 Papers; Maurice Forge to Armand Scala, Dec. 21, 1949, Folder 34, Forge Papers.
59. Charles Smolikoff to Maurice Forge, Feb. 5, 1949, Folder 41, Forge Papers.
60. Dave Lippert to Maurice Forge, Sept. 29, 1949, Folder 71, Forge Papers; Mohl, "Blacks, Jews, and the Civil Rights Movement in Miami"; Graff, "Historic Continuity of the Civil Rights Movement"; Graff, personal interview by Lichtenstein, May 18, 1992; Horne, *Communist Front,* 192–93; *Forum: The Magazine of the Florida Humanities Council* 18 (Winter 1994–95). On the NAACP and the AFL, see the correspondence between Herbert Hill and Howard Dixon, NAACP Papers on microfilm, Series 13, Part A, Reel 3.
61. Fred Swick to Maurice Forge, Oct. 3, 1958, Folder 63, Forge Papers; James R. Robinson to Mrs. Philip Stern, Oct. 13, 1958, Box 10, Series 5, Local Chapters, Congress of Racial Equality Papers, Wisconsin State Historical Society, Madison.

The CIO and the Limits of Labor-based Civil Rights Activism: The Case of Louisiana's Sugar Workers, 1947–1966

Rick Halpern

In the decade after World War II, black sugar workers in Louisiana, in alliance with the progressive national leadership of the United Packinghouse Workers of America (UPWA), fought off challenges to the biracial unions that the CIO had organized during World War II. While successful CIO organization in 1942 had brought both black and white sugar workers significant economic gains, it was not until these locals became affiliated with the UPWA in 1947 that blacks perceived opportunities to use union-based activism to challenge segregation and to move against discriminatory pay and workplace treatment. In the 1950s, dissident segregationist whites, relying heavily on anti-Communist appeals and gaining support from national CIO functionaries, sought reversal of the black-UPWA initiative. The success of civil-rights activists in beating back this challenge and their achievement of important, if limited, gains in the sugar mills and communities, reveals much about the possibilities and limitations of biracial unionism in the postwar South.[1]

In recent years, the "new" labor history has begun to come to terms with the ways in which the issue of race has complicated the experience of class in America. Partly owing to the rich outpouring of studies of the civil rights movement, and partly because the 1980s and 1990s have brought intensified racial polarization and renewed awareness of the persistence of racially based inequalities, labor historians have engaged in a vibrant debate about the dynamics of race relations among workers and the relationship of even the more liberal trade unions, especially those affiliated with the Congress of Industrial Organizations (CIO), to the struggle for black equality.

The debate about the character of the CIO is part of a larger controversy that addresses not only the relationship of class and race in American history but also the viability of the concept of class as a basis for understanding the activity and consciousness of working people. Some scholars' continuing preoccupation with the role of the Left in addressing issues of racial discrimination and attempting to build links between the labor and civil rights movements has rendered the debate even more complex and controversial. In 1988, an important and provocative article by Robert Korstad and Nelson Lichtenstein argued that the conditions generated by World War II sparked the emergence of a "very different sort of civil rights movement," led by the Left and characterized both by a focus on issues of economic equality and by a dynamic alliance between CIO unions and the black community. Other historians have argued that even some of the CIO's mainstream unions had an authentic commitment to the cause of racial equality.[2]

This characterization of the CIO's record on race has elicited vigorous dissent from scholars who argue that the vast majority of the CIO unions, including those with strongly worded commitments to racial equality and a record of support for civil rights at the national level, were unable to serve as authentic allies of the black freedom struggle because they functioned as institutions to protect the privileged position of white workers in the occupational hierarchy. Most unions, concludes Herbert Hill, the most outspoken of these critics, "either actively discriminated against blacks or, at best, regarded their nonwhite membership as a problem to be contained or controlled."[3]

The experience of Louisiana sugar workers in the postwar period casts additional light on this debate. It reveals that even cautious biracial unionism could advance the economic interests of both whites and blacks. At the same time, however, it reveals the difficulty of achieving a strong and vibrant biracial union presence when blacks began to pose plausible threats to white workers' privileged access to better-paying jobs. In Louisiana, white workers eventually acquiesced in a progressive civil-rights union program, but not until they had nearly destroyed the union and only at the price of their withdrawal from all but nominal participation in the surviving organizations.

• • •

Mack Scott had been working at American Sugar's Chalmette refinery, located just outside New Orleans, for only a few weeks in the autumn of 1943 when he came face to face with the hard realities of job segregation. A year earlier, the refinery's nine hundred workers had voted in the CIO. In accordance with the recently signed contract, the company posted all job openings on a bulletin board adjacent to the main entrance. Familiar with the practice of job bidding from his earlier employment on the unionized New Orleans waterfront, and seeking to transfer away from his back-breaking job of loading hundred-pound sacks of refined sugar, Scott approached a union official and asked about the lighter, better-paying machine-tending positions. "That's a white boy's job, you can't get that job," came the reply. Surprised because the company's postings did not carry racial designations, Scott retreated. Later, he recalled that he "didn't have the nerve enough to ask him why."[4]

Well into the CIO era, informally maintained but remarkably rigid job segregation characterized the employment patterns in virtually all of the sugar mills and refineries around New Orleans and out in the bayou country. With a workforce equally divided between African Americans and whites, the latter group predominantly Cajun, Louisiana's sugar industry relentlessly reproduced the Jim Crow practices of the South. Whites operated all machines in the refineries except for those in the hot and unpleasant filtering department and the unwieldy bulk packaging equipment. Moreover, blacks operating these machines found themselves in lower wage brackets than whites performing similar or even identical work. Elsewhere, when black workers filled labor shortages and tended machinery usually maintained by whites, the employer designated them as "helpers" and paid only a fraction above the unskilled common-labor rate. The vast majority of black refinery workers, however, provided simple muscle power. They moved cane to the grinders, transported raw sugar from one department to the next, and muscled heavy sacks in the all-black shipping department which loaded railcars with the finished product. Foremen and lower-level management posts were the preserve of whites, although here finer racial distinctions favored Anglos over Cajuns. Some refineries even made special allowance for illiterate whites, placing them above black workers in the hierarchy by employing them as "oilers" charged with roaming the plant and lubricating machinery.[5]

Gender dynamics complicated and reinforced this system of job segregation. The larger refineries, such as American at Chalmette, and Godchaux and Colonial out in the bayou country, employed a significant number of women, most of whom worked in the packaging departments. White females operated machines that filled and sealed small bags of sugar, while African-American women wielded brands with which they affixed the company's trademark to the hundred-pound sacks destined for industrial consumers. Management and union alike considered branding a black job. Indeed, so strong was the commitment to racial hierarchy that, when the white female packagers suffered layoffs, veteran workers later recollected, the company "would have a black man branding before they would put a white woman on it."[6]

The logic of segregation permeated the social relations of the workplace, extending beyond the usual separate water fountains and dressing rooms. Separate pay lines were the norm at most refineries. Thus, at Godchaux Sugar, whites waited under a roof, shielded from both sun and rain, as the paymaster distributed weekly wages, while black workers queued up in an open yard only a few yards away. Smaller plants with only a single pay window scheduled separate hours for black and white employees. Refineries that ran cafeterias operated them on a strictly Jim Crow basis, while at plants without eating facilities workers scattered at meal times to separate neighborhood cafes. Godchaux provided no toilets for black workers. American supplied uniforms for whites, while black employees had to furnish their own work clothing. African Americans sharply resented these indignities.[7]

This system reached its fullest expression in the company-dominated towns out in the bayou, notably Reserve, where Godchaux was based, and Gramercy and Matthews, where both Colonial and South Coast operated growing and processing facilities. Company-owned housing, company stores, and company-provided water and electricity allowed for a full-blown American apartheid. Racial thinking reached absurd extremes, a situation illustrated by the widely circulated story that, in Reserve, blacks could not go into the company store and ask for Prince Albert tobacco; they had to request "Mr. Prince Albert." Indeed, the only true beneficiaries of economic and social segregation were the refiners. Basic wage rates in southern sugar lagged considerably behind those in the North, allowing Louisiana's producers an edge on their competitors. In the early 1940s, when the CIO first enrolled southern refinery workers, the North-South differential stood at forty-one cents an hour; a decade later, it had been reduced by only nine cents, still providing southern sugar producers a significant operating advantage. "It was a plantation set up," one worker recalled, "only for the whites it was a little bit better. Maybe they had houses and not shacks. Maybe they got paid a penny more. But all of them was hurting and being kept down."[8]

Indeed, African Americans bore a heavier burden, not simply in terms of the social costs of segregation but materially as well. Discriminatory wage rates at Colonial Sugar's Gramercy refinery were typical. While the *average* hourly pay of black workers lagged 12.5 cents behind that of whites, in critical departments such as the boiling house, semiskilled whites earned as much as 37 cents an hour more than black laborers. Likewise, in the centrifugal department, where high-speed machines separated out impurities and crystallized the sugar, white machine tenders earned 17 cents more per hour than the blacks who mixed the sugar and cleaned the machines between batches. In the tradesmen's gangs responsible for maintaining the machinery and the physical plant, African-American "helpers" earned two to three cents more than the base rate of 81 cents, while white electricians, machinists, carpenters, masons, and welders formed a sort of labor aristocracy, with hourly wages ranging from $1.02 to $1.15. Because these better-paying jobs were exclusively the preserve of whites, black workers faced an effective wage ceiling that insured that their earnings would remain significantly below those of even the lowest paid white worker.[9]

Initially, the unionization of the refineries did not alter the racial division of labor or significantly narrow the gap between black and white income. However, from the outset, the CIO addressed the North-South wage differential and succeeded in raising the hourly rates of all southern sugar workers. Equally important, early CIO unionism quickly diminished wage differentials *within Louisiana,* bringing smaller bayou area refineries in line with larger producers. In addition to helping to rationalize the distended economics of the industry, these gains meant that workers at small plants in places such as Tallieu, Franklin, and Harvey saw their basic wage rates rise by as much as 60 percent in four years.[10]

Common concerns about wages provided the ground upon which black and white workers came together in the project of unionism. Organizers who brought the refinery workers into the CIO in local industrial unions in the fall of 1942 did not target the arrangements that reserved the better jobs for whites and dictated segregated dressing rooms and other facilities. To have done so would have threatened the privileged position of whites and alienated them. Instead, CIO representatives pitched a narrower but safer economic appeal to all workers. Black rank-and-file activists such as Isaac Shaw at American and Chester Driver at Godchaux, who helped bring the union to their plants, were acutely aware of discriminatory practices but understood this imperative. "The thing was so fragile," one worker recalled, "you just didn't have black and white together in that sort of way."[11]

CIO interracialism was indeed limited and cautious. Even so, blacks and whites shared membership in the same local unions. They divided positions on local executive boards among themselves, and they defended each other's economic rights. "Limited as it was," recalled a black activist, "it was powerfully threatening to a lot of people."[12]

Even racially traditionalist white unionists recognized that violations of black workers' rights threatened all sugar workers. Thus, in 1944, a year after commencing work at American Sugar, Mack Scott was fired unfairly. The local union's business agent, a white woman named Hazel Behenna, fought for seven months to have him reinstated. She succeeded, and Scott, now a strong union supporter, returned to American with nearly $1,500 in back pay. As he later recalled, "I said to myself, 'Hey, if the union can do that, it's a good thing. Don't matter about those jobs for white boys or any of that stuff.'"[13]

Interracialism, however, had sharp limits. While blacks and whites now shared membership in the same locals, their union meetings, picnics, and other social functions remained segregated. Indeed, the depth of sugar workers' commitment to segregation occasionally surprised other CIO unionists. Frank Wallace, a packinghouse worker from Fort Worth familiar with the range of southern racial practice, remembered first arriving in the bayou in the early 1950s and discovering that, at union meetings, "there would be a section of whites sitting here, a section of blacks sitting here, another section of brown blacks sitting here, another section of light colored blacks sitting there. So you had discrimination of four different segments of people all in one building."[14]

Throughout the South, segregation did more than simply separate workers from one another. It paralyzed union programs and weakened southern labor's ability to act as a progressive force. Segregation and black disfranchisement hobbled the activities of the CIO's Political Action Committee (PAC). Not only did African-American workers not participate in union-led political efforts, but they resented the commitment of local energy and resources to such campaigns. "How can I collect PAC dollars?" Chester Driver of the Godchaux local asked at a regional meeting. "What can I say to my people?" As a result, southern sugar locals played only a minimal role in the politics of their respective parishes, where, given their relative numbers and potential strength in the immediate postwar period, they could have made a significant difference.[15]

White racism also weakened southern locals by distancing them from the national CIO and parent international unions. Southern locals often declined to take advantage of training schools and other educational opportunities because these were offered on an integrated basis. At other times, small locals in the midst of contract negotiations or caught up in complex arbitration proceedings refused the services of black international union officials. For example, when Ed Shanklin, a black packinghouse official, showed up at Penick and Ford, a small sugar processing plant in Harvey, Louisiana, the white local president balked at entering the conference room at his side. Presiding over a biracial local union, and not known for extreme views, the president was painfully aware of the opprobrium he courted by appearing subordinate to an African American. "I sincerely doubt you are aware of the local situation," he wrote to a regional official, explaining that to present Shanklin to his members or to the company would risk dissolving the union and making him "the laughing stock of town, subject to much ridicule in this very prejudiced parish."[16]

In the sugar refineries, it was the racial attitudes of white workers, not the formal mechanisms of the union contract, that maintained discriminatory employment and promotion practices. While blacks and whites shared power in the local unions, they did so on the basis of a tacit understanding that racial practices at work were not subject to change. Speaking of white union leaders, one black worker recalled that few of them were "hard" racists and many even proved willing to soften their belief in social segregation, but "when it came down to ending that stuff *in* the plant, they wouldn't meet it, they couldn't see ending any of that stuff." Generally good leaders, "fair" persons who were "straight on the issues," they drew the line at sharing their job privileges with black unionists.[17]

When, in 1947, Louisiana's sugar locals exchanged their status as CIO local industrial unions for membership in the United Packinghouse Workers of America, refinery workers did not anticipate change in the racial status quo. Indeed, very few southern officials knew much about the new parent union. Northern sugar workers in Boston, New York, Philadelphia, and Baltimore had initiated and pursued affiliation; the southern locals simply were caught up in the movement. They expressed some concerns, but these arose from perceived threats to their local autonomy and not from unease about the UPWA's aggressive civil rights policies or its left-wing leadership. Moreover, the tremendous appeal of the high wages and benefits that UPWA had negotiated for its southern packinghouse members more than offset these reservations.[18]

For their part, the Packinghouse Workers expressed little real enthusiasm for the sugar workers' affiliation. Flush with their 1946 strike victory over the packers, and anticipating another national showdown in 1948, UPWA officials concentrated on the slaughterhouses and stockyards where the overwhelming bulk of the union's members labored. Indeed, the officials were so preoccupied with meatpacking that none investigated the racial dynamics or the existing patterns of discrimination in southern sugar, a surprising oversight given the union's recent establishment of an anti-discrimination, or "A-D," department and the black insurgency developing in its militant Chicago locals. UPWA leaders considered the sugar affiliation a welcome but ultimately unimportant addition to the union, a source of added dues revenue that would require little servicing. "They probably thought of the sugar locals as a kind of backwater," Ed Shanklin surmised. "Hell, I doubt that any one of them could have found Gramercy or Reserve on a map."[19]

Within a few years, UPWA's officials would have no difficulty locating Gramercy or Reserve on a map of Louisiana—or Houma, Labadieville, or Tallieu, either. The union's A-D program, brought to the fore in the wake of the disastrous 1948 meatpacking strike, set it on a collision course in its southern sugar locals. By the early 1950s, several factors—an internal factional struggle, the first stirrings of the southern civil rights movement, and the increasingly strident anti-communism of the CIO itself—had combined to place the Louisiana sugar locals uppermost in the minds of UPWA leaders.

Soon after their affiliation with the UPWA, within the sugar locals the balance of power began to shift. The initial catalyst, a series of sociological surveys of racial attitudes that the parent union commissioned shortly after the 1948 strike, seemed innocuous. On the national level, these surveys were part of an effort to rebuild the union, crippled by its recent strike defeat, around its large African-American membership.[20] One of the last surveys conducted, the Louisiana study revealed to union officials the depth of white prejudice and racism in its sugar locals. However, it also served as a vehicle through which black sugar workers learned about the UPWA's formal "A-D" policies and became aware of potential allies in the northern packing centers and within the international bureaucracy itself.

Even before fieldwork commenced in the New Orleans area, union officials realized that these sugar locals were different from the ones in meatpacking. Not directly affected by the strike defeat and largely cut off from the rest of the union, local leaders balked at cooperating with the field representatives and sociologists charged with carrying out the survey. "We found the membership in this area to be extremely cautious," an official noted, adding that, even after traveling into the bayou and meeting with area unionists, "it was apparent that no agreement from individual locals would be forthcoming." More than southern distrust of northern officialdom or healthy suspicion of academic sociology was at work here. It was clear that the survey was designed to go beyond simply describing racial ideology and practice; it would highlight the different perceptions of black and white workers with an eye toward identifying specific problems in need of redress. The findings of fact obtained from the survey, its director declared, were meant to provide a "springboard" for the "prosecution of a vigorous action program."[21]

Carried out in the late spring and summer of 1950, the New Orleans area survey starkly revealed the different worlds of black and white sugar workers. Not only did relatively few whites believe that discrimination and inequality were general problems, more than 97 percent reported that black workers received equal treatment *within* the union. Although roughly half of the white respondents indicated an awareness of segregation in union social affairs, very few thought that this situation needed remedying. Perhaps most revealing were the findings pertaining to whites' attitudes about working with African Americans. Almost three-quarters of the whites surveyed expressed no objection to working in close proximity to blacks, as long as they were in a lower job classification. Yet two-thirds declared their opposition to African-American coworkers of higher status; and only a quarter were willing to contemplate laboring under a black foreman.[22]

Not surprisingly, the opinions of blacks were at odds with these beliefs in virtually every category. Racism and discrimination were omnipresent. Nearly half of black workers questioned thought about their unequal status on a daily basis; and while close to 40 percent believed their unions were doing "something" about racial discrimination, a greater proportion (44 percent) felt that the local was not doing enough.[23]

The most dramatic disparity between black and white, and the one most indicative of the social gulf between the races, concerned public amenities and consumer services in the wider community. Whether the subject was taverns and restaurants, transportation and cinemas, or barber shops and pool halls, African Americans expressed a profound sense of grievance, while all but a small proportion of whites clung to the fiction of "separate but equal." In the category "protection of citizenship," a mental apartheid was evident, with most whites professing a belief in equal justice before the law and claiming to be unaware of Jim Crow's violent underside. For African-American respondents, however, police brutality was a feature of everyday life, and mob attacks were regular occurrences.[24]

The UPWA self-surveys prompted an institutional reaction on the part of the international union and marked a shift in the thinking of black sugar workers. The Louisiana findings alarmed UPWA officials, and not simply because they revealed a level of prejudice unacceptable within the packinghouse workers' union. Like the surveys conducted in the meatpacking centers of Omaha and Kansas City, the Louisiana study pointed to an uncomfortable gap between union policy and actual implementation on the local level in virtually every sphere.

This was true of matters other than standard union functions such as education, political activity, and the workings of the steward system. The surveys "really opened the eyes" of international officials to the paralysis and "structural weaknesses" plaguing the union, admitted a 1951 internal memo. Russell Lasley, the black international vice-president who oversaw the union's civil-rights program, soberly told the Executive Board that it must abandon the idea of a proactive anti-discrimination policy until the UPWA could reinvigorate local union structures and launch a thorough educational program.[25]

However, not all was doom and gloom. Overall, the surveys demonstrated that black workers supported the international's "A-D" policy and believed that their locals at least potentially were vehicles in the struggle for equality. Although in Louisiana both white and black workers were active in union affairs, elsewhere white participation had declined precipitously since the 1948 strike, leaving many locals in the hands of African Americans. International officials decided to build upon this foundation and rehabilitate the union by placing black workers and their needs at its center.[26]

Demographic factors, perhaps only dimly discernible at the time, assisted this strategy. Beginning with the defense mobilization of the early 1940s, white ethnics had been leaving meatpacking for cleaner, lighter jobs in other sectors. Hiring and promotion barriers in booming defense industries meant that African Americans enjoyed no such mobility and remained in packing, where, after the war, renewed migration from the South augmented their numbers in northern centers. This expanding black membership base provided an impetus from below for intensified struggle against discrimination at precisely the moment when the union bureaucracy committed itself to the same orientation. The confluence of institutional and social dynamics produced a powerful and clearly articulated program, one that had a profound impact in the "backwater" of Louisiana sugar.[27]

The first manifestations of the UPWA's rehabilitation scheme were the creation of a Program Department under the direction of black activist and writer Richard Durham and the strengthening of educational activities. Since union leaders believed that successful implementation of policy depended upon rank-and-file participation, they devoted special attention to the training of stewards and committeemen. Regional program coordinators, who reported directly to the international office in Chicago rather than to racially conservative district directors, implemented the program. Not only did these functionaries provide the international with first-hand information in the two southern districts, they acted as powerful counterweights to ineffectual directors who slighted the renewed and intensified "A-D" campaign.[28]

In addition to conducting classes for officers, stewards, and active members, the program coordinators developed a close relationship with the Highlander Folk School in Monteagle, Tennessee. They held regular sessions there which brought together activist-minded workers from a wide geographical area. In fact, Highlander's director and guiding spirit, Myles Horton, served briefly as UPWA educational director. His tenure was stormy, owing largely to unorthodox methods, but Horton did ensure that civil-rights issues received priority under the new setup and that complacent regional bureaucrats could not succeed in neutralizing initiatives flowing from mobilized rank-and-file workers.[29]

Nationally, the effectiveness of these initiatives was uneven. They produced positive results in many of the major packing centers, most notably Chicago and Kansas City, where a large critical mass of black workers labored. In more rural sections, however, inertia and rank-and-file indifference (and occasional hostility) prevailed. Regardless of its outcome in terms of policy implementation, however, the push from above was a boon for black sugar workers. Attending day schools or after-work steward classes raised workers' awareness of the International's resources and of its commitment to combat discrimination. Highlander weekends brought sugar workers in contact with activist-minded unionists from other locals. And when the two southern districts, under pressure from the International, began holding annual conventions in the early 1950s, sugar delegates began to move into alliance with progressives eager to replace the regional bureaucracy with officials committed to civil rights.

The new A-D program ended black sugar workers' isolation. Greater contact with the International helped black sugar workers replace feelings of resignation with a mood of optimism and possibility. Ed Shanklin recalled representing the American Sugar local at the first District Eight convention in 1953 and listening to packinghouse workers report on their progress in breaking down segregation in and around their plants. Late in the day, Fort Worth's black-led contingent succeeded in subverting an anti-Communist resolution by amending it to include the Ku Klux Klan and other race-hate groups. "Us sugar boys were sitting in listening to this and we liked what we heard! Guys like Mack Scott and myself, we liked what we heard, what we saw, so we wanted a piece of that action too."[30]

Generational dynamics played an important role in the mobilization of black sugar workers. Shanklin was ten to fifteen years younger than the founders of his local union, and his cohort expanded in the late 1940s, as black war veterans came to work in the Chalmette refinery. In the early 1950s, Korean war veterans further swelled this number. The race consciousness of these workers differed significantly from that of their elders. According to David Leonard, who returned to the U.S. after two years in Korea, "We was a little hungrier, a little more anxious to see things change." Although an industrial accident kept Shanklin from military service, he spent the war years laboring at a New Orleans roofing factory organized by the racially progressive International Longshoremen's and Warehousemen's Union, where he was exposed to a militant style of unionism that vigorously addressed the needs of its black members. "That's where I really had my baptism in unionism. . . . I really got a taste for the labor movement and militancy and I liked it," he recalled.[31]

For Shanklin and others like him, the growing racial activism of the UPWA provided tremendous encouragement. When "I found out about the packinghouse workers and what they stood for," he explained, it was "right down my alley!" Back in their local unions, young militants began agitating for the creation of A-D committees, a move mandated by the International, and raising questions about the racial status quo. In Shanklin's local, their most notable success came in early 1953, with the winning of a clause in the 1953 contract with American Sugar, prohibiting the union, its members, or the company from discriminating "against any employee because of race, creed, color or national origin." Long a standard feature of packinghouse contracts that enabled activists to use the established grievance machinery to attack discriminatory practices, this was the first time the clause found its way into southern sugar agreements.[32]

The efforts of rank-and-file activists received a boost in the autumn of 1953, when the International union pressured District Eight, which covered the states of Louisiana, Texas, Oklahoma, and Colorado, to convene an Anti-Discrimination Conference. Meeting in Fort Worth, this gathering formulated a comprehensive "action program" covering a wide range of issues. It aimed at the termination of segregated hiring, upgrading, and transfer within plants, the elimination of separate facilities such as dressing rooms and cafeterias, the upgrading of female wage rates, and the enhancement of women's role in the union. It called, in addition, for recognition of the special needs of Hispanic workers and an assault on discriminatory practices in the wider community.[33]

More than simply high-minded rhetoric, this ambitious agenda grew from struggles already under way in the packinghouses. The center of southwestern dynamism was the Fort Worth Armour plant, where contractually mandated desegregation had brought down dining-room partitions and locker-room walls, while sparking a political realignment inside the local that soon spilled over into the district at large.[34] By early 1954, other large packinghouse locals in the South were beginning to make progress on A-D as well. In Oklahoma City, the Armour local fought to integrate the cafes surrounding the stockyards and contemplated setting up its own eatery where blacks and whites could mingle. In Atlanta, union pressure forced Armour to hire black women in previously lily-white departments; while in Birmingham, against tremendous odds and intransigent opposition, locker-room desegregation was proceeding apace and black activists removed Jim Crow signs over water fountains.[35]

This activism antagonized many white workers and threatened the prevailing racial balance of power in the sugar locals. While the reaction of one woman in the Atlanta Armour plant who threatened to pay her dues money to the Klan instead of the union was extreme, the sentiment she expressed was widespread. By late 1953, field representatives across the South were reporting whites' resistance to A-D initiatives and marked difficulty in coaxing them into even sitting on committees where civil-rights matters were discussed. Cajoling truculent workers into participating often backfired, as happened when two white delegates to a national A-D conference in Chicago returned to their Birmingham plant and triggered howls of protest when they misinformed fellow workers that blacks would be hired in each department, even at the cost of laying off whites currently employed. "All hell broke out," an observer reported.[36]

The obstinacy of many white field representatives in the region was even more damaging. Beholden to the district directors but responsible for overseeing the implementation of policy, these minor officials were caught among bureaucratic imperatives bearing down on them from above, reactions of local white workers, and the increasing restiveness of African Americans. Generally racial moderates, they reacted to these pressures by urging a cooling down of the union's A-D crusade. After attending a Highlander-sponsored staff school, A. J. Shippey, a former stockhandler and longtime lieutenant of District Eight Director Alvin Pittman, asserted that "on AD discussion we were making much better progress before discussion got blunt" and offended white workers. Staffers servicing sugar locals counseled a gradualist approach, fearing that to "push too hard" would roll back the limited progress made since the locals joined the CIO.[37]

The situation took a dramatic turn for the worse when, in 1953, the issue of Communism became entangled with union-led civil-rights activity. While a long-established left-center coalition governed the UPWA nationally, Communist strength was concentrated in the Chicago packinghouses and extended no further afield than a few scattered cadre in Kansas City and Omaha.[38] Nevertheless, the notion of "Communist domination" provided many southern whites with a way of making sense of the International's aggressive civil-rights program; it also allowed committed white supremacists to cloak their racism in an acceptable anti-communist mantle and, temporarily at least, secure powerful allies within the CIO. By early 1954, a number of southern locals, including twelve in sugar, were in open rebellion against the Packinghouse Workers, seeking to disaffiliate and either return to CIO local industrial union status or join up with AFL unions willing to reverse A-D gains. The International's response to this crisis, and the activities of white and black sugar workers, show how the politics of race and anti-Communism were intertwined within the CIO.

The rebellion did not begin in the sugar-producing region or in the southern packinghouses, although it had its greatest impact there. It started late in 1953 within the midwestern UPWA and was largely a reaction to the distribution throughout the union of a pamphlet, "The Road Ahead," in which leftist activists in the union expressed vigorous dissent from CIO support for Cold War foreign policy. Coupled with lingering resentment over the conduct of the 1948 strike, "The Road Ahead" in turn galvanized the UPWA's right wing for another round of confrontation with the administration. Dubbing themselves the "Kansas City Committee," after an organizational meeting held there in August 1953, this group sought to pressure the national CIO to "clean out the Communists" in the UPWA or, failing that, to issue a charter for a rival organization. Allying themselves with former UPWA officials now employed by the CIO, and with anti-communist officials close to new CIO President Walter Reuther, the "Kansas City Committee" reached out to southern locals for support at precisely the moment when union A-D activity and the first stirrings of community-based civil-rights initiatives combined to trigger a powerful white backlash.[39]

The CIO's initial intervention into the factional dispute focused on the Communist issue. Reuther commissioned a committee, headed by Jacob Potofsky of the Clothing Workers, to investigate the charges leveled by the Kansas City group. Although the committee, in the spring of 1953, cleared the UPWA, its hearings legitimized concerns about the extent of Communist participation in the union, generated copious publicity, and emboldened southern dissidents. "Deep in the heart of Chicago stockyards . . . some union members and officials would butcher American democracy the first moment they could," trumpeted Victor Riesel's syndicated column, "Inside Labor," in what was a typical, if particularly vicious, piece of reportage.[40] When the UPWA International struck back at its enemies by firing field staff close to Director Pittman in the southwestern district and by removing A. O. McKinney, the director of the southeastern region, Reuther again bowed to right-wing pressure and in October 1953 impaneled another investigatory committee, this one chaired by Emil Mazey of the Auto Workers. While the Mazey body set about its work, southern packing locals began an open revolt.[41]

The Louisiana sugar locals stood at the center of the rebellion. The Southern Sugar Council, a vestigial body left over from the period when affiliation was directly with the CIO, coordinated the movement. The council's chairman, Antoine Songy, president of the Godchaux local and an ally of District Director Pittman, demanded new local industrial union charters and, adroitly combining anti-Communism with expressions of long-standing concerns about autonomy, engineered disaffiliation referendums in virtually every local on the bayou and in New Orleans.[42]

Regional CIO officials abetted this movement. Lorne Nelles, Southern Organizing Committee director, encouraged the sugar locals to disaffiliate from UPWA, assuring the dissidents that the move had the full backing of the Congress. CIO Executive Vice-President John Riffe, Nelles's predecessor, even went so far as to speak to one local meeting via long-distance telephone hookup, urging that the local bolt from the parent union. Acting independently, C. H. Gillman, another southern CIO director, along with Dave Burgess, the executive secretary of the Georgia CIO Council; W. H. Crawford of the Steel Workers; and Ray Nixon of the Rubber Workers, issued a damning report clearing ousted UPWA Southeastern District Director McKinney of charges of racial discrimination and accusing the UPWA of using the race issue for political purposes.[43]

Within southern locals, workers responded to the disaffiliation movement in a racialized way. White union leaders and rank and filers saw secession from the UPWA as a means of preserving the fading status quo and embraced the rebellion. C. B. McCafferty, whose father vainly attempted to dissuade white workers from leaving the UPWA, remembered that appeals to solidarity and references to the UPWA's militant tradition fell upon deaf ears. "They didn't know what he was talking about. The only thing they knew was that the Communists and niggers were coming in to take their jobs." Black workers responded differently, seeing the movement as a threat to the limited but meaningful progress they had made in recent years. Anti-communist rhetoric failed to move them, since, in Ed Shanklin's words, "they would call you Red anytime you'd push integration." As a result, Frank Wallace explained, "Communism wasn't the big bad wolf" in the minds of African-American workers; "it didn't catch on like wildfire like Pittman and his group thought it would."[44]

Black sugar workers mobilized independently of their local unions to counter the revolt. As late as January 1954, UPWA officials were concentrating their efforts upon retaining the loyalty of packinghouse and stockyard locals, feeling that the depth of anti-administration sentiment in sugar rendered that sector a lost cause. However, black unionists in the large refineries brought about a dramatic shift in the International's strategy when they impressed upon International officers the degree of support they enjoyed among African Americans. Chester Driver, one of the few blacks on the Sugar Council and an officer of the Godchaux local, wrote directly to the union's President Ralph Helstein: "I am hoping that you will not release us because thousands of Negroes are of the opinion that the Southern group are trying to dodge the A.D. program." At American Sugar, Isaac Shaw, Mack Scott, and Ed Shanklin worked with the International through George Thomas, a recently appointed black field representative charged with stemming the disaffiliation tide. Traveling up and down the bayou, they prepared black sugar workers for upcoming disaffiliation ballots, met with other influential loyalists such as Chester Ackers at Colonial and Silas Richardson at Henderson, and attempted to counter the not-so-subtle threats that members had best "vote right or it will be hard on your job."[45]

Black loyalists worked hard and successfully to split liberal white supporters from the secessionist movement. For instance, in New Orleans, local attorney Fred Cassibry had counseled the rebels and facilitated their contacts with regional CIO officials. But black unionists from American, with whom he had worked in the past, persuaded him that the movement was primarily motivated by racist concerns and not anticommunism. "I didn't know y'all had this opposition," Shanklin remembers Cassibry telling the dissenters; "I can't go with you." Similarly, black lobbying convinced Father Louis Twomey, an anti-Communist but pro-labor priest, to distance himself from the rebels and to persuade other leaders of the church, who wielded great power in small bayou towns, to adopt a neutral position. "This is not a communist issue; this is a civil rights issue. This is about the rights of black people." That was the message that black activists took to liberal whites within and close to the sugar locals.[46]

In May 1954, the rebellion peaked. The Supreme Court's Brown decision, the launching of White Citizens Councils, and an upsurge in racial violence all combined to create a supercharged atmosphere. Shanklin remembered that, in the American refinery prior to the disaffiliation vote, blacks responded to the appearance of Citizens Council buttons on the breasts of whites by affixing NAACP pins to their overalls. Racial violence threatened, and many workers carried barely concealed weapons to union meetings. "They was some rough times," one recalled.[47]

Yet, by the end of the month, the tide of rebellion had receded. The UPWA did lose three locals, but it held the four large refineries—American, Godchaux, Colonial, and Henderson—and five smaller mills. Moreover, the margins of victory in these cases indicated that a substantial portion of the white membership had voted to retain the affiliation with the UPWA, thus indicating at least tacit acceptance of the anti-discrimination program that was a key issue in the rebellion. In some locals, in which African Americans accounted for half of the membership, the vote went 5:1 against disaffiliation, indicating, as Chester Driver put it, that "we have conscious-minded [*sic*] white workers, but they are just not willing to come to the forefront." Of course, supporting the UPWA still did not mean endorsement of the union's battle against discrimination. It was the UPWA's militant unionism and its bread-and-butter appeal that effectively neutralized the racist opposition. For many whites, admitted UPWA president Helstein, "Civil rights was something they put up with because the union meant higher wages, paid holidays, and sick benefits."[48]

The referendum results did not mark the end of the rebellion. Throughout late 1954, the AFL Machinists and Meatcutters both conducted raids that plagued the UPWA and promised white sugar workers an end to "nigger unionism." But the revolt subsided as the CIO backed away from interfering in the affairs of its packinghouse affiliate. The spring referendums, though, did signal a new politics of power in the larger sugar locals, as black workers brokered the election of new executive boards. These bodies still were comprised largely of whites, but the new officers now were willing to accommodate the A-D program flowing down from the International and activated on the local level by black workers. In other locals, most notably Godchaux, older white leaders held onto power but moderated their opposition to civil-rights initiatives. Helstein named black unionist Emerson Mosely, a West Indian–born sugar worker from Baltimore, sugar director; and sugar-local votes helped George Thomas defeat A. J. Pittman for the District Eight directorship. The Communist "issue" never again figured as a potent factor in Louisiana sugar.[49]

A crucial reason for the dissipation of white opposition to black civil rights was a new round of industrial conflict beginning in the 1954 grinding season and peaking in 1955 with a bitter fourteen-week strike against Godchaux and Colonial. While the employers hoped to capitalize on racial divisions within the workforce, the experience of successful common struggle had the opposite effect. The entrenched positions of Godchaux and Colonial, the repressive measures enacted by state and local authorities, and the considerable financial and tactical support lent by the nation's packinghouse workers pushed sugar workers toward solidarity rather than fragmentation. Indeed, during the strike, unionists achieved significant civil-rights gains. Local unions eliminated segregated seating at their meetings, and union activists gained integration of local eateries. In several communities, the sugar locals launched unprecedented efforts to gain registration of black voters.[50]

The 1955 strike ostensibly was fought over economic issues, but in fact the larger fight had as much to do with social equality as with wages. The two, of course, were inextricably linked. As one unionist eloquently explained, "It's a whole lot easier for a white worker to see that the privileges of color are a sham when his belly is full, his rent is paid, and his kids have shoes on their feet than when he scared about where the next dollar is coming from."

Of course, common cause on economic issues did not guarantee progressive racial policies. Few white rank-and-file sugar workers lent active support to the union's A-D activities. More important, however, was the fact that, after 1954–55, very few actively *opposed* those efforts. Further gains in the late 1950s included the opening up of the most highly prized jobs to qualified applicants regardless of color, the employment of significant numbers of black women for the first time, the cautious involvement of local unions in community-based civil-rights activities, and the sugar unions' emergence as a potent black voice within the Louisiana AFL-CIO. White workers responded to these developments by withdrawing from participation in union affairs. Although groups of malcontents flirted with disaffiliation, and although certain events triggered vocal grumbling—the election of Leo Scott, a black, as president of the American local in 1966, for instance—whites acquiesced in black union activism around civil-rights issues.[51] They continued to pay their dues, they used the grievance machinery, they put in their time, and they took home their pay. They left the union and its programs to their black coworkers. Although racial separatism persisted, a new and vastly different equilibrium now prevailed, one predicated upon the continued ability of the union to "deliver the goods."

Notes

1. For the distinctive history of black workers in the meatpacking industry and the racial dynamics of packinghouse unionism in the 20th century, see Rick Halpern, *Down on the Killing Floor: Black and White Workers in Chicago's Packinghouses, 1904–1954* (Urbana: Univ. of Illinois Press, 1997); Roger Horowitz, *"Negro and White, Unite and Fight!": A Social History of Unionism in Meatpacking, 1930–1990* (Urbana: Univ. of Illinois Press, 1997); and Rick Halpern and Roger Horowitz, *Meatpackers: An Oral History of Black Packinghouse Workers and Their Struggle for Racial and Economic Equality* (New York: Twayne, 1996). In an earlier article, I charted this dynamic process in one southern locale: Rick Halpern, "Interracial Unionism in the Southwest: Fort Worth's Packinghouse Workers, 1937–1954," in *Organized Labor in the Twentieth-Century South,* ed. Robert H. Zieger (Knoxville: Univ. of Tennessee Press, 1991), 158–82.
2. Robert Korstad and Nelson Lichtenstein, "Opportunities Found and Lost: Labor, Radicals, and the Early Civil Rights Movement," *Journal of American History* 75, no. 3 (Dec. 1988): 245–86. The best illustration of the latter trend is Judith Stein, "Southern Workers in National Unions: Birmingham Steelworkers, 1936–1951," in Zieger, *Organized Labor in the Twentieth-Century South,* 183–222. For overviews of the ongoing debate, see Michael Goldfield, "Race and the CIO: The Possibilities for Racial Egalitarianism During the 1930s and 1940s," *International Labor and Working-Class History* 44 (Fall 1993): 1–32; and Rick Halpern, "Organised Labour, Black Workers, and the Twentieth-Century South: The Emerging Revision," *Social History* 19, no. 3 (Oct. 1994): 359–83.
3. Herbert Hill, "Race, Ethnicity and Organized Labor: The Opposition to Affirmative Action," *New Politics* 1, no. 2 (Winter 1987): 31–82; and Herbert Hill, "Mythmaking as Labor History: Herbert Gutman and the United Mineworkers of America," *International Journal of Politics, Culture and Society* 2 (Winter 1989): 132–200. See also Robert J. Norrell, "Caste in Steel: Jim Crow Careers in Birmingham," *Journal of American History* 73 (Dec. 1986): 669–94. A more balanced critical position is staked out in Bruce Nelson, "Organized Labor and the Struggle for Black Equality in Mobile," *Journal of American History* 80, no. 3 (Dec. 1993): 952–88. Quotation from Herbert Hill, *Black Labor and the American Legal System: Race, Work, and the Law* (Washington, D.C.: Bureau of National Affairs, 1977), 273.
4. Mack Scott, interview by Rick Halpern, New Orleans, La., Sept. 18, 1994, audiocassette and transcript in author's possession. The only published account of initial union organization in sugar is a brief reference in Thomas Becnel, *Labor, Church, and the Sugar Establishment: Louisiana, 1887–1976* (Baton Rouge: Louisiana Univ. Press, 1980), 63.
5. David Leonard and Mack Scott, interview by Rick Halpern, Sept. 18, 1994; Edward Shanklin, interview by Rick Halpern, Sept. 18, 1994, New Orleans, La., audiocassette and transcript in author's possession.
6. David Leonard and Mack Scott, interview by Rick Halpern, Sept. 18, 1994.

7. Field Report, Edward Sutton, Nov. 28, 1953, United Packinghouse Workers of America (UPWA) Papers, State Historical Society of Wisconsin, Madison, Wisc. (hereafter cited as UPWA Papers), Box 347, Folder 3; Minutes, 7th National UPWA-CIO Sugar Conference, May 1–2, 1954, UPWA Papers, Box 361, Folder 4; Catherine Brosnan to Alvin Vicknair, Jan. 13, 1955, UPWA District 8 Collection, Special Collections, Univ. of Texas at Arlington Library (hereafter the collection is cited as UPWAUTAL, the library as UTAL), 51-88-7; Edward Shanklin to Russell Lasley, June 17, 1955, UPWAUTAL, 51-83-13. Additional information on separate pay lines from Shanklin, interview by Halpern, Sept. 18, 1994; Ralph Helstein, interview by Rick Halpern and Roger Horowitz, Chicago, Ill., July 18, 1983, transcript, State Historical Society of Wisconsin, Madison, Wisc.; Charles Hayes, interview by Les Orear, Sept. 1993, transcript, Illinois Labor History Society, Chicago, Ill.
8. For a detailed description of living conditions in these communities, see National Agricultural Workers Union, *The Louisiana Sugar Cane Plantation Workers vs. the Sugar Corporations, U.S. Dept. of Agriculture et al.: An Account of Human Relations on Corporation-Owned Sugar Cane Plantations in Louisiana under the Operation of the U.S. Sugar Program, 1937–1953* (Washington, D.C.: Inter-American Educational Association, 1954). For more recent treatments, see Robin Myers, *Louisiana Story, 1964: The Sugar System and the Plantation Workers* (New York: National Advisory Committee on Farm Labor, 1964); and Patsy Sims, *Cleveland Benjamin's Dead: Struggle for Dignity in Louisiana's Cane Country* (New York: Dutton, 1981). For the Prince Albert Story, see Anti-Discrimination Department "Report to the International Executive Board," Apr. 22, 1953, UPWA Papers, Box 98, Folder 4. Plantation quotation from Shanklin, interview by Halpern, Sept. 18, 1994. A *regional* differential between Louisiana's large and small refineries, averaging 18¢ an hour in 1947 (and as great as 34¢), further complicated the economics of the sugar industry: "Proceedings of the CIO Sugar Workers Conference," Nov. 19, 1941, United Sugar Workers, UTAL, 51-1-4; untitled chart in United Sugar Workers Collection, UTAL, 54-1-11; "Status of Sugar and Allied Product Locals," UPWA Papers, Box 78, Folder 5; Program, 6th Annual Sugar Conference (1951), UPWA Papers, Box 78, Folder 2.
9. Figures calculated from "Schedule A" [Colonial Sugar, Gramercy, La., 1948], United Sugar Workers, UTAL, 51-27-11a, in conjunction with interview with Edward Shanklin by Halpern, Sept. 18, 1994. The generality of these findings is borne out by data for the larger New Orleans–Bayou region, presented in John Hope II, "Human Relations in New Orleans, La.: 1951," UPWA Papers, Box 344, Folder 6.
10. "Details of Local Union Status in Louisiana" [chart], UPWA Papers, Box 78, Folder 3.
11. Jerome Arceneux, telephone interview by Rick Halpern, Sept. 3, 1994, audiocassette in author's possession.
12. Ibid.
13. Mack Scott, interview by Halpern, Sept. 18, 1994; Mack Scott, telephone interview by Rick Halpern, Sept. 20, 1994, audiocassette; and Frank Wallace,

interview by Rick Halpern and Roger Horowitz, Fort Worth, Tex., Mar. 17, 1986, abstract and audiocassette in UPWA Oral History Project, State Historical Society of Wisconsin, Madison, Wisc. (hereafter cited as UPWAOHP).

14. Wallace, interview by Halpern and Horowitz, Mar. 17, 1986; Hayes, interview by Orear, Sept. 1993. For segregation of social functions, see Russell Lasley to Alex Summers, Sept. 13, 1954, UPWA Papers, Box 113, Folder 2.
15. Driver quoted in Minutes, First Constitutional Convention, District Council No. 8, July 17–19, 1953, UPWAUTAL, 51-60-10, p. 61. Four white sugar unionists ran for local office in Lafourche and Assumption parishes in 1951. All went down to defeat in the absence of black voting strength: *Sugar News,* n.d. [1951], UPWA Papers, Box 78, Folder 4.
16. Burbank V. Richard to Alex Summer, Oct. 16, 1954, UPWAUTAL, 51-76-5.
17. Shanklin, interview by Halpern, Sept. 18, 1994.
18. Indeed, several UPWA officials recalled that the easiest method of recruiting unorganized workers was to distribute at the plant gate copies of recently signed contracts. See, e.g., A. J. Pittman, interview by Halpern and Horowitz, Aug. 23, 1986, UPWAOHP. For southern sugar reservations, see the summary in Ralph Helstein to J. A. Beirne, Jan. 20, 1954, UPWA Papers, Box 150, Folder 9. See also Alex Summers to Frank Ellis, n.d. [June 1947], UPWA Papers, Box 514, Folder 11; Frank Ellis to Antoine Songy, Feb. 12, 1947, UPWA Papers, Box 438, Folder 1; and Frank Ellis to A. G. Jenevein, Apr. 11, 1947, UPWA Papers, Box 438, Folder 1.
19. For establishment of the UPWA's Anti-Discrimination Dept., see the material in CIO, Secretary-Treasurer Files, Box 113, Folder 2, Archives of Labor and Urban Affairs, Wayne State Univ., Detroit, Mich. (hereafter cited as CIO-ST Papers). For discussion of the Chicago situation and the civil rights activities of the large locals there, see Halpern, *Down on the Killing Floor*; and Halpern and Horowitz, *Meatpackers.* Parallel developments in the Kansas City packinghouses are treated in Horowitz, *Negro and White.* Shanklin, telephone interview by Rick Halpern, Aug. 26, 1994.
20. For discussion of this rebuilding, see Halpern, *Down on the Killing Floor*; Horowitz, *Negro and White*; and esp. Halpern, "Interracial Unionism," 170–71.
21. "Report of the Anti-Discrimination Dept." [1951], UPWA Papers, Box 344, Folder 6. On design of the surveys, see John Hope II, "The Self-Survey of the Packinghouse Union," *Journal of Social Issues* 9, no. 1 (1953): 3–24; John Hope II, *Equality of Opportunity: A Union Approach to Fair Employment* (Washington, D.C.: Public Affairs Press, 1956). Final quotation from Hope, "Human Relations in New Orleans."
22. Hope, "Human Relations in New Orleans," 9, 19, 26–27.
23. Ibid., 7, 9.
24. Ibid., 30–36, esp. charts A and D. The UPWA also conducted a survey in the Fort Worth, Tex., area in 1951. There, the disparity between white and black opinions in this final category was even more pronounced. See John Hope II, "Human Relations in Fort Worth, Texas: 1951," UPWA Papers, Box 344, Folder 6.

25. "Report of the Anti-Discrimination Dept." [1951], UPWA Papers, Box 344, Folder 6. Transcript, International Executive Board Meeting, Nov. 21, 1950, 179–82, UPWA Papers, Box 33, Folder 2.
26. International Executive Board, Sept. 28, 1950, Transcript, 61–62, UPWA Papers, Box 32, Folder 5. "Historically, we are paralleling in some areas the 1921 situation[,] with the races reversed," noted Education Director Louis Krainock at this meeting, making reference to the collapse of the post–World War I organizing drive, which saw black packinghouse workers desert the union *en masse.* The rebuilding of the union in the years after 1948 is chronicled in Halpern, *Down on the Killing Floor,* and Horowitz, *Negro and White.*
27. Wartime demographic changes in a number of packing centers are analyzed in Horowitz, *Organizing the Negro and White*; for post-strike black rank-and-file insurgency in Chicago and its impact upon the union bureaucracy, see Halpern, *Down on the Killing Floor*; Sam Parks interview by Rick Halpern and Roger Horowitz, Oct. 3, 1985, Chicago, Ill.; Chuck Pearson interview by Rick Halpern and Roger Horowitz, July 17, Peoria, Ill.; Anna Mae Weems interview by Rick Halpern and Roger Horowitz, May 9, 1986, Waterloo, Iowa; Jimmy Porter interview by Rick Halpern and Roger Horowitz; May 8, 1986, Waterloo, Iowa; and Eddie Humphrey, interview by Rick Halpern and Roger Horowitz, March 18, 1986, Fort Worth, Tex. All these interviews exist as abstracts and on audiocassettes at UPWAOHP.
28. The best insights into the role of the new program coordinators and their positions vis-à-vis district directors are found in Marion Simmons, interviews by Rick Halpern and Roger Horowitz, Aug. 21 and 25, 1986, Kansas City, Kans., in UPWAOHP.
29. For Highlander, see John M. Glen, *Highlander, No Ordinary School, 1932–1962* (Lexington: Univ. Press of Kentucky, 1988); and Aimee I. Horton, *The Highlander Folk School: A History of Its Major Programs, 1932–1961* (Brooklyn: Carlson, 1989). See Michael K. Honey, *Southern Labor and Black Civil Rights: Organizing Memphis Workers* (Urbana: Univ. of Illinois Press, 1993), 118, *passim,* for Highlander's relationship with Leftist CIO unions. For Horton's employment with the UPWA, see Horton to Ralph Helstein, Dec. 10, 1951, UPWA Papers, Box 75, Folder 3; Myles Horton, "Education Dept. Report by Myles Horton," Mar. 20, 1952, UPWA Papers, Box 346, Folder 24; and Myles Horton to Ralph Helstein, Mar. 14, 1953, UPWA Papers, Box 98, Folder 4. Horton liked to call his approach to education the "percolater system," explaining that "ideas will come from the workers up, and not as in the drip system, from the top down"; Horton, "Education Dept. Report." A number of UPWA workshops held at Highlander in the early 1950s were recorded and form an invaluable source. See esp. Tapes 79 and 80, Highlander Research and Education Center Records, State Historical Society of Wisconsin, Madison, Wisc.
30. Minutes, First Constitutional Convention, District Council No. 8, UPWA-CIO, July 17–19, 1953, UPWAUTAL, 51-60-10; Shanklin, interview by Halpern, Sept. 18, 1994.
31. Edward Shanklin, interview by Halpern, Sept. 18, 1994; David Leonard,

interview by Rick Halpern, Sept. 18, 1994; David Leonard, telephone interview by Rick Halpern, Sept. 20, 1994. The wartime cohort's impact in Fort Worth is discussed in Halpern, "Interracial Unionism," 172. See also Halpern, "Organized Labour, Black Workers, and the Twentieth-Century South"; and Eddie Humphrey interview by Halpern and Horowitz, Mar. 18, 1986, UPWAOHP; Chuck Pearson interview by Halpern and Horowitz, July 17, 1986, UPWAOHP, for further detail on this dynamic. A suggestive account of the impact of Korean military service upon African Americans is George Lipsitz, *A Life in the Struggle: Ivor Perry and the Culture of Opposition* (Philadelphia: Temple Univ. Press, 1988). On the ILWU in New Orleans, see David Lee Wells, "The ILWU in New Orleans: CIO Radicalism in the Crescent City, 1937–1957" (M.A. thesis, Univ. of New Orleans, 1979); a different view of the longshore union is presented in Bruce Nelson, "Class and Race in the Crescent City: The ILWU, from San Francisco to New Orleans," in *The CIO's Left-Led Unions,* ed. Steve Rosswurm (New Brunswick, N.J.: Rutgers Univ. Press, 1992), 19–45.

32. "Anti-Discrimination Department Report to the International Executive Board," Apr. 22, 1953, UPWA Papers, Box 98, Folder 4; "Concessions Granted to UPWA Local 1101," Mar. 18, 1953, UPWA Papers, Box 514, Folder 12. For Chicago locals' use of the no-discrimination clause to attack discriminatory practices, see Kelley to Russell Lasley and Charles Hayes, June 22, 1950, UPWA Papers, Box 342, Folder 7; UPWA Press Release, Dec. 21, 1950, UPWA Papers, Box 345, Folder 12; and the *Packinghouse Worker,* Dec. 1951. For the ways in which contractual provisions assisted women workers in their struggle for equality, see Bruce R. Fehn, "Striking Women: Gender, Race, and Class in the United Packinghouse Workers of America, 1938–1968" (Ph.D. diss., Univ. of Wisconsin, 1991), 166–78.
33. For International pressure on the regional bureaucracy, see A. T. Stephens to A. J. Pittman, July 22, 1953, UPWAUTAL, 51-66-19. For the action program, see "First Anti-Discrimination Conference, District Council No. 8," Oct. 24, 1953, United Sugar Workers Papers, UTAL, 54-2-2; and related material on specific workshop sessions, in UPWAUTAL, 51-60-8. The program largely followed the one under way in the major packinghouse chains. For a summary, see Anti-Discrimination Dept. to All Armour, Cudahy, Swift, and Wilson Locals, Nov. 18, 1952, UPWA Papers, Box 345, Folder 21.
34. See Halpern, "Interracial Unionism," for full treatment.
35. On Oklahoma City, see A. T. Stephens to Steve Mauser, Feb. 2, 1954; A. T. Stephens to Richard Durham, Feb. 17, 1954; and Richard Durham to Steve Mauser, Feb. 19, 1954, all in UPWA Papers, Box 350, Folder 16. On Atlanta, see report dated Apr. 6, 1953, UPWA Papers, Box 101, Folder 1; and A. O. McKinney to Russell Lasley, Nov. 3, 1952, UPWA Papers, Box 345, Folder 22. On Birmingham, see Field Reports of Ada Lee Howell and John Henry Hall, Dec. 1953, UPWA Papers, Box 347, Folder 3. See also local progress reports in "National Anti-Discrimination Conference, UPWA-CIO," Chicago, Oct. 30–31 and Nov. 1, 1953, UPWA Papers, Box 349, Folder 5.
36. John Henry Hall, Field Report, Dec. 19, 1953, UPWA Papers, Box 347, Folder

3. Other enraged whites said that they would "go to Governor Talmadge"; Field Report, Apr. 6, 1953, UPWA Papers, Box 101, Folder 1. See also Field Reports of Ada Lee Howell, John Miller, and Archie Brookins, Dec. 1953, UPWA Papers, Box 357, Folder 15.

37. A. J. Shippey to A. T. Stephens, June 2, 1953, UPWAUTAL, 51-66-26; "Anti-Discrimination Dept. Report to the International Executive Board," Apr. 22, 1953, UPWA Papers, Box 98, Folder 4.

38. On the Left-Center coalition, see Halpern, *Down on the Killing Floor*; and Horowitz, *Negro and White, passim.*

39. For "The Road Ahead," see various drafts in UPWA Papers, Box 98, Folder 4. For reaction to the document, see C. B. McCafferty, interview by Rick Halpern and Roger Horowitz, Mar. 18, 1986, Fort Worth, Tex., UPWAOHP. On UPWA internal politics in this era, see "Short History of Factional Attacks," UPWA Papers, Box 50, Folder 8; and Russell Lasley to Ralph Helstein, Aug. 26, 1953, UPWA Papers, Box 352, Folder 2. CIO involvement was centered around CIO Secretary-Treasurer James Carey and Reuther's assistant, John Riffe. See esp. CIO Policy Faction, Glenn Chinander et al. to Walter Reuther, 8 Sept. 1953, CIO-ST Papers, Box 114, Folder 6; and correspondence from various packing locals in CIO-ST Papers, Box 292, Folders 12 and 17.

40. For the Potofsky Committee, see Minutes, UPWA International Executive Board, Apr. 25, 1953, UPWA Papers, Box 100, Folder 2. See also Ralph Helstein to Walter Reuther, May 20, 1953; John Riffe to Helstein (telegram), May 15, 1953; Helstein to Jacob Potofsky, May 29, 1953; and "Report on Meeting with the CIO Special Committee," June 4, 1953, all in UPWA Papers, Box 100, Folder 3. Southern rebels did their part to publicize the investigation—see, e.g., A. J. Pittman to all Local Unions and Field Representatives, May 8, 1953, United Sugar Workers Collection, UTAL, 54-3-14. Victor Riesel, "Inside Labor," *Dallas Morning News,* Nov. 4, 1953.

41. The incident leading to McKinney's removal was a segregated union dinner held in Atlanta. See "Charge Plot to Sabotage UPWA's Equal Rights Policy," *Packinghouse Worker,* Aug. 1953; G. R. Hathaway to Local Unions in District 9, Aug. 20, 1953, UPWA Papers, Box 358, Folder 6; Statement by A. O. McKinney, Oct. 1, 1953, UPWA Papers, Box 352, Folder 4; Helstein to McKinney, Oct. 17, 1953, UPWA Papers, Box 352, Folder 2; and related correspondence. The African-American press covered the union's response to the dinner. See, e.g., *The Call* (Kansas City, Mo.), Aug. 14, 1953; and the *Chicago Defender,* Aug. 15, 1953. For firing of field staff, see A. J. Pittman to All Local Unions, Sept. 14, 1953, United Sugar Workers, UTAL, 54-3-14. On the second CIO investigation (Mazey), see material in CIO-ST Papers, Box 114, Folder 10; and material in Papers of Walter Reuther, UAW President, Wayne State Univ., Box 292, Folders 17 and 21.

42. Antoine Songy to Walter Reuther, Jan. 4, 1954, CIO-ST Papers, Box 178, Folder 21; Songy to all local unions affiliated with the Southern Sugar Council, Aug. 14, 1953, United Sugar Workers Collection, UTAL, 54-2-2; Local 399 Minutebook, Special Executive Board Meeting, Dec. 7, 1953, United Sugar Workers Collection, UTAL, 54-OS152-2. Ralph Helstein to J. A. Beirne,

Jan. 20, 1954, UPWA Papers, Box 150, Folder 9; Carey Haigler, "Summary Report," n.d. [early 1954], Box 150, Folder 9.

43. For Nelles's and Riffe's interference, see Local 399 Minutebook, Special Meetings of Local, Dec. 8, 1953, Jan. 1954, Apr. 20, 1954, and May 25, 1954, United Sugar Workers Collection, UTAL, 54-OS152-2. For Gillman Committee report, see UPWA Papers, Box 352, Folder 2; and W. H. Crawford et al., "To Whom It May Concern," Aug. 5, 1953, United Sugar Workers Collection, UTAL, 54-3-14.

44. C. B. McCafferty, interview by Halpern and Horowitz, Mar. 18, 1986; Frank Wallace, interview by Halpern and Horowitz, Mar. 17, 1986; Edward Shanklin, interview by Halpern, Sept. 18, 1994. McCafferty believed that "blacks basically know that it's a smokescreen for lack of progress in civil rights. They viewed anti-Communism as a negative force in their personal view, or in their advancement."

45. Chester Driver to Ralph Helstein, Dec. 9, 1953; and A. T. Stephens to Chester Driver, Dec. 9, 1953, both in UPWA Papers, Box 113, Folder 1; Edward Shanklin, interview by Halpern, Sept. 18, 1994; David Leonard, interview by Halpern, Sept. 18, 1994; and Mack Scott, interview by Halpern, Sept. 18, 1994. According to Shanklin, "It looked at that time like the International was more or less ready to throw in the towel. They figured they'd lost us until they got the letter. Then they said, 'Hey! Wait a minute! We got some sympathizers down there.'" George Thomas and Alex Summers to Ralph Helstein, May 14, 1954, UPWAUTAL, 51-72-22; Frank Wallace, interview by Halpern and Horowitz, Mar. 17, 1986. For threats and intimidation, see George Thomas to Carey Haigler, May 14, 1954; Haigler to Thomas, May 18, 1954, and attached reports; Alex Summers to A. T. Stephens, May 17, 1954 (quotation); and Ralph Helstein to John Riffe, May 18, 1954, all in UPWA Papers, Box 150, Folder 9. See also Moses Adedeji, "Crossing the Colorline: Three Decades of the United Packinghouse Workers of America's Crusade Against Racism in the Trans-Mississippi West, 1936–1968" (Ph.D. diss, North Texas State Univ., 1978), 143–44.

46. Edward Shanklin, interview by Halpern, Sept. 18, 1994; David Leonard, interview by Halpern, Sept. 18, 1994; and Mack Scott, interview by Halpern, Sept. 18, 1994.

47. Edward Shanklin, interview by Halpern, Sept. 18, 1994; David Leonard, interview by Halpern, Sept. 18, 1994; Frank Wallace, interview by Halpern and Horowitz, Mar. 17, 1986. Adedeji, "Crossing the Colorline," 144.

48. Ralph Helstein to Emil Mazey, Feb. 17, 1954, UPWA Papers, Box 113, Folder 1; Carey Haigler to George Thomas, May 18, 1954, and attached reports, UPWAUTAL, 51-77-1; Minutes, 7th National UPWA-CIO Sugar Conference, Sioux City, Iowa, May 1–2, 1954, esp. 8–11, UPWA Papers, Box 514, Folder 10. On the "bread and butter appeal," see Helstein to "Dear Fellow Member," Jan. 8, 1954, UPWA Papers, Box 113, Folder 1.

49. On raiding, see Alvin Vicknair to Alex Summers, June 15, 1954, UPWAUTAL 51-76-5. Summers to A. T. Stephens, July 13 and 16, 1954; and Ralph Helstein to R. J. Thomas, Aug. 5, 1954, all in UPWA Papers, Box 113, Folder

2. The most serious raid in sugar, an attempt by the IAM at the American refinery, blatantly played the race card; see IAM to Fellow Workers of American Sugar Refinery, June 28, 1954, and other material in UPWAUTAL, 51-67-19. For the southeastern district, where the AFL's Meatcutters were active, see "Report to the International Officers on District 9 Situation," Nov. 19, 1954, UPWA Papers, Box 108, Folder 3 and materials in Folder 1. On new leadership, see Edward Shanklin, interview by Halpern, Sept. 18, 1994, and David Leonard, interview by Horowitz, Sept. 18, 1994. Local 1101, List of Officers for 1955, UPWAUTAL, 51-77-11. For Pittman's defeat, see Halpern, "Interracial Unionism," 175; Frank Wallace, interview by Halpern and Horowitz, Mar. 17, 1986; A. J. Pittman, interview by Halpern and Horowitz, Aug. 23, 1986, UPWAOHP; and Mary Salinas, interview by Halpern and Horowitz, Mar. 18, 1986, UPWAOHP. *Proceedings of the United Packinghouse Workers of America* (Chicago, WPWO, 1954).

50. The best overview of the 1955 strike is "Southern Sugar Strike 1955," Reuther Papers, Box 292, Folder 22. See also "The Southern Sugar Strike—1955" and "Fact Summary Sheet," Sept. 19, 1955, both UPWA Papers, Box 369, Folder 4. On strike violence and legal repression, there is good coverage by *New Orleans Times-Picayune* (June 18, 19, 29, and 30 and July 2 and 5–9, 1955). Anti-discrimination advances are discussed in Frank Wallace, interview by Halpern and Horowitz, Mar. 18, 1986; and Charles Fischer, interview by Halpern and Horowitz, Chicago, Ill., Jan. 27, 1986, UPWAOHP; Edward Shanklin, interview by Halpern, Sept. 18, 1994; and David Leonard, interview by Horowitz, Sept. 18, 1994. See also Adedeji, "Crossing the Colorline," 188–89.

51. On AD gains, see Edward Shanklin to Russell Lasley, June 17, 1955, UPWAUTAL, 51-83-13; Minutes, 3rd Constitutional Convention, District Council No. 8, Mar. 26–27, 1955, UPWAUTAL, 51-78-20; Minutes, 4th Constitutional Convention District Council No. 8, Oklahoma City, Okla., Mar. 10–11, 1956, UPWAUTAL, 51-93-13; Edward Shanklin, interview by Halpern, Sept. 18, 1994; and David Leonard, interview by Halpern, Sept. 18, 1994. See also Adedeji, "Crossing the Colorline," 157, 198. For continued disaffiliation sentiment, see George Thomas to Vicknair, Shanklin, and Mack Scott, Oct. 7, 1966, UPWAUTAL, 51-226-11; and A. P. Stoddard and C. J. Stephens to Members of UPWA Local 1101, Feb. 27, 1967, UPWAUTAL, 51-239-12. On Leo Scott, see Petition, June 17, 1966; Edward Shanklin to George Thomas, June 20, 1966; and Thomas to Helstein, Aug. 16, 1966, all in UPWAUTAL, 51-226-11. Adedeji, "Crossing the Colorline," 169–70, provides a typically idiosyncratic account.

5

"CIO Meant One Thing for the Whites and Another Thing for Us": Steelworkers and Civil Rights, 1936–1974

Bruce Nelson

During World War II, when the fight against fascism gave a special urgency to the rhetoric of democracy, and an unprecedented labor–civil rights alliance began to take shape, CIO President Philip Murray embraced the cause of racial equality as a "holy and a noble work . . . that all right-thinking citizens should dedicate themselves to." Murray, who was also the president of the United Steelworkers of America (USWA), helped make the CIO an important voice in support of fair employment practice and a wider civil rights agenda. He was so proud of the industrial union federation's commitment and achievements in this regard that he told the 1944 CIO convention, "God help the Negro in America, and God help the minority groups of America, were it not for the splendid work that is being done by this great institution of yours and mine. We don't confine ourselves to the mere adoption of resolutions in meetings of this kind; we make those resolutions effective and workable."[1]

Murray was expressing the widely shared belief that the CIO meant something new and significant for race relations in American society, and for the cause of African-American equality in particular. And the CIO *did* win important gains for blacks. Relative to their counterparts who remained trapped in casual and low-wage sectors of the labor market, unionized black workers gained significant benefits. Moreover, blacks often had a stronger commitment to the CIO than whites did. In some instances, CIO unions with a substantial African-American membership and a left-wing leadership played a vital role in the struggle for black equality, both on the job and in the larger society.[2]

Eventually, however, most CIO affiliates were caught in a paralyzing dilemma. Rhetorically, their leaders adhered to the industrial union federation's commitment to racial equality. Cautiously, and as much as possible in conjunction with employers and government, some of them sought to implement anti-discrimination policies in the workplace. But for the most part, they chose not to allow these concerns to jeopardize the institutional survival of their organizations, which were dependent upon the allegiance of white workers and generally reflected their consciousness. Ultimately, they faced the contradiction between a narrow democracy that privileged the interests of the white majority and a more inclusive vision that promised to bestow equal rights on white and black alike. While the CIO's rhetoric often invoked the latter ideal, its practice far more often reflected the former.[3]

This essay explores the working out of this contradiction in the steel industry, and in the relationship between black and white workers—most of them members of United Steelworkers Local 2401—at the Atlantic Steel Company in Atlanta, Georgia. In Atlanta, black insurgency, white backlash, and an international union leadership caught between a formal commitment to racial justice and reluctance to confront a local union's intransigent white majority combined to reveal the limitations of the racial progressivism Murray so eloquently proclaimed.

In the realm of employment, the steel industry was a multilayered world that reflected generations of ethnic succession and racial gerrymandering. Its job structure was bewildering in variety and scale—because the process of making steel was complex; because the mills were vast; and because the giants of the industry turned out a wide array of products, often in the same location. Thus, innumerable occupational categories and many "lines of progression" characterized each workplace. From a social standpoint, the industry was more a mosaic than a melting pot. Immigrant steelworkers in Pittsburgh remembered "a Ukrainian department, a Russian department, a Polish department," and judged it "a beautiful thing." In Youngstown, local union president Sam Camens painted a vivid portrait of the ethnic—and racial—layering at U.S. Steel's Ohio Works. "The blast furnace was basically black," he recalled. "The machine shop was English and German. The open hearth was Irish and Scotch. . . . The primary mills . . . were mostly East Europeans. The masons, bricklayers, were all Italians. . . . The riggers were all [Hungarians]. . . . That's the way the plant was. . . . It was all little islands of ethnic concentrations."[4]

Over time, ethnicity became less important in defining workers' positions in the mills' occupational hierarchies. As immigrant workers and their sons became more fully American, they also relinquished their status as "in-between people" and became unambiguously "white." This transition occurred at different times for different ethnic groups, but the escalating pace of the struggle for black equality during and after World War II sharpened European immigrants' sense of their status as white and their determination to maintain the limited but nonetheless real entitlements that came with that status. Joseph Bazdar, local union president at the Bethlehem Steel plant in Steelton, Pennsylvania, observed that, in many departments, before the coming of the USWA "it was necessary for workers belonging to the 'wrong' group to curry favor with their foremen by plying them with material gifts, including cash, or by the old fashioned method known as 'bootlicking' in order to retain even the lowest paid and most menial of jobs." In this case, the "wrong" groups were "workers of the colored race, recent immigrants or sons of immigrants, workers of the wrong religious denomination, workers who did not belong to certain fraternal lodges and even workers who did not live in the same neighborhood as their foreman." Generally speaking, Bazdar said in 1950, "limitations on the promotion of white workers have been largely wiped out." But "a definite ceiling exists on job opportunities for the majority of our negro workers on a level slightly above the floor."[5]

In the South, race was the one factor that mattered. In 1965, NAACP Labor Secretary Herbert Hill observed that the "racial practices" at U.S. Steel's Ensley Works blast furnace were typical of those that had long prevailed in the Birmingham–Bessemer area of Alabama. According to Hill, black workers were concentrated in a racially segregated "labor pool" and had separate, and limited, seniority rights only within its confines; while whites were "automatically promoted on the basis of seniority, skills and job vacancies into a variety of production and craft operations." "As a result of the operation of separate seniority lines which are codified by the local supplementary agreement between the union and the company," Hill concluded, "Negro workers are permanently locked in menial and unskilled job classifications. White workers with less seniority are promoted into more desirable jobs and there are, of course, significant differentials in the average earnings between Negro and white workers."[6]

The union was by no means solely responsible for this pattern. The companies and the United Steelworkers negotiated seniority provisions at the local level, and there were instances in which the intervention of the union created openings for black workers in what had been all-white lines of progression. But often the seniority agreements that USWA locals negotiated served to limit opportunity for black workers; sometimes they further racialized the distribution of jobs in the plants. Writing on behalf of a "group of colored workers" at the U.S. Pipe and Foundry Company in Bessemer, the local union president complained in 1950 that "we hold no skill[ed] jobs and are losing semi-skilled jobs every year." Before the organization of the plant by the United Steelworkers, Charles Alford reported, "the Negro held many sub-foremen jobs and many skill[ed] jobs." But now "he is restricted to common labor and semiskill[ed jobs] the white[s] do not desire to fill." This pattern was also evident, on a much larger scale, at Pullman-Standard's railroad car manufacturing plant in Bessemer. After the signing of a collective bargaining agreement in 1941, the number of "one-race" departments at Pullman-Standard actually increased; and in the mid-1950s, when the local union proposed a change from occupational to departmental seniority, seven new "one-race" departments were created. Attorneys for the NAACP Legal Defense Fund estimated that, by 1964, "96% of the employees in the Bessemer plant were located in racially identifiable departments."[7]

Formally, at least, the top leaders of the United Steelworkers were committed to racial equality, and periodically they issued pronouncements reminding the membership of the union's stance on this issue. In 1954, the USWA's president, vice-president, and secretary-treasurer declared unequivocally that "any collective bargaining contract which either by its terms or its actual operation permits discrimination on account of race, creed, color or nationality violates the policy of this union." But in practice, the leadership was caught in a bind, for seniority—the key to the job structure's racial character and monetary rewards—was negotiated locally, and the union's white majority displayed little if any commitment to changes in the mills' employment patterns. On the contrary, the seniority system that local unionists negotiated reflected the determination of the most entrenched and (relatively) privileged sections of the workforce to maintain the status quo, which in racial terms meant the determination of whites to keep blacks subordinate. One district director admitted that "the customs of the past have been to allow the colored worker to progress just so far and then the road to advancement is closed to him." Those customs would not change easily, even in the face of an unprecedented wave of struggle for racial equality.[8]

The conflict generated by the civil rights movement only added to the union's travail and the leadership's dilemma. As early as 1950, when President Philip Murray issued an order calling for the desegregation of the USWA's facilities and events, the response from white unionists in Birmingham was one of outrage; threats of "secession" were widespread. Alabama District Director Reuben Farr informed Murray, "Yesterday I was notified that there was a petition for decertification being circulated [at] Fairfield Steel. It was also reported to me that practically every employee that this petition has gone to has signed." At Stockham Valve and Fitting Company, where a collective bargaining agreement was scheduled for imminent renewal, Farr reported that a large number of white employees were actively seeking to terminate their membership in the union via a fifteen-day escape clause in the contract. "It looks as though our union is completely torn asunder," he concluded.[9]

Murray also received a letter from seven local union presidents in the Birmingham area, warning him that continued tampering with the "feelings, wishes, customs and beliefs" of southern white workers would "sound the death knell of the Union in the South." The USWA president got the message. When Murray delivered a Labor Day address to thousands of steelworkers in Birmingham the following September, Police Commissioner Bull Connor and his men strung a heavy piece of rope down the center of the hall. Whites sat on one side; blacks, on the other. Although Murray continued to insist that Jim Crow signs be removed from all offices and meeting halls of the United Steelworkers, Herbert Hill reported in 1953 that "white and colored" signs for toilets and drinking fountains remained in most local unions, and that a pattern of segregated seating prevailed in "all union membership meetings." Clearly, the volatile situation in Birmingham and much of the South made the international union exceedingly cautious about challenging the segregationist mores of its white membership.[10]

In the North, year by year, the official culture was becoming more committed to the goal of racial equality. Here the USWA became an important ally of the increasingly powerful civil rights lobby in Washington, D.C., in state capitals, and in many municipalities. The union supported the creation of fair employment practice legislation at every level; and, in conjunction with prestigious academicians, it conducted "human relations" seminars on university campuses. At the same time, however, the Steelworkers' leadership remained reluctant to confront an employment structure that—in the North as well as the South—favored the white union majority at the expense of the black minority.

Indeed, some black steelworkers came to believe that the union's highly visible activity on behalf of civil rights in northern communities was intended as a substitute for confronting racial stratification in the mills. Oliver Montgomery, a black steelworker from Youngstown, recalled that, when the union leadership assigned him to his local's civil rights committee, "the word was if I would just not touch the jobs in the plant . . . I could [write] my own ticket. I could have been gone almost every day. I could have been on [union business] full time, just going around to civil rights meetings. . . . But don't touch the plant. We never would buy that. That's why we were at odds with [the union leadership] almost continuously."[11]

Black workers' growing disenchantment with the union—at the local, district, and international levels—was paralleled by increasing strains in the relationship between civil rights organizations and the United Steelworkers. Tension grew partly from changes in the leadership of the Steelworkers' union and the labor movement as a whole. With the merger of the American Federation of Labor (AFL) and the CIO in 1955, the center of gravity in organized labor shifted decisively toward the AFL, which always had been more conservative on the issue of race than the CIO. Under AFL-CIO President George Meany's leadership, organized labor functioned more than ever as an interest group that lobbied at the top for incremental change rather than as a social movement that challenged the existing relations of power through mass mobilization at the grassroots level. In the United Steelworkers, David J. McDonald, who succeeded Philip Murray as president in 1952, was in the Meany mold, temperamentally and ideologically. He candidly acknowledged that "I never regarded myself as a social reformer," and during his presidency the USWA became increasingly disengaged from the day-to-day struggles of the civil rights movement. Frank Shane, executive secretary of the union's Civil Rights Committee, complained bitterly, with regard to two of the movement's most pivotal moments, the 1963 March on Washington and the Selma-to-Montgomery pilgrimage of 1965, that "only two [USWA] district directors were present in Washington and none in Montgomery." Speaking of the union's top leadership, he concluded that "these armchair strategists muff[ed] the chance of a lifetime to really stand up and be counted when the chips were down."[12]

Such transgressions probably could have been forgiven had the union made major strides in confronting the burning issue of racial discrimination in the steel industry employment structure. But with black workers demanding justice and whites clinging to their monopoly of skilled jobs, "We are," said one district director, "placed in the position of being 'Damned if you do and damned if you don't.'" The union frequently assured civil rights organizations of its good intentions and promised that change was imminent. And there were some changes, but for the most part the discriminatory structure remained intact.[13]

• • •

The case of the Atlantic Steel Company and United Steelworkers Local 2401 offers important insights into the dynamics of this growing conflict and provides a clear sense of the role that each of the main actors played over time. Although southern steel production was centered in the Birmingham area, by the end of the 1950s, Atlanta—and Atlantic Steel—had become the center of racial controversy in the industry. Incorporated in 1901 to make steel bands for cotton bales and hoops for turpentine casks, Atlantic Steel dramatically expanded its production over the years. By the early 1950s, it was turning out more than two hundred thousand tons of steel ingots and a wide variety of steel products annually. At that time, it employed two thousand workers, about 90 percent of whom were members of Local 2401 of the United Steelworkers of America. In 1953, when Glenn Gilman and James Sweeney, from the School of Industrial Management at Georgia Tech, conducted an in-depth study of labor relations at Atlantic Steel, they characterized the company as an outstanding example of labor-management cooperation and mutually beneficial collective bargaining.[14]

Insofar as this was true, it represented a dramatic change for Atlantic Steel, which had long been a bastion of the open shop and had once employed the fanatically anti-union Tom Girdler as its general superintendent. (Girdler had gone on to become the president of Republic Steel and the leading national symbol of corporate hostility to unionism during the CIO era.) In 1907, Girdler had broken a strike by an AFL union; but he was long gone in 1941, when the Steel Workers Organizing Committee succeeded in winning a representation election. On the eve of the election, the Ku Klux Klan staged a parade of some six hundred cars through the Negro section of Atlanta, burning crosses along the way, in an attempt to intimidate the black workers who formed the strongest bloc of union supporters. But they refused to be intimidated. Because they were relegated to unskilled jobs, at a maximum wage of 72 cents an hour compared to $3.50 for skilled whites, blacks no doubt believed that they had the most to gain from the unionization of Atlantic Steel. They were the leading participants in the strike for union recognition that followed the election, and during the war years they continued to make up about 60 percent of the union membership, even though they constituted only about 30 percent of the workforce in the plant. Initially there had been separate locals for blacks and whites; and Bill Crawford, who served as the Steelworkers' district director in Atlanta from 1942 until his death in 1954, worried that "there seems to be a lot of the old Klan spirit still alive in this plant." Crawford gradually succeeded in merging the two locals into one, and in bringing most of the white workers into the union as well. By 1953, the team of industrial relations specialists from Georgia Tech concluded that Atlantic Steel had "no race problem." According to Gilman and Sweeney, Local 2401 was working toward a solution of "the Negro problem in the South . . . within the framework of southern tradition and custom, rather than by attempting revolutionary action." This meant that the local accepted "the policies of segregation that are practiced at the plant in deference to southern mores" but also was willing to "put the entire resources of the union behind an employee who has been subjected to individual discrimination because of his color."[15]

That Gilman and Sweeney could reach such a conclusion suggests that they spent very little time talking to black workers, or perhaps that black workers did not yet feel free to express their growing dissatisfaction with the racial separation and inequality that continued to characterize the plant's employment pattern. The timing of their observations may also suggest that, in much of the South, there was a moment of fragile equilibrium when the Steelworkers and other CIO unions were able to avoid racially divisive issues and to serve the perceived needs of their black and white memberships at the same time. In 1953, Herbert Hill captured the reality, and the ambiguity, of this equilibrium in a report on relations between the CIO and the NAACP in the Birmingham-Bessemer area. He acknowledged that staff representatives and local officials of the Steelworkers were doing an "excellent job on behalf of Negro workers in the processing of grievances against management." But he also perceived a growing disenchantment among black workers. Speaking of the CIO, and the Steelworkers in particular, Hill reported that "many Negro workers indicated a sense of despair and futility because the one important institution operating in the South that they hoped would provide the bridge across the divide of color was not doing so."[16]

Events beyond the workplace soon demonstrated that even this fragile equilibrium could not last, for it was constructed upon a foundation of sand and was subject to pressures that union leaders could not contain. The historic *Brown* decision hit the Deep South like a bolt of lightning in 1954, precipitating an era of "massive resistance." Then the civil rights movement found its mass base, first in Montgomery in 1955 and gradually across much of the South and the nation, triggering interconnected waves of black insurgency and white backlash that inevitably penetrated the unions and troubled the relations between black and white workers. As whites rallied to the defense of segregation, blacks proved increasingly unwilling to accept incremental gains within the framework of a separate and unequal status quo. Labor leaders across the South continued to express the hope that the "issue [of civil rights] will soon blow over and . . . conditions will return to normal." But there was no returning to "normal." In Atlanta, a self-proclaimed "oasis of tolerance" that was "too busy to hate," several locals of the United Auto Workers became bastions of the Ku Klux Klan; one of them even boasted the Georgia Klan's Grand Dragon as a member. When former USWA official Morton Elder visited the city in 1956 to conduct a race relations survey for the Southern Regional Council, he found that, while other industrial unions in the area had managed to avoid the insurrectionary backlash that had engulfed the UAW locals, their leaders admitted to "rather strained relations on the job, with communication between the races becoming less and less frequent."[17]

This was the context in which the "race problem" reemerged at Atlantic Steel. The person who served as the catalytic agent was the Rev. Joseph Rabun, a Baptist minister who had been employed at the plant since 1949, first as a production worker and then, briefly, as a foreman. In the aftermath of the lynching of fourteen-year-old Emmett Till and the acquittal of his murderers in Mississippi, Rabun wrote a letter of protest to the *Atlanta Constitution*. Published in October 1955 under the heading, "Atlanta Preacher Calls Till Trial a Lynching," the letter declared: "With what humility and shame we 'supreme' whites should bow our heads and implore God's mercy when we think of our own share of responsibility for the outrageous murder and the jury's cowardly verdict." "As long as we remain silent and inactive before the corruption of justice," Rabun concluded, "all of us are criminal."[18]

As his letter suggests, Joe Rabun was hardly a typical employee of Atlantic Steel. He had lost his pulpit in McRae, Georgia, in 1947, after speaking out against the racial policies of the congregation's most famous member, Gov. Eugene Talmadge, one of the Deep South's most virulent and outspoken segregationists. At the urging of USWA District Director Bill Crawford, who shared his deep religious faith and at least some of his racial liberalism, Rabun had made an unsuccessful run for governor in 1948. Then, with no church and no prospect of one, he had turned to Crawford, who helped him secure employment at Atlantic Steel. He was, by his own account, a "faithful member of 2401," until September 1955, when he had the opportunity to become a turn foreman in the Wiredrawing Department.[19]

After a little more than a month on his new job, Rabun recalled, "lightning struck without warning." The cause was his letter to the *Atlanta Constitution*. When he came to work the next evening, he noticed immediately that someone had posted his letter on a bulletin board and had written, "Why the hell don't you go to Mississippi and tell them this?" Soon agitated workers were calling him a "nigger lover," and several of the men under his supervision went to other departments to spread the word of his heresy. Before long, there was a work stoppage and, when confronted by the local union president and the company's director of industrial relations, the strikers announced that they would not return to work as long as Rabun remained their foreman. He was told to "go home," allegedly to allow matters to cool down, and then removed from his job, on the grounds that he "did not get along with the employees under his supervision." Rabun appealed to the United Steelworkers, including President David McDonald, for help. But, taking the position that, as a foreman, he was not a member of the bargaining unit, the district and international union leaders washed their hands of the matter. It was not, after all, a "union problem."[20]

In the narrowest and most technical sense, perhaps it was not. But the combination of external stimuli and internal grievances was pushing black employees of Atlantic Steel in a direction that would make Local 2401 one of the most contentious in the United Steelworkers' jurisdiction. In April 1957, after concluding that the local leadership was unwilling to address their concerns, eight black workers met with the Labor and Industry Committee of the Atlanta NAACP and unveiled a long list of grievances. They complained that blacks received a maximum wage of $2.13 per hour, while the maximum among whites was $4.95; that even black workers who did the same work as whites received lower wages; that whites with low seniority were upgraded to more skilled and better-paying jobs, while high-seniority black workers were bypassed; and that there were no black union officials in Local 2401. Blacks paid the same dues as whites, they said, but had "no voice" in the union.[21]

Soon the national office of the association—above all, Labor Secretary Herbert Hill—became deeply involved in the case. A veteran of the labor and civil rights movements, Hill was one of the few whites on the staff of the national NAACP or any other civil rights organization. Before his appointment at the NAACP in the late 1940s, he had worked in a steel plant and for the United Steelworkers. Ultimately, he would become famous for his criticism of the unions' failure to live up to their declared commitment to racial equality; indeed, one unionist would characterize him as "completely anathema to almost everybody in the trade union movement." But in the late 1940s and early 1950s, he played a central role in strengthening the alliance between organized labor and the emerging civil rights movement. Even then, however, he was becoming acutely aware of the growing discontent among black steelworkers. As their despair gave way to anger, and anger fueled activism, there was no doubt in Hill's mind about which side he was on. He became a tribune of black workers in their fight to achieve equality on the job.[22]

His probe into the Atlantic Steel situation revealed Hill's changing perspective. After a lengthy investigation, he painted a clear portrait of racial segregation and discrimination at the Atlanta facility, which by the late 1950s employed twenty-five hundred workers, about nine hundred of whom were African Americans. In May 1958, he reported that there were "separate lines of progression for white and Negro employees." Blacks were "hired exclusively into a classification designated as 'common laborer'" and did not enjoy seniority or promotional rights in the higher-paying and more skilled classifications. Whites, meanwhile, were hired into production and craft positions that were "completely closed" to blacks.[23]

A subsequent investigation by the U.S. Commission on Civil Rights not only bore out Hill's observations but added additional detail to what would become a searing indictment. The commission found that, in a "sample department" with 30 job classifications, only whites held occupational seniority in 19 of the classifications, and only blacks held seniority in the rest. Within the department, the pay grades ranged from 1 to 26. None of the black workers had attained a pay grade above 8, and more than half of the 64 blacks remained at pay grade 4 or lower. The commission concluded that "a similar picture prevails throughout the plant."[24]

In the summer of 1957, Hill conferred with USWA international representative Boyd Wilson, the union's liaison with the civil rights community, about the Atlantic Steel case. He then met with black steelworkers in Atlanta and—again—sought to inform Wilson of the urgency of the situation. He warned that, because of the Local 2401 leadership's "continuing indifference" to the pattern of racial discrimination in the mill, "a number of Negro workers are desirous of quitting the Steelworkers Union under the Georgia 'Right to Work' law." Together with the president of the Atlanta NAACP branch, Hill spent several hours persuading them not to abandon the USWA, but he also promised that, in return, representatives of the international union would meet with them and seek to resolve their grievances.[25]

Hill acknowledged that the company was "at least equally responsible" for the maintenance of Jim Crow seniority lines. In fact, at management's initiative, many forms of segregation were operative in the plant. The company maintained separate time clocks for black and white employees, with a partition between them. There also were separate water fountains, restrooms, bathhouses, and locker rooms; and a segregated cafeteria, which the company eventually abolished and replaced with vending machines.[26]

But the local union also bore some responsibility for this situation. Industrial relations specialists Gilman and Sweeney had observed in 1953 that collective bargaining between the company and the union was informal, continuous, and remarkably broad in scope. One union official informed them that "the company has never yet refused to bargain with us over any issue we've brought up." In a 1959 letter to the USWA staff man who serviced Local 2401, a company vice-president expressed willingness to bargain over issues of race and insisted only that "measures to correct any unfairness to any of the negro Employees be initiated by your Union." Of course, this may have been a subterfuge or a simple passing of the buck. Given the general climate of massive resistance in the late 1950s and the potential for disruption on the shop floor and in the union hall, it is likely that both management and the union were reluctant to confront these issues. As black workers organized to demand change and racial polarization in the plant intensified, Ku Klux Klan literature and recruiting posters appeared on company bulletin boards and remained up, in at least one instance, for as long as a month. Blacks believed that this could not have happened without the acquiescence of the local union leadership and that, in general, Local 2401 and the company were in collusion to maintain a pattern of racial discrimination in the plant.[27]

In this situation, it became the responsibility of the international union to act. Indeed, Hill was convinced that only forthright intervention by Boyd Wilson and other international representatives would prevent the aggrieved black steelworkers from quitting the USWA. Wilson's response, however, was disappointing. He reported that management and the union had agreed to conduct a Company Wage Study (CWS), a comprehensive investigation of all of the jobs in the mill in order to evaluate their comparable worth, which he applauded as a "splendid approach" to the problem. But while such a study almost certainly would lead to an adjustment in wage rates, it would not resolve the issues of segregated lines of progression and seniority that were at the heart of the conflict at Atlantic Steel. Moreover, given the complexity of the steel industry job structure, the CWS process was bound to be a lengthy one; in this case, it took several years. In the meantime, Wilson could only recommend that black protesters make use of the union's grievance procedure and become more active in the affairs of the local. "Your president . . . wants to be re-elected," he wrote to a leader among the black workers. "Your group may well have the balance of power to decide this question."[28]

Wilson was the highest-ranking black official in the United Steelworkers. A native of Missouri and a high school graduate with two years of college, he had been working at Scullin Steel in St. Louis when the Steel Workers Organizing Committee (SWOC) targeted the plant in 1940. In order to solidify its position among the black workers who constituted the majority of the labor force at Scullin Steel, SWOC hired Wilson as a staff representative. In 1942, Philip Murray appointed him to the international staff and assigned him the nebulous responsibility of "developing the proper kind of human relations that ought to exist between colored and white workers." For the first two years of his tenure, Murray admitted, Wilson was "required to carry his office around in his pocket." He had no secretary, and his mailing address was "usually a train or a hotel room somewhere." Murray finally gave him a secretary and an office in Pittsburgh, and Wilson became the most visible African American in the Steelworkers' hierarchy. Even so, his high visibility only accentuated the fact that his role was largely symbolic. Power in the USWA was concentrated among its top leaders and district directors. Beyond conducting investigations and issuing educational literature, even the union's Civil Rights Committee had little or no authority; characteristically, the committee was run entirely by whites. Wilson was a token member whose alleged role was to serve as the USWA's ambassador to the black community and to represent the interests of the union's African-American membership. But in reality he was caught between his obligations to the international union on the one hand and to an increasingly restive rank-and-file constituency on the other. While the latter demanded that he be an agent of change, the former insisted that he be an instrument of containment.[29]

Whatever his sentiments may have been, Wilson knew where his bread was buttered and acted accordingly. At Atlantic Steel, his goal was to fend off the NAACP and keep black protest within the channels of the union. As relations between the USWA and the NAACP became more acrimonious, Wilson informed black workers that he resented "Hill's interference" and warned that "too many cooks spoil the brew." Hill, in turn, became increasingly incensed at Wilson's failure to "take a prompt and honest stand"; he concluded, after more than a year of NAACP involvement in the case, that "absolutely no progress has been made."[30]

Meanwhile, black workers continued to press their grievances. Veteran unionists Nathaniel Brown and J. C. Wynn attended the United Steelworkers convention in 1958 and informed Hill of their intention to "give Mr. Wilson a reasonable amount of time to work this out within the framework of the union." But by now Wilson was impaled on the horns of his dilemma and therefore was virtually useless. As a loyal servant of the Steelworkers' bureaucracy, he had tried to keep the NAACP at bay, only to find that more powerful forces within the union were marginalizing him. On several occasions, District 35 Director Lorne Nelles refused to allow Wilson to come to Atlanta to meet with black workers who urgently had requested his presence. Union protocol required that an international staffer receive the district director's permission to enter his domain. And to Nelles, Wilson had become an "outside person" whose meddling only created political problems.[31]

Stymied by the white majority in Local 2401 and frustrated at the district leadership's acquiescence in the status quo, black workers decided to go directly to the international union. In the summer of 1960, they raised the money to send Nathaniel Brown to Pittsburgh to plead their case. But, according to the *Pittsburgh Courier,* he was "refused admission to a meeting . . . where the race problem was being discussed." Afterwards, a clearly disillusioned Brown told the *Courier* that racial discrimination at Atlantic Steel was "the fault of the union." "The company has been willing to eliminate the discriminatory practice," he said, but union officials continued to insist that "employment be 'within the framework of tradition and custom.'" Brown charged that David McDonald was "aware of the situation and has done nothing about it" and that Boyd Wilson was "sitting on his fingers" and offering little if any cooperation to his aggrieved constituents. Thus, black workers developed a new protest strategy and planned "to take the[ir] case to the courts" as soon as they had exhausted all avenues within the USWA. The clear implication was that the union, rather than Atlantic Steel, had become the target of their wrath.[32]

Actually, since April 1960, members of the USWA Civil Rights Committee had been meeting with the bargaining committee of Local 2401 in an attempt to develop new contract language that would alleviate the problem of racially separate lines of progression. Specifically, the international union took the position that "no line of progression should be composed exclusively of either white or colored workers." Negotiations with the company on this matter and others dragged on for well over a year, and a new agreement incorporating this principle was ratified by the local union membership in the summer of 1961. The contract appeared to create unprecedented opportunities for black workers, and by June 1962, seventeen African Americans, thirteen in one department and four in another, were employed in jobs that formerly had been closed to them. This was a modest beginning, to be sure, but a member of the Civil Rights Committee informed Herbert Hill that "the present local union officers are determined to make the new pattern work and we are certainly going to give them the fullest opportunity to do so."[33]

But for many black workers, incremental gains of this kind represented no improvement at all. The problem, or a large part of it, had to do with the way the principle of seniority was applied in the steel industry. Seniority long had been occupational or departmental, rather than plantwide. The more seniority a worker earned in one department or line of progression, the less likely he (or, occasionally, she) would be to transfer, even to a higher-paying job in another department or line, because such a move meant giving up one's accumulated seniority and starting over again. In order to create the necessary freedom of movement, the principle of retroactivity, along with a policy of plantwide seniority, would have to prevail. But low-seniority workers who held desirable jobs were overwhelmingly opposed to any changes in the seniority system that would make them vulnerable to downgrading and layoffs. In practice, not only at Atlantic Steel but throughout the industry, this meant that white workers were opposed to contractual innovations that would facilitate black mobility. In most places, a racialized democracy pitted the white majority against the black minority, and the union leadership was not about to jeopardize its own security by siding with the minority. Thus, when the new contract created nonracial lines of progression at Atlantic Steel, it was no surprise that the international union took the position that "retroactivity could not be enforced" in upgrading employees into jobs from which they had been excluded.[34]

What the union saw as progress, black workers saw as sham and betrayal. Led by Brown and Wynn, many of them bitterly opposed the ratification of the 1961 contract and its renewal in 1962. Few black workers, especially the high-seniority men who had been among the founders and most faithful members of the union, were willing to sacrifice decades of seniority for a higher-paying job in which they would be vulnerable to layoffs. The fact that the steel industry was still mired in a sustained period of stagnation when the 1961 contract was signed undoubtedly contributed to their concern, as did the fact that, as racial polarization at the plant intensified, Atlantic Steel simply stopped hiring black workers.[35]

Apparently some African Americans—especially younger and lower-seniority workers—joined the union in seeing the new regime as a step forward. But others now were so disillusioned that they were ready to quit the United Steelworkers. From 1959 to 1961, Nathaniel Brown had served on the bargaining committee, but he was replaced by a white worker when he vigorously protested the terms of the contract that the union was negotiating. Acidly, District Director Nelles noted that Brown had failed to attend the union meeting that voted to ratify the 1961 agreement. To Nelles, this meant that he was a mere malcontent. But speaking to Herbert Hill, Brown poignantly and compellingly articulated not only his own sense of grievance but that of his fellow workers as well. "When the union first came," he said,

> most of the whites were afraid, but we Negroes . . . wore the CIO button. We were the first to come out for the union. We helped get it started here. . . . But now they—the whites—get all the benefits and we are left behind again. Turned out CIO meant one thing for the whites and another thing for us. The union don't handle our grievances, we are stuck with Jim Crow seniority, back-breaking jobs and we get less pay than they do. . . . White boys just hired off the street get treated better than we do after twenty years. That's what we get for bringing in the union here.[36]

After the ratification of the 1962 contract, black workers met with representatives of the NAACP and decided to petition the National Labor Relations Board for a decertification election. This was an extraordinary step. It meant that some of the men who had been most loyal and active in building the Steelworkers' union now were prepared to dismantle it. In taking this step, Brown and his fellow workers had the full support of the NAACP, which had authorized such an initiative at its annual convention in 1960. On October 30, 1962, accompanied by Georgia Field Secretary Vernon Jordan, Hill filed a decertification petition on behalf of thirteen members of Local 2401.[37]

The Steelworkers reacted with surprise and dismay. General Counsel David Feller complained to the NAACP that the USWA had not been forewarned of this move, despite a long-standing agreement between the two organizations to consult before acting on discriminatory practices of "mutual interest." After reviewing the history of the case from the union's perspective, Feller offered up a by-now-familiar refrain: "We have, perhaps, not been able to do enough but we have continued to make progress." But NAACP Executive Secretary Roy Wilkins disagreed. He countered with an eloquent summary of the nearly six years of frustration that had accumulated in the Atlantic Steel case. "The conditions existed long before they were brought formally to our attention," he said. "Every possible method (short of NLRB proceedings) has been employed to try to redress the grievances. . . . Piles of correspondence with the USWA have accumulated. Numerous conferences have been held, high-level, low-level and in-between." And yet, in all that time, "nothing has produced a meaningful change."[38]

• • •

To understand the inner sense of urgency, frustration, and disillusionment that led to the filing of the decertification petition at Atlantic Steel, and the NAACP's unflinching support for this action, it is important to probe the larger national environment in which the struggle for black equality was evolving. Among liberals, there was a widespread assumption in the 1950s and early 1960s that the "American Dilemma" soon would be resolved in favor of racial equality—because, said Harvard psychologist Gordon Allport, most Americans "deep inside their consciences do approve [of] civil rights and anti-discrimination legislation." Liberals also tended to believe that the rising tide of postwar prosperity would lift even the "boats" of the black sharecroppers and day laborers who were being displaced by the mechanization of cotton agriculture and pushed toward cities south and north. It became an article of faith that northward migration automatically would improve the economic circumstances of African Americans, who then would be in a position to play their assigned role as the "last of the immigrants." Anthony Lewis of the *New York Times* voiced several of these assumptions when he wrote in 1962 that "in almost every aspect of American life it is possible to point to dramatic improvements in the status of the Negro." In the economic realm, in particular, he noted "striking progress."[39]

But many African Americans did not share this optimism, in large measure because persistent racial discrimination and far-reaching but largely unforeseen economic developments limited their opportunities and clouded the horizon. Despite an undeniable surge in the Gross National Product, important sectors of the industrial economy remained sluggish, and—as always—the fruits of economic dynamism were experienced unevenly. In Detroit, the number of manufacturing jobs fell from 338,000 in 1947 to 200,000 in 1963. The city's East Side lost ten plants and more than 70,000 jobs between 1953 and 1960, at a time when black migration to Detroit was increasing rapidly. In Ohio, a major steel-producing state, the number of jobs in basic steel declined from 205,517 in 1940 to 154,941 in 1960, a loss of more than 50,000 in twenty years, even though the net capacity of the state's producers increased by 43.4 percent in the 1950s alone. Overall, employment in auto, steel, tobacco, and mining, all industries that had provided significant employment for African Americans, declined 12 percent in the 1950s. And the black unemployment rate, which had been about 60 percent greater than that of whites in the late 1940s, began to grow, in absolute and relative terms. By 1962, a labor economist reported, "nonwhite men in both the 25–34 and 35–44 age brackets . . . recorded unemployment rates about three times as high as for white men." Clearly, then, the ongoing "Great Migration" was nowhere near the unalloyed blessing that liberals had predicted. In the words of economist Gavin Wright, black migrants "were not moving into areas where jobs were waiting for them, where the industrial employment structure and the educational system were geared to integrating them as quickly as possible into the economy. Instead, they were moving into places where . . . the economy had relatively little use for them."[40]

African Americans confronted not only a precarious economic environment but also a growing backlash that incorporated broad segments of the southern white population and often was characterized by the aggressive participation of white workers and their local unions. This development could not help affecting the attitudes of black workers toward the labor movement. A survey conducted in 1958 noted that, in a Birmingham Steelworkers' local with about fifteen hundred white and a thousand black members, the blacks had "practically stopped" attending meetings, because the whites, led by the local union officers, had become so open and virulent in their opposition to "integration and social justice." Three years later, Herbert Hill reported that "the Ku Klux Klan and White Citizens Council forces . . . have moved into many local unions and made them, in effect, virtual extensions of segregationist organizations," with the result that "Negro workers throughout the South are experiencing an acute sense of alienation . . . from organized labor."[41]

Meanwhile, the Democratic party that had claimed the allegiance of many blacks during the Roosevelt and Truman eras proved reluctant to do battle with the Dixiecrats in its ranks. And in the trade union movement, the national leadership spoke the language of racial equality but was unwilling to launch a frontal assault upon the deeply rooted patterns of inequality in trades and industries where labor's strength was greatest. What had begun as a historical moment of great promise for blacks—who greeted the *Brown* decision as a "second Emancipation

Proclamation"—became tinged with bitterness, as more and more African Americans experienced the sharp disparity between the rhetoric of change and the reality of tokenism and backlash.[42]

It was in these circumstances that A. Philip Randolph, the president of the Brotherhood of Sleeping Car Porters and the nation's preeminent black trade unionist, spoke out with uncompromising clarity about the failure of the AFL-CIO to set its house in order. In return, he received the taunt from George Meany, "Who the hell appointed you as the guardian of all the Negroes in America?" For thousands of black trade unionists in the trenches of the struggle against racism, the brickbat Meany launched at Randolph in 1959 only served to enhance the reputation of a man they already revered. He understood their disappointment and frustration; he spoke for them. They flocked to his banner when he formed the Negro American Labor Council (NALC) in 1960. "We are in rebellion," Randolph bravely declared. "The NALC reflects within organized labor the same rebellion that finds its expression in the student lunch counter demonstrations in the South."[43]

In close collaboration with Randolph, the NAACP also was moving toward a more direct confrontation with its trade union allies over what it regarded as the glacially slow pace of change in organized labor. Wilkins acknowledged that "labor has done a magnificent job in the general civil rights field." But the AFL-CIO's failure to take similar action "within its own house" was galling, as was the continual recitation of the progress that unions allegedly were making in addressing issues of race. In a widely publicized report on "Racism Within Organized Labor," Hill concluded that "five years after the AFL-CIO merger, the national labor organization has failed to eliminate the broad pattern of racial discrimination and segregation in many important affiliated unions." He characterized efforts in this direction as "piecemeal and inadequate," complaining that the federation was more interested in maintaining a "'liberal' public relations image" than in confronting racism in its ranks. In an unguarded moment, Hill called the AFL-CIO Civil Rights Department an "empty ritual" and a "complete fraud."[44]

The growing perception that the NAACP was "at war" with organized labor intensified when the association brought formal charges against two large and powerful unions—the USWA and the International Ladies' Garment Workers' Union (ILGWU)—that had been closely associated with the cause of civil rights. Historically a predominantly Jewish organization that took pride in its Socialist heritage, the ILGWU had grown increasingly diverse since World War II. Blacks and Hispanics now constituted a significant minority of its membership nationally, and a majority in New York City, the union's heartland. But Jews continued to dominate the leadership of the ILGWU and the ranks of the skilled cutters' locals. As early as 1953, one scholarly observer had detected a "crisis of leadership" in the union that reflected the "cleavage between two membership generations, differing very considerably in composition, background, and outlook." By 1957, there were mass picket lines of black and Hispanic workers at the international union headquarters, protesting "sweetheart contracts." That same year, ILGWU members who worked in garment shops in the Bronx filed a decertification petition with the NLRB, in this instance apparently without the explicit support of the NAACP.[45]

But the association was bound to offer the hand of solidarity to workers of color in their fight against racial discrimination. Thus, in 1961, with the active support of the NAACP, African-American garment worker Ernest Holmes filed a complaint with the New York State Commission for Human Rights, charging that the union had blocked his attempt to join Cutters Local 10 and learn the cutters' trade. In 1962, at the behest of Harlem's U.S. Rep. Adam Clayton Powell, a congressional subcommittee held public hearings to investigate "nefarious practices" in the garment industry and heard accusations, from Herbert Hill among others, that the ILGWU was partly responsible for a pattern of "de facto racial segregation" in the industry.[46]

Trade union leaders and representatives of the Jewish community rushed to the ILGWU's defense. ILGWU Vice-President Charles Zimmerman called Hill's charges "demonstrably untrue, . . . malicious and tinged with anti-Semitism." "The fact that Mr. Hill is white and Jewish," said Zimmerman, "does not mitigate this in the least." The *Jewish Daily Forward* accused the NAACP labor secretary of a "racist assault" on the ILGWU and of spreading "anti-Semitic poison." Emanuel Muravchik of the Jewish Labor Committee also raised the specter of anti-Semitism and questioned whether "it is any longer possible to work with the NAACP." Finally, the president of the AFL-CIO weighed in. In a speech to the Negro American Labor Council, George Meany denounced Hill's "smears" and "falsehoods," defended the ILGWU as "a union whose record shines like a beacon in the history of human progress," and dismissed the NAACP's case against the United Steelworkers as "fantastic." According to the *New York Times*, his words were "blunt, bitter and scornful."[47]

But Roy Wilkins refused to blink. The NAACP's forty-eight-member national board already had come to Hill's defense, concurring publicly with his charges against the ILGWU. Now Wilkins himself defended Hill against the "baseless allegation" of anti-Semitism and the accusation that he was an "irresponsible individual" whose conduct threatened to "destroy" the alliance between the labor and the civil rights movements. Unlike Emanuel Muravchik and other liberal allies of labor, Wilkins said, Hill was "not for trade unions first and Negro workers second." His sole job was "to serve the interests of the Negro worker through the NAACP." If, in carrying out this task, he jeopardized the "unity" of civil rights groups, as Muravchik charged, this was no "calamity" but rather a "blessed clearing of the air." As for Meany's barbs, Wilkins simply pointed to the "disgraceful" pace of "desegregation in the labor movement" and reminded the AFL-CIO president that "a Negro worker needs the patience of Job, the hide of an elephant, plus a crowbar to get into Mr. Meany's own union—the plumbers."[48]

• • •

Given the precarious economic status of African Americans, their growing determination to achieve "Freedom Now," and the increasing strain in the labor–civil rights alliance, it is hardly surprising that black workers at Atlantic Steel repudiated the union they had helped to build and turned instead to a civil rights organization and the federal government as allies in their fight against racial discrimination. In this case, however, the government initially sided not with the aggrieved black workers but with the USWA. The National Labor Relations Board took the position that the issue of pay inequity had been resolved (apparently as a result of the Company Wage Study) and that, because of recent changes in the collective bargaining agreement, blacks had won and in some cases exercised transfer rights into skilled jobs previously held only by whites. This was a very narrow perspective that ignored some of the petitioners' main complaints, especially the issue of retroactivity in transferring from one job to another. After the passage of the 1964 Civil Rights Act, the newly created Equal Employment Opportunity Commission (EEOC) took a radically different stance on this matter, ruling in 1967 that the "effect of [the company's] transfer policy is to . . . segregate the various jobs according to race." But the union's role in maintaining this pattern had become less clear than the company's, and in

1963 the NLRB credited the United Steelworkers with seeking "even greater concessions regarding equal job opportunities" than management had been willing to grant.[49]

The NAACP vigorously dissented from the NLRB's reasoning. But the Association already was involved in another case that raised the same issues even more sharply. The Hughes Tool Company long had maintained two racially separate and manifestly unequal locals of the Independent Metal Workers Union in Houston, Texas. The company and the white local collaborated in the exclusion of black workers from skilled work, and management refused to bargain with the black local over this issue. This constituted a clear and unambiguous example of unfair representation, and rather than appeal the Atlantic Steel case, the NAACP decided to concentrate its resources on Hughes Tool. The NLRB's July 1964 order decertifying the segregated locals at Hughes Tool represented what Hill would later call a "major turning point" in the evolution of NLRB policy and a new willingness to protect the rights of black workers.[50]

At Atlantic Steel, however, the issue of racial discrimination remained unresolved. The company did make important concessions on the vital issue of transfer rights but then proceeded in at least some instances to take back with one hand what it had given with the other. In the hoop mill, for example, management agreed to the use of departmental seniority as the basis of job upgrading in a previously all-white line of progression and then unilaterally imposed a second criterion requiring that employees take tests to determine whether they were qualified for the jobs in question. A number of black workers failed the tests, which apparently had little practical relationship to the performance of these jobs, and were denied promotions on that basis. The overall effect of company policy was to maintain a clear pattern of *de facto* segregation in the distribution of jobs in the plant. As of July 1967, only 353 African Americans were employed at Atlantic Steel, and 98.3 percent of them worked in semiskilled and service occupations. Among the 383 skilled craftsmen in the plant, only 5 were black; and there were no blacks among the 40 female employees. Long after the passage of the Civil Rights Act of 1964, the company continued to segregate locker rooms, bathhouses, and other facilities. Although in January 1965 Atlantic Steel announced that it would apply a policy of equal opportunity to "all phases of personnel activity," it did not desegregate the facilities on its premises until March 1968.[51]

The local union acquiesced in some of these practices, but it vigorously opposed the use of tests, except in the skilled trades, as a means of judging workers' qualifications for jobs in the plant. Overall, the longstanding dilemma of the trade-union movement remained operative at Atlantic Steel, as it did throughout most of the United Steelworkers' jurisdiction. In a meeting with black workers, District Director Nelles admitted that "the white union workers want their jobs to remain white." Faced with a white majority—in this case a growing white majority—that remained uncommitted to the goal of racial equality, Local 2401 and the USWA refused to get too far out in front of their principal constituency.[52]

The union did encourage black workers to make use of the grievance machinery, especially in cases where they believed that racial discrimination was involved, but this was hardly pure altruism on the Steelworkers' part. For, after the passage of the Civil Rights Act of 1964 and the creation of the Equal Employment Opportunity Commission in 1965, black workers repeatedly turned to the EEOC as a means of resolving their grievances and in the process often filed complaints against both the company and the union. What was particularly frustrating to USWA representatives was that, even when they believed they were making a good-faith effort to serve their members, black workers tended to bypass the union and go right to the EEOC. This was true at times even of black union representatives on the shop floor, who would file grievances on behalf of their fellow workers and themselves and then, before the grievances had been resolved, turn to the EEOC and implicate the union as well as the company in their complaints. "Plaintiff has . . . refused to use the grievance procedure" became an all too common lament on the union's part in cases involving charges of racial discrimination.[53]

But, from the black workers' standpoint, turning to the EEOC made good sense. Before an issue was resolved, the grievance process could drag on for years; and, perhaps more importantly, many blacks remained unconvinced that the union was really on their side. For high-seniority workers like Nathaniel Brown and J. C. Wynn, who once had been among the most active and loyal unionists, a bond had been severed, and their sense of betrayal was not overcome by the union's practice in the remainder of the 1960s. Brown served for a time as a grievanceman in his department but also was one of the first to turn to the EEOC. Although the commission was underfunded, understaffed, and devoid of enforcement power, it was sympathetic to the civil rights community's agenda and responsive to the complaints of black workers. In 1967, the EEOC identified a clear pattern of "discriminat[ion] on the basis of race" in the allocation of jobs at Atlantic Steel and, in an even more sharply worded decision in 1969, declared that the company's method of applying seniority to job classifications plainly did not constitute "a 'bona fide seniority system.'" This case and others like it echoed across the length and breadth of industrial America, reinforcing an old polarity and creating a new set of alliances that pitted black workers, the NAACP, and federal administrative agencies against white workers, unions, and corporate management.[54]

What is most unusual at Atlantic Steel is that black unionists sought to decertify their local union as the collective bargaining agent for the company's employees. But otherwise the case epitomizes a pattern that occurred in steel, in the North as well as the South, during the 1950s and 1960s. Black workers often were deeply committed unionists; they took the union at face value when it spoke of its commitment to racial equality. But eventually they found that the gap between rhetoric and reality added up to a cruel hoax. As the civil rights movement gained momentum in the larger society, black workers began to see the union, as well as the employer, as an obstacle to the achievement of their objectives. Although most black steelworkers chose to remain members of the USWA, they began to organize autonomously on behalf of their own demands, often in alliance with civil rights organizations such as the NAACP, and to sue both the company and the union for persistent violations of the law. Indeed, one journalist contended in 1968 that "more complaints of restrictive seniority and promotion practices have been filed against the United Steelworkers and the steel industry than any other group."[55]

In retrospect, it is clear that the Steelworkers' union reflected, and to some degree reinforced, the racial segmentation and cleavages that had characterized American society for centuries. Recognizing the determination of the union's white majority to maintain the "wages of whiteness" in the face of black demands for equality, USWA leaders at virtually every level bowed to the dictates of a racialized democracy and chose institutional equilibrium over the cause of racial justice. The result was that the issue of racial discrimination in employment and seniority finally was addressed comprehensively not by the United Steelworkers but by an alliance of the federal government, the NAACP, and black rank and filers from Birmingham to Buffalo, in a sustained campaign that targeted the companies and the union. The long road from the founding of the Steel Workers Organizing Committee in 1936 to the steel industry Consent Decree of 1974 suggests that Nathaniel Brown's experience in Atlanta was no anomaly. On the contrary, he spoke not only for himself but for many black workers of his generation when he declared that the "CIO meant one thing for the whites and another thing for us."[56]

Notes

Anyone who takes even a cursory glance at the notes that follow will recognize my great indebtedness to Herbert Hill, who shared with me his extraordinary collection of documents on the steel industry and on the NAACP's role in advancing the cause of black workers, and who allowed me to interview him on his career as labor secretary of the NAACP. Thanks also to Bob Dinwiddie, Cliff Kuhn, Mary Lydon, and John Pellettieri.

1. Philip Murray, quoted in St. Clair Drake and Horace Cayton, *Black Metropolis: A Study of Negro Life in a Northern City* (1945; reprint, Chicago: Univ. of Chicago Press, 1993), 341.
2. Robert Korstad and Nelson Lichtenstein, "Opportunities Found and Lost: Labor, Radicals, and the Early Civil Rights Movement," *Journal of American History* 75 (Dec. 1988): 786–811; Rick Halpern, "Interracial Unionism in the Southwest: Fort Worth's Packinghouse Workers, 1937–1954," in *Organized Labor in the Twentieth-Century South,* ed. Robert H. Zieger (Knoxville: Univ. of Tennessee Press, 1991), 158–82; Michael K. Honey, *Southern Labor and Black Civil Rights: Organizing Memphis Workers* (Urbana: Univ. of Illinois Press, 1993).
3. Bruce Nelson, "Organized Labor and the Struggle for Black Equality in Mobile during World War II," *Journal of American History* 80 (Dec. 1993): 955.
4. John Bodnar, Roger Simon, and Michael P. Weber, *Lives of Their Own: Blacks, Italians, and Poles in Pittsburgh, 1900–1960* (Urbana: Univ. of Illinois Press, 1982), 62; Sam Camens, interview by Bruce Nelson, Youngstown, Ohio, Sept. 22, 1991, audiotape in author's possession.
5. James Barrett and David Roediger, "In-between Peoples: Race, Nationality, and the New Immigrant Working Class" (paper presented at the Commonwealth Fund Conference, University College London, Feb. 18, 1995); David R. Roediger, "Whiteness and Ethnicity in the History of 'White Ethnics' in the United States," in *Towards the Abolition of Whiteness* (London: Verso, 1994), 181–98; Joseph Bazdar to Thomas Shane, Mar. 9, 1950, Records of the United Steelworkers of America (USWA), Civil Rights Dept., Box 7, Folder 21, Historical Collections and Labor Archives, Pattee Library, Penn State Univ., University Park, Pa. (hereafter cited as HCLA/PSU).
6. Robert J. Norrell, "Caste in Steel: Jim Crow Careers in Birmingham, Alabama," *Journal of American History* 73 (Dec. 1986): 669–94; Herbert Hill to Roy Wilkins ("Memorandum Re: United States Steel Corporation and United Steelworkers of America, AFL-CIO[,] Birmingham, Alabama"), Sept. 13, 1965,

Records of the National Association for the Advancement of Colored People, Group III, Box A195, Manuscript Division, Library of Congress, Washington, D.C. (hereafter cited as NAACP Papers).

7. Judith Stein, "Southern Workers in National Unions: Birmingham Steelworkers, 1936–1951," in Zieger, *Organized Labor in the Twentieth-Century South,* 183–222; Charles Alford to Thomas Shane, Mar. 12, 1950, USWA, Civil Rights Dept., Box 3, Folder 21; Jack Greenberg et al., "In the Supreme Court of the United States, Oct. Term, 1981, Pullman-Standard, a Division of Pullman Incorporated, Petitioner, No. 80-1190, United Steelworkers of America, AFL-CIO and Local 1466, United Steelworkers of America, AFL-CIO, Petitioners, No. 80-1193, v. Louis Swint and Willie Johnson et al, . . . Brief for Respondents," n.d. [1981], Personal Papers of Herbert Hill, Madison, Wisc.
8. David J. McDonald, I. W. Abel, and James G. Thimmes, "To All USA District Directors, Staff Representatives and Local Union Recording Secretaries" ("Re: Union Policy Against Racial Discrimination in Plants"), Aug. 31, 1954; W. H. Crawford to David J. McDonald, Dec. 4, 1953, USWA, Civil Rights Dept., Box 7, Folder 52.
9. Arthur J. Goldberg to All CIO Regional Directors and CIO Industrial Union Councils ("Subject: Segregated Facilities in CIO Offices and Halls"), Apr. 24, 1950, USWA, Civil Rights Dept., Box 5, Folder 27; R. E. Farr to Philip Murray, May 19, 1950, USWA, Civil Rights Dept., Box 3, Folder 13.
10. E. T. Earp et al. to Philip Murray, June 12, 1950, USWA, Civil Rights Dept., Box 3, Folder 13; Norrell, "Caste in Steel," 685; Herbert Hill to Walter White ("Confidential Memorandum Re: Birmingham, Bessemer Area CIO-NAACP Relations"), May 8–17, 1953, USWA, Civil Rights Dept., Box 6, Folder 27.
11. United Steelworkers of America, *Proceedings of the Fifth Constitutional Convention,* Atlantic City, N. J., May 9–12, 1950, 89–91; Francis C. Shane to David J. McDonald ("Re: Report of United Steelworkers of America Committee on Civil Rights, Jan. 1, 1952, through Dec. 31, 1952"), Jan. 1, 1953, USWA, Civil Rights Dept., Box 5, Folder 25; United Steelworkers of America, *Report of Officers to the 8th Constitutional Convention,* Los Angeles, Sept. 17–21, 1956, 82–102; Francis C. Shane to Roy Wilkins, Apr. 24, 1956, NAACP Papers, Group 3, Box A195; Dennis C. Dickerson, *Out of the Crucible: Black Steelworkers in Western Pennsylvania, 1875–1980* (Albany, N.Y.: State Univ. of New York Press, 1986), 190; Oliver Montgomery, interview by Bruce Nelson, Pittsburgh, Oct. 22, 1990, audiotape in author's possession.
12. William H. Harris, *The Harder We Run: Black Workers Since the Civil War* (New York: Oxford Univ. Press, 1982), 140–42; Robert H. Zieger, "George Meany: Labor's Organization Man," in *Labor Leaders in America,* ed. Melvyn Dubofsky and Warren Van Tine (Urbana: Univ. of Illinois Press, 1987), 334, 342–44; David J. McDonald, *Union Man* (New York: Dutton, 1969), 15; "Statement by Francis C. Shane, Retired Former Executive Secretary, Committee on Civil Rights, United Steelworkers of America," May 23, 1967, in author's possession (courtesy of John Hoerr).
13. Crawford to McDonald, Dec. 4, 1953.
14. Glenn W. Gilman and James W. Sweeney, *Atlantic Steel Company and United*

Steelworkers of America: A Case Study, Causes of Industrial Peace Under Collective Bargaining, Case Study No. 12 (Washington, D.C.: National Planning Association, 1953), 1–18.

15. Ibid., 12, 16–22; Tom M. Girdler with Boyden Sparkes, *Boot Straps: The Autobiography of Tom M. Girdler* (New York: Scribner's, 1943), 148–62; Noel R. Beddow to David J. McDonald, Aug. 27, 1941, USWA, David J. McDonald Papers, Box 17, Folder 10, HCLA/PSU; *Atlanta Constitution,* Oct. 24, 1941, 7; W. H. Crawford to Noel R. Beddow, Mar. 18, 1942, USWA, District 36 Papers, Box 4, Folder on W. H. Crawford, 1941–42, HCLA/PSU. On Crawford, see USWA, "International Executive Board Proceedings," Washington, D.C., Mar. 2–4, 1955, 353–55, in USWA, International Executive Board (USWA-IEB) Proceedings, Box 45, HCLA/PSU.
16. Hill to White ("Confidential Memorandum Re: Birmingham, Bessemer Area CIO-NAACP Relations"), May 8–17, 1953.
17. Alton Hornsby, Jr., "A City That Was Too Busy to Hate: Atlanta Businessmen and Desegregation," in *Southern Businessmen and Desegregation,* ed. Elizabeth Jacoway and David Colburn (Baton Rouge: Louisiana State Univ. Press, 1982), 120–36; Alan Draper, *Conflict of Interest: Organized Labor and the Civil Rights Movement in the South, 1954–1968* (Ithaca, N.Y.: ILR Press, 1994), 28; Morton T. Elder, "Labor and Race Relations in the South" (a report to the Southern Regional Council), Oct. 1956, in Fund for the Republic Papers, Box 108, 10–12, Seeley G. Mudd Manuscript Library, Princeton Univ., Princeton, N.J.
18. Joseph A. Rabun to David J. McDonald, n.d. [Nov. 1955], United Steelworkers of America, District 35 Records, 1940–73, Box 718, Folder 31, Southern Labor Archives, Georgia State Univ., Atlanta (hereafter cited as SLA/GSU); *Atlanta Constitution,* Oct. 4, 1955, p. 4. On the Till case, see Stephen J. Whitfield, *A Death in the Delta: The Story of Emmett Till* (New York: Free Press, 1988).
19. Rabun to McDonald, n.d. There is a brief portrait of Rabun in John Egerton, *Speak Now Against the Day: The Generation Before the Civil Rights Movement in the South* (New York: Knopf, 1994), 423–24.
20. Rabun to McDonald, n.d.; Lorne H. Helles to David J. McDonald, Dec. 14, 1955, USWA, District 35 Papers, 1940–73, Box 718, Folder 31. Crawford died in Dec. 1954 and was succeeded by Lorne Nelles as director of District 35.
21. Report of Labor and Industry Committee [Atlanta Branch, NAACP], Apr. 7, 1957, Personal Papers of Herbert Hill.
22. Herbert Hill, interview by Bruce Nelson, Madison, Wisc., Aug. 19–21, 1994, audiotape in author's possession; Karen Budd, "An Interview with Jimmy Jones," Philadelphia, May 4, 1971, HCLA/PSU; Hill to White ("Confidential Memorandum Re: Birmingham, Bessemer Area CIO-NAACP Relations"), May 8–17, 1953; [Jonathan Comer] to Herbert Hill, Oct. 4, 1973, Personal Papers of Herbert Hill.
23. "Memorandum to Mr. Wilkins from Herbert Hill: Re: The Atlantic Steel Company, Atlanta, Georgia," May 27, 1958, NAACP Papers, Group 3, Box A184.
24. U.S. Commission on Civil Rights, *Employment: 1961 Commission on Civil Rights Report* (Washington, D.C.: USGPO, 1961), 137.

25. Herbert Hill to Boyd L. Wilson, Aug. 1, 1957, Personal Papers of Herbert Hill.
26. Herbert Hill to J. H. Calhoun, Aug. 6, 1958, and Nathaniel Brown et al. to President's Committee on Equal Employment Opportunity, Sept. 11, 1961, both in Personal Papers of Herbert Hill; U.S. Commission on Civil Rights, *Employment*, 136–37.
27. Gilman and Sweeney, *Atlantic Steel Company*, 62–66, quotation on 64; Wilbur F. Glenn to United Steelworkers of America, June 17, 1959, and David E. Feller to Roy Wilkins, Nov. 9, 1962, both in NAACP Papers, Group 3, Box A195; "Memorandum to Mr. Wilkins from Herbert Hill: Re: The Atlantic Steel Company, Atlanta, Georgia," May 27, 1958; Robert L. Carter and Maria L. Marcus, "Memorandum Supporting Motion," in the case of Atlantic Steel Company and United Steelworkers of America, Local 2401, Before the National Labor Relations Board, Oct. 29, 1962, both in Personal Papers of Herbert Hill; U.S. Commission on Civil Rights, *Employment*, 137.
28. Boyd L. Wilson to Herbert Hill, Aug. 15, 1957; Wilson to Hill, Nov. 15, 1957; Wilson to Hill, Apr. 9, 1958; and Wilson to Julius C. Wynn, Mar. 28, 1958, all in Personal Papers of Herbert Hill; Boyd L. Wilson to Lorne H. Nelles, Aug. 15, 1957, USWA, District 35 Records, 1940–73, Box 718, Folder 21; "Memorandum to Mr. Wilkins from Herbert Hill: Re: The Atlantic Steel Company, Atlanta, Georgia," May 27, 1958; U. S. Commission on Civil Rights, *Employment*, 138.
29. Dennis C. Dickerson, "Wilson, Boyd L.," in *Biographical Dictionary of American Labor*, ed. Gary Fink, 2d ed. (Westport, Conn.: Greenwood, 1984), 586–87; Jack Spiese, "An Interview with Boyd Wilson," Oct. 23, 1967, HCLA/PSU, pp. 1–6; "Proceedings of the International Executive Board, United Steelworkers of America," Cleveland, Ohio, May 5, 1944, 94–104, quoted on 95–96, USWA-IEB Proceedings, Box 41; Dickerson, *Out of the Crucible*, 195–99.
30. Boyd L. Wilson to Julius C. Wynn, Aug. 21, 1958; Herbert Hill to J. H. Calhoun, Aug. 6, 1958, both in Personal Papers of Herbert Hill. For a general statement about the dilemma Wilson faced, see William Kornhauser, "The Negro Union Official: A Study of Sponsorship and Control," *American Journal of Sociology* 57 (Mar. 1952): 443–52.
31. Nathaniel Brown and J. C. Wynn to Herbert Hill, Nov. 3, 1958; J. H. Calhoun to Herbert Hill, May 31, 1958, both in Personal Papers of Herbert Hill; "Memorandum to Mr. Wilkins from Herbert Hill: Re: The Atlantic Steel Company, Atlanta, Georgia," May 27, 1958. As late as 1973, black steelworker Jonathan Comer complained that intervention by the USWA Civil Rights Dept. "must be . . . ok'd by the District Directors, which in most cases just does not happen. When it does happen you are monitored very closely by the District Director, or other staff persons in that district." [Comer] to Hill, Oct. 4, 1973.
32. Trezevant W. Anderson, "G[eorgi]a Steelworkers Say Union Is 'Selling Out,'" *Pittsburgh Courier*, July 23, 1960, copy in USWA, Howard R. Hague Papers, Box 13, Folder 15, HCLA/PSU.

33. Francis C. Shane to Herbert Hill ("Subject: United Steelworkers of America-National Association for the Advancement of Colored People Joint Committee"), June 30, 1960; Francis C. Shane to Herbert Hill, June 1, 1962, both in NAACP Papers, Group 3, Box A195.
34. Shane to Hill, June 30, 1960.
35. Roy Wilkins to David E. Feller, Dec. 13, 1962, NAACP Papers, Group 3, Box A195; Nathaniel Brown et al. to President's Committee on Equal Employment Opportunity, Sept. 11, 1961; Jerome A. Cooper to Bernard Kleiman, Jan. 20, 1967, United Steelworkers of America, District 35 Records, 1945–1987, Box 2900, Folder 3, SLA/GSU. Cooper, an attorney representing Local 2401, pointed out that, from the beginning of the union's efforts to resolve the matter, black workers had wanted opportunities for promotion but "did not wish in any way to jeopardize their accumulated seniority on their old jobs."
36. Wilkins to Feller, Dec. 13, 1962; Lorne H. Nelles to David J. McDonald, Aug. 1, 1961, USWA, McDonald Papers, Box 49, Folder on District No. 35, Lorne H. Nelles, June 1961–May 31, 1963; Nathaniel Brown, interview by Herbert Hill, Atlanta, Oct. 21, 1962, in Personal Papers of Herbert Hill, typescript in Herbert Hill's possession.
37. Wilkins to Feller, Dec. 13, 1962; Stuart Rothman to Robert L. Carter, Apr. 8, 1963, USWA, District 35 Records, 1945–1987, Box 2888, Folder 2; Roy Wilkins to George Meany, Dec. 7, 1962, in Personal Papers of Herbert Hill; *New York Times,* Oct. 31, 1962, 13; Herbert Hill to author, Feb. 6, 1995, in author's possession.
38. Feller to Wilkins, Nov. 9, 1962; Shane to Hill, June 30, 1960; Wilkins to Feller, Dec. 13, 1962.
39. Gordon Allport, quoted in Walter A. Jackson, *Gunnar Myrdal and America's Conscience: Social Engineering and Racial Liberalism, 1938–1987* (Chapel Hill: Univ. of North Carolina Press, 1990), 183. Jackson's chapter on "The Rise and Fall of a Liberal Orthodoxy," 172–211, is indispensable for understanding liberal attitudes toward race in the postwar era. Irving Kristol, "The Negro Today Is Like the Immigrant of Yesterday," *New York Times Magazine,* Sept. 11, 1966, cited in Stephan Thernstrom, *The Other Bostonians: Poverty and Progress in the American Metropolis, 1880–1970* (Cambridge, Mass.: Harvard Univ. Press, 1973), 177–78; Lewis quoted in Alan B. Batchelder, "Decline in the Relative Income of Negro Men," *Quarterly Journal of Economics* 78 (Nov. 1964): 526.
40. Thomas J. Sugrue, "The Structure of Urban Poverty: The Reorganization of Space and Work in Three Periods of American History," in *The "Underclass" Debate: Views from History,* ed. Michael B. Katz (Princeton, N.J.: Princeton Univ. Press, 1993), 102–5; Richard L. Rowan, *The Negro in the Steel Industry,* pt. 4 of Herbert R. Northrup et al., *Negro Employment in Basic Industry: A Study of Racial Policies in Six Industries* (Philadelphia: Wharton School, Univ. of Pennsylvania, 1970), 273, 279; David M. Gordon, Richard Edwards, and Michael Reich, *Segmented Work, Divided Workers: The Historical Transformation of Labor in the United States* (Cambridge, England: Cambridge Univ. Press, 1982), 209; Matthew A. Kessler, "Economic Status of Nonwhite Workers,

1955–62," *Monthly Labor Review* 86 (July 1963): 783; Gavin Wright, *Old South, New South: Revolutions in the Southern Economy since the Civil War* (New York: Basic Books, 1986), 246–47. See also Hugh Davis Graham, *The Civil Right Era: Origins and Development of National Policy, 1960–1972* (New York: Oxford Univ. Press, 1990), 100–102; and Harris, *The Harder We Run,* 127–33.

41. Numan V. Bartley, *The Rise of Massive Resistance: Race and Politics in the South During the 1950s* (Baton Rouge: Louisiana State Univ. Press, 1969), 305–12; Robert J. Norrell, "Labor Trouble: George Wallace and Union Politics in Alabama," in Zieger, *Organized Labor in the Twentieth-Century South,* 250–72; "Local Union Questionnaire, United Steelworkers of America LU 'A,' Birmingham Ala.," n.d. [1958], Emory Via Papers, Box 1277, SLA/GSU; Herbert Hill, "Racism Within Organized Labor: A Report of Five Years of the AFL-CIO, 1955–1960," *Journal of Negro Education* 30 (Spring 1961): 110. See also "NAACP Attacks Bias in Unions," *Business Week,* Jan. 10, 1959, 78, 80.

42. Harvard Sitkoff, *The Struggle for Black Equality, 1954–1980* (New York: Hill and Wang, 1981), 23, 37–39, 83–85.

43. George Meany quoted in Jervis Anderson, *A. Philip Randolph: A Biographical Portrait* (1972; reprint, Berkeley: Univ. of California Press, 1986), 302; Montgomery, interview by Bruce Nelson, Oct. 22, 1990; Jim Davis, interview by Bruce Nelson, Niles, Ohio, Feb. 18, 1989, audiotape in author's possession; "Negro Pressure on Unions," *Business Week,* Apr. 30, 1960, p. 139; Paula F. Pfeffer, *A. Philip Randolph, Pioneer of the Civil Rights Movement* (Baton Rouge: Louisiana State Univ. Press, 1990), 218. Randolph was referring to the wave of student-led sit-ins in restaurants and other public accommodations that began in Greensboro, N.C., in Feb. 1960 and spread like wildfire across much of the South.

44. Roy Wilkins to A. Philip Randolph, Feb. 6, 1959, Personal Papers of Herbert Hill; Hill, "Racism Within Organized Labor," 109–18, quoted on 109; Joseph Wershba, "Closeup: NAACP's Labor Secretary Herbert Hill," *New York Post,* Dec. 14, 1959, quoted in Pfeffer, *A. Philip Randolph,* 230; Hill to author, Feb. 6, 1995.

45. Wilkins to Randolph, Feb. 6, 1959; Herbert Hill, "The ILGWU—Fact and Fiction: A Reply to Gus Tyler," *New Politics* 2 (Winter 1963): 8; Will Herberg, "The Old-Timers and the Newcomers: Ethnic Group Relations in a Needle Trades Union," *Journal of Social Issues* 9 (1953): 12–19; Herbert Hill, "Race, Ethnicity, and Organized Labor: The Opposition to Affirmative Action," *New Politics,* new series 1 (Winter 1987): 53–54.

46. Hill, "Race, Ethnicity, and Organized Labor," 55; *New York Times,* July 8, 1962, p. 66; Sept. 20, 1962, p. 23.

47. *New York Times,* Oct. 12, 1962, p. 20; Oct. 19, 1962, p. 15; Nov. 10, 1962, pp. 1, 13. Hill, "The ILGWU—Fact and Fiction," 26; Roy Wilkins to Emanuel Muravchik, Oct. 31, 1962, Personal Papers of Herbert Hill. On the development of the controversy between the ILGWU and the NAACP, see also Herbert Hill, "The ILGWU Today—The Decay of a Labor Union," *New Politics,* no. 1 (Summer 1962): 6–17; Gus Tyler, "The Truth about the ILGWU," *New Politics,* no. 2 (Fall 1962): 6–17; Hill, "The ILGWU—Fact and Fiction," 7–27. For

an early attempt at a dispassionate summation, see Ray Marshall, *The Negro and Organized Labor* (New York: John Wiley and Sons, 1965), 73–79.

48. *New York Times,* Oct. 12, 1962, p. 20; Wilkins to Muravchik, Oct. 31, 1962; Roy Wilkins to George Meany, Dec. 7, 1962, Personal Papers of Herbert Hill; Peter B. Levy, *The New Left and Labor in the 1960s* (Urbana: Univ. of Illinois Press, 1994), 20; *Atlanta Daily World,* Nov. 23, 1962, p. 5.
49. Rothman to Carter, Apr. 8, 1963; "Order Granting Request," in the case of Atlantic Steel Company and Local Union no. 2401 of the Steel Workers' Organizing Committee, Oct. 23, 1963, in USWA, District 35 Records, 1945–1987, Box 2888, Folder 2; Equal Employment Opportunity Commission, "Decision," in the case of Nathaniel Brown et al., Charging Parties, v. Atlantic Steel Company, Respondent, July 19, 1967, USWA, District 35 Records, 1945–1987, Box 2900, Folder 4.
50. Herbert Hill, *Black Labor and the American Legal System: Race, Work, and the Law* (1977; reprint, Madison: Univ. of Wisconsin Press, 1985), 131. On the role of the NLRB in cases of racial discrimination, see Michael I. Sovern, "The National Labor Relations Act and Racial Discrimination," *Columbia Law Review* 62 (Apr. 1962): 563–632; Herbert Hill, "The National Labor Relations Act and the Emergence of Civil Rights Law: A New Priority in Federal Labor Policy," *Harvard Civil Rights–Civil Liberties Law Review* 11 (Spring 1976): 299–360; Hill, *Black Labor and the American Legal System,* 93–169.
51. Cooper to Kleiman, Jan. 20, 1967; U.S. Equal Employment Opportunities Commission, "Decision," in the case of Nathaniel Brown et al., July 19, 1967; "Exhibit 'A,'" attached to Benjamin L. Erdreich to Charles Mathias, Mar. 6, 1968, USWA, District 35 Records, 1945–1987, Box 2900, Folder 4.
52. Cooper to Kleiman, Jan. 20, 1967; SCLC to President's Committee on Equal Employment Opportunity ("Memorandum Re: Discriminatory Practices within Atlantic Steel"), June 8, 1963, USWA, District 35 Records, 1940–73, Box 718, Folder 32.
53. Cooper to Kleiman, Jan. 20, 1967; Jerome A. Cooper to Equal Employment Opportunity Commission, July 6, 1966; Cooper to Michael H. Gottesman, July 26, 1966 (quoted), USWA, District 35 Records, 1945–1987, Box 2900, Folder 3; *Atlanta Constitution,* July 23, 1966, p. 3.
54. U.S. Equal Employment Opportunities Commission, "Decision," in the case of Nathaniel Brown et al., July 19, 1967; U.S. Equal Employment Opportunities Commission, "Decision," in the case of Nathaniel Brown, Charging Party, vs. Atlantic Steel Company and Local Union 2401, United Steelworkers of America, Respondents, Jan. 17, 1979; Nathaniel Brown to Atlantic Steel Company Union Local No. 2401, Apr. 16, 1970, in USWA, District 35 Records, 1945–1987, Box 2900, Folder 4. On the EEOC, see Graham, *Civil Rights Era,* 147–49, 157–59, 234–53.
55. Norrell, "Caste in Steel," 689–90; Thomas O'Hanlon, "The Case Against the Unions," *Fortune* 77 (Jan. 1968): 188. Nearly ten years after O'Hanlon's observation, legal scholar William Gould stated that "probably no industrial union has faced more Title VII trouble than the United Steelworkers of

America." See William B. Gould, *Black Workers in White Unions: Job Discrimination in the United States* (Ithaca, N.Y.: Cornell Univ. Press, 1977), 395–400, quotation on 395.

56. Brown, interview by Hill, Oct. 21, 1962; David R. Roediger, *The Wages of Whiteness: Race and the Making of the American Working Class* (London: Verso, 1991). Bruce Nelson, "Class, Race, and Democracy in the CIO: The 'New' Labor History Meets the 'Wages of Whiteness,'" *International Review of Social History* 41 (Dec. 1996): 351–74, elaborates upon the theme of race and democracy in the United Steelworkers and other industrial unions.

Martin Luther King, Jr., the Crisis of the Black Working Class, and the Memphis Sanitation Strike

Michael Honey

On the twenty-fifth anniversary of the death of Martin Luther King, Jr., several hundred people from across the nation met at the National Civil Rights Museum in Memphis. Built on the site of the Lorraine Motel, where King was shot on April 4, 1968, in an impoverished district where he helped to lead a strike of black sanitation workers, the museum highlights King's deep commitment to movements of the poor. In this setting, participants at a three-day symposium on King criticized popular treatments of him, which typically focus on his role in the early desegregation struggles and victories from 1955 to 1965 and cite his "I Have a Dream" speech in 1963 as the high point of his career. While affirming the importance of King's early role, participants viewed King not as a dreamer but as a pragmatist and a movement strategist, one who had an economic analysis and who sought to mobilize movements from below. King's radicalism became especially apparent during his later career from 1965 to 1968 and particularly during the Poor People's Campaign and the Memphis sanitation workers' struggle in the last months of his life. Many symposium participants felt that King must be understood more fully, as a minister to the poor and the working class, as well as a civil rights leader, if his legacy is to be useful to new generations struggling with blatant disparities between rich and poor. This perspective suggests, among other things, the need for closer assessment of the significance of King's role in the events in Memphis and of the struggles of black workers in that city.[1]

By the time of the sanitation strike in 1968, King believed that movements by those at the bottom, allied with unions and middle-class people of good will, could regenerate what seemed to be a flagging struggle for freedom and equality. Since the mid-1950s, he had put his life on the line repeatedly to end southern segregation, but increasingly he had come to believe that desegregation by itself could not end black oppression. The Watts rebellion and other uprisings of the urban black poor after 1965 forced King to focus on questions of economic justice. In numerous speeches and writings of this period, he repeatedly warned of economic trends throwing black workers into crisis, even as they strode toward legal and civic freedom. He spoke of the deep roots of black economic distress in slavery and segregation. He probed the effects of a global economy which increasingly mechanized and marginalized people of color, the uneducated, and the poor; and he criticized unions for failing to address the needs of African Americans. He saw trends creating a crisis of the poor and the black working class that neither civil rights organizations nor the established labor unions by themselves could address. King hoped that poor people's movements would focus renewed energy on reforming an oppressive racial and economic order that placed disproportionate numbers of African Americans on the bottom. He saw the Memphis sanitation strike as one such movement.[2]

King's focus on economic and class issues did not emerge during the sanitation strike, nor during the Poor People's Campaign. As a graduate student, King recalled his first-hand experience of the Depression as one source of his "anti-capitalist feelings," and in his early graduate school papers he displayed some sympathy for Karl Marx's critique of capitalism, while opposing Marx's moral relativism and historical materialism. As a minister, King certainly empathized with the working class and the poor, despite his Ph.D. and relative affluence. As a civil rights leader, King had a long-standing concern for economic issues. Civil rights legislation, he repeatedly wrote and said, was but a downpayment on, and not a fulfillment of, the American dream of economic security and civic equality.[3] In 1957, he told civil-rights activists at Highlander Folk School: "I never intend to adjust myself to the tragic inequalities of an economic system which will take necessities from the masses to give luxuries to the classes." At that early date, King said that he sought the "complete realization" of democratic principles in the United States, emphasizing that "we must not rest until segregation and discrimination have been liquidated in every area of our nation's life."

King initially may have hoped that civil rights gains themselves would rectify economic inequalities, but later in his career he increasingly called for national economic compensation for centuries of slavery and segregation, as well as for a continuing moral commitment to ending racism.[4]

Nor did King's relationship with unions evolve only later in his life. During the Montgomery Bus Boycott and after it, King gained from unionists some of his knowledge of organizing and considerable financial support. He drew support not only from the AFL-CIO and the United Auto Workers (UAW), but also from smaller activist unions with leftist leaders and sizable black memberships, among these the United Packinghouse Workers, headquartered in Chicago. Throughout the 1960s, he continued to go to these unions and to others, such as Local 1199 Hospital Workers Union in New York City, for funds and organizational support. By observing the active civil-rights programs of these unions and using his own creative analysis, King early in his career developed a positive advocacy of organized labor that might be described as "civil-rights unionism." This form of unionism saw equal-rights struggles and labor struggles as complementary and mutually reinforcing, rather than as antagonistic and divisive.[5]

Although King spent most of his time working in the top-down organizational style of the Baptist Church, via the Southern Christian Leadership Conference (SCLC), his Ghandian understanding of the role of masses in history caused him to view both labor and the civil rights movements, at their best, as grassroots rebellions evolving from the bottom up. Long before the 1968 sanitation strike, King had made speech after speech to unions, pointing to the common methods and goals of labor and civil rights movements, and calling for a grand alliance of the two. He presumed not only that civil rights and voter registration would break segregation, but also that black and white workers' votes would combine to end state restrictions on union organizing and replace reactionary southern legislators with liberals. The high point of his own alliances with unions came in June 1963, with a mass freedom march in Detroit, cosponsored with the UAW, with over 125,00 participants; and with the August 28 March on Washington, to which the UAW and many other unions (although not the AFL-CIO) gave crucial support. By 1965, King and SCLC even went so far as to propose to UAW President Walter Reuther that unionists collaborate with SCLC to train a new generation of southern organizers for placement in the field, to "bring Unions into every sphere of labor activity here in the South w[here] Unions do not now exist."[6]

King relished the glowing promise of a civil rights–labor alliance, but he also expressed growing unease with its limitations, which became more apparent as the 1960s wore on. Unions and the civil rights movement needed each other but often had separate and competing concerns. Like other black leaders, King saw unions as fundamental allies in the freedom struggle, but he also recognized clearly the role white unionists frequently played in marginalizing blacks economically. Moreover, in the second half of the 1960s, King increasingly worried that a growing economic crisis among black workers would continue to drive ghetto rebellions in the cities. These uprisings forced King's attention to the North and in 1966–67 drew him into a frustrating and largely fruitless campaign for black economic advancement and open housing in Chicago. In speeches to union gatherings, he repeatedly described the cause of black economic crisis as rooted partly in automation, which in the 1950s and 1960s eliminated hundreds of thousands of unskilled jobs. After a long history of employer and union discrimination, these positions had only begun to provide accessible, high-wage, unionized employment for black workers; racism still blocked African-American advancement into more skilled production and craft jobs. In his speeches, King stressed the vulnerability of the black working class and called upon unions to do away with all vestiges of discrimination within their own organizations.[7] If the unions did not find a way to raise the living standard of all workers, and not just those under union contract, the proportion of unionized workers would continue to shrink; black workers would continue to be impoverished; and the strength of both labor and civil-rights organizations would ebb.[8]

The growing inequality of blacks in the 1960s that King highlighted in his labor speeches was starkly documented in economic statistics. These figures showed that, since the mid-1950s, black economic fortunes had declined. In the 1940s, the access of black workers, both male and female, to industrial employment had increased dramatically compared to previous decades, giving rise to a generally higher standard of living and greater black longevity.[9] But the Korean War was the last period of relatively low unemployment for black males (4.4 percent). Since then, relative economic decline had characterized the plight of black male workers. Their income had averaged 37 percent of the level for white males in 1939, 54 percent in 1947, and 62 percent in 1951; by 1962, though, it had dropped to 55 percent, about where it had been in 1945. Between 1959 and 1964, the most rapid job growth occurred in professional, technical, and clerical work; but these white-collar jobs remained largely closed to blacks. Throughout the 1950s, while some black males did gain semiskilled and skilled jobs as factory operatives, most black male workers remained in the constricting sector of unskilled labor.[10] In the 1940s and 1950s, black women also had made advances as factory operatives, and in the 1960s, to a greater extent than black men, some of them also made their way into the lowest-paid white-collar work as teachers, clerks, and office workers. Still, most employed black women remained stuck in domestic, laundry, and restaurant work.[11]

Constricted job opportunities not only drove down black income levels relative to those of whites; lack of employment opportunity, too, contributed to massive black unemployment. Males suffered most, with an unemployment rate two to three times that of whites and rising rapidly by the mid-1960s. In 1947–48, black unemployment had been 5 percent, relative to a white rate of 3 percent; by 1964, the respective rates were 10 percent and 5 percent. Counting hidden unemployment, however, the gap between white and black was much wider.

These conditions especially irritated the youngest and best-educated blacks, concentrated in the North, who had great difficulty finding jobs to match their training. Northern working-class blacks increasingly fell into two broad categories: a unionized group, who in the period 1940–53 had gotten and, protected by seniority provisions, for the most part kept industrial jobs classified as semiskilled and unskilled; and a younger and often better-educated group of workers, who after the Korean War could find no such employment security.[12] In the mid-1960s, economist Charles Killingsworth summed up the frustrating situation for black workers: "In the past decade changing technology and changing regional and industrial growth patterns have made opportunity far less equal for Negroes than it was a quarter century ago." Killingsworth believed that only a massive program to create jobs could "fit the size and shape of the problem" of black employment disadvantage. Clearly, failure to generate jobs in the inner cities, along with blatant police brutality, lay at the heart of the ghetto uprisings that punctuated the late 1960s.[13]

Black workers in the South suffered grievously as well. Millions of African Americans had left the region in search of work, but a reverse flow also had begun, as industries were fleeing unionized areas of the North for the non-unionized South. Between 1940 and the 1960s, manufacturing employment in the latter region increased by 80 percent, and during World War II blacks had gained an increasing share of these jobs. But after the war, industrial employers increasingly "whitened" their workforce, seeking workers who were better educated and less willing to organize than blacks. At the same time, agricultural employment declined by 60 percent, as the percentage of cotton harvested by machines went from 5 percent in 1950 to 50 percent by 1960 and 95 percent by 1970. Mechanization of cotton production gutted rural employment in the Mississippi Delta surrounding Memphis, forcing black farm laborers to flee to the city or to remain behind in unremitting poverty. Although the rate of industrial growth in the South exceeded that in the North, most of the new jobs were nonunion and concentrated in white, suburban areas. Partly as a result of these trends, the 1959 median income of black men in the South remained half that of black men in other regions. And in contrast to the 1940s, when southern blacks' income rose relative to that of whites, in the 1950s it fell by ten percentage points. Whereas growing industrial employment once had engendered hope, contracting rural employment and stagnant urban manufacturing employment in the 1960s aroused anger and frustration among southern African Americans. Moreover, their declining fortunes came during a period in which many white southerners, and white Americans generally, were doing better than ever.[14]

Vast and growing economic disparities between African Americans and whites came into high relief in the Mississippi Delta and in its urban capital, Memphis. Always grim, life for black migrants to the city deteriorated in the 1960s. Those escaping mechanization in the cotton fields had little education and few marketable skills to bring to Memphis, at a time of slack demand for unskilled labor. Entrenched barriers of racial discrimination and poor education in the city barred most African Americans from white-collar jobs, although a few black men and women worked as teachers, while a thin stratum of professional and business people provided political and social leadership. But most employed black men continued to work in the declining labor-intensive cotton and wood-related extractive and manufacturing industries, or in service work that paid equally poorly; the lucky ones worked at Firestone Tire, International Harvester, and a few other unionized industrial plants. Most employed African-American women continued to work as domestics and laundresses or in other lowly occupations, as this group made only token advances into white-collar employment. To avoid paying the higher wages required by federal minimum-wage laws, labor-intensive industries eliminated many unskilled positions normally filled by blacks and replaced these workers with machines, usually tended by whites. African-American men, the mainstay of unskilled factory employment in Memphis, suffered especially: as late as 1969, an astounding 86 percent of black men in Memphis still performed unskilled and service work. African Americans as a whole remained worse off by occupational distribution in Memphis than in many other parts of the urban South, to say nothing of the rest of the country.[15]

As a cumulative effect of these conditions, 57 percent of the black population lived below the poverty line in Memphis in the 1960s, compared to 13.8 percent in the white community. Although African Americans comprised less than 40 percent of the Memphis population, they made up 86 percent of the residents of the city's poverty areas. Other statistics showed disproportionately high rates of death, malnutrition, and family disorganization among African Americans. One of the greatest gaps between white and black Memphians remained in education, the single most telling index of discrimination and unemployment. Twenty-four percent of the people in poverty areas were functionally illiterate; fewer than 17 percent of them had finished high school (compared to 45 percent for white Memphis); fewer than 7 percent of them, compared to a 17.5 percent rate for whites, went on to college. Schools remained highly segregated, and white males generally obtained nearly four years more schooling than black males, while an eighth-grade education in African-American schools was roughly equivalent to a sixth-grade education in white schools. Inferior, segregated education continued to block the movement of African Americans into the growing sector of white-collar employment, even though significant desegregation of public places had occurred after numerous protests in the early 1960s.[16]

These devastating conditions fit easily into the history of a place that, like other southern cities, had a long record of virulent white supremacy. Slavery and then segregation had inculcated in most whites a deep belief in black inferiority. In Memphis, a small number of elite families had built a racial and economic order based on commerce, land ownership, extractive and processing industries, cheap labor, and unreconstructed white supremacy. Cemented into place by the poll tax and by political boss E. H. Crump, who ran the town on behalf of these families from before World War I until his death in 1954, the racial-economic system of white supremacy insured wealth for a few and poverty for the many. From the late 1930s on, black and white workers had contested their common victimization through industrial unions. Yet Memphis also had a long history of craft union exclusion, while its industrial unions, though interracial in membership, for the most part remained firmly controlled by whites. In some cases, as at the International Harvester plant, White Citizens Council and Ku Klux Klan influence remained strong. White workers resisted efforts of black workers to break down segregation in factory facilities, in seniority lines, and in union halls. "Massive resistance" to desegregation and the post–World War II Red Scare combined to defeat organizing drives and to drive progressives from the unions. In the 1960s, the unions still failed to reach beyond the core of organized industries and into the service sector to organize the least skilled, lowest-paid workers, most of them black and many of them women.[17]

The union movement once had promised much more, but by the 1960s the labor movement was in decline in Memphis. Although blacks composed about one-third of the city's union members, and by the 1950s the AFL and CIO unions had combined memberships of some 50,000 to 60,000, this total represented only about 23 percent of potential union membership, in a city with 540,000 people. Black influence in union leadership remained marginal, while the percentage of all workers organized into unions had begun to decline. Indeed, the situation in Memphis provided an archetypal example of how racism, mechanization, and a flagging labor movement combined to keep African-American workers poor, powerless, and exploited.[18]

Memphis exhibited all the racial and economic problems which King had pointed to in his speeches before union audiences. It is not surprising, then, that in the winter and spring of 1968 the mounting socioeconomic grievances of African-American workers erupted into a dramatic and far-reaching confrontation. In February, more than thirteen hundred black sanitation men launched what became a sixty-four-day strike, seeking nothing more than what many other workers had gained long before: union recognition, decent conditions, improved wages and benefits. The uprising of such men shocked white Memphians, as even those older workers who presumably had resigned themselves to their condition rose *en masse* to support the strike. The strike quickly developed into a stark confrontation, pitting supporters of the old racial-economic order against practically the entire Memphis African-American community and major portions of the city's organized labor movement.[19]

The condition of the thirteen hundred sanitation men who worked for the city epitomized the plight of the black urban poor. Many sanitation workers lived below the poverty level, even as they worked two or more jobs. A large portion of them came from rural Fayette County, Tennessee, where control of the cotton economy had shifted from planters using black unskilled labor to corporations using machines. There black unemployment reached nearly 70 percent, and 80 percent of the housing lacked plumbing. According to one of the men who moved from Fayette County to become a sanitation worker in Memphis, "There is no worst job. I would take anything." Such individuals usually obtained sanitation work through friends or family members already employed. At one time, rural blacks had used low-wage jobs in Memphis as stepping stones to jobs in Chicago or elsewhere in the North. But as employment opportunities in northern cities slackened, those who remained in Memphis were locked into dead-end jobs. They soon discovered that, no matter how long they might work as sanitation men, they remained classified as unskilled day laborers and could not become foremen or supervisors. Only whites held these positions, and most of them had little more than contempt for African Americans, who did backbreaking work compensated by low wages, few benefits, and no job security. Forty percent of sanitation workers were so poor that they qualified for welfare to supplement their salaries. In the 1960s, conditions worsened, as successive city governments economized by sending them home without pay on rainy days (it typically rained 60 inches a year in Memphis), refusing to replace obsolete and dangerous trucks and other equipment, and refusing to increase wages even to keep up with the cost of living.[20]

Unionization for these men represented a break from their past of peonage and sharecropping in the countryside and urban poverty and caste-system status in the city. Their organizing efforts also directly conflicted with long-entrenched anti-union policies of the city government. True, the Crump machine always had used craft unions as a vehicle for patronage and as a political auxiliary, and the machine had allowed whites to organize in the building trades and other areas where the city let contracts. Even then, however, it had made its agreements with the white unionists orally. It had violently resisted industrial unions, encouraging and even organizing beatings and expulsion of organizers. It also totally opposed public employee unions, and city officials repeatedly had vowed never to sign an agreement with a labor organization. In the 1930s and 1940s, when city employees, including teachers, firefighters, and police, tried to organize, the municipal authorities fired and blacklisted them. From the 1930s into the 1960s, municipal judges issued injunctions freely, crippling organizing campaigns and disrupting even the most militant strikes of white workers. Given this history, the idea that poor black sanitation workers would breach the barriers to form a public employee union seemed unthinkable.[21]

Union organizing among sanitation workers reflected the heroic and dogged efforts of a few individuals. In 1947 and again in 1960, outsiders had attempted to unionize sanitation workers, but both times city authorities had scared them off. However, with help from the Retail Clerks International Association, garbage worker T. O. Jones, a Memphis native who had returned to the city in 1958 when a recession in West Coast shipyards had eliminated his job, began another attempt to help the sanitation workers. In 1963, acting on the basis of on tips from informants, the Public Works Department fired Jones and thirty-three other workers. Over the next several years, however, Jones continued to meet with workers in their homes and to collect union dues. By 1964, aided by ministers and a black businessman and civic leader, O. Z. Evers, Jones and a number of workers had formed an Independent Workers Association of Memphis. With help from Secretary-Treasurer Bill Ross of the Memphis Trades and Labor Council, Jones succeeded in getting several of the dismissed unionists rehired. The American Federation of State, County, and Municipal Employees (AFSCME) put him on its payroll as an organizer, and he soon succeeded in gaining a charter for Local 1733. The Trades and Labor Council supported this initiative and called on the city to grant a written contract and dues check-off. City Commissioners rejected the council's demand, claiming that the city charter forbade formal recognition of any union.[22]

City politics also helped the sanitation workers to press their case. Unlike their counterparts in most of the South, Memphis's African-American citizens never had been disfranchised, although for decades the poll tax and the Crump machine had controlled their vote. Civil rights protesters had made modest gains in desegregating the downtown stores, and in 1964 black voters provided the winning margin in the election of racial moderate William Ingram as mayor, giving Jones encouragement to press on. Hoping for a reasonable response, in August 1966, the workers were on the verge of a strike. But even during Ingram's regime, the courts issued a severe injunction, and the Public Works Department threatened to replace the workers if they ignored it. At this point, black community leaders remained reluctant to endanger that progress toward desegregation that had been made during Ingram's regime and took little action to support the union.[23]

By 1968, however, things had changed dramatically. By now, many blacks no longer viewed the sanitation workers' struggle as simply a labor dispute. Organizing among sanitation workers had become a struggle of African Americans as a group for the right to be treated with human dignity by the white power structure. But which side one took in this struggle depended a great deal upon perceptions of the past, and these perceptions differed dramatically for whites and blacks. [24] Prior to 1968, many whites, and even some blacks, had held that Memphis had no race problem. In the 1950s and 1960s, these people pointed out, blacks had voted in significant numbers. Desegregation of public facilities had occurred earlier and more peacefully there than in any other major city in the Deep South. Yet, beneath a veneer of civility and white paternalism, brutality at the hands of an overwhelmingly white police force was a fact of daily life for blacks; so was widespread poverty and exclusion from any of the real centers of economic power or political decision making. In the mid-sixties, racial progressives saw signs of real change under Mayor Ingram. The 1966 shift from a commission to a mayor-council form of municipal government would, they believed, facilitate Ingram's progressive reforms. And in 1967 three blacks gained seats on the new city council. At the same time, however, the 1967 mayoral election split black and working-class white voters. Previously they had joined to elect Ingram, but now the black vote divided between incumbent Ingram and black mayoral candidate A. W. Willis, while Henry Loeb won by campaigning openly as a white supremacist, gaining virtually no support from the eighty thousand African-American voters. Loeb's election hardened white resistance to further black gains and especially frustrated and angered the city's historically moderate black middle class and religious leaders. "After all these years of being cooperative citizens, there were not enough white people to join with us to give us a decent mayor," recalled Rev. Benjamin Hooks.[25]

Under Loeb, a fiscal conservative who vowed to cut the city's costs, conditions worsened considerably for both the sanitation workers and the African-American community. The city's refusal to provide modern equipment meant that workers had to carry leaking tubs of garbage on their heads. White residents considered these workers "garbage men," not hard-working fellow citizens providing essential services. In the neighborhoods, they were treated as servants who should be grateful for gifts of cast-off clothing as a "fringe benefit" of the job. City authorities refused to entertain the idea that their work might be worth more than $1.60 an hour. To save money, Loeb's administration reduced the workforce in the sanitation division of the Public Works Department, an act that vastly increased the workloads of those who remained and forced them to toil extra hours without compensation. Loeb also appointed as Director of Public Works his political crony Charles Blackburn, a man with little tact and few negotiating skills, who repeatedly affronted the workers' sense of dignity. In one episode at the end of January, the sanitation division sent black workers home without pay during a rainstorm, while allowing the few white supervisors and drivers who worked for the division to remain on the job and collect wages. Such behavior by white bosses was typical, as was their refusal to allow blacks to take shelter during storms. On February 1, this disdain for black workers' safety and comfort had tragic consequences, when two African-American sanitation workers took refuge from a storm in a truck's compactor, which malfunctioned and crushed them to death. Having no insurance, the men's families were left destitute, while the city took more than a week to pay for their burial expenses. Meanwhile, the deeply racist Loeb regime continued to scorn—when it did not simply ignore—black sanitation workers' efforts to organize and thus seek to ameliorate their condition.[26]

Following a chain of accumulated grievances, the deaths of the two black workers and the failure of the Public Works Department to pay wages to the men sent home in January set off a spontaneous walkout by outraged workers on February 12. Almost immediately, the local chapter of the National Association for the Advancement of Colored People (NAACP) and many black ministers voiced their support for the job action. In response, for the next two months, Loeb's government refused to bargain with the men as long as they were on strike and hauled out every means at its disposal to break the union. Its methods included an injunction that prohibited union leaders from almost all public activities, continual police intimidation of strikers and their supporters, permanent replacement of many strikers by scabs of both races, and refusing to talk to union representatives or to recognize the right of city workers to organize. The city's two daily newspapers supported these policies and ignored the perspectives of the strikers and the black community. The press failed to explain the underlying causes of the strike and ran racist cartoons and headlines that further offended black sensibilities. Powerful city elites saw the dispute as an opportunity to teach lower-class blacks that while their counterparts in other places, such as Detroit and New York, might demonstrate and strike, this could not happen in Memphis. White citizens seemed to support Loeb's hard-line stance, helping with garbage collection and applauding the city's intransigent stance. The city government even gave the impression that those who interfered with strike-breakers might be shot in the streets, as newspapers pictured white replacement workers carrying guns while they picked up garbage.[27]

Confusion on the part of the city council heightened tensions. Its Committee on Public Works first told strike supporters that it would recommend a settlement to the council, but instead the council, on February 23, without permitting public comment, adopted a hostile substitute resolution. Finding the council meeting closed, strikers and their supporters flooded from the City Hall into the streets for a march, only to be attacked by truncheon-wielding, mace-spraying police. This incident, more than any other, demonstrated the limits of the black political empowerment and civil rights victories that had been achieved in Memphis. It demonstrated in a visceral way that black economic powerlessness remained the main fact of life, and it fused festering economic grievances with fundamental questions of civil and human rights.

The blatant racism of the city administration now galvanized black ministers, politicians, and civil rights leaders and energized a hitherto somnolent local labor movement. On the day after the police attacks, black community leaders and organizations, long at odds with each other, put aside their divisions and organized a group called Community on the Move for Equality (COME). Over the next six weeks, this organization proceeded to unite the African-American community behind the strikers with mass meetings, daily picketing, and a boycott of downtown businesses (particularly targeting the Loeb family's laundries), and the newspapers. Whites and blacks from the Memphis Trades and Labor Council and the United Rubber Workers and other industrial unions joined to support the strike.[28]

All in all, the walkout triggered a degree of mobilization of both the African-American community and progressive whites rarely seen in Memphis or anywhere in the South. As the conflict in Memphis became both more dramatic and more desperate, the struggle drew in Roy Wilkins of the NAACP, Bayard Rustin of the AFL-CIO's A. Philip

Randolph Institute, and AFSCME President Jerry Wurf, as tacticians and speakers at huge mass rallies. On March 14, a crowd variously estimated at between nine thousand and twenty-five thousand Memphians attended a rally featuring Wilkins and Rustin. Behind the scenes, debates whirled over whether to emphasize the strike as a workers' struggle, with hopes of drawing in more white unionists, or as a civil rights struggle, in order to solidify the black community behind it. For AFSCME, the outcome of the struggle represented the success or failure of its efforts to organize blue-collar public workers, especially in the South. For national civil rights leaders, the struggle in Memphis provided a crucial test of white America's willingness to come to grips with black economic demands or to recognize the dignity of African Americans in a more general sense. Many local people concluded that the strike was *both* a labor and a civil rights struggle and that the two could not be separated. With this perspective in mind, on March 17, Rev. James Lawson, a longtime Memphis religious and civil-rights leader, called his friend and colleague Martin Luther King, Jr., for the second time to ask him to come to the city and speak on behalf of the workers.[29]

King's labor perspective led him naturally to support the Memphis union struggle. His staff at SCLC, in the midst of frenzied preparations for the Poor People's Campaign, opposed his involvement in Memphis, while King identified the situation as emblematic of the dilemmas facing poor people and especially poor blacks. As workers, the sanitation men fought for union recognition; for the right to vacations, decent wages and benefits, rest breaks, and health and safety precautions; and for recognition of their right to belong to a union. King commented that these men, like most of the working poor, had none of the benefits that made a job worthwhile. Yet, more than that, he realized, black sanitation workers fought for dignity and respect as human beings. King understood that the conditions of the Memphis strikers typified the harsh realities facing the black working poor and unemployed all over America.[30]

On March 18, when King made his first speech to the workers and the Memphis community, the strike already had been under way for five weeks. King's role was to break the national news blackout of what was developing into one of the most dynamic labor and civil-rights struggles of the 1960s. He proceeded to put the situation into a context that could help people understand the strike as something with larger implications. Thereby the support of both unions and civil rights organizations across the country might be mobilized.

King used Memphis as an example of how the nation had devalued the labor of the working poor. "You are reminding the nation that it is a crime for people to live in this rich nation and receive starvation wages . . . this is our plight as a people all over America," King said. "We are living as a people in a literal depression," but one unrecognized by most whites or the government. "Do you know that most of the poor people in our country are working every day?" he asked the crowd. "And they are making wages so low that they cannot begin to function in the mainstream of the economic life of our nation. These are the facts which must be seen, and it is criminal to have people working on a full-time basis and [in] a full-time job, getting part-time income." It was the powerlessness of workers and the unemployed, especially people of color, said King, that accounted for the widespread poverty in America. "We are tired of being at the bottom," he said; we are tired of "wall-to-wall rats and roaches" instead of wall-to-wall carpeting; "we are tired of smothering in an airtight cage of poverty in the midst of an affluent society. We are tired of walking the streets in [a] search for jobs that do not exist."[31]

King also explained the sanitation strike as emblematic of the freedom movement's evolution from civil-rights demands to more systemic demands. According to King, the struggle for black equality logically had brought the movement to Memphis. While the Selma march and the Voting Rights Act of 1965 had brought to an end one phase of the struggle, "now our struggle is for genuine equality, which means economic equality. For we know that it isn't enough to integrate lunch counters. What does it profit a man to be able to eat at an integrated lunch counter if he doesn't earn enough money to buy a hamburger and a cup of coffee?" Civil rights gains had been only a down payment on the fulfillment of the American Dream. Returning to a theme of his 1963 "I Have a Dream" speech, King demanded payment on the "promissory note" for life, liberty, and happiness that originated in the documents of the American Revolution. "We are saying now is the time," King told Memphians, "to make real the promises of democracy."[32]

King's plea for African-American racial unity in support of working-class demands resonated deeply in Memphis; his call for the "haves" to join hands with the "have-nots" already had become a central theme of the strike. Even before his appearance, the confrontation between ill-treated workers and a racist city administration had lessened divisions based upon conflicting political loyalties and organizational turf battles among African-American leaders in Memphis, particularly among black ministers. As Rev. Ralph Jackson, a key leader and negotiator in the conflict, later told interviewers, he and other members of the black middle class had been distant from black workers and had not understood their plight at all. His eyes had been opened by thirteen hundred sanitation strikers carrying placards proclaiming "I Am a Man" and demanding to be treated not as "boys" or as servants but as citizens with rights equal to those of the wealthy and white. Moreover, the experience of being maced by the police had brought Jackson and other better-off blacks sharply up against the racial system and taught them how it felt to be both black and poor. The strike drew ministers and professionals away from a focus purely on civil-rights concerns and into the daily lives of poor people, where economic and racial injustice went hand in hand. Thus, a struggle that the poorest of the poor had initiated became central to the achievement of intraclass black unity in the Memphis of the late 1960s.[33]

The March 18 mass meeting validated King's poor people's strategy and released him from the brooding depression, anxiety, and exhaustion that increasingly had weighed him down. Rev. Lawson, the leading minister organizing support for the strikers, pointed out that, despite the "sardine atmosphere" in Mason Temple and the rising militancy of younger black activists who rejected nonviolence as an absolute principle, the Memphis crowd showed complete support for King's mission of nonviolent mass struggle. "Martin was visibly shaken by all this," said Lawson, "for this kind of support was unprecedented in the Movement. No one had ever been able to get these numbers out before." King became so inspired by the rally that he vowed to return to lead a mass march and called for a one-day general strike in support of the sanitation workers. At this point, the Memphis strike seemed to offer powerful testimony supporting King's belief that movements of the working poor and the unemployed represented the next phase of the freedom struggle.[34]

King had placed the sanitation strike not only into the context of the movement for black unity, but into an almost classic labor context. King's presence in Memphis awoke the national media to the importance of the strike there and brought many international unions into the picture. More than any other group, AFSCME, whose future in the South, if not nationally, hung on the outcome of the strike, provided the core of support. In addition, however, once King and other civil-rights leaders had made the strike a national issue, the AFL-CIO and its member unions sent substantial financial support—well over one hundred thousand dollars by the end of the strike. Fifty union officials from ten southern states meeting in Memphis for an AFL-CIO Social Security conference backed the strike and called the conduct of the city government "a throw-back to the Dark Ages."[35]

At the local level, attention from the national AFL-CIO galvanized many white union leaders to take a stronger position in support of the strike. The white-led Memphis Trades and Labor Council, the local AFL-CIO coordinating body, backed the strike with donations of funds and by mobilizing a March 4 march of some five hundred white unionists. The *Memphis Union News,* edited by Bill Ross, sharply and repeatedly denounced Mayor Loeb and "the ultra-conservative community leaders" he represented and supported the boycott of downtown stores and "the labor-hating press." The Labor Council and its Amalgamated Meat Cutters and Butcher Workman's Union President Tommy Powell called for a petition drive to recall Loeb. And some local white leaders challenged white workers' racism. George Clark, white president of United Rubber Workers of America Local 186, responded to criticism from white members of his union with a ringing denunciation of "the right-wing people in our plant, that are supposed to be union members," stating that they "will not prevent this union from supporting this, or any other group of workers, in their efforts to have a union."[36]

Black unionists also were forthright in their support of the strike. Leroy Clark, president of Local 282 of the United Furniture Workers of America, and other African-American trade unionists encouraged community and union picketing and support, while black members of the rubber workers' local provided space for meetings and moral support to the sanitation workers from the beginning. William Lucy played a key role as an international AFSCME organizer. George Holloway and a few other black members of UAW Local 988 at the International Harvester plant supported the strike wholeheartedly, despite the disapproval of whites at the plant. One perspective, then, held that a labor–civil rights coalition had in fact been created in Memphis. Labor economist F. Ray Marshall, for example, concluded that the support of organized labor, black and white, combined with an aroused civil-rights community, provided "a significant element leading to the [eventual] settlement of the dispute."[37]

However, at the same time that labor and civil rights solidarity seemed to be growing, white workers' responses were ambivalent, even contradictory. While some white unionists engaged in arms-length solidarity, others expressed outright hostility to the strike. The AFL-CIO's regional political organizer Dan Powell recalled that African-American workers could win only when their strike became a racial issue, making it possible to mobilize the African-American community behind them. Yet, as he and AFSCME leader Lucy noted, while white union leaders supported the strike as an economic issue, as soon as it became a racial struggle, many rank-and-file whites abandoned it. AFSCME organizer Jesse Epps and Rev. Lawson both observed that white workers generally stayed out of the struggle. On March 4, when they did march in support of the sanitation workers, white workers began their march separately from blacks, took a different route, and stayed to themselves when the groups came to a common destination. Worse, the building trades and many craft unions, always a conservative force in Memphis, took no official position on the sanitation strike but unofficially sided with Mayor Loeb. Many white workers did not want to pay the increased taxes that wage increases for sanitation workers would have necessitated. Nor did national union support necessarily translate into support at the local level. Although the national UAW had a strong record of support for Dr. King, for example, whites in UAW Local 988 had a long history of militant racism and largely opposed the sanitation workers' struggle. In short, the resistant racialized consciousness of the white working class surfaced clearly during the strike.[38]

The schizophrenic character of organized labor in Memphis reflected a growing racialization of white worker consciousness in the late 1960s which had become apparent to King, who found himself increasingly at odds with many white union members and much of the established union leadership. The 1955 merger of the AFL craft unions and the CIO industrial unions may have strengthened organized labor; but, as Lucy later commented, its leadership, starting with AFL-CIO President George Meany, "was not vested in the more progressive side of labor." King wanted labor leaders to take up the challenge of poverty in America, but he felt that, for the most part, they had not done that. King's opposition to the Vietnam War and his unwillingness to condemn Black Power also distanced him, and many grassroots activists, from mainstream liberals, especially many top union leaders with institutional ties to the American foreign-policy establishment.

At the same time that King struggled with these contradictions between the "movement" and the labor bureaucracy, Black Power advocates criticized him for his ties to liberals and integrationists. In 1967, when King spoke in Chicago of a "Negro-Labor alliance," blacks booed him. Such responses forced King to speak less about alliances with labor and more about independent black action. Thus, while King assumed the role of a labor militant in Memphis, his ties to many of the international unions, and certainly to the AFL-CIO, increasingly frayed.[39]

Long before the Memphis strike, King had realized that the coalition he sought between the civil rights movement and the unions was problematical. At the same time, King lacked a real grounding in the labor movement, making it difficult to conceive or execute the Poor People's Campaign, which included few unions in the coalition of the poor. Neither King nor his lieutenants had built a strong working-class base for the campaign, nor did they seem to know how to do so. King's conception of the campaign rested on the idea of an alliance among poor whites and poor people from racially oppressed minorities, few of whom belonged to unions and many of whom were without jobs. Most unions in high-wage sectors of the economy, on the other hand, long since had opted out of poor people's politics.

Even more worrisome to King, the ability of such racial polarizers as George Wallace to stimulate "backlash" among white voters had increasingly come to define two-party politics. In a May 1967 speech titled "Civil Rights at the Crossroads," delivered to shop stewards of the Teamsters Union, which in the past had pledged funds to SCLC, King identified the racial undercurrents eroding potential coalitions. Few whites, unionized or not, said King, recognized or welcomed the new phase of the movement that had opened after the passage of the Voting Rights Act in 1965. Once basic civil rights had been won, blacks began to look for the second phase, which King called "the realization of equality," meaning economic and social equality as well as civil rights. King realized that his effort to end widespread economic disparities had no guarantee in the Constitution or Bill of Rights and would cost billions of dollars in taxes, at a time when many in the white population, including many white workers, increasingly saw their interests as being in conflict with those of the poor and people of color. "To put it in plain language," King told the Teamsters, "many Americans would like to have a nation which is a democracy for white Americans but simultaneously a dictatorship over black Americans."[40]

King's move into the second phase of the civil rights revolution had elicited hostility toward him from many quarters, particularly the media and the federal government. The Federal Bureau of Investigation long had orchestrated a smear campaign against him in the press, and during the Memphis campaign its surveillance of King and all his associates escalated. On March 28, media hostility climaxed after black Memphis teenagers began breaking store windows on Beale Street during an attempted mass march led by King. Using this disorder as their excuse, Memphis police unleashed an indiscriminate and violent attack against all marchers and citizens in the area of the march. In their enthusiasm to repress the gathering, police killed black youth Larry Payne with a shotgun and beat scores of others. Following this incident, the mayor placed the African-American community under curfew, and the state brought in four thousand members of the National Guard, while the courts enjoined King from leading any more marches. With FBI encouragement, both federal officials and national news media barraged the public with unfavorable images of King's abilities and character. The events in Memphis now brought King's national leadership into question. This onslaught convinced King that he must defy the court order against him and return to Memphis to lead a massive and nonviolent public demonstration, even under the most unfavorable of circumstances. Failure to do so, he feared, would destroy the Poor People's Campaign and his own status as a national leader.[41]

The Memphis strike thus brought King, and in many ways the movements of the 1960s, to a point of crisis that entailed both opportunity and danger. On the night of April 3 at Mason Temple in Memphis, King, on the verge of complete exhaustion, offered the world his last speech. In it he offered both a pessimistic and an optimistic vision of the future. King still believed that the direction of events favored the freedom movement. "Something is happening in our world. The masses of people are rising up" all over the world in a "human rights revolution." He saw this rising up as a positive thing, not as something to be repressed, and the sheer force of numbers involved in the revolution meant that people did not need violence to bring about change if they were united. But he also warned that Pharaoh had prolonged slavery by keeping the slaves fighting each other, whereas in truth "either we go up together or we go down together." King reviewed the great history of achievements and change the freedom struggle had wrought in his lifetime; and his own life flashed before him, as he more or less predicted his death at the hands of some of "our sick white brothers." In a climax of emotionalism, King issued his last testament before the black poor and dispossessed of Memphis, saying, "I may not get there with you, but I want you to know tonight that we as a people will get to the promised land."[42] The next day he was dead, victim of an assassin's bullet.

King's death led to massive bad publicity for Memphis and to rapid defeat for Mayor Loeb, who had resisted or sabotaged every effort by the city council or citizens to resolve the sanitation strike. On April 2, white business leaders already had begun to pressure Loeb to soften his opposition to collective bargaining; after King's death, a delegation of them came to him and demanded that he settle the strike. Meanwhile, cities all over the U.S. went up in flames in response to King's death. In Memphis alone, nearly a million dollars in property damage (including 275 stores looted) and three deaths resulted from turmoil in the streets. On April 7, some eight thousand Memphians, most of them white, held a "Memphis Cares" memorial. Then, on April 8, thousands of labor, civil rights, and religious leaders converged on the city from around the country for a completely silent march by between twenty and forty thousand people. Some one hundred thousand people marched the next day at King's funeral procession in Atlanta. At the Memphis rally, the UAW's Walter Reuther pledged fifty thousand dollars to the sanitation workers, and the AFL-CIO's Meany set aside twenty thousand dollars as the first installment in a special fundraising drive among unions to support the sanitation strike. President Lyndon B. Johnson sent Undersecretary of Labor James Reynolds to impress upon local officials the urgency of the need for a strike settlement; Tennessee's Gov. Buford Ellington likewise pressed for resolution of the dispute. Although unrepentant to the end, Loeb finally removed himself as an obstacle to negotiations, and on April 16 union members ratified a proposed settlement in which the city capitulated to virtually all of the union's demands, including union recognition and dues check-off. The union had won.[43]

At the national level, however, King's death destroyed whatever chance the Poor People's Campaign had had for success, and removed from national life the one figure who still had the capacity to unite progressives in America. In a real sense, it brought to an end one phase of the movements of the 1960s. American history indeed turned in a direction that King had greatly feared. Mass uprisings in urban ghettoes, the assassination of Robert Kennedy, police riots in the streets of Chicago, and the election of Richard Nixon as U.S. president all followed on the heels of King's murder. Subsequent years saw the creation not of a progressive coalition of black and white workers, but the Republican party's "southern strategy" to split white workers and the white middle class away from the Democratic party, using racism to rationalize growing racial-economic inequality. White racial identity, forged through centuries of propaganda and white economic advantage over people of color, continued to undermine both unions and larger political coalitions, turning "Populism" into a rhetorical prop for business interests.

Twenty-five years after King's death, participants at observances in Memphis noted some of the consequences of failing to attend to the agenda he laid out in 1968. In predominantly black cities such as Memphis, African Americans continued to lose ground in a disintegrating economic order on which they had a slippery foothold at best. Employers and the state have repressed, discouraged, and in other ways whittled away the gains of both unions and the organized black freedom movement, while the economic fortunes of many African Americans have sunk to the lowest level since the Great Depression of the 1930s. These conditions remain nowhere more apparent than in the American South.[44]

On the other side of the historical ledger, King's struggles in the last year of his life have left an important and positive legacy. Black leader Rev. H. Ralph Jackson recalled that bringing King into Memphis was the key to the strike's outcome; the strike would have remained lost "as long as it was a local affair." In the aftermath of the strike victory, the black community and civil rights forces in Memphis surged forward. AFSCME 1733 became the largest single local in the city, consolidating nearly six thousand members, 90 percent of them black. In 1969, Local 1733, along with other Memphis unions, the NAACP, and the black community went on to instigate support of union organizing at Saint Joseph's Hospital. Although this drive failed, the city eased its opposition to collective bargaining; and in 1972 and 1973, white fire fighters and, ironically, the police (the vast majority of them white) created officially recognized unions. In 1978, both groups won strikes. In the early 1970s, an aroused African-American community elected blacks to the school board and elected the first black congressmen from the Mid-South since Reconstruction. By virtue of their prestige and the size of their union, the lowly sanitation workers became power brokers of a sort. In 1975, according to scholar Thomas Collins, "Local 1733 was the largest and by far the most powerful black political organization in town." As late as 1982, he felt that "the sanitation workers are in a position of power capable of making demands on the city political system quite independent of the black middle class," although the union's political power weakened in subsequent years. The racial divide in Memphis remained deep, and intraclass unity among blacks dissipated as well. Yet the strike victory and its aftermath brought a significant change in power relations in Memphis, leading in the 1990s to the election of an African American, Willie Herrenton, as mayor and also to a degree of black-white power sharing.[45]

The 1968 strike victory had ramifications beyond Memphis as well. "A new kind of respect and a new kind of recognition" of the role of garbage workers in municipal economies emerged after the Memphis strike, according to William Lucy. An upsurge of sanitation-worker organizing in several southern cities followed the Memphis struggle, and public-employee unionism became the fastest-growing sector of the union movement in the 1970s. According to Lucy, "a new enthusiasm to organize really went across sanitation workers across the country." The Memphis formula of maximum community involvement in union battles, the "Memphis spirit," as Lucy called it, also inspired other efforts to build labor–civil rights coalitions, most notably in the dramatic struggle between black hospital workers organized into Local 1199B Hospital Workers Union, joined by King's Southern Christian Leadership Conference, and white city leaders in Charleston, South Carolina, in 1969.[46]

By the end of the 1970s, the upsurge in civil-rights unionism had receded, along with the SCLC itself. The Charleston strike, for example, led to no consolidation of union power. The model of a labor–civil rights coalition and of maximum community involvement in strikes remained, but their implementation seemed uncertain. Nonetheless, the death of King amid a labor struggle in Memphis left an ideological imprint on history which is an important legacy of the 1960s. Memphis and the Poor People's Campaign represent the culmination of King's search for a means to shake the foundations of American racism and economic injustice. No one mounted as ambitious an effort to deal with the deep-seated ills of society or provided as universalistic a response to the forces of economic fragmentation and the disintegration of community. King sought to turn the civil rights movement toward an economic agenda that finally would address black economic demands that the United States had neglected ever since Reconstruction. At the same time, he tried to bring together the economic grievances of poor whites, blacks, and other people of color. The legacy of civil rights unionism remained uncertain in a subsequent era in which Republican and corporate strategies of divide-and-rule dominated the American landscape. Nonetheless, King's struggle to counter such strategies with coalition politics aimed at uniting poor and working people with other potential allies continued to offer an alternative road map for labor, civil rights, and reform movements, one based on King's admonition to striking sanitation workers in Memphis: "We can all get more together than we can apart . . . and this is the way we gain power."[47]

Notes

The author revised this article as a fellow at the National Humanities Center, Research Triangle Park, North Carolina, 1995–96.

1. Conference on "Twenty-Five Years Since Martin Luther King, Jr.: Rebuilding Movements for Social Change," National Civil Rights Museum, Memphis, Tenn., Apr. 2–4, 1993, audiotapes of addresses by Cornel West, C. T. Vivian, Charles McDew, Martha Norman, and others, in author's possession. For King's global concerns and focus on the poor, see his last book, Martin Luther King, Jr., *Where Do We Go from Here: Chaos or Community?* (New York: Harper and Row, 1967), esp. 161–91.
2. I have developed these themes in unpublished papers drawing upon King's speeches before unions in the 1950s and 1960s: Michael K. Honey, "Coalition and Conflict: Martin Luther King, Civil Rights, and the American Labor Movement," paper presented at North American Labor History Conference, Detroit, Mich., Oct. 1992; and Michael K. Honey, "Labor and Civil Rights Movements at the Crossroads: Martin Luther King, Jr., Black Workers, and the Poor People's Campaign," paper presented at Annual Meeting of the Organization of American Historians, Atlanta, Ga., Apr. 1994. For details of King's later development, see David J. Garrow, *Bearing the Cross: Martin Luther King, Jr., and the Southern Christian Leadership Conference* (New York: William Morrow, 1986), 357–624; Adam Fairclough, *To Redeem the Soul of America: The Southern Christian Leadership Conference and Martin Luther King, Jr.* (Athens: Univ. of Georgia Press, 1987), 253–384; Adam Fairclough, *Martin Luther King, Jr.* (Athens: Univ. of Georgia Press, 1990), 105–22. Charles H. Cone, *Martin and Malcolm and America: A Dream or a Nightmare?* (Maryknoll, N.Y.: Orbis Books, 1991), also discusses King's commitment to the poor, 219–27. On King's heartbreaking struggles in Chicago, see James R. Ralph, Jr., *Northern Protest, Martin Luther King, Jr., Chicago, and the Civil Rights Movement* (Cambridge, Mass.: Harvard Univ. Press, 1993).
3. See Martin Luther King, Jr., "I Have a Dream," text in James M. Washington, ed., *Testament of Hope: The Essential Writings of Martin Luther King, Jr.* (New York: Harper and Row, 1986), 217–30; Clayborne Carson et al., eds., *The Papers of Martin Luther King, Jr.*, vol. 1: *Called to Serve, Jan. 1929–June 1951* (Berkeley: Univ. of California Press, 1992), 31, 41, 54, 359, 435–36; and Taylor Branch, *Parting of the Waters: America in the King Years, 1954–63* (New

York: Simon and Schuster, 1988), 79–87. See also Martin Luther King, Jr., *Stride Toward Freedom: The Montgomery Story* (New York: Ballantine, 1958), 164–67, 183; and Martin Luther King, Jr., *Why We Can't Wait* (New York: Penguin, 1963), 130–33, 140–43, 146–55.

4. Martin Luther King, Jr., "The Look to the Future," an address delivered at the 25th Anniversary of the Highlander Folk School, Monteagle, Tenn., Sept. 2, 1957, Box 6, Folder 28, Sanitation Strikers' files, Mississippi Valley Collection, Brister Library, Univ. of Memphis, Memphis, Tenn. (hereafter cited as SSFMVC/UMT). Labor organizer and southern Communist Party activist William E. Davis rode in a car with King and Anne Braden from the Highlander meeting, and he recalled that King seemed quite aware of the economic aspects of racism and of the Leftist critique of capitalism. William E. Davis, interview by Michael Honey, Memphis, Tenn., May 21, 1989, notes in author's possession. In *Where Do We Go From Here,* 93, and in speeches, King pointed out that, in the process of emancipation, the nation never created an economic base for African Americans.
5. Union supporters such as E. D. Nixon, Jack O'Dell, Stanley Levison, Bayard Rustin, A. Philip Randolph, Myles Horton, Carl and Anne Braden, and Ralph Helstein all had a good deal of early contact with King. In 1957, Helstein turned over to King $11,000 created as a "fund for democracy" in the South, raised by UPWA locals across the country. The UPWA already had launched one of the most impressive efforts of any union to root out racism from within the ranks of its members and their communities, and was one of the earliest and most persistent financial supporters of the Montgomery Bus Boycott and of King's subsequent work in the South. King supported the union when some called it "Communist," and in a 1962 speech before the UPWA, he declared that, had other unions followed the example of the Packinghouse union, "the civil rights problem would not be a burning national shame, but a problem long solved." See King's addresses at 4th Biennial Wage and Contract Conference, 3rd National Anti-Discrimination Conference, and 3rd National Conference on Women's Activities, all United Packinghouse Workers of America, AFL-CIO, Sept. 30–Oct. 4, 1957, Chicago; in UPWA Conferences, Box 526, as well as other items, UPWA Collection, Wisconsin Historical Society, Madison. See also his "Address Before the United Packinghouse Workers of America," May 21, 1962, in Martin Luther King, Jr., Papers, Martin Luther King, Jr., Institute for Nonviolent Social Change, Atlanta, Ga. (hereafter cited as MLK Papers).
6. King's speeches to unions are collected in Martin Luther King, Jr., Papers, Series 3, speech files, Martin Luther King, Jr., Institute, Atlanta. They are analyzed in Honey, "Coalition and Conflict." See also Branch, *Parting of the Waters,* 842–43; and King to Walter Reuther, May 23, 1962, on black-labor voting, in Walter P. Reuther Papers, Box 523, Folder 1, Archives of Labor History and Urban Affairs, Wayne State Univ., Detroit, Mich. (hereafter cited as WRP); and King to Reuther, July 19, 1965, enclosing a proposal, "To All Union Representatives," in WRP, Box 523, Folder 2. For material on the March on Washington, see WRP, Box 494, Folders 8–10.

7. Honey, "Coalition and Conflict." See also King's only speech to a national AFL-CIO convention, "If the Negro Wins, Labor Wins" (1962), printed in Washington, *Testament of Hope,* 201–7. See also King, *Why We Can't Wait,* 129.
8. Manning Marable, "The Crisis of the Black Working Class: An Economic and Historical Analysis," *Science and Society* 66, no. 2 (Summer 1982): 130–61, describes many of the characteristics of the crisis also described by King. King made his most critical statements about unions in "Civil Rights at the Crossroads," an address to the shop stewards of Local 815 of the Teamsters, New York, May 2, 1967, and in "The Other America," a speech before Local 1199 at Hunter College, New York, Mar. 10, 1967, both in King Speeches, MLK Papers, Atlanta.
9. According to Charles Killingsworth, between 1900 and the 1960s, life-expectancy for blacks doubled, with the largest change in the white-black health differential occurring in the 1940s. This development coincided not just with employment in manufacturing but also with a movement of rural people to the cities. Killingsworth, "Negroes in a Changing Labor Market," in *Employment, Race, and Poverty,* ed. Arthur M. Ross and Herbert Hill (New York: Harcourt, Brace and World, 1967), 55.
10. Arthur M. Ross, "The Negro in the American Economy," in Ross and Hill, *Employment, Race, and Poverty,* 18–19, and Killingsworth, "Negroes in a Changing Labor Market," 51–52, 57–71; William H. Harris, *The Harder We Run: Black Workers Since the Civil War* (New York: Oxford Univ. Press, 1982), 82.
11. Harris, *The Harder We Run,* 159–60; Jacqueline Jones, *Labor of Love, Labor of Sorrow: Black Women, Work and the Family, from Slavery to the Present* (New York: Random House, 1986), 260–62, 277.
12. Killingsworth, "Negroes in a Changing Labor Market," 59, 58, 62, 60, 69.
13. Police brutality often sparked upheavals rooted in more systemic problems. The Detroit riot of 1967 provided the most devastating example. See Sidney Fine, *Violence in the Model City: The Cavanaugh Administration, Race Relations, and the Detroit Riot of 1967* (Ann Arbor: Univ. of Michigan Press, 1989); and Killingsworth, "Negroes in a Changing Labor Market," 73, 72.
14. On percentages of agricultural and industrial employment, see Vivian W. Henderson, "Region, Race, and Jobs," in Ross and Hill, *Employment, Race, and Poverty,* 80. On the disparity in median black income North and South as of 1959, see Killingsworth, "Negroes in a Changing Labor Market," 68. See Gavin Wright, *Old South, New South: Revolutions in the Southern Economy since the Civil War* (New York: Basic Books, 1986), 243, 247, 255, on the mechanization of southern agriculture. See F. Ray Marshall, "Industrialization and Race Relations in the Southern States," in *Industrialization and Race Relations: A Symposium,* ed. Guy Hunter (New York: Oxford Univ. Press, 1965), 91, on the decline in black median income relative to that of whites.
15. See Bruce Williams, Michael Timberlake, Bonnie Thornton Dill, and Darryl Tukufu, "Race and Economic Development in the Lower Mississippi," Research Paper No. 15, Center for Research on Women, Univ. of Memphis, Memphis, Tenn., 1992; John M. Brewster, *Labor and Power Utilization at Cotton Seed Oil Mills,* U.S. Dept. of Agriculture Marketing Research Report

218 (Washington, D.C.: USGPO, 1958); James E. Fickle, *The New South and the "New Competition": Trade Association Development in the Southern Pine Industry* (Urbana: Univ. of Illinois Press, 1980), 314–35 (on mechanization in extractive industries); and Arvil Van Adams, "The Memphis Labor Market," in *Negro Employment in the South,* ed. F. Ray Marshall, Manpower Research Monograph no. 23 (Washington, D.C.: USGPO, 1971), 2:9–18. On the industrial configuration, see Michael Honey, *Southern Labor and Black Civil Rights: Organizing Memphis Workers* (Urbana: Univ. of Illinois Press, 1993), 13–64.

16. F. Ray Marshall and Arvil Van Adams, "Negro Employment in Memphis," *Industrial Relations: A Journal of Economy and Society* 9, no. 3 (May 1970): 308–23; Donald D. Stewart, *Poverty in Memphis: Report of a Preliminary Study* (Memphis, Tenn.: Dept. of Sociology and Anthropology, Memphis State Univ., 1964), 23, 40; David M. Tucker, *Memphis Since Crump: Bossism, Blacks, and Civic Reformers, 1948–1968* (Knoxville: Univ. of Tennessee Press, 1980), 118–42.
17. See Honey, *Southern Labor and Black Civil Rights,* 245–91; Michael Honey, "Industrial Unionism and Racial Justice in Memphis," in *Organized Labor in the Twentieth-Century South,* ed. Robert H. Zieger (Knoxville: Univ. of Tennessee Press, 1991), 135–57; Michael Honey, "Operation Dixie: Labor and Civil Rights in the Postwar South," in *Mississippi Quarterly* 45, no. 4 (Fall 1992): 439–52; and Michael Honey, "Labor, the Left, and Civil Rights in the South: Memphis during the CIO Era, 1937–1955," in *Anti-Communism: The Politics of Manipulation,* ed. Judith Joel and Gerald M. Erickson (Minneapolis, Minn.: MEP Publications, 1987), 57–87. See also Alan Draper, *Conflict of Interests: Organized Labor and the Civil Rights Movement in the South, 1954–1968* (Ithaca, N.Y.: ILR Press, 1994), 29, on the segregationist and right-wing movement among white workers in the South, and in Memphis.
18. Earl Green, Jr., "Labor in the South: A Case Study of Memphis—The 1968 Sanitation Strike and Its Effect on an Urban Community" (Ph.D. diss., New York Univ., 1980), 79, 90, 94; Joan Turner Beifuss, *At the River I Stand: Memphis, the 1968 Strike, and Martin Luther King* (Memphis, Tenn.: B and W Books, 1985), 54; and Richard P. Schick and Jean J. Courtier, with Thomas W. Collins, "Memphis, Tennessee: Sanitationmen's Bargaining Climate in 1975 Compared with 1968," in *The Public Interest in Government Labor Relations,* ed. Richard P. Schick and Jean J. Courtier (Cambridge, Mass: Ballinger Publishing Co., 1977), 69–104.
19. For a dramatic account of the situation in 1968, see Beifuss, *At the River I Stand,* passim, and also Garrow, *Bearing the Cross,* 575–624.
20. Thomas W. Collins and L. B. Brooks, "Regional Migration in the South: A Case Analysis of Memphis," paper presented at the Annual Meeting of the American Anthropological Association, New Orleans, La., Nov. 30, 1973, in author's possession; and Thomas W. Collins, "An Analysis of the Memphis Garbage Strike of 1968," in *Anthropology for the Eighties: Introductory Readings,* ed. Johnetta B. Cole (New York: Free Press, 1982), 353–62.
21. Strike incidents led by white workers included a six-month walkout of Dixie Greyhound bus workers in 1946, the American Snuff factory strike in 1950,

and construction strikes in the 1950s involving confrontations on picket lines and even bombings and shootings. However, the city resorted to injunctions to break unions, no matter who inspired the violence or, indeed, whether or not violence was involved. See Honey, *Southern Labor and Black Civil Rights,* 72–73, 75–78, 93, 149, 181, 208–9, on AFL and Crump, and 260–63 on the American Snuff strike; and Green, "Labor in the South," 70–73, on the Greyhound strike.

22. Green, "Labor in the South," 102–24.
23. On the city's civil rights history, see Green, "Labor in the South"; Gerald D. McKnight, "The 1968 Memphis Sanitation Strike and the FBI: A Case Study in Urban Surveillance," *South Atlantic Quarterly* 83, no. 2 (Spring 1984): 138–56; and Tucker, *Memphis Since Crump,* 118–42.
24. For accounts of the strike and its meaning, see J. Edwin Stanfield, *In Memphis: More Than a Garbage Strike* (Atlanta, Ga.: Southern Regional Council, Mar. 22, 1968); Beifuss, *At the River I Stand;* Schick and Courtier with Collins, "Memphis, Tennessee"; and Green, "Labor in the South." See also the sparest and most direct account: Philip S. Foner, *Organized Labor and the Black Worker, 1619–1973* (New York: International Publishers, 1974), 378–85. A good short account is in Joseph Goulden, *Jerry Wurf: Labor's Last Angry Man* (New York: Macmillan, 1982), 142–82. See also Anne Trotter, "The Memphis Business Community and Integration," in *Southern Businessmen and Desegregation,* ed. Elizabeth Jacoway and David R. Colburn (Baton Rouge: Louisiana State Univ. Press, 1982), 282–300; and one of the most pointed and thorough accounts, F. Ray Marshall and Arvil Van Adams, "The Memphis Public Works Employees Strike," in *Racial Conflict and Negotiations, Perspectives and First Case Studies,* ed. W. Ellison Chalmers and Gerald W. Cormick (Ann Arbor, Mich.: Institute of Labor and Industrial Relations et al., 1971), 75–216.
25. See Trotter, "Memphis Business Community," 286–89; Sandra Vaughn, "Memphis: Heart of the Mid-South," in *In Search of the New South: The Black Urban Experience in the 1970s and 1980s,* ed. Robert D. Bullard (Tuscaloosa: Univ. of Alabama Press, 1989), 98–120; and Stanfield, *In Memphis: More Than a Garbage Strike,* 3. Hooks is quoted in Beifuss, *At the River I Stand,* 57.
26. Green, "Labor in the South," 119, 127–40, and Beifuss, *At the River I Stand,* 28–31.
27. Green, "Labor in the South," 140–64; Beifuss, *At the River I Stand,* passim; Garrow, *Bearing the Cross,* 575–624; and Goulden, *Jerry Wurf.*
28. Green, "Labor in the South," 190–93, 197; *Memphis Union News,* Mar. 8, 1968.
29. Green, "Labor in the South," 190–93, 197. For a dramatic account of how the issues around the strike developed into broader concerns, see the film version of Beifuss, *At the River I Stand,* as shown on the Public Broadcasting System, Apr. 2, 1993, and distributed by California Newsreel.
30. Garrow, *Bearing the Cross,* 616; and "Address of Rev. Martin Luther King, Jr., on Mar. 18, 1968, at Mason Temple Mass Meeting in Memphis," Box 6, Folder 29, SSFMVC/UMT.

31. "Address of Rev. Martin Luther King, Jr., on Mar. 18, 1968, at Mason Temple Mass Meeting in Memphis," Box 6, Folder 29, SSFMVC/UMT.
32. Ibid.
33. H. Ralph Jackson, interview by F. Ray Marshall and Arvil Van Adams, July 21, 1969, in Marshall and Van Adams, "Memphis Public Works Employees Strike," 169–79.
34. On King's state of mind, see Garrow, *Bearing the Cross,* 570–610. James Lawson, interview by F. Ray Marshall and Arvil Van Adams, July 21, 1969, in Marshall and Van Adams, "Memphis Public Works Employees Strike," 179–85, quotation on 181.
35. *Memphis Union News,* Jan. through May 1968, carried heavy supportive coverage of the strike. The quoted views are in the Mar. 1968 issue. See also an article in the national periodical of the American Federation of State, County and Municipal Employees, *Public Employee* 33, no. 4 (Apr. 1968): 12, on union contributions.
36. *Memphis Union News,* issues of Mar. and Apr. 1968.
37. Leroy Clark, recorded interview by Michael Honey, Mar. 27, 1983, Memphis; George Clark, recorded interview by Michael Honey, Oct. 30, 1984, Memphis; Clarence Coe, recorded interview by Michael Honey, May 28 and 29, 1989, Memphis; and George Holloway, recorded interview by Michael Honey, Mar. 23, 1990, Baltimore; all in author's possession. Clark quotation in "A Report to Members of Local 186 from G. W. Clark, President," mimeographed, ca. Mar. 1968, in Box 5, Folder 12, SSFMVC/UMT. Marshall and Van Adams, "Memphis Public Works Employees Strike," 100.
38. Concerning the depth of the problem of white union racism, see Honey, *Southern Labor and Black Civil Rights,* passim. William Lucy, recorded interview by Michael Honey, Apr. 2, 1993, Memphis, in author's possession; and Holloway, interview by Honey, Mar. 23, 1990. Epps, interview by Marshall and Van Adams, July 8, 1969, 165–69; James Lawson, interview by Marshall and Van Adams, July 21, 1969, 179–83; and Dan Powell, interview by Marshall and Van Adams, June 11, 1969, 183–85.
39. On the waning of the CIO and its merger with the AFL, see Robert H. Zieger, *The CIO, 1935–1955* (Chapel Hill: Univ. of North Carolina Press, 1995), 333–56. In the turmoil within the civil rights movement in 1966 and 1967, Bayard Rustin and other liberals and unionists remained silent about the war in Vietnam and became increasingly vocal in criticizing movement radicalism, thus discrediting themselves in the eyes of militants. King, on the other hand, refused to condemn the more militant wing of the movement, even while he criticized the Democratic party for its failure to provide a real vehicle for change. See Fairclough, *To Redeem the Soul of America,* 327, and Foner, *Organized Labor and the Black Worker,* 366, 376. See also King's speech, "Civil Rights at the Crossroads, an Address to the Shop Stewards of Local 815," and Honey, "Coalition and Conflict."
40. King, "Civil Rights at the Crossroads, an Address to the Shop Stewards of Local 815." During the Chicago struggles, Teamsters President James Hoffa

had pledged $50,000 to SCLC, but it is unclear whether he came through with the funds. Garrow, *Bearing the Cross,* 536.

41. See McKnight, "The 1968 Memphis Sanitation Strike," on the role of the FBI; and Beifuss, *At the River I Stand,* 211–42, on the Mar. 28 altercations. The film *At the River I Stand* graphically depicts these events. See also Garrow, *Bearing the Cross,* 611–16; and David Garrow, *The FBI and Martin Luther King, Jr.: From "Solo" to Memphis* (New York: Norton, 1981), 173–203. The clippings files in SSFMVC/UMT make clear the role of the media in exacerbating King's difficulties.
42. See the film *At the River I Stand* and King, "Mountaintop Speech," Apr. 3, 1968, in SSFMVC/UMT, Box 6, Folder 29.
43. Beifuss, *At the River I Stand,* 333–42; Trotter, "Memphis Business Community and Integration," 295–97; *Memphis Union News* 9 (Apr. 1968), on donated union funds; and Goulden, *Jerry Wurf,* 181.
44. See Honey, *Southern Labor and Black Civil Rights,* 279–91; and Michael Honey, "King's Unfinished Agenda: Economic Justice," paper delivered at conference on "Twenty-Five Years Since Martin Luther King, Jr.: Rebuilding Movements for Social Change," at National Civil Rights Museum, Memphis, Tenn., in author's possession, Apr. 2–4, 1993.
45. Jackson quotation from Marshall and Van Adams, "Memphis Public Works Employees Strike," 176; Trotter, "Memphis Business Community and Integration," 298; Schick and Courtier with Collins, "Memphis, Tennessee," 69–72, 75, and quotation on 80; second quotation is from Collins, "An Analysis of the Memphis Garbage Strike," 361.
46. William Lucy, interview by Honey, Apr. 2, 1993, in author's possession. See the positive assessment of the strike's outcome in Marshall and Van Adams, "Memphis Public Works Employees Strike," 83, 106–7. See also Foner, *Organized Labor and the Black Worker,* 378–96; Leon Fink and Brian Greenberg, *Upheaval in the Quiet Zone: A History of Hospital Workers' Union Local 1199* (Urbana: Univ. of Illinois Press, 1989), 128–58; and Leon Fink, *In Search of the Working Class: Essays in American Labor History and Political Culture* (Urbana: Univ. of Illinois Press, 1994), 51–85.
47. "Address of Rev. King," Mason Temple Mass Meeting, Mar. 8, 1968.

Gender, Race, Work Culture, and the Building of the Fire Fighters Union in Tampa, Florida, 1943–1985

Mark Wilkens

Between the end of World War II and the mid-1980s, the fire fighters of Tampa, Florida, built a strong and lasting tradition of union activism in one of the nation's premier anti-union states. During this period, a skeletal organization, maintained by a handful of activists, grew into a vigorous local of over five hundred members who exerted political power in the larger community in order to exploit changes in state collective bargaining law and win a large measure of control at the workplace. The foundation for the activism of fire fighters, which made them among the most union-conscious and militant public workers both in Tampa and throughout the nation, was the unique occupational culture of the profession. This culture, which bound fire fighters together into a tightly knit community with a cooperative, fraternal outlook and a shared masculine identity, was both created and sustained by the need to live and work together for long periods. Although, as a uniformed service, fire fighting necessarily has been hierarchical, the intimate living arrangements, the tendency to promote through the ranks, and the need for close cooperation in the face of a dangerous work environment tempered divisions between officers and men. It was this combination of close quarters, hazardous work, and professional pride that generated support among fire fighters for unions and bred a remarkable degree of resistance to civilian managers.[1]

Fire-fighter solidarity, however, also buttressed ethnic, racial, and gender discrimination. As in industries as diverse as cigar making and construction, fire fighters' organizations built on the basis of cohesive male work cultures also enforced prevailing ethnic and gender norms.[2] In the 1940s, Tampa's largely Anglo fire fighters resisted the entry of descendants of Hispanic and Italian immigrants into their ranks, while in the 1960s and 1970s African-American applicants fought to open the ranks further. The entry of women into the department in 1978 posed a more fundamental challenge to the fire fighting community because of its emphasis upon cultivating a highly masculine sense of self and service. As a consequence, fire fighters in Tampa have had to struggle to reconcile the legacy of an exclusionary work culture with the realities of an increasingly diverse workforce.

The history of professional fire fighting in Tampa dates to May 10, 1895, when the city council authorized the creation of a fire department of paid employees. Although the early fire fighters enjoyed the benefits of increased job security, they also labored in an environment that imposed long hours and low pay. The "one platoon" system employed by the city in the early twentieth century forced fire fighters to work shifts that lasted for six straight days, punctuated by a single day off. The city gradually improved hours over the next several decades, but as late as 1959, Tampa's fire fighters still were working a "two-platoon" system that required firemen to work forty-eight hours on, followed by twenty-four hours off. During the Great Depression, even the cherished benefits of economic security faded away, as the collapse of the local economy forced the city to close several fire stations, slash expenses, and either lay off or demote many of the department's employees. By the time the economic crisis came to an end during World War II, the remaining firemen were overworked, lived in rundown housing, and had to risk their lives with dilapidated equipment.[3]

It was conditions such as these that prompted the fire fighters in 1943 to organize as Local 754 of the International Association of Fire Fighters (IAFF). This was not the first example of activism on the part of the Tampa fire fighters, though. More than forty years earlier, they had organized themselves into a union, the Firemen's Protective Benevolent Association, and affiliated with the American Federation of Labor (AFL). Shortly thereafter, in January 1903, a dispute with the city over the firing of the union head and three other fire fighters prompted Tampa's firemen to launch the nation's first department-wide strike of fire fighters.[4] The city fired the striking fire fighters, though, and was able to hire replacements, thereby defeating this early attempt at unionization. It took another forty years before the Tampa fire fighters were able to organize a union under the auspices of the IAFF.

By the standards of most public employee unions, the IAFF was a venerable organization. As early as 1901, the AFL had begun chartering independent unions of fire fighters, and by 1918 there were eighty-two locals claiming the allegiance of one-quarter of the nation's forty thousand professional fire fighters. These unions, which opened their ranks to all uniformed personnel, often faced competing jurisdictional claims by the International Brotherhood of Teamsters and the Union of Steam and Operating Engineers. In 1918, this dispute helped prompt the AFL to establish the IAFF as a separate international union, granting it authority over the fire fighting community. From the union's very inception, therefore, the solidarity of the IAFF was rooted in its members' common identity as fire fighters, rather than in their distinct craft skills.[5]

While the birth of Local 754 provided the Tampa fire fighters with a valuable organizational advantage, the concerted opposition of the federal and state governments and the courts inhibited the activities of public employee unions. Even during the explosion of labor militancy in the 1930s, government workers gained few formal rights from the New Deal. The National Labor Relations Acts (NLRA) of 1935 and 1947, which revolutionized labor relations and institutionalized collective bargaining in the private sector, explicitly excluded federal, state, county, and municipal employees. Despite organized labor's protestations that these provisions violated public workers' right to equal protection, the federal courts consistently denied that government employees could enjoy the benefits of the NLRA.[6]

In Florida, the legislature and courts mirrored the federal government's efforts to circumscribe the rights of public employees. Even though a 1943 amendment to the Florida Constitution guaranteed workers the right to join a union and engage in collective bargaining, the courts ruled that public employees were exempt from its protections. The state legislature pursued a similar path, failing to include government workers in Florida's equivalent of the NLRA. In 1959, the legislature finally passed legislation giving state and local workers the right to join unions, but the courts and the state attorney general limited the law's impact by interpreting it so as to prohibit municipalities from engaging in collective bargaining. As a 1959 state attorney general's opinion noted, a public employee union had to "restrict [itself] to the representation of its members in the presentation of petitions and grievances connected with employment."[7] Under these conditions, the Tampa fire fighters union's activities were limited to lobbying council members, publicizing fire fighters' grievances, and exploiting the protections offered by the municipal civil service system.[8]

During the 1960s, however, opportunities for public employee unions expanded dramatically. In the case of the Tampa fire fighters, three developments were particularly crucial in strengthening the power of the union. First, starting in 1959, the city dramatically expanded the size of the fire department. Second, in 1965 the TFFU ushered in an era of increased political activism by forming a political action committee to fund the campaigns of sympathetic candidates. Most importantly, in 1967 the Florida legislature passed the Fire Fighters Collective Bargaining Act, thereby providing the TFFU with the right to engage in collective bargaining. Consequently, by the end of the decade, the nature of the relationship between the union and the city had changed dramatically.

The 1960s and 1970s were a period of historic change for public sector unionism. At the national level, the key development was President John F. Kennedy's Executive Order 10988, which reaffirmed the right of federal workers to organize unions and, for the first time, granted them the right to engage in collective bargaining. A similar transformation occurred at the state level where, beginning in 1959 with Wisconsin, an increasing number of states began passing laws that required government employers to engage in collective bargaining with their organized workers. Unions quickly exploited the legal reforms of the 1960s and enrolled a flood of new recruits. Whereas in 1960 only one million government employees belonged to unions, by 1976 that number had tripled, accounting for 80 percent of all new workers who joined unions during this period.[9]

The explosion in the growth of public employee unions in the 1960s was prompted in large part by the changing attitudes of many Americans, including the workers themselves, toward unions in the public sector. As the public sector expanded in size, government employees often faced an environment that was increasingly bureaucratic, impersonal, and unresponsive.[10] To many workers, organizing a union and becoming more militant seemed to be the only way to get the state to respond to their concerns. Echoing this sentiment, in 1969 the president of the TFFU declared, "Duty and service are two-way streets . . . [The] relationship in which the city plays the role of the benevolent

Massa and its employees, his faithful servants, can no longer be tolerated."[11] Employees of the state even began finding allies for these views among the general public: in an era that was increasingly rights-conscious, many citizens became more sympathetic to claims that the inferior legal status of public workers was unjust.[12]

For the TFFU, the emerging revolution in public-sector labor relations began in October 1965, when several hundred fire fighters descended on a church in Tampa's Ybor City to organize the Fire Fighters Service League, a political action committee. The city had improved conditions in 1959, when it instituted the three-platoon system, which established a schedule of twenty-four hours on, forty-eight hours off. This schedule shortened the typical work week to fifty-six hours, but grievances by fire fighters against the administration of the department continued to accumulate. Despite recent improvements in equipment and stricter building codes, the dangers facing the men of the Tampa Fire Department actually increased during the 1950s, a decade in which the small fire fighting community suffered the loss of five of its members in the line of duty. As Tampa's skyline rose, so did the hazards facing the men who struggled to battle fires in the new towers of concrete, glass, and steel that rose in the city's business district. Even more dangerous to fire fighters was the growing use of plastics, synthetics, and chemicals in construction materials and furnishings, which forced firemen to battle through deadly fumes with primitive gas masks.[13]

The violent unrest in the nation's cities in the 1960s also had an impact on safety conditions for fire fighters. Several fire fighters were killed and hundreds more injured in what one national magazine referred to as "the undeclared war on the nation's firemen."[14] The anger that many African Americans felt toward fire departments that were a privileged white preserve boiled to the surface in Tampa as well. On June 11, 1967, a violent protest broke out in the city's African-American community, and when the fire department responded to the emergency, residents met many of the fire fighters with a hailstorm of bricks and bottles. Nationally, fire safety statistics reflected the increasing dangers of the postwar era: between 1964 and 1970, fire-fighter deaths in the line of duty increased every year, and by 1970 fire fighting was the deadliest profession in the nation.[15]

In addition to concerns over safety, fire fighters in Tampa in the 1960s also worked to eliminate the role of partisan politics and personal favoritism in hiring and promotion practices. In October 1966, the discontent, which had contributed to the creation of the Fire Fighters Service League, prompted fire fighters under the auspices of the league to file a complaint with the city against Fire Chief Ken Ayers. The city council's final report, issued on November 30, 1966, led Mayor Nick Nuccio to demote Ayers, but it also charged the league with engaging in "political activities and threats, . . . [creating] dissension . . . [and] the suborning or inciting of insubordination and disrespect for authority."[16] The council urged Tampa's legislative delegation to press for a state law to restrict city workers from participating in any political party or campaign, but area legislators rejected the admonitions of the city council, forcing city hall to reconcile itself to the presence of an increasingly assertive and influential fire fighters' union.[17]

Of all the developments that marked the 1960s as a watershed era for the growing political power of the TFFU, the most significant event occurred in 1967, when the Florida legislature passed the Fire Fighters Collective Bargaining Act. The passage of the act demonstrated that the Florida Professional Firefighters (FPF), which was formed in 1944 as the state counterpart of the IAFF, had developed into a surprisingly potent lobby at the state capital. The FPF's accomplishments were particularly impressive because Florida, like most southern states, long had been inhospitable terrain for unions. By 1968, the Sunshine State ranked forty-fourth in the nation in the proportion of its workers who were organized. In this environment, the FPF learned that it was often easier to advance its cause by limiting its identification with the labor movement. During the debates over the fire fighters' collective bargaining legislation, the FPF neither asked for nor received assistance from other labor unions, and at the time it was not even affiliated with the state AFL-CIO. Instead, the organization relied upon the grassroots lobbying efforts of its member locals, who had spent decades cultivating the friendship of state legislators.[18]

In 1967, the persistence of the FPF finally bore fruit when the state legislature passed the Fire Fighters Collective Bargaining Act, which covered the state's most populous counties. Describing this momentous event, a past president of the FPF explained that the fire fighters found that the victory was simply a consequence of "cashing in the chips" that had accrued from years of hard work.[19] Five years later, additional legislation extended the reach of the act to the rest of the state; and in 1974, the legislature completed the revolution in labor relations, when it passed the Public Employee Relations Act (PERA), guaranteeing all government workers the right to engage in collective bargaining. The combination of lobbying by fire fighters and teachers, a progressive governor, and a court system that provided public employees with a sympathetic interpretation of the state's new constitution helped to generate the South's first comprehensive labor relations act for public employees. Spurred by the new legal climate in Florida, public employee unions quickly expanded throughout the state, and by the end of the 1970s, a majority of the state's public employees had availed themselves of the right to collective bargaining.[20]

The Tampa Fire Fighters Union quickly benefited from the flurry of activity by the state legislature. Although the first contract between the city and the TFFU in 1969 was a brief document, only a single page, within three years it had expanded to twenty-seven pages. Although union leaders focused their energies on winning wage increases for their members, the TFFU also sought to use the bargaining process to protect the union's ability to operate free of city interference and to promote a safer workplace. Some of the more exceptional provisions required the city to maintain minimum manpower levels on vehicles and to meet certain requirements for equipment. If manpower requirements were not met, the station captain had the authority to put a truck out of service rather than operate it while short of personnel.[21]

The early spirit of cooperation between the union and the city quickly collapsed, however, following the mayoral race of 1974, when insurance executive William Poe defeated the union's ally, city council member Joe Kotvas. Rather than being settled in private, the politically charged disputes between the city and the TFFU were played out in public before an arbitrator, as dictated by the terms of the 1974 Public Employees Relations Act. The arbitrator's decision was not binding, though, so if either side rejected the settlement, the dispute had to be resolved by the local legislative body, which was the city council. Although arbitration hearings were an elaborate and involved process, the final decision still remained in the political arena, a factor that the administration and the TFFU both realized. Contract negotiations, which had been amicable, now became an annual conflict in which the union fought against the city's attempts to rein in wages and assert greater control over the operations of the department and of the union.[22]

Despite the considerable powers of the mayor's office, Poe and his allies found the fire fighters to be formidable opponents, because they had spent years cultivating the sympathy of the city council's seven representatives. On three different occasions, the TFFU was able to deflect many of the mayor's plans to curb spending and reorganize the department. After one particularly venomous debate in 1979, the *Tampa Times* published a scathing editorial that spoke of the "Firemen's Four" on the city council who "continue to sing the same old tune under the baton of Sam Sinardi and his fire fighters union."[23] Although the editorial, which spoke of the "overpaid and underworked" fire fighters, did not perfectly mirror public sentiment, it did demonstrate that many Tampans had grown to resent the politicization of public employees and their growing influence in municipal government.

Like public employee unions throughout the nation, the Tampa fire fighters found that their success in influencing the political process proved to be a double-edged sword, as it helped to draw out anti-union opponents. If the 1960s marked the birth of public employee unions as a major force in society, then the 1970s undoubtedly were their troubled adolescence. The growth in size and assertiveness of public sector unions in the late 1960s prompted concern and in some cases even fear among a growing number of Americans. Academic studies warned that "excessive power" in the hands of public employees could distort the bargaining process and "overwhelm the needs of others" within the municipal community.[24] Putting it more succinctly, the title of an article in the popular monthly *Reader's Digest* queried, "Can Public Employee Unions be Controlled?"[25] Locally, critics of public sector unionism found the TFFU an obvious target. By the early 1970s, editorialists of local papers were warning that the precedent set by the fire fighters could turn elections into "a competition to see which candidate could promise to do most for the public [employees] with the biggest slush fund and largest army of poll workers."[26] Even the local television stations joined the chorus with editorials charging that the TFFU was on a "treasure hunt" and warning that offering arbitration to the fire fighters would be "disastrous for democratic self-government."[27]

In Florida, public apprehension about the growing militancy of government workers rose most dramatically after 1968, when a statewide teacher's strike was only the most notable of six public employee walkouts that resulted in 354,000 lost worker-days.[28] Two years later, Florida's Gov. Claude Kirk painted a frightening vision of a future in which the power of public employee unions was unbridled: "A strike by public employees brings to mind the vision of heaps of unsanitary garbage . . . menacing the health of the people. . . . Of prisons without guards. . . . Streets without policemen. Fires with no one to fight them. Complete chaos and an open invitation to anarchy. Clearly, public service is . . . above and beyond the ability to collectively bargain . . . which can only encourage illegal strikes."[29] Eight years later, in Memphis, Tennessee, Kirk's predictions appeared to come true, when fire fighters and police officers staged a simultaneous walkout. For the eleven days that the strike persisted, National Guardsmen enforced a dusk-to-dawn curfew with loaded rifles, while hundreds of fires swept through the city, causing millions of dollars in damage. The following January, the *Tampa Tribune* published a feature article on the strike, previewing it with the chilling question, "Memphis—could it happen here?"[30]

The growing popular sentiment against the influence of public employee unions meant that, by the 1980s, unions like the TFFU faced a uniformly inhospitable environment. If John F. Kennedy's Executive Order 10988 symbolized the rise of public employee unions, then Ronald Reagan's destruction of the air traffic controllers' union during its 1981 strike was a somber counterpart. The election of Reagan in 1980, however, was only the culmination of a growing conservative movement that gained momentum in the late 1970s by championing lower taxes and reduced spending on public services.[31] When combined with a recession-bound economy and a stagnant tax base, this "revolt of the haves" placed enormous budgetary pressures on government and made its workers an increasingly vulnerable target.[32]

In Tampa, the move towards fiscal restraint began with Poe's administration. Even as he was losing battles with the "Fireman's Four," the mayor was able to shrink the size of the fire department's workforce dramatically through attrition. Between 1974 and 1979, the number of uniformed employees dropped from 650 to 564, eroding the union's popular base. As the union's president wryly observed, "We [are] paying for our own pay raise by a cut in manpower."[33] The austerity continued under Poe's successor, Bob Martinez, who held office from 1979 to 1986. Despite his background as a longtime leader of the local teachers' union, Martinez aggressively attacked the municipal payroll, slashing several dozen more positions from the fire department.[34]

Had they retained their support on the city council, the fire fighters' union might have weathered Martinez's regime much as they had Poe's. Unfortunately for the TFFU, however, the 1979 municipal elections ushered in a more conservative council. Following the union's capitulation during the 1980 contract negotiations, one local columnist observed that "the president of the Tampa firefighters' union local did a political headcount of the City Council and took a dive," having lost the battle at the voting booth, not the negotiating table.[35] Throughout his tenure, Martinez continued to press his advantage, secure in the knowledge that he had the backing of the city council. Even the *Tampa Tribune,* a longtime nemesis of the fire fighters' union, questioned the mayor's actions, sensing that "it's almost as if he were trying to pick a fight."[36] Although Martinez's behavior puzzled the *Tribune,* the more conservative political climate of the 1980s, when the "Fireman's Four" had become a much less imposing "Fireman's Three," made his actions exceedingly pragmatic. From Ronald Reagan to Bob Martinez, political leaders of the 1980s realized that often they could expect to win more support among voters by challenging public employees than by cooperating with them.

In spite of the setbacks of the late 1970s and the 1980s, the Tampa Fire Fighters Union still could claim to have established itself as a formidable, and permanent, force in the realm of local politics. In contrast to the era before the 1960s, Tampa's fire fighters no longer felt the need to remain guarded and surreptitious in expressing their support for sympathetic officials. In addition to assisting in electoral campaigns, the TFFU also magnified its voice in local government by adeptly marshaling public opinion on its behalf. The union frequently mobilized hundreds of fire fighters, their families, and their supporters to attend the city council meetings that decided contract disputes. Furthermore, fire fighters worked to make sure that the community was aware of their services and that the local populace continued to have a positive image of the department. Fire fighters frequently traveled into the community to educate the populace on fire safety issues and participated in charity functions such as collecting for muscular dystrophy. In an era in which Americans were increasingly disenchanted with the service of government employees, fire fighters worked hard to maintain their image as one of the few occupations that enjoyed public favor.[37]

The ultimate source of the strength of the TFFU, however, lay neither in the size of the union's bank account nor in its skillful tactics, but in the profession's unique occupational culture. Fire fighters were not simply employees of a municipal department; they were members of a tightly knit community. Much of this closeness derived from the safety risks inherent in the job. Fire fighters frequently faced situations fraught with enormous danger, and even though individual acts of heroism are central to the experience and mythology of fire fighting, it also is essential that the individuals work quickly and effectively as a team. Furthermore, in the course of performing their jobs, fire fighters often dealt with heart-rending tragedy, and only other fire fighters could understand this aspect of the job. As one writer and former fire fighter explained, "It's more the things you see, the shared grief, . . . the loss of a child at a fire, the unspeakable things . . . you can't bring home and tell your family. . . . With other firemen, you don't have to graphically explain. . . . You just look into each other's eyes."[38]

Another factor contributing to the close social relations among fire fighters was the need to remain on duty for extended periods. To fire fighters, the fire station house was not simply a workplace, it was a shared living space—what one veteran referred to as a "home away from home."[39] An almost universal refrain among fire fighters is that their comrades are as much a member of their family as they are coworkers. One former fire fighter, recalling the era of the two-platoon rotation, put it simply: "We lived with these guys twenty-four hours and then we lived with our wife twenty-four hours."[40] Even with the introduction of the three-platoon system, fire fighters still spent close to one-third of their working life in the close quarters of the fire station.

Although official responsibilities took up much of a fire fighter's shift, he or she also had the time to engage in a number of practices that normally are thought of as being "domestic," such as cooking, eating, cleaning, sleeping, reading, playing games, and watching television or listening to the radio. Taking advantage of this time away from work, fire fighters had the opportunity to build strong friendships under casual circumstances and to discuss their problems and grievances. The station house also was the site of frequent pranks and jokes that lightened the mood of veterans and served as vehicles for initiating rookies into the profession. Even something as mundane as the process of cooking, eating, and cleaning up after meals helped to reinforce communal bonds by demanding a constant process of cooperation and allowing opportunity for socializing. Typically, either fire fighters would rotate the responsibility for preparing meals, or someone would volunteer to cook regularly in return for free meals or being freed from cleanup duties. In all instances, fire fighters would divide the burdens and costs of shopping and cleaning. Meals long have been a central part of the ritual life of fire fighters, and, as one veteran pointed out, the first shock for rookie fire fighters often came when faced with the need to cook for a station full of hungry critics.[41]

Another characteristic of fire fighting that helped to contribute to the sense of community was that lines of authority were not sharply drawn. The labor-management dichotomy so central to most other workplaces was less distinct in the fire service, where the department's leaders had more in common with a hoseman or plugman than they did with the civilian managers in the mayor's office. All the men and women of the Tampa Fire Department, from the greenest recruit to the fire chief, had started as a trainee and had experienced service as a combat fire fighter. Furthermore, since turnover was low and transfers almost unheard of, most of the officers had served with each other and with the men in their department for many years.[42] The nature of the living arrangements for fire fighters also tended to weaken the divisions between officers and men. Most employees in Tampa, even district fire chiefs, lived, worked, and slept together according to the platoon-shift system. In an environment where it was possible to see a station captain cleaning dishes, traditional social barriers between labor and management often were irrelevant; "There's no rank in the kitchen" has been a common refrain among fire fighters in Tampa.[43]

Fire fighters also exercised a remarkable degree of autonomy within the station house, and this sense of empowerment further provided them with an intense attachment to the workplace and their comrades. This was largely a result of the domestic nature of fire fighting life, which made it impractical to impose strict scrutiny over the activities of fire fighters. Taking advantage of this freedom, fire fighters frequently took liberties at work that would have been unimaginable in most other occupations. Given the loose regulation of the workplace, fire fighters frequently would swap shifts on an informal basis without having to go through a complicated process of administrative approval. If a fire fighter needed a place to stay temporarily because of a personal mishap or a domestic squabble, it was often the fire station that served as a refuge. Illustrating the national scope of the fire fighting community, one Tampa veteran recalled that, in past years, it was common practice to allow fire fighters visiting the area to stay at the station house, using it as an impromptu hotel.[44] On certain occasions, particularly during holidays, fire fighters even invited their families into the station house for meals and celebrations. In return, if a fire fighter needed help with a major project at his home on an off day, he often could expect to find his stationmates on his doorstep. In a world in which the boundaries between work and home were becoming ever more impermeable, fire fighters sought to ensure that those between the station and the household would remain flexible and under their control.

Underlying the occupational culture of fire fighters was the need to make sure that everyone "fit in." Proving oneself in the field, however, was only a partial step toward gaining acceptance in the community of fire fighting. Given that fire fighters often worked at the same station or even with the same crew for years at a time and had to trust each other with their lives, good working relations were not just a desirable goal, they were crucial to the safe operation of the department. There was only so much tolerance of serious personality conflicts within the fire station before the administration would have to step in and consider transferring personnel. As one former fire fighter observed, "If you did not fit into the pattern then it was best that you move to another station where you did."[45] Fire fighting allowed little room for serious dissent from the social norms and expectations of the community.[46]

Although it helped to provide a vital source of strength for fire fighters, the closely knit community that existed within fire departments served as a barrier against the intrusion of outsiders into the workforce. This was true of Tampa as well, where the fire department was a privileged enclave for native white males amid a diverse population that included African Americans and the descendants of Italian, Spanish, and Cuban immigrants. Although the Tampa Fire Department continues to be dominated by white men, the increased political power of these previously marginalized communities has dramatically changed the ethnic, racial, and gender composition of the workforce.

Until the 1940s, fire fighting in Tampa was almost exclusively the domain of native whites. In the 1940s and early 1950s, a few "Latins," the sons of Italian, Spanish, and Cuban immigrants from the cigar-making districts of Ybor City and West Tampa, managed to enter the department, but they received a cold welcome from their comrades. In the Tampa of the Jim Crow South, the arrival of Italian and Hispanic Catholic immigrants unsettled the city's Protestant, Anglo-Saxon natives and their biracial world view. Tampa's natives were even resistant to noting the multiethnic character of the city's immigrants, referring to these "nonwhite" Europeans as "Latins," a collective identity that the Italians, Spaniards, and Cubans soon appropriated for themselves. At first, native whites treated the Latins much as they did their African-American neighbors, marking off many public accommodations with "No Dagoes" signs and targeting prominent activists with vigilante violence. Despite considerable enmity, though, Tampa's native whites never were willing or able to enforce upon the Latin community the stigma of being black, particularly since many of the city's civic leaders were cigar magnates of Spanish or Cuban extraction. Consequently, by the 1940s, second-generation immigrants began making inroads into public arenas such as the fire department, although one Latin fire fighter recalled that native whites often harassed their ethnic counterparts, noting that the epithet "Cuban nigger" was common in the station houses.[47]

By the mid-1950s, however, the Anglo-American community's attitude towards Latins was changing, particularly following the victory of Nick Nuccio in the mayor's race of 1956. The election of Nuccio, the son of Sicilian immigrants, marked the growing power and assertiveness of the Latin community within Tampa, and this change was reflected in the ethnic composition of the fire department. By the late 1950s, Latin fire fighters were a common sight in Tampa, and ethnic tensions within the department rapidly declined. Latins soon became key figures within the leadership of the union, and by the 1970s government statistics reveal that Hispanic fire fighters were overrepresented among the senior ranks of the department.[48]

Like the Latins before them, African Americans faced formidable obstacles to entering the community of fire fighters. Unlike Latins, however, blacks did not have the necessary leverage within municipal government to facilitate integration, because they did not gain widespread access to the ballot until the 1960s. Furthermore, the endemic racism that was a historic legacy of segregation proved to be a much more powerful barrier for blacks than the barrier of ethnicity had been for the Latins. Consequently, it was not until 1968, four years after the passage of federal civil rights legislation, that the city finally hired its first African-American fire fighters.

In addition to facing the typical hazing that was a part of any rookie's effort to win acceptance within the firehouse, the early black fire fighters also had to endure racial epithets and ostracism by many of their white counterparts. In particular, the presence of African Americans within the intimate living arrangements of the city's fire stations violated generations-old taboos against contact between the races. The first black fire fighter recalled coworkers silently getting up and leaving when he sat down at the table to eat, and some whites even brought their own coffee mugs rather than share with an African American. Another black veteran, recalling the cold welcome, explained that he kept to himself at first, intimidated by the legendary clannishness of the nearly all-white fire department.[49]

Despite the imposing barriers of race, the communal ethic of the fire fighting community also held the potential to act as a vehicle for inclusion. By demonstrating their competence and bravery in the field, black fire fighters were able to win acceptance by many within the "family," although lowering social barriers within the station house was a more difficult and time-consuming task. One early black fire fighter noted, though, that tensions gradually subsided, once he had established himself within the station house: "Once you're in, you're in."[50] As the years progressed, racism continued to find a home within the Tampa Fire Department, but it was more likely to express itself in the form of an unguarded comment rather than in any systematic resistance to the presence of blacks.

By the mid-1970s, many individual African Americans had won grudging acceptance into the ranks of the Tampa Fire Department, but the racial composition of the department had changed very little. Although the city had ended formal discrimination, the department had an anemic hiring program that did little to encourage members of Tampa's black community to apply to become fire fighters. By 1975, seven years after integration, the department employed fewer than ten African Americans, and conditions did not improve until the following year, when the threat of a lawsuit by the federal Equal Employment Opportunity Commission forced the city to institute a more aggressive affirmative action program.[51]

Although the department accelerated the hiring of African Americans with little opposition from whites, conflicts within the union between white and black fire fighters soon developed over efforts to increase promotional opportunities for blacks. Hiring programs that favored African Americans were frequently of little concern to white fire fighters, because job candidates were not yet a part of the fire fighting community. In contrast, many white fire fighters saw affirmative action promotional policies as striking at the heart of an occupational culture that demanded that its members win the respect of their peers and advance without invoking the assistance of outsiders. As a consequence of the resultant clash between society's efforts to remedy past injustices and a workplace ethic that privileged white veterans, fire fighters nationwide soon became renowned for their opposition to affirmative action. By the late 1980s, the IAFF held the distinction of having initiated more reverse discrimination suits than any other organization in the country.[52]

The TFFU did not escape the raging controversy over affirmative action policies. In October 1981, thirteen white fire fighters filed suit in U.S. district court, challenging the city's policy of using separate promotional lists for black men, white men, and women. The union later joined the suit, arguing, in the words of its attorney, that the system led to "greater hostility among the classes" and that it provided the opportunity for increased favoritism by reducing dependence on test scores. The union also took the same position in its contract negotiations, demanding that the city eliminate any policies that undermined the principle of promoting strictly on the basis of test scores.

Although black fire fighters had learned to tolerate sporadic hostility on the part of individual fire fighters, the TFFU's intervention in the affirmative action debate undermined their faith in the union's ability faithfully to reflect the interests of the entire community. Calling themselves the "New Breed," the small but growing group of black fire fighters affiliated with the International Association of Black Professional Fire Fighters (IABPFF). They then went to the TFFU's leaders and threatened permanently to withdraw their members from the union unless it established a seat for an African American on the executive board and dropped its appeal of the affirmative action program. The union, which already had had its demands dismissed by both a judge and an arbitrator, ended up conceding to the dissidents, providing a seat on the board, and dropping further appeals of affirmative action policies. Facing a hostile legal system and a potential revolt from within, the TFFU's leaders ended their confrontational stance. As the leader of the black fire fighters later noted, "Once we made a show of unity and strength, everything else took care of itself."[53]

Although the "New Breed" and the union ended up resolving their differences, the incident was fraught with the potential for creating a fatal rift within the department. The debate over affirmative action has been a frequent and occasionally explosive source of tension between white and female and minority fire fighters throughout the nation. In nearby Miami, black fire fighters seeking to end the stranglehold of whites on promotion and hiring in the department clashed repeatedly with the union and its members. In 1988, after the local chapter of the

IABPFF publicly threatened to negotiate directly with the city and bypass the local IAFF chapter, the union retaliated by expelling all sixty-two black fire fighters.[54]

Even as racial tensions were tearing some fire departments apart, though, relations within Tampa remained comparatively civil. Possibly influenced by the fire fighting community's experience reconciling native whites and Latins, the TFFU's leadership ended up taking a conciliatory stance. Despite the severity of its grievances, the New Breed group also sought to remain cooperative and made a point of preserving the public image of unity within the union by refusing to air their demands in public. The conflict was, in many ways, representative of the delicate compromises that fire fighters throughout the country were having to make in the wake of the civil rights movement. Defending core values of the fire fighting profession that slowed the entrance of minorities, whites also sought to incorporate African Americans into the fire service. Black fire fighters, in turn, challenged traditional patterns of authority and behavior, threatening dissolution even as they sought integration, and publicly affirmed the unity and inviolability of the fire fighting community. In Tampa, as well as in the rest of the United States, the tensions produced by relations between blacks and whites clearly have illuminated the contradictory tendencies of inclusion and exclusion that are an integral part of the fire fighting profession.[55]

While the introduction of African Americans into the ranks of fire departments has been a shock to the fire fighting community, the integration of women has been even more profoundly disturbing to many in the fire service. Beginning in the United States in 1974, and in Tampa in 1978, the federal government and the courts have forced municipal fire departments to open their ranks to women. The change has been difficult because fire fighting was one of the last bastions of traditional notions of manliness in a society where work provided few outlets for men to display physical prowess and courage. Since the days of the boisterous volunteer fire companies of the nineteenth century, the occupational culture of fire fighting has celebrated physical strength, fraternal camaraderie, and the heroic quality of fire fighters' contest with that most elemental of opponents, fire.[56] Nowhere was the masculinity of the culture of fire fighting expressed more clearly than in the station house: a place filled with bawdy jokes, playful highjinks, and boastful tales of valor; where fire fighters purged themselves after "eating" smoke; and where, on occasion, they mourned the passing of comrades stricken in the line of duty. It was, in other words, a place and an occupation that, almost by definition, male fire fighters believed was off-limits to women.

One of the most basic concerns of male fire fighters about the introduction of women into the fire service has been that they are not physically strong enough, and particularly that they lack upper-body strength. A fire fighter charging into combat with full gear, including a hose, must carry over one hundred pounds of equipment. When women first began applying for jobs in fire fighting, their performance on eligibility tests almost universally was dismal, but a series of court challenges in Florida and elsewhere forced changes in these tests. Although women generally were accurate in charging that these requirements did not directly test for job-related skills, the validity of their claims did little to improve the attitudes of male fire fighters. Regardless of whether or not the challenges were technically correct, the appearance was that women were forcing changes in generations-old testing standards, altering the rules to make up for their own shortcomings. In a culture where fire fighters expect that their coworkers will be both willing and able to save an injured comrade from the perils of a fire, the conflict over changing physical requirements has helped erode the trust that binds together the members of a station house.[57]

Another controversial issue raised by the introduction of women into the fire service has been a general concern about men and women living together under the intimate conditions of the station house. The wives and girlfriends of male fire fighters typically were most vocal in raising these concerns. The exuberant masculinity of the fire fighting profession led many to assume that firemen would have difficulty controlling their sexuality in a situation where the two sexes would be sharing sleeping quarters, showers, and bathrooms. Conversely, others feared that female fire fighters would take advantage of the situation to seduce their male counterparts, since any woman willing to work in such a masculine profession must be aggressive. As a consequence of these fears, the female spouses and partners of firemen frequently were vocal critics of hiring women. In one national survey conducted in 1981, 40 percent of the female fire fighters surveyed said they had suffered harassment at the hands of firemen's wives.[58] Tampa's first female fire fighters were no stranger to this hostility, with many of them experiencing complaints and harassment from firemen's spouses when they first entered the station house. Noting the phenomenon, the union president declared that he hadn't met "one wife who said they thought women should be in the stations," and he even claimed that there were more complaints from wives than from firemen.[59]

In addition to more tangible concerns about the physical strength of women or their living arrangements in the station house, the integration of women into fire departments also has demanded that firemen examine how, if at all, their behavior should change with the introduction of women. In contrast to another male-dominated occupation such as construction work, which often is openly sexist and misogynist, fire fighters long have cultivated a public image stressing the fire service's sense of honor, propriety, and politeness, especially towards potential victims such as women. In contrast to this public persona, life in the fire station is exuberantly masculine and often vulgar, featuring obscene language, scatological humor, and even the occasional pornographic film or pinup. As one former firemen and a chronicler of the lives of fire fighters recalled, the language there could be as risqué as an "Eddie Murphy monologue . . . But put a firefighter in mixed company, and it is like he's dressed in a cassock and surplice and ready to serve Mass. A male firefighter will not curse in front of a woman."[60] The introduction of women into the fire station, however, deprived fire fighters of the ability to separate these two personas. Taught to behave one way around women and another way around their comrades, male fire fighters struggled to develop a new set of social norms for behavior around the unimaginable: a female comrade.

Fundamentally, though, the challenge posed by women was not just one of facing the need to adapt personal behavior to the realities of integrated workplaces, but also of having to ask whether this change would fatally compromise the masculine identity of all of the profession's members. Society's heroic image of the fireman exists in large part in relation to its defenseless victims, which include women. If women could assume this role, then it followed that this nobility no longer was distinctively the preserve of men. There would no longer be an elevated status for the male fire fighter. Furthermore, the very values that previously were central to the strength and vitality of the profession, its expressive, fraternal masculinity, now were being criticized as backward and sexist. Noting the quandary faced by male fire fighters, New York City's fire commissioner lamented in the early 1980s that "fire fighters are the last bastion of something that used to be called chivalry, and is now called chauvinism."[61]

In the case of Tampa, the city's female fire fighters did not face the extreme opposition that met many of their counterparts elsewhere in the nation. After a period of adjustment, most came to appreciate the job, noting with affection the sense of family that existed within the station house. Nevertheless, women still found that they were laboring in an environment where many of their comrades would not fully accept them. Despite the appearance of a new generation that has matured in the era following the women's rights movement, the male work culture of the fire department has been remarkably persistent. As one of Tampa's first female fire fighters pointed out, "The young men that are coming on now with the women, they're more accepting . . . and then once they get on the job they may not be so accepting anymore because . . . you've got the old guard that brainwash the younger ones."[62] As a consequence, women fire fighters in Tampa still are apt to feel that their presence is something that is to be tolerated rather than embraced.

The uneasiness of women in the department is exacerbated by the fact that the subtle resistance of men helps to insure that any woman who is too distinctly assertive and outspoken will abandon the profession or modify her behavior. One female fire fighter in the early 1980s explained that "if a girl comes on to a station and she's a supporter of women's lib . . . she won't be accepted . . . They could make life miserable for you."[63] Under these circumstances, women, unlike African Americans before them, have been loathe to challenge the union to protect their interests: "Women on this job aren't apt to grieve things a lot to the union . . . [because] they don't want to make waves because they don't want to get a bad name. So we're still trying to fit in after sixteen and a half years," explained one female fire fighter.[64] Once again, the persistence of the traditional occupational culture, which has been such a powerful foundation for the strength of community within fire fighting, also has served as a means to sustain the exclusivity of that community.

During the course of the twentieth century, the fire fighting community has established itself as one of the most active and best organized segments in the public employee union movement in the United States. The TFFU was the first municipal union in Tampa; the FPF, along with the teachers, were the driving force behind the success of collective bargaining legislation in Florida; and the IAFF is the oldest international union in the country for state and local workers. Excluded by the labor law reforms of the New Deal, fire fighters and other public workers continued to press their case in the political arena in the decades following World

War II, transforming the legal environment for public employees in the process. In contrast with their private-sector counterparts, however, public employees never forced the passage of comprehensive national labor legislation. Consequently, as the case of the fire fighters in Tampa demonstrates, the crucial battlegrounds in the public-sector labor movement have been, and continue to be, at the state and local level.

The importance of state labor law reforms in determining the ability of public employees to organize successfully is clearly demonstrated when comparing Florida with the rest of the South. According to government statistics, in 1972, before the passage of the PERA, Florida had one of the lowest rates of union organization in the public sector of any state in the nation. Among the eleven states of the old Confederacy, only Mississippi had lower rates of organization than Florida.[65] Fifteen years later, the Sunshine State, the only state in the region where the state constitution protected public employees' right to engage in collective bargaining, had become a novelty among its southern neighbors. Florida's percentage of organized public workers was at 38.3 percent, only 7 percent behind the national rate and nearly double the figure for the rest of the South (which was 21.2 percent). Even more striking, of the 684 collective bargaining contracts between public employees and state and local governments in effect in the South in 1987, 458, or two-thirds, were in the state of Florida.[66]

While fire fighters unquestionably benefited from changes in labor law, it is important to remember that the historical experience of fire fighters also demonstrates the ability of a community of workers to build and sustain organizations despite a hostile legal environment. Drawing upon an occupational culture that stressed the values of community and autonomy, fire fighters have achieved astonishingly high rates of participation in unions, both in Tampa, where they were usually over 95 percent, and in Florida and the United States as a whole.[67] Even in the rest of the South, which has remained comparatively hostile to the existence of public employee unions, fire fighter unions have been unusually successful. In 1987, at a time when only 21.2 percent of public workers in these states were organized, nearly one-third of the fire fighters in the region belonged to unions.[68] Fire fighting, with its self-reliant occupational culture and its unique system of organization, has proven itself well suited to creating a strong union capable of protecting its interests through political mobilization.

Despite its achievements, though, the fire fighting community and its union also have had to endure profound internal changes that have weakened the occupation's strong communal ties. Most significantly, the fire service in Tampa and the rest of the nation has become more diverse, introducing different ethnic groups, African Americans, and women into the station house. Membership in the fire fighting community no longer intersects so neatly with that part of the population that is white and male. To some degree, an increased emphasis upon building the occupation's professional identity and standards has become a surrogate for these cultural bonds. Although contemporary fire fighters no longer share a common ethnicity, race, or gender, they do share the pride in a profession that consistently has raised the levels of education, training, and technical proficiency of its members since the early part of the century. Even professionalization, however, has had its costs in the form of expanded workplace regulations that have undermined the autonomy and sense of community within the department. Systems of more frequent rotation, for example, have helped to break up the stability of social life in station houses, even as they have increased the variety of experiences in the field. Shift swapping is more highly regulated, and even something as seemingly beneficial as expanded safety regulation has lessened fire fighters' control over the types of equipment they use. Finally, the persistence of the debate over affirmative action has made it difficult for fire fighters to achieve any stable consensus over the full meaning of professional training and standards in the modern era.[69]

To a certain extent, Tampa's fire fighters also have become victims of their own success. Shorter hours have lessened the importance of work to many fire fighters; the average work week in Tampa now is a little over fifty hours—a far cry from the era of the two-platoon system, when they would spend over seventy hours a week together. Higher wages also have played a small role, providing fire fighters with the means to live far away from their stations and their coworkers. One survey in the early 1980s found that over 60 percent of Tampa's fire fighters did not even live within city limits.[70] Increasingly generous pension plans also have undermined the generational stability of the fire fighting community by prompting large numbers of the fire department's employees to depart when they qualify for retirement after twenty years. Fire fighters have even found that the contracts made possible by collective bargaining have become a means by which the city could increase its influence in the workplace, through management rights clauses. It also has allowed the city to fragment the unity of the employees of the fire department by removing senior officers from the bargaining unit, and by contracting out for maintenance and service personnel. Reflecting on the changes, a former president of the TFFU noted that "in the old days . . . we were one group, we represented everybody. But when they started some of these laws, the administration took that to say, well, this guy is an administrator, he cannot belong to your union. So, that started the division between the ranks, between the fire fighter and the administration."[71]

Despite the profound transformations in the nature of fire fighting, the occupation is still marked by some powerful continuities. For example, despite the increasing diversity of the workforce, the fire department still has a comparatively homogenous composition. In 1989, slightly more than three-quarters of the department's employees were white men, and only 3.4 percent were women. In contrast, two-thirds of Tampa's police officers were white males, and 15 percent were female.[72] As the experience of women has demonstrated, fire fighting still has a potent work culture that unites its employees while deterring the entry of outsiders.

More importantly, the basic elements of the life of the fire fighting community remain, thereby helping to sustain the social bonds of an occupational culture that has made the profession a unique force in the history of public employee unionism. Tampa's fire fighters still spend two or three days a week away from their homes, living with their stationmates. There they continue to have the opportunity for a shared social life as well as a common work experience. Fire fighters still are promoted through the ranks, and they can depend on a level of informality that mutes the divisions between officers and men in the station house. Finally, fire fighting remains a dangerous profession which demands a high level of cooperation and trust among its members.

In the midst of all the changes that have occurred in the station houses in Tampa, the union is another constant, available to draw fire fighters together and unite them in defense of their interests. With the gradual weakening of station house bonds, the union has become an important means of drawing fire fighters together to work for a common end. Particularly in light of the legal regime under which the TFFU operates, where contract arbitration is nonbinding and disputes are settled by the city council, most fire fighters realize that the union's activities are vital to the continued prosperity of the Tampa fire department's workers. As long as it can negotiate the pitfalls of internal conflicts over race, gender, and affirmative action and faithfully represent the interests of the entire community, it is likely that the union will continue to play an important function in institutionalizing the communal bonds between fire fighters.

Notes

1. Portions of this paper appeared in Mark Wilkens, "'With Pride and Valor': The Tampa Fire Fighters Union, 1943–1979," *Tampa Bay History* 15 (Spring-Summer 1993): 30–52, and are reproduced with permission.
2. See, e.g., Joshua Freeman, "Hardhats: Construction Workers, Manliness, and the 1970 Pro-War Demonstrations," *Journal of Social History* 26 (Summer 1993): 725–44; and Patricia Cooper, *Once a Cigar Maker: Men, Women, and Work Culture in American Cigar Factories, 1900–1919* (Urbana: Univ. of Illinois Press, 1987).
3. Karl H. Grismer, *Tampa: A History of the City of Tampa and the Tampa Bay Region of Florida* (St. Petersburg: St. Petersburg Printing Co., 1950), 192–93, 203; George J. Richardson, *Symbol of Action: A History of the International Association of Fire Fighters, AFL-CIO-CLC* (New York: International Association of Fire Fighters, 1974), 2; Edgar Gray, *Tampa Firefighter* (Tampa: Paleveda Printing Co., 1972), 45, 57, 62, 67, 74; *Tampa Times,* Apr. 15, 1976, Aug. 13, 1944; clipping dated Jan. 20, [1945?], from the vertical file, Florida Room, Hillsborough County Library, Tampa, Fla. (this library hereafter cited as HCL).
4. *Tampa Tribune,* Apr. 2, 1995.
5. David Ziskind, *One Thousand Strikes of Government Employees* (New York: Columbia Univ. Press, 1940), 53; Gary M Fink, ed., *Labor Unions* (Westport, Conn.: Greenwood Press, 1977), 103–4; Richardson, 4–5, 7–8.
6. Theodore Kheel, "Introduction: Background and History," *Public Employee Unions: A Study of the Crisis in Public Sector Labor Relations,* 2d ed., ed. A. Lawrence Chickering (San Francisco: Institute for Contemporary Studies, 1977), 1-13; Richard W. Ervin, "Attorney General's Opinion No. 059–164, August 20, 1959," *Biennial Report of the Attorney General, State of Florida, from January 1, 1959, through December 31, 1960* (Tallahassee: 1961), 241–47.
7. Ervin, "Attorney General's Opinion," 244–45.
8. *Constitution of the State of Florida, Adopted by the Convention of 1885 (As Amended)* (Tallahassee: 1954), 10; Ervin, "Attorney General's Opinion," 241-47; Raymond G. McGuire, "Public Employee Collective Bargaining in Florida—Past, Present and Future," *Florida State Univ. Law Review* 1 (Winter 1973): 26, 35; Gray, *Tampa Firefighter,* 3; Charles Hall, former vice-president of the International Association of Fire Fighters (IAFF), 1968–79, personal interview by Mark Wilkens at Florida International Univ., Miami, Nov. 4, 1991; notes in author's possession. Also see Sam Sinardi, Tampa fire fighter, 1957–81, and former president of the Tampa Fire Fighters Union (TFFU), and Frank Urso, Tampa fire fighter, 1952–79, and former vice-president of

the TFFU, joint interview in person by Mark Wilkens, Tampa, Fla., Nov. 23, 1991; notes in author's possession.

9. Henry S. Farber, "Evolution of Public Sector Bargaining Laws," *When Public Sector Workers Organize,* ed. Richard B. Freeman and Casey Ichniowski (Chicago: Univ. of Chicago Press, 1988), 129–30; Mark H. Maier, *City Unions: Managing Discontent in New York City* (New Brunswick, N.J.: Rutgers Univ. Press, 1987), 5, 9; Michael Goldfield, "Public Sector Union Growth and Public Policy," *Policy Studies Journal* 18 (Winter 1988–89): 404–20.
10. Robert A. Nisbit, "Public Unions and the Decline of Social Trust," in Chickering, *Public Employee Unions,* 30.
11. *Tampa Tribune,* May 22, 1969.
12. George Meany, "Union Leaders and Public Unions," in Chickering, *Public Employee Unions,* 169–70.
13. Gray, *Tampa Firefighter,* 80, 85, 130; National Commission on Fire Prevention and Control, *America Burning: The Report of the National Commission on Fire Prevention and Control* (Washington, D.C.: USGPO, 1973), xi, 53–59; Sinardi and Urso, interview by Wilkens, Nov. 23, 1991. City of Tampa, Fire Department, *Annual Report,* 1963, in Nick Nuccio Papers (2d term), Box 12-3-F-11, Tampa Archives; City of Tampa, Fire Department, *Annual Report,* 1964, in HCL; Aubrey Grant, Tampa City fire fighter, 1959–92, and deputy fire chief, audiotaped interview by Mark Wilkens, Tampa, Fla., Feb. 21, 1992; tape in author's possession.
14. Sid Ross and Herbert Kupfberg, "The Undeclared War on the Nation's Firemen," *Parade Magazine,* reprinted in *International Fire Fighter* 54 (Nov. 1971): 18–22.
15. "Annual Death and Injury Survey of the Professional Fire Fighter in the United States and Canada," *International Fire Fighter* 54 (Nov. 1971): 4–9.
16. "Report of the City Council upon the Investigation by the City Council of the Fire Dept.," Nov. 30, 1966, in Box 12-3-F-1, Tampa Archives, p. 3.
17. Ibid., 9; Gray, *Tampa Firefighter,* 96; *Tampa Times,* Aug. 5, 1975; *Tampa Tribune,* Oct. 11 and Oct. 12, 1966. The city council was arguing for what was known as a "little Hatch Act," a local counterpart to the original Hatch Act, which was passed by the U.S. Congress in 1939 to prevent federal employees from taking part in political campaigns. See "Regulation of Partisan Political Activities of Public Employees—The Hatch Act," in *Labor Relations in the Public Sector: Cases and Materials,* 3d ed., ed. Harry T. Edwards et al. (Charlottesville, Va.: Michie Co., 1985), 858–80.
18. Harry P. Cohany and Lecretia M. Dewey, "Union Membership among Government Employees," *Monthly Labor Review* 93 (July 1970): 19; *Tampa Tribune,* May 11, 1969; Sinardi and Urso, interview by Wilkens, Nov. 23, 1991; Eddie Hoffman, West Palm Beach fire fighter, 1948–70, and former president of the Florida Professional Fire Fighters (FPF), 1969–77, telephone interview by Mark Wilkens, Nov. 15, 1995; notes in author's possession.
19. Hoffman, telephone interview by Wilkens, Nov. 15, 1995.
20. William F. McHugh, "The Florida Experience in Public Employee Collective Bargaining, 1974–1978: Bellwether for the South," *Florida State Univ. Law Review* 6 (1978): 264. In 1979, 44.2 percent of Florida's public employees

were in bargaining units; by the next year, 53.3 percent were. U.S. Bureau of the Census, *Labor-Management Relations in State and Local Governments: 1979,* Series GSS No. 100 (Washington, D.C.: USGPO, 1980), 36; U.S. Bureau of the Census, *Labor-Management Relations in State and Local Governments: 1980,* Series GSS No. 102 (Washington, D.C.: USGPO, 1980), 28.

21. Contract for 1969 (agreement 4145) and for 1972 (agreement 4145D), esp. Articles 4, 15, 16, and 23, in Box 9-3-E-11, Tampa Archives; Sinardi and Urso, interview by Wilkens, Nov. 23, 1991.
22. Sinardi and Urso, interview by Wilkens, Nov. 23, 1991. For newspaper accounts of the contract disputes, see Tampa Fire Dept. clipping file, HCL.
23. *Tampa Times,* May 30, 1979.
24. The former quotation is from Paul F. Gerhart, *Political Activity by Public Employee Organizations at the Local Level: Threat or Promise?* Public Employee Relations Library No. 44 (Chicago: International Personnel Management Association, 1974), 70. The latter quotation is from Harry H. Wellington and Ralph K. Winter, Jr., *The Unions and the Cities,* Studies of Unionism in Government Series (Washington, D.C.: Brookings Institution, 1971), vii.
25. Kenneth Tomlinson, "Can Public Employee Unions Be Controlled?" *Reader's Digest* 110 (Apr. 1977): 141–42.
26. *Tampa Tribune,* Sept. 30, 1971.
27. Editorials of WTVT-TV, Channel 13, on May 22 and Apr. 11, 1977, in Personal Papers of Sam Sinardi.
28. State of Florida, House of Representatives, Committee on Labor and Industry, *Collective Bargaining in Public Employment: A Study Report of the Committee on Labor and Industry* (Tallahassee: 1970), 15.
29. Press release of Claude Kirk, Mar. 25, 1970, quoted in ibid., 61.
30. *Tampa Tribune,* Jan. 6 and Jan. 7, 1979.
31. See Kenneth Fox et al., eds., *Crisis in the Public Sector: A Reader,* (New York: Monthly Review Press, 1981).
32. Robert Kuttner, *Revolt of the Haves: Tax Rebellions and Hard Times* (New York: Simon and Schuster, 1980).
33. *Tampa Times,* June 27, 1979; *Tampa Tribune,* June 10, 1980.
34. *Tampa Times,* Mar. 20, 1980; James Covington and Debbie Lee Wavering, *The Mayors of Tampa: A Brief Administrative History* (Tampa: The Social Sciences Division of the University of Tampa, 1987), 90–91.
35. *Tampa Tribune,* Dec. 3, 1980; *Tampa Times,* Dec. 3, 1980.
36. *Tampa Tribune,* Mar. 26, 1984.
37. *Tampa Times,* Sept. 1, 1973; Sinardi and Urso, interview by Wilkens, Nov. 23, 1991; Sam Sinardi, audiotaped interview by Mark Wilkens, Mar. 25, 1992, Tampa; tape in author's possession.
38. Miriam Lee Kaprow, "Magical Work: Firefighters in New York," *Human Engineering* 50 (Spring 1991): 97–103; Dennis Smith, *Firefighters: Their Lives in Their Own Words* (New York: Doubleday, 1988), 105.
39. Grant, interview by Mark Wilkens, Feb. 21, 1992.
40. Etelvino Fernandez, Tampa fire fighter (1951–72), audiotaped interview by Mark Wilkens, Tampa, Mar. 28, 1992; tape in author's possession.
41. Ibid. For an excellent analysis of fire station life, including the role of meals,

see Robert McCarl, *The District of Columbia Fire Fighters' Project: A Case Study in Occupational Folklife* (Washington, D.C.: Smithsonian Institution Press, 1985), 38–64. For local accounts of meals in the fire station, see *Tampa Tribune,* Nov. 30, 1975, and July 11, 1978; *Tampa Times,* May 23, 1973.

42. In 1961–62, for example, the turnover rate in the Tampa Fire Dept. was 2.4 percent. The rate for the Police Dept. was 13.8 percent and for the Sanitation Dept. 18.9 percent. The rate for city employees as a whole was 13.7 percent. Results in the 1970s were much the same. City of Tampa, Civil Service Board, *Annual Report,* 1963, and *Annual Report,* 1976, both in HCL. A factor contributing to this tendency was that pension credits could not be transferred between fire departments or among the various municipal services, a practice prevalent throughout the U.S. Sinardi, interview by Wilkens, Mar. 25, 1992; National Commission on Fire Prevention and Control, *America Burning,* 37.
43. Holly Boggs, Tampa fire fighter, 1978–95, interview by Mark Wilkens, Tampa, Fla., Jan. 5, 1995; audiotape in author's possession.
44. Fernandez, interview by Wilkens, Mar. 28, 1992.
45. Sinardi, interview by Wilkens, Mar. 25, 1992.
46. These observations on station life are drawn from Fernandez, interview by Wilkens, Mar. 28, 1992; Hall, interview by Wilkens, Nov. 4, 1991; Sinardi and Urso, interview by Wilkens, Nov. 23, 1991; Grant, interview by Wilkens, Feb. 21, 1992; Eddie Hoffman, telephone interview by Wilkens, Nov. 15, 1995; Sinardi, interview by Wilkens, Mar. 25, 1992; Boggs, interview by Wilkens, Jan. 5, 1995; and Steve Anderson, Tampa fire fighter, 1972–84, telephone interview by Mark Wilkens, Jan. 5, 1994; notes in author's possession. See also Smith, *Firefighters*; and McCarl, *District of Columbia Fire Fighters.*
47. Fernandez, interview by Wilkens, Mar. 28, 1992; Gary R. Mormino and George E. Pozzetta, *The Immigrant World of Ybor City: Italians and their Latin Neighbors in Tampa, 1885–1985* (Urbana: Univ. of Illinois Press, 1987), 302–4.
48. In the late 1960s, for example, the union's president and vice-president, and the president of the Fire Fighters Service League all were of Latin descent. In 1975, the proportion of Hispanic workers in the main fire fighter job classifications (deputy fire chief, district fire chief, fire captain, driver-engineer, and fire fighter) was 11.5 percent (of 593 total). In the cases of deputy fire chief (16.7 percent), district fire chief (15.8 percent), fire captain (13.8 percent), and driver-engineer (18.4 percent), they were overrepresented. Only 5.5 percent of the 274 employees with the lowest rank, fire fighter, were Hispanic. No statistics were kept for Italian-American employees. "EEOC Detail, June 30, 1975," in Records of the Equal Employment Opportunity Office (EEOO), City of Tampa (hereafter cited as Tampa EEOO).
49. *Tampa Tribune,* June 22, 1986; Anderson, interview by Wilkens, Jan. 5, 1994.
50. *Tampa Tribune,* July 11, 1987; McCarl, *District of Columbia Fire Fighters,* 103; Fernandez, interview by Wilkens, Mar. 28, 1992; and Anderson, interview by Wilkens, Jan. 5, 1994.
51. In 1975, of 274 men holding the rank of fire fighter, only 6 were African-American, and of the 185 men who were driver-engineers, only 1 was black.

Higher ranks were the exclusive domains of whites. By 1982, 1 black had reached the rank of captain and 4 the rank of driver-engineer, and 27 were fire fighters. "EEOC Detail, June 30, 1975," and "Work Force Analysis, May 13, 1982," in Records of Tampa EEOO. See also "Conciliation Agreement" between the U.S. Equal Employment Opportunity Commission and the City of Tampa, May 20, 1976, in HCL.

52. Paul Rockwell, "Fighting the Fires of Racism," *Nation* 249 (Dec. 11, 1989), 714; Smith, *Firefighters,* 118; *Guardian* (England), Mar. 11, 1995; *New York Times,* Apr. 17, 1992.
53. *Tampa Tribune,* Apr. 29, June 2, Aug. 13, and Nov. 2, 1983; Anderson, interview by Wilkens, Jan. 5, 1994.
54. Rockwell, "Fighting the Fires of Racism," 714–18; Alfred Whitehead, "Where There's Smoke . . . ," *Nation* 250 (Mar. 5, 1990): 294.
55. *Tampa Tribune,* Nov. 6, 1983; McCarl, *District of Columbia Fire Fighters,* 106–7; Smith, *Firefighters,* 139.
56. Kaprow, "Magical Work," 99–100; Bruce Laurie, *Working People of Philadelphia, 1800–1850* (Philadelphia: Temple Univ. Press, 1980), 58–61; Mark Tebeau, "Community, Capital, and the Built Environment in the 19th Century," 3–20, paper presented at the 8th Symposium of the George Meany Memorial Archives, Silver Spring, Md., Feb. 11–12, 1996. Tebeau's paper is drawn from his dissertation-in-progress at Carnegie-Mellon Univ. on fire fighting, fire protection, and fire insurance in St. Louis and Philadelphia, 1850–1950.
57. *Tampa Times,* Apr. 23, 1981.
58. Terese Floren, "Women Fire Fighters Speak," pt. 2, *Fire Command* (Jan. 1981): 22.
59. *Tampa Times,* Apr. 23, 1981.
60. Smith, *Firefighters,* 102; Joshua Freeman, "Hardhats," 730.
61. Karen Stabiner, "The Storm over Women Firefighters," *New York Times Magazine,* Sept. 26, 1982, p. 105.
62. Boggs, interview by Wilkens, Jan. 5, 1995.
63. *Tampa Times,* Apr. 23, 1981.
64. Boggs, interview by Wilkens, Jan. 5, 1995.
65. All figures are for full-time public employees. U.S. Bureau of the Census, *1972 Census of Governments: Public Employment: Management-Labor Relations in State and Local Government,* vol. 3, no. 3 (Washington, D.C.: USGPO, 1974). For purposes of this paper, I am defining the South as Alabama, Arkansas, Florida, Georgia, Louisiana, Mississippi, North Carolina, South Carolina, Tennessee, Texas, and Virginia.
66. U.S. Bureau of the Census, *1987 Census of Governments: Public Employment: Management-Labor Relations in State and Local Government,* vol. 3, no. 3 (Washington, D.C.: USGPO, 1991).
67. No precise figure is available for the TFFU, but interviewees consistently provided this approximate figure. In 1987, the rate of unionization of fire fighters in Florida was 62.3 percent, while in the U.S. as a whole it was 64.9 percent. The overall rate of unionization for public employees was 45.3 percent in the U.S. and 38.3 percent in Florida. Ibid.

68. Ibid. These figures are for the South, excluding Florida.
69. Kaprow, in "Magical Work," 100–101, also sees an increasing rationalization and regulation of fire fighting in New York City, which she claims suggests an increasing "proletarianization" of the occupation.
70. *Tampa Tribune,* Aug. 25, 1983.
71. Sinardi, interview by Wilkens, Mar. 25, 1992.
72. "City of Tampa: Job Group Analysis, Jan. 3, 1989," in Records of Tampa EEOO.

The Florida Teacher Walkout in the Political Transition of 1968

James Sullivan

On the Monday morning of February 19, 1968, almost half of Florida's public school teachers did not show up for work, leaving some 750,000 pupils without instructors and closing about one-third of the state's schools. Over 27,000 elementary and secondary school teachers had "walked out." They demanded that Gov. Claude Kirk convene a special session of the Florida Legislature to increase the education budget. Three weeks later, the first statewide teachers' strike in the United States and the largest labor action in Florida history collapsed in defeat.[1]

The outcome of the Florida teacher walkout depended largely on changes in the national political culture.[2] By 1968, four years of racial violence in U.S. cities, coupled with the perception of failure in Vietnam, had derailed popular support for the ambitious initiatives of Democratic presidents John Kennedy and Lyndon Johnson. During the 1968 presidential campaign, Republican Richard Nixon sensed this shift in public sentiment and presented himself as a conservative champion of traditional values. In November of that year, he won the election. A disillusioned majority rejected the liberal ideals embodied in the administrations of Kennedy and Johnson; American voters had become unwilling to "pay any price" and "bear any burden" in an uncertain quest for a better world. They responded instead to a Republican candidate who stressed a return to the time-tested truths of American conservatism: hard work, family, government by law, and peace through strength.

In the first months of 1968, leaders in the Florida Education Association (FEA) failed to understand this shift in political culture and called a strike premised upon the assumptions and ideals of a disintegrating liberal consensus. FEA teachers justified their walkout with high-minded appeals to professional responsibility and calls for sacrifices on behalf of the "dream of quality education."[3] But politicians, school administrators, and others who opposed the FEA mobilized an emerging conservative majority disillusioned with the promises of reform. Striking teachers, they argued, were disregarding their duties, deserting their pupils, and attempting to coerce the government. Thus, FEA opponents equated the walkout with problems troubling the nation at large, while styling themselves as the guardians of traditional American values. Florida's politicians and school administrators thereby invited the public to act on national frustrations associated with domestic unrest and foreign failure by rallying against their local FEA and crushing the teacher walkout.

As the changing political culture of 1968 played a key role in determining the course of the strike, the strike also reveals something of the changing political culture. Though emphases vary, historians agree that 1968 represented a political "turning point." Interpretations of that turn, however, have focused on the national level.[4] Although useful as overviews, these works necessarily gloss over the particulars of how such a political transition took place and was manifested in the daily lives of Americans. By focusing on a politically charged conflict in a single state in the first quarter of 1968, this study seeks a more detailed understanding of the broader shift in political culture. How did the war in Vietnam and the riots in American cities affect political events in the U.S. at the state and local levels? In what particular ways did Americans perceive, act in, and thereby constitute the national political transition of 1968?

• • •

A national tide of reform in the organization of teachers cleared the way for the walkout in Florida. Before the 1960s, the FEA had been a junior partner of the state superintendent's office. School administrators led the association and encouraged a prim professionalism among teachers, who joined as a matter of course.[5] But throughout the 1950s, teachers and other public employees had grown increasingly restless with their low-wage status in an expanding economy. Union membership among public employees edged upward, and nervous legislators sought ways of containing public workers' growing dissatisfaction. Thus, in 1959, Wisconsin enacted the first collective-bargaining law for public employees, and in 1962 President Kennedy issued Executive Order 10988 which facilitated collective bargaining among federal employees.

Over the next decade, public employee strikes, once practically unheard of, became regular features of the American scene. The 1968 garbage strikes in St. Petersburg and Memphis linked the concerns of low-wage African-American workers with civil rights issues. In the spring of 1969, hospital workers in Charleston, South Carolina, challenged paternalistic and repressive public authorities in another walkout that highlighted the plight of low-wage minority workers. A massive wildcat strike of federal postal workers in the summer of 1970 further attested to public worker militancy.[6]

Teachers were major participants in this ferment. In 1961, a strike led by the American Federation of Teachers established collective bargaining for New York City's teachers. During the following decade, in the FEA and other teacher organizations across the nation, reform-minded educators transformed professional associations into more unionlike organizations capable of bargaining for better salaries and working conditions. By the early 1970s, teacher strikes had become regular features of the fall season. Indeed, some of these, such as the 1968 Ocean Hill–Brownsville dispute in New York City, were bitter and complex disputes. The surge in public-employee unionism knew no regional boundaries, as fire fighters, police, sanitation workers, and teachers south of the Mason-Dixon Line joined their counterparts elsewhere in demanding union recognition as well as improved wages, benefits, and personnel policies.[7]

In Florida, FEA Executive Director Phil Constans symbolized the rising aspirations of teachers. The son of educators and a former teacher himself, Constans earned a doctorate in education before going to work for the FEA. In 1967, Constans, a tall, thin man of forty years, became the association's executive director. His easygoing southern accent belied his earnest dedication to reform. Energetic and convinced of the rightness of his cause, Constans spoke "the language of teachers," according to one of his close associates, and scorned the hat-in-hand etiquette his FEA predecessors had adopted around the state's political leadership.[8]

Meanwhile, Floridians elected Claude Kirk governor of Florida, the first Republican to win that office in ninety-four years. A self-made millionaire in the insurance business and a natural at what he called "the politics of confrontation," Kirk also entered office in 1967. He was forty-two years old and a large, roughly handsome man whose truculent wit made good press, while his unbothered boosterism appealed to Florida's growth industries. Throughout his flamboyant and aggressive campaign, Kirk promised to "make Florida first in education" while opposing any tax increase. Kirk favored administrative restructuring in education and referred to teachers as "hired help."[9]

In the four years before the strike, conditions in Florida's schools had deteriorated sharply. In 1964, the Southern Association of Colleges and Secondary Schools withdrew accreditation from Jacksonville's high schools because these schools could not meet minimum standards.[10] In 1965, a new state statute rescheduled Florida's gubernatorial elections and thereby disrupted a pattern of raising taxes in one legislative session and "holding the line" in the next; campaign-minded politicians postponed unpopular tax increases, despite the strain on public services.[11] In 1966, a National Education Association study concluded that Florida's "political atmosphere" was detrimental to its public school system.[12] By 1967, Florida ranked tenth in the nation in personal income per capita, but thirty-fifth in per-capita expenditures for public schools, thirty-seventh in expenditures per pupil, and forty-eighth in teacher-pupil ratio.[13] That fall, in St. Petersburg the school board informed parents that bus service would be curtailed because of "inadequate allotment of school funds from the state."[14] The board also limited enrollment for kindergarten. At several schools parents camped in line all night to register their children, and by 8:30 the next morning, quotas were filled.[15] Around the state, outdated textbooks were common, and churches volunteered space for classrooms as swelling student populations overwhelmed existing facilities.[16]

These same years were traumatic for most of the nation. Violent white resistance to the civil rights movement marked the early sixties, and in 1964 rioting in Harlem and other urban areas prefaced four years of black rebellion in cities such as Los Angeles, Chicago, Detroit, Newark, Atlanta, and Tampa. In 1967 alone, eighty-three people died in urban riots. According to polls at the end of that year, a majority of Americans felt that "crime and lawlessness" was the most important problem facing the nation. Then, on January 30, 1968, Vietcong forces launched a wave of surprise attacks against dozens of U.S. installations and South Vietnamese cities. Though ultimately a military failure for the Vietcong, the Tet offensive illuminated the murderous failure of U.S. policy in the region and dealt a psychological blow to Americans, the majority of whom had supported the war. In the first months of 1968, polls showed "Vietnam" replacing "crime and lawlessness" as the most important problem in America.[17]

On January 29, just as the Tet offensive began, Governor Kirk convened a special session of the Florida legislature with a speech calling upon lawmakers to raise taxes, to increase the budget for education, to restructure educational administration, and to submit these changes to the public in a single referendum.[18] When the special session adjourned on Friday, February 16, the bill presented to the governor envisaged financing education with new sales taxes but ignored Kirk's demand for administrative restructuring and for a referendum.[19] Kirk opposed the new legislation, and the FEA attacked the bill for raising revenues in the name of schoolchildren, when only part of the new funds would go to education. The bill raised approximately $350,000,000 in new taxes, yet only about $200,000,000 of this money was slated for education. The rest of the money relieved property taxes and supported other services. All in all, teachers got about one-half of the funding they had asked for, and on Saturday, the FEA announced that a statewide walkout was on for the following Monday.[20] Because a "strike" by public employees was illegal in the state of Florida, FEA teachers would simply "resign" *en masse*.

Over the weekend, Kirk marshaled opposition to the strike in terms resonant with the hopes and fears of a beleaguered American majority. In a Saturday "Open Letter," Kirk argued that it would be "our children" who suffered in the event of a walkout and pleaded with FEA teachers to "put yourselves in the place of the parents of Florida students. . . . Please don't desert your children."[21] By equating the professional obligations of an educator with the boundless responsibilities of a parent and implying that teachers who left the classroom were no better than mothers who deserted their children, Kirk simultaneously defined the contest over education in terms inimical to the FEA and cast himself as the patient champion of traditional family values. As social commentators focused attention on the decay of the family among the urban poor, the thought of maternal desertion raised fears associated with abandoned children and the integrity of society. On Sunday, Kirk addressed these fears again, calling for "a mother's march of volunteers" to "man" the schools during the strike. Ignoring the specifics of the situation, Kirk spoke instead to "the crisis," concluding that "the time is now, the crisis is at hand, the people of Florida can be counted on to meet the crisis."[22] In the context of escalating domestic unrest and the Tet offensive, many in the U.S. felt the sense of crisis Kirk invoked, and the family, epitomized in traditional motherhood, emerged as a rhetorical rallying point.[23]

Constans, on the other hand, mistakenly assumed that the justice of the FEA walkout was self-evident and failed to frame the issues to the teachers' advantage. He declared that "raising taxes in the name of the schools and not having the money get to the schools is inadequate—just prima facie inadequate" and believed that "parents are going to be just as furious as the teachers" when they learn of the legislative "fraud." In response to the question "What does the FEA want?" Constans wandered through a medley of education issues: professional negotiations, professional standards, tenure procedures, retirement benefits, and adequate funding, noting that "we, of a purpose, haven't gotten locked into any particular amount of money."[24] Concerned that a simple emphasis on finances would seem selfish, Constans listed a confusing array of concerns but offered no popular agenda. Although the FEA walkout most directly affected the general public, immediately posing a problem of childcare for more than a million parents, Constans did not ask the people of Florida to do, or not do, anything in particular. Only those already familiar with the conflict knew that the central demand of the strike was another special legislative session. Meanwhile, millions of Floridians did not understand why the FEA had disrupted their lives.[25]

In the absence of clear demands or workable solutions, FEA teachers ennobled their efforts with characterizations of personal sacrifice for high ideals, a theme that had moved many Americans to support social reform in the 1960s. When the walkout began, FEA teachers invoked rhetoric that echoed John Kennedy's inaugural address. A teacher in Miami, for example, explained that teachers were "willing to sacrifice our homes, our professional careers, our families' security, our very livelihood" to realize "quality education."[26] And FEA President Dexter Hagman promised that "the teachers . . . are more determined than ever to achieve improvements in education in Florida—whatever the cost or personal sacrifice."[27] By expounding upon the sacrifices made by striking teachers, the FEA offered an innovative interpretation of a traditional theme. Teachers had always sacrificed, but usually a teacher's sacrifice meant enduring difficult working conditions and putting in extra hours in order that students might truly learn. The FEA extended this logic, arguing that teachers had sacrificed themselves precisely to secure improvements in education for the students. Teachers, they tried to explain, had quit teaching in order to improve education. Thus, the strike was consistent with "the highest ideal of professional service."[28]

But in a changing political culture, the theme of personal sacrifice worked against the FEA in at least three ways. First of all, the language of sacrifice and "service" hindered FEA teachers in terms of gender. Secondly, such language hurt the striking teachers precisely because they were teachers. Finally, discussions of sacrifice proved especially volatile because of the ongoing war in Vietnam. At another time, the striking teachers' rhetoric of sacrifice may well have met with the public acceptance the FEA expected, but in early 1968, the many meanings inherent in this rhetoric proved unstable and open to reinterpretation by FEA detractors.

Invoking a theme of personal sacrifice and professional service proved problematic for striking teachers, in that teaching is a feminized occupation, both in the sense that elementary and secondary school teachers are predominantly female and in the sense that school teaching commonly is associated with traits and values understood as feminine. In 1968, women comprised an overwhelming majority of teachers in Florida and a majority of those who walked out.[29] When FEA teachers emphasized their personal sacrifices, they traded on a traditional ideal of feminine morality in order to stir the public conscience. In other words, when striking teachers framed their demands in terms of their sacrifices, they claimed their entitlement as teachers because they had fulfilled their duties as women. Strikers in a masculinized occupation—sanitation workers, for instance—could not expect such a posture to be effective.

But playing a feminine role also restricted the striking teachers, because to play the role credibly they had to maintain the deferential comportment expected of women. Here Florida's striking teachers encountered a problem familiar in all the feminized occupations in which practitioners sought professional status. In male-dominated professions, an ethos of service (principled, disinterested, and public) signals autonomy, the *sine qua non* of professionalism; but in feminized occupations that same ethos of service easily devolves into the too-familiar tradition of feminine subservience, the antithesis of autonomy.[30] For FEA teachers, therefore, the gendered meanings inherent in the language of personal sacrifice and professional service ultimately subverted, rather than legitimized, their protest.

For example, on Monday, February 19, when Cornelia Hanna, president of the Alachua County Teachers Association, delivered a seven-pound bundle of resignations to the school board, she read a prepared statement explaining why teachers had walked out. "We have cried for help, have been humble, quiet, polite, and served unselfishly under the misguided concept of dedication," she explained. "The truth is we have let the children down and now we face our ultimate responsibility—we resign in hopes that our children may profit from our loss. Now, we are truly dedicated, though, paradoxically, unemployed."[31] Rejecting the traditional role of a dedicated teacher as "misguided," Hanna nevertheless explained a teacher's "ultimate responsibility" as a willingness to sacrifice for "our children." Presumably the old concept of dedication was "misguided" because the legislature ignored long-suffering teachers when they "cried for help," but Hanna's nine-paragraph statement never mentioned the legislature. Indeed, in Hanna's text, it was not the legislature that had offended but rather "we," the teachers, who had "let the children down."[32] Other FEA leaders remained deferential as well, insisting upon a "nonvindictive approach" and even praising hostile school administrators for their professional performance during such difficult times.[33] Such feminine deference underscored the nobility of the teachers' sacrifice but obscured the legitimacy of the teachers' grievance. Yet, as the war and domestic unrest generated rising concern over social order, FEA teachers proved unwilling to shed traditional gender roles.

Secondly, the language of sacrifice worked against striking teachers because they were teachers. In the American ideal (at least), the "symbol of the schoolhouse" guarantees the equality of opportunity that legitimates the social order.[34] When FEA teachers walked out of their classrooms, they stepped out of their traditional roles and politicized the sphere of education; they not only stayed away from work, they desecrated an American icon. Floridians anxious to reaffirm the social ideal reasserted the traditional meaning of a teacher's sacrifice and reassigned teachers to the classroom "where they belong."[35] A postman in Miami, for example, opposed the walkout, arguing that teaching meant "accepting a job that requires a certain amount of dedication and sacrifice."[36] A school board member in Alachua County explained that understaffed schools would not be closed, because such action would affect those "good and dedicated" teachers who had stayed in the classroom.[37] A high school student in Tallahassee argued that if teachers "really cared about the students they would be in the classrooms teaching instead of trying to get more money."[38] Such shrill defenses of the conventional role of a teacher reflected both a cherished idealization of American education and the widespread fear that such traditional ideals were at risk.

Finally, invocations of sacrifice carried a particularly serious weight because of the war in Vietnam. When the walkout began, more than eighteen thousand U.S. soldiers already had died in Southeast Asia, and the U.S. had just experienced its bloodiest week of the war. For many, the young Americans who were dying in Southeast Asia were the ones making the "ultimate" sacrifice, while the teachers' rhetoric seemed selfish and unpatriotic.[39] In a letter printed in the *Tampa Tribune* under the headline "Our Servicemen in Vietnam Are Paid Less Than Teachers," a "mother of three boys" observed: "I have not heard any of the teachers complaining that our servicemen aren't paid enough. I wonder if they realize what these boys are giving up so they can earn what they now make." She suggested that "maybe those able-bodied men teachers that have turned their backs on our school children would be willing to trade places with our sons and husbands in Vietnam."[40] Another letter asked, "What would become of our country if all the boys in the service should strike? I am sure they do not have the wages or working conditions that the teachers have here at home." This writer lamented that "my grandson is in Vietnam and it makes me sick at heart to see the kind of people he is giving his life for."[41] In the same issue, the *Tribune* reported that "Kirk said he hoped the Selective Service board would look into the draft status of teachers who make the final decision to quit their jobs."[42] By February 1968, a once-generous notion of sacrifice had become a bitter question of who would give up what and for whom.

The war itself provided a potent metaphor for FEA critics intent on associating the FEA with problems troubling the nation at large. On February 8, during the special legislative session, the *Tallahassee Democrat* and newspapers around the nation ran photographs of the police chief of Saigon holding a gun to the head of a suspected Vietcong soldier and then summarily executing his prisoner. A few pages away, a *Democrat* editorial fumed that "some legislators find it difficult to admit the real culprit is the FEA, which put a gun to the head of the commission and refused to wait for any thorough, time consuming study."[43] Governor Kirk made the analogy explicit. When criticized for being out of the state when the walkout began, he asked, "Does President Johnson have to be in Vietnam to handle the situation in Vietnam?"[44]

Characterizations of striking teachers as deserting soldiers appeared regularly. The *Tampa Tribune* headlined the strike as a "battle," beginning a front-page item with the announcement that "Florida teachers will be asked to desert their classrooms Monday by the FEA."[45] The following day, the *Tribune* began its lead story: "School administrators in most Florida counties hoped yesterday they could muster enough of their own kind of minute-men to stand off the expected rebellion tomorrow of teachers."[46] A cartoon appearing in the *Tallahassee Democrat* depicted a man facing himself in the mirror and preparing to shave. He represented "G.I.'s who desert their country in time of trouble" under a heading declaring that "it must be a difficult time of day." Immediately below this illustration, the *Democrat* arranged a series of letters about the walkout under the headline "Striking Teachers Showing True Colors." One letter from a high school student appeared under the heading "Teachers, please don't desert us."[47] That day's paper contained no news of military desertion or any reference to disloyal soldiers or even draft dodgers. Instead, the cartoon appeared right above text that criticized FEA teachers for deserting their classrooms. By literally bringing together these disparate topics, the editors elided the differences between the war in Vietnam and the struggle in Florida. Editorials referring to FEA teachers as "AWOL" rendered the connection explicit.[48]

By depicting the walkout in imagery borrowed from the struggle in Vietnam, FEA opponents invited Floridians to act upon frustrations associated with the war by opposing the strike. For example, on the third day of the walkout, the *Tampa Tribune* headline read "All But 5 Hillsborough Schools Reopen Today." The middle part of the front page covered developments in Vietnam under the headline "Escalation of U.S. War Effort Appears Certain," and immediately under this article, across the bottom of the front page, appeared an "Editorial: You Can Fight in This Battle."[49] The piece began by citing several concerns including "proper education" and "the spreading evidence of lawlessness in this country" and then asked "have you often asked yourself in frustration: What can I do about the situation?" The editors asserted that "you have the opportunity now to do something; to become an active soldier in a battle whose outcome can affect the whole pattern of life in your community, state, and nation." The walkout presented this opportunity: "You can enlist in the fight to keep open the public schools of Florida." And the *Tribune* affirmed that "this is a battle which must not be lost. It WILL NOT be lost if the citizens who have a care for . . . the future of this nation, respond to the call." Calling upon Floridians to "volunteer" and to "encourage former teachers to enlist," the *Tribune* editors reminded that "in a time of war, men and women on the home front readily volunteer to roll bandages or serve as air raid wardens. Well, this is a war—a war of wills." The editorial concluded by intoning that "the battlefront runs by your door."[50]

Such analogies brought the war home. In the grim dawn of Tet, polls reported that 49 percent of Americans had begun to believe that U.S. involvement in Vietnam was a "mistake."[51] On the evening of February 27, in a special one-hour CBS television report from Vietnam, Walter Cronkite described the situation as a "quagmire."[52] Disillusionment with the claims of the Johnson administration deepened. In Florida, concerned citizens could at least symbolically resolve their anxieties about the war by winning the "fight" to keep the schools open. In Tampa and across the state, volunteers did, in fact, keep the state's school system running. When FEA opponents framed the efforts of these volunteers in a military analogy, they spoke to the growing frustration many Americans felt concerning the war.

In early 1968, especially in the South, the perception of failure in Vietnam only added to the tensions brought to the fore by the civil rights movement. As Martin Luther King, Jr., planned for a "Poor People's March on Washington," many embittered whites worried that King's movement had merely opened the way for ungrateful, militant blacks to advance themselves at the expense of the white middle class. For many whites, in both North and South, four summers of escalating urban riots had eroded all tolerance for demanding minorities, racial or otherwise.

True, the FEA walkout was related only tangentially to the civil rights movement. In 1966, black and white teachers had merged their hitherto separate organizations, hoping that their professional consolidation would ease the tardy integration of Florida's schools, and each weekday during the walkout, striking teachers convened in twenty-six FEA district meetings, which for many teachers were the first integrated public gatherings they had ever attended. The FEA leadership, however, remained almost exclusively white and did not draw attention to similarities between the teachers' movement and the civil rights movement.[53]

Nevertheless, FEA opponents maligned the walkout by associating it with the controversy surrounding the struggle for racial justice. As the walkout began, the *Miami Herald* predicted that Kirk would "play the strike-breaking role," explaining that, "in a nation plagued with strikes and demonstrations, such a victory would label him a politician who will stand up to all types of protesters, be they labor unions or civil rights groups."[54] Another article suggested that the FEA was employing "many of the same principles that worked so well in the early, undiluted days of the American civil rights movement" and explained that, "just as the early civil rights leaders found rationalizations to justify the breaking of laws," so FEA teachers "feel their walkout this week adheres to a higher morality and ethic."[55] Likewise, the *Gainesville Sun* described popular reaction to the walkout as "reminiscent of the anguish of 1964 when the Civil Rights Act was passed. There was a feeling that it would all go away in due time."[56]

Other critics of the FEA were less circumspect. A disgruntled citizen in Tallahassee agreed that the walkout "reminds me of the civil rights movement" and complained that "beggars are never satisfied."[57] At least one Floridian worried that, "with those other recent demonstrations and marches and riots, I'm afraid [the walkout] will accomplish about the same results," while one pundit wanted to "kick the FEA and all of its followers out of the state. Let them join with the Rap Browns and Stokely Carmichaels where they belong."[58] The Panhandle community of Panama City witnessed an enactment of the comparison. There the president of the Bay County Classroom Teachers Association awoke to find a six-foot wooden cross burning in his front yard.[59] Despite their studied silence on the issue, FEA teachers could not avoid the question of race, and among the many condemnations of the strike could be heard the voice of white backlash against the civil rights movement.

When not specifically tied to issues of race, criticism of the strike frequently related the FEA to the general proliferation of protest and the breakdown of law. In a meeting of the Alachua County school board, a Gainesville citizen argued that striking teachers "have violated the law" and that "the whole country is losing law and order. You can't yield to pressure by violators of the law who are trying to close the schools."[60] A letter in the *Gainesville Sun* opposed the walkout in the name of "democracy" and "all this great country stands for." Criticizing the FEA for employing "methods which are uncommon to us and our representative type of government," this writer warned his "citizen friends" to guard "the God-given right to govern yourself."[61] A radio commentator in Tallahassee complained that education "is not going to be served by teacher-inspired anarchy."[62] The editors of the *Tampa Tribune* agreed: "The battle that is now joined pits the supporters of government-by-law against the disciples of government-by-intimidation. In this battle, every open school represents a victory for law, every closed school a defeat."[63] Thus, in a political culture preoccupied with domestic unrest, the FEA's public protest evoked stern remonstrations.

Though Constans had predicted that an overwhelming majority of schools would shut down, only twenty-two of Florida's sixty-seven counties closed all schools, and four more counties closed a portion of their schools. On Monday, the first day of the walkout, the State Board of Education claimed that only 556,155 pupils out of a total of 1,300,000 were not in their classrooms.[64] Teachers had not walked out in the numbers the FEA had hoped for, but on Tuesday reports from several urban counties indicated a slight increase in the number of regular teachers off the job.[65] On Wednesday, challenges to the FEA multiplied across the state. House Speaker Ralph Turlington accused the FEA of deliberately misleading teachers with grossly inaccurate dollar figures, and the State Department of Education reported a slight weakening in the ranks of striking teachers statewide; 533 more teachers were at work than on Monday.[66] Though this was a decline of only about 2 percent, it was the beginning of a steady erosion in the FEA's position, now exacerbated by a spate of injunctions. Late Tuesday, a circuit judge ordered all Lee County teachers back to work, and on Wednesday school boards in several counties filed for similar injunctions. The school board in Miami announced that any teachers not back at work by the end of the month would face legal action.[67]

By Wednesday, February 21, the Florida teacher walkout itself had become a national issue. With the 1968 presidential election only nine months away, Republican presidential hopeful Richard Nixon worried that Alabama Gov. George Wallace's third-party campaign would draw conservative votes away from the Nixon ticket, especially in the South. When Kirk turned a colorful underdog candidacy into a southern Republican gubernatorial win, the party enlisted him to stump for Nixon against Wallace. Kirk stood squarely behind the party, and, amid speculation that Nixon would ask him to be his running mate, Kirk crisscrossed the nation, claiming that a vote for Wallace was as good as a vote for the Democrats. But amid Kirk's whirlwind tour, a bunch of Florida teachers was ruining his image—an image the Florida Development Commission paid publicist William Safire ninety thousand dollars a year to manage.[68] On Wednesday, Kirk assured the NBC evening news that there would be no special session of the legislature, as the FEA demanded.[69] A keen student of political culture, Kirk decided to "play the strike-breaking role," as the *Miami Herald* had suggested, and on Wednesday night he flew to Miami to make his position clear to a mass meeting of FEA teachers.[70]

The stage of Miami Marine Stadium actually was a floating platform on Biscayne Bay. On Wednesday night, February 19, a cold wind blew off the water and up through the amphitheater, as some six thousand teachers assembled for the encounter with the governor. Predicting that the governor would stage a fashionably late, dramatic entrance via helicopter, the FEA arranged a comparably impressive entrance for their representatives. When Kirk arrived as anticipated, colleagues quickly shushed the few teachers who clapped for him, but the uncomfortable quiet ended in a deafening cheer when Dade County Teacher Association President Janet Dean and Executive Secretary Pat Tornillo stepped directly onto the stage from a hydrofoil.[71]

From the beginning, the meeting went poorly. Kirk opened by suggesting, "Let's have a good boo for the governor and get it out of your systems," but the crowd of thousands sat in icy silence.

"How about a little hiss then?" Kirk rebounded.

"How about getting down to business!" someone shouted, and the stadium erupted in applause.[72]

Clearly not among friends, Kirk delivered a rambling three-hour speech that choked any hopes for a dialogue. Brooking only occasional interruptions from the audience, Kirk told the crowd that he would not recall the legislature and that teachers should return to their classrooms immediately. Tornillo did manage to read the most succinct statement of the FEA position on record; in three sentences, he explained to Kirk the conditions under which teachers would return to work, but by then it was too late.[73] Kirk had branded the walkout an illegal strike and attacked any efforts to involve the FEA in negotiating a settlement. After Wednesday, the third day of the strike, FEA teachers were fighting a losing battle.[74]

Multiple complications further weakened the FEA's position. On Friday, police in Coral Gables arrested sixteen FEA teachers for distributing handbills.[75] On the same day, Dr. B. Frank Brown, superintendent in Brevard County, formally accepted his teachers' resignations and immediately notified the draft board of all male teachers who no longer had jobs.[76] At the end of the first week of the walkout, legal attacks on the FEA multiplied, and a steady erosion of confidence had reduced the number of teachers off the job by some 7 percent, to 23,824.[77] On Monday, February 26, an FEA press release from Tallahassee reflected the worsening situation. First among five conditions for a settlement was the demand that every teacher be reinstated without reprisal. The call for another special legislative session had dropped to number four.[78]

In the second week of the walkout, Kirk made good on his promise to block any efforts at involving the FEA in negotiations. The five-member State Board of Education, composed of Governor Kirk, Attorney General Earl Faircloth, Superintendent Floyd Christian, Secretary of State Tom Adams, and State Treasurer Broward Williams, exercised the highest authority over education in Florida. On Wednesday evening, February 28, in a closed meeting, the four Democratic board members (everyone except Kirk) met with Constans and National Education Association President Braulio Alonso and worked out a deal: the board would require county school boards to adopt formal procedures for professional negotiations with teacher representatives, and the FEA would call off the walkout. The proposed resolution also called for the establishment of a professional standards board and the release of $10,200,000 in education funds previously withheld because of a budget deficit. Confident that his Democratic majority would overrule Kirk's objections, Superintendent Christian called a meeting of the board for six o'clock that evening, and the FEA summoned representatives from every county to Tallahassee for a vote on the settlement. That evening, however, Kirk found out about the meeting between the Democrats and the FEA, the negotiated settlement, and the impending board meeting. He immediately called Christian into his office, and a heated exchange audible to reporters waiting outside took place. Upon emerging, Christian postponed the board meeting until Friday.[79]

In a press conference the following morning, Kirk threw down the gauntlet. Before an audience of journalists from around the nation, he positioned himself as the bold champion of an embattled democratic tradition, responding to the deeply felt frustrations of an American majority angered by the degradation of values they cherished. The governor explained that because the "striking teacher under FEA control demands a veto," he would allow the education bill served up by the legislature to become law without his signature on March 7, still one week away. "This action thwarts the efforts of the striking teachers," he explained. Kirk held that "the issues that are at stake in Florida today are important and they are basic" and asserted that the response of his administration to the strike "is important not only to our future in Florida, but also to the future of our national life in America, which up to now has been built on the observance of the law by all people."[80] Kirk blasted the Democrats for their "secret negotiations," an action which "condones law breaking," and warned that "there can be no compromise with illegal action."[81] Kirk finished with an attack on the FEA: "There is nothing for any coercive or militant group to negotiate with the state."[82]

Before his press conference, Kirk had contacted Safire, his image consultant, who reportedly recommended that Kirk take a hard line against the FEA, basing his advice on the political fallout from the recent strike by sanitation workers in New York City. There, on February 8, Mayor John Lindsay had taken a tough stand against striking sanitation workers, even calling for the National Guard to break the strike, but New York Gov. Nelson Rockefeller had refused Lindsay's plea and instead reached a settlement with the union. Most observers felt that Lindsay emerged from the conflict as a man ready to stand up for the everyday citizen against the demands of militant groups, whereas Rockefeller's negotiated settlement appeared a dangerous surrender to the tactics of public coercion.[83] Determined to avoid Rockefeller's error, Kirk moved against the FEA by condemning any "secret negotiations," a familiar phrase associated with ignoble compromises overseas, and carefully tailored his image to match the national mood.[84]

On Thursday morning, the governor's calculated statements challenged the Democrats on the Board of Education to follow through with their negotiated settlement, but later that afternoon each member of the board received a letter prompting reconsideration. The two-page letter from John C. Lee, executive vice president of the Associated Industries of Florida (AIF), included a list of that organization's officers and the corporations which these men represented. A veritable "who's who" of major industry in Florida, the list included names from the First National Bank, General Electric, Honeywell, Boeing, Martin Marietta, Standard Oil, National Airlines, Pan American Airways, United States Sugar, Southern Bell, Dupont, Occidental of Florida, St. Joe Paper, Florida Power Corporation, and Florida Steel Corporation, among others.[85]

The AIF letter urged each board member immediately to accept all resignations of striking teachers. The AIF claimed that "the magic word 'Florida' in job placement advertisements" would solve potential recruiting problems and brushed aside objections to having substitute teachers finish the current school year. "In the interest of fairness . . . and the future of representative government," the AIF maintained, "it is far better to endure pain briefly now while effecting a cure, than to allow a cancerous growth to erode our basic system of government. Let us not achieve the fate of some sister states to the north which lacked the foresight to properly treat the disease when it first appeared." In this way, the leaders of Florida's business community, men who controlled the flow of hundreds of thousands of dollars in campaign contributions, made their wishes known to Florida's elected leadership.[86]

On the following day, in Friday's meeting of the Board of Education, three of the four Democrats backed away from the resolution they had agreed to two nights before, pleading that "mail" was running one hundred to one against the proposal.[87] The board postponed action on the resolution, and hopes for a negotiated settlement vanished. In a press conference following the meeting, an exultant Kirk reported, "Fortunately, they don't have the guts to follow through on what they agreed behind closed doors to do."[88] When asked if Christian's resolution would not have settled the strike by getting teachers back into classrooms, Kirk replied, "I can get all the boys home from Vietnam too, if we want to give up to the Communists."[89]

In Florida, a state with a large military-based population, anxiety concerning "Vietnam" and "crime and lawlessness" was conspicuous in the opposition to the teacher walkout. On Saturday, a letter printed in the *Gainesville Sun* echoed the sentiments of the AIF. Comparing the FEA to "an infiltrating cancer," the writer denounced the walkout as "a flagrant violation of the law" aimed at subverting the government. "Riots in the streets of our cities" and the walkout demonstrated that "the mob" would use any and all means to obtain "'civil' rights, no matter how uncivilized it may be." This writer saw the strike as "analogous to half the U.S. Army walking off the job, going AWOL, because of low salaries or poor living conditions." Asserting that "the American public would be incensed" if soldiers deserted in Vietnam, this writer urged the same anger toward those "teachers who revolt against the government."[90] Expressions such as these, which directly linked the walkout to the conflict in Southeast Asia, bolstered Kirk's get-tough grandstanding.

For the FEA, the overall situation continued to deteriorate. On Monday in the third week of the walkout, the number of teachers out dropped to 19,378.[91] On Tuesday, someone leaked the AIF letter to the press.[92] The next day, only 18,000 teachers stayed away from their classrooms.[93] On Thursday, Kirk allowed the education bill to become law without his signature.[94]

Only the state Board of Education seemed at all responsive to the teachers' concerns. On Friday, March 8, the board adopted a statement of principles that included releasing the $10,200,000 that had been slated for education but delayed by the budget deficit. The FEA leadership seized upon this positive development to announce an honorable end to the strike, although in fact none of its major demands had been met.[95]

Despite this effort at face-saving, the strike clearly had failed. There was no second special session of the legislature and no agreement on professional negotiations or any of the other FEA concerns.[96] Although most teachers returned to their classroom without reprisal, school boards in several counties moved to punish FEA teachers. In Lee County, the school board required teachers to forfeit a one-hundred-dollar fine for reemployment.[97] In other counties, school boards and administrators drew up blacklists, and many teachers lost their jobs.[98] Moreover, the FEA's mismanagement of the walkout served as an invitation for the American Federation of Teachers, the National Education Association's chief rival, to begin organizing in Florida. Organizational rivalry soon divided Florida's teachers, further reducing their influence in the legislature.[99]

The struggle over education in Florida also illuminates a transition in political culture. FEA teachers positioned themselves by reference to the liberal ideals that earlier had moved many Americans to support social reform. With a good conscience as their only sure reward, FEA teachers sacrificed themselves for the "dream of quality education," hoping that their earnest example would justify their cause and inspire support.[100] Many Floridians responded to the teachers' appeal and supported the walkout, but an emerging conservative majority had lost patience with such idealism. By the first months of 1968, widely felt fears of escalating domestic unrest merged with the perception of failure in Vietnam to undermine support for the liberalism of John Kennedy and Lyndon Johnson, and Americans turned their attention from the noble challenges of the future to the grim threats of the present.

In Florida, the language of FEA opponents asserted the new conservatism. To mobilize opposition to the FEA, Florida's politicians and school administrators defended traditional social roles, extolled the duties of patriotism during wartime, and linked the strike with crises troubling the nation at large. Thus, during the walkout, Republican State Sen. L. A. Bafalis had predicted the FEA's defeat. "I think Americans basically are tired of compromising, tired of giving in," he explained.

"They have become tired of losing."[101] When Bafalis and other FEA opponents invited Floridians to act in the education crisis as they would in the national crisis, they provided a frustrated and disillusioned majority the opportunity to reaffirm its cherished values and to achieve a longed-for but elusive victory. Florida's popular rejection of the teachers' appeal thereby foreshadowed a national transition in political culture, a transition confirmed in November of that year with the election of Richard Nixon to the U.S. presidency.

Notes

1. Clif Cormier, "School's Closed: The Great Florida Teacher Walk Out of '68," *Gainesville Sun,* Feb. 18, 1973. The exact number of regular teachers out on strike was a matter of contention. The author thanks Kimberly Brodkin, John Chambers, Ronald Formisano, Suzanne Kaufman, Susan Kent, Jackson Lears, Alice Kessler-Harris, David Oshinsky, Scott Sandage, and Joan Scott for advice on earlier drafts of this essay, and John Dykes for generously providing research material. Persisting weaknesses are my own.
2. Close attention to the language deployed by both sides during the walkout reveals connections between particular political statements made in Florida and the national political culture from which these statements derive significance. The term *political culture* here refers to the changing configuration of values, assumptions, and expectations relevant to authority and manifest in language. *Language* here encompasses words and symbols, as well as posturing, role playing, and other symbolic aspects of behavior. In the Florida walkout, participants struggled over the meanings of particular ethical positions and policy options. Their struggle illuminates a transition in political culture. On political culture, see Ronald Formisano, "Deferential-Participant Politics: The Early Republic's Political Culture, 1789–1840," *American Political Science Review* 68 (June 1974): 486–87; and Harry Eckstein, "A Perspective on Comparative Politics, Past and Present," in *Comparative Politics: A Reader*, ed. Harry Eckstein and David Apters (New York: Free Press, 1963), 26. On culture, see Clifford Geertz, *The Interpretation of Cultures* (New York: Basic Books, 1973), 3–30, 193–233. On language, see Mary Poovey, *Uneven Developments: The Ideological Work of Gender in Mid-Victorian England* (Chicago: Univ. of Chicago Press, 1988), 1–23; Joan Scott, *Gender and the Politics of History* (New York: Columbia Univ. Press, 1988), 1–11.
3. This quotation appears frequently in Florida Education Association (hereafter FEA) literature. See, e.g. "FEA Action," internal memorandum, Feb. 14, 1968, photocopy in author's possession.
4. For diverse perspectives on the shift in 1968, see William H. Chafe, *The Unfinished Journey: America since World War II* (New York: Oxford Univ. Press, 1986); Alan Crawford, *Thunder on the Right: The "New Right" and the Politics of Resentment* (New York: Pantheon, 1980); Lewis J. Gould, *1968: The Election that*

Changed America (Chicago: Ivan R. Dee, 1993); Godfrey Hodgson, *America in Our Time* (New York: Doubleday, 1976); Charles Kaiser, *1968 in America: Music, Politics, Chaos, Counterculture, and the Shaping of a Generation* (New York: Weidenfeld and Nicholson, 1988); Allen J. Matusow, *The Unraveling of America: A History of Liberalism in the 1960s* (New York: Harper and Row, 1984); Kim McQuaid, *The Anxious Years: America in the Vietnam-Watergate Era* (New York: Basic Books, 1989); William O'Neill, *Coming Apart: An Informal History of America in the 1960s* (Chicago: Quadrangle Books, 1971); Richard Slotkin, *Gunfighter Nation: The Myth of the Frontier in Twentieth-Century America* (New York: Atheneum, 1992); Barbara Tischler, "Promise and Paradox: The 1960s and American Optimism," in *The Legacy: The Vietnam War in the American Imagination,* ed. D. Michael Shafer (Boston: Beacon, 1990), 30–32; Irwin Unger and Debi Unger, *Turning Point: 1968* (New York: Charles Scribner's Sons, 1988).

5. FEA, *History of the Florida Education Association* (Tallahassee: FEA, 1958), xi, 1, 72, 81, 87–89; David Tyack, Robert Lowe, and Elisabeth Hansot, *Public Schools in Hard Times: The Great Depression and Recent Years* (Cambridge, Mass.: Harvard Univ. Press, 1984), 42–43; Arthur White, *One Hundred Years of State Leadership in Florida Public Education* (Tallahassee: Univ. of Florida Presses, 1979), 15–16, 126–43; Donald D. Chipman, "The Development of Florida's State System of Public Education, 1922–1948" (Ph.D. diss., Florida State Univ., 1973); Wayne Cole Malone, "The Development, Operation, and Evaluation of the Statewide Teachers' Walkout in Florida" (Ph.D. diss., Univ. of Florida, 1969), 36–41.
6. Joan Turner Beifuss, *At the River I Stand,* rev. ed. (Memphis, Tenn.: St. Luke's Press, 1990); Leon Fink and Brian Greenberg, *Upheaval in the Quiet Zone: A History of Hospital Workers' Union, Local 1199* (Urbana: Univ. of Illinois Press, 1989), 129–58; Peter Rachleff and the Work Environment Project, *Moving the Mail: From a Manual Case to Outer Space* (N.P.: Work Environment Project, 1982); Darryl Paulson and Jane Stiff, "An Empty Victory: The St. Petersburg Sanitation Strike of 1968," *Florida Historical Quarterly* 57, no. 4 (Apr. 1979): 421–33. See also Michael Goldfield, "Public Sector Union Growth and Public Policy," *Policy Studies Journal* 18, no. 2 (Winter 1988–89): 404–20.
7. Robert H. Zieger, *American Workers, American Unions,* 2d ed. (Baltimore, Md.: Johns Hopkins Univ. Press, 1994), 163–66; Susan Lowell Butler, *The National Education Association: A Special Mission* (Washington, D.C.: National Education Association, 1987), 60; Cavit C. Cheshier, "Professional Sanctions by the National Education Association and Its Affiliates" (Ph.D. diss., George Peabody College for Teachers, 1965), 1; William Robert Sullins, "Characteristics and Attitudes of Secondary School Teachers as Related to Support or Nonsupport of Teacher Militant Activities" (Ph.D. diss., Univ. of Florida, 1968), 1–24. Also see Stephen Cole, *The Unionization of Teachers: A Case Study of the UFT* (New York: Praeger, 1969); Dorothy Kerr Jessup, *Teachers, Unions, and Change: A Comparative Study* (New York: Praeger, 1985); Martin Lawn, *Servants of the State: The Contested Control of Teaching, 1900–1930* (New York: Falmer Press, 1987); David Selden, *The Teacher Rebellion* (Washington, D.C.: Howard Univ. Press, 1985); Wayne J. Urban, *Why Teachers Organized* (De-

troit, Mich.: Wayne State Univ. Press, 1982); Donald Warren, ed., *American Teachers: Histories of a Profession at Work* (New York: Macmillan, 1989).

8. *New York Times,* Feb. 21, 1968; *Orlando Sentinel,* Feb. 21, 1968; Malone, "Development, Operation, and Evaluation," 84; *Gainesville Sun,* Feb. 18, 1973; FEA, "How Florida Slept: Background on the Developing Florida School Crisis," FEA press release, n.d., p. 1, in Series D2, M86-011, Box 3, Florida State Archives, Tallahassee (hereafter cited as FSAT); White, *Florida's Crisis,* 35–38.
9. James Cass, "Politics and Education in the Sunshine State," *Saturday Review,* Apr. 20, 1968, pp. 63–65, 76–79; David Halberstam, "Claude Kirk and the Politics of Promotion," *Harper's,* May 1968, pp. 33–40. Kirk is quoted in FEA, "How Florida Slept," 1.
10. *Duval County, Florida, Public Schools* (Nashville, Tenn.: Division of Surveys and Field Services, George Peabody College for Teachers, 1965), 5; FEA, "How Florida Slept," 1.
11. Cormier, "School's Closed."
12. National Commission on Professional Rights and Responsibilities, National Education Association of the United States, *Florida: A Study of Political Atmosphere as It Affects Public Education* (Washington, D.C.: National Education Association of the United States, 1966).
13. *St. Petersburg Times,* Aug. 23, 1967.
14. Jan Andrews to Gov. Claude Kirk, n.d., Series 923, RG 102, Box 38, FSAT. This quotation appears in a notice from the local school board, which Andrews used as stationery.
15. Joe Hunter to Gov. Claude Kirk, n.d., Series 923, RG 102, Box 38, FSAT; *St. Petersburg Times,* Aug. 23, 1967.
16. Mrs. William E. Kirk to Gov. Claude Kirk, Aug. 23, 1967, Series 923, RG 102, Box 38, FSAT; Malone, "Development, Operation, and Evaluation," 44–45; Urban, "Ideology and Power," 141; FEA, "How Florida Slept," 2; Phil Constans to Clif Cormier, Jan. 31, 1973, printed in its entirety in the *Gainesville Sun,* Feb. 18, 1973.
17. On Tet and public opinion, see Peter Braestrup, *Big Story: How the American Press and Television Reported and Interpreted the Crisis of Tet 1968 in Vietnam and Washington* (New Haven, Conn.: Yale Univ. Press, 1977); Philip E. Converse and Howard Schuman, "'Silent Majorities' and the Vietnam War," *Scientific American* 222 (June 1970): 17–25; George C. Herring, *America's Longest War: The United States and Vietnam, 1950–1975* (New York: Knopf, 1979), 183–89; Guenter Lewy, *America in Vietnam* (Oxford, England: Oxford Univ. Press, 1978), 76, 127, 434; John E. Mueller, "Trends in Popular Support for the Wars in Korea and Vietnam," *American Political Science Review* 65 (June 1971): 358, 364–65; Donald Oberdorfer, *Tet!* (Garden City, N.Y.: Doubleday, 1971), ix, xii, 238–51, 273–75, 329–30, 335; Truong Nhu Tang, *A Vietcong Memoir* (New York: Vintage Books, 1985), 122–23, 142–43, 154; Tischler, "Promise and Paradox," 33; William C. Westmoreland, *A Soldier Reports* (Garden City, N.Y.: Doubleday, 1976), 334; Marilyn Young, *The Vietnam Wars, 1945–1990* (New York: Harper Collins, 1991), 216–25.

    Contemporary sources include the *Wall Street Journal,* Feb. 6, 8, 12, 19, and 23, 1968; "New Signs of Growing Discontent Over War," *U.S. News and World Report,* Mar. 25, 1968, p. 13; H. Sidey, "Shaken Assumptions about the War," *Life,* Feb. 16, 1968, p. 32b; "Defeat?," *Saturday Evening Post,* Apr. 20, 1968, p. 20; "Translating Disgust," *Commonweal,* July 12, 1968, p. 452. For opposing views, see "Sizing Up the Public on the War," *Business Week,* Feb. 24, 1968, p. 37; "Crest or Gulf," *National Review,* Feb. 27, 1968, p. 174. On public opinion, see Philip E. Converse, Jean D. Dotson, Wendy J. Hoag, and William H. McGee, III, eds., *American Social Attitudes Data Sourcebook, 1947–1978* (Cambridge, Mass.: Harvard Univ. Press, 1980), 416, 429; *Gallup Opinion Index* 33 (Mar. 1968): 3, 5–6, 14; *Gallup Opinion Index* 34 (Apr. 1968): 12–15; *Gallup Opinion Index* 35 (May 1968): 1, 19–21; *Gallup Opinion Index* 38 (Aug. 1968): 1; Louis Harris, *The Anguish of Change* (New York: Norton, 1973), 62–65, 168–99.

18. *Miami Herald,* Jan. 30, 1968; *Tallahassee Democrat,* Jan. 30, 1968.
19. *Miami Herald,* Feb. 17, 1968; *Gainesville Sun,* Feb. 18, 1973; FEA, "How Florida Slept," 1; *Tampa Tribune,* Feb. 9, 1968.
20. *Tallahassee Democrat,* Feb. 17, 1968; Phil Constans to Clif Cormier, Jan. 31, 1973, printed in its entirety in the *Gainesville Sun,* Feb. 18, 1973; FEA, "How Florida Slept," 2; Urban, "Ideology and Power," 136–37; FEA, "Analysis: Taxes and Appropriations, Estimated Revenue," n.d., photocopy in author's possession. The exact budget figures were matters of contention.
21. Kirk, "Open Letter to the Teachers of Florida," Feb. 17, 1968, photocopy in author's possession.
22. Kirk, press release, Feb. 17, 1968, photocopy in author's possession; *Gainesville Sun,* Feb. 19, 1968, and Feb. 18, 1973.
23. On public opinion in the first quarter of 1968, see n. 17 above.
24. *Miami Herald,* Feb. 20, 1968; *St. Petersburg Times,* Feb. 20, 1968.
25. Urban, "Ideology and Power," 133–36, 140–45.
26. *Miami Herald,* Feb. 23, 1968.
27. Dexter Hagman, press release, Feb. 24, 1968, photocopy in author's possession.
28. The quotation is from the "Code of Ethics of the Education Profession in Florida" and appears in the *Gainesville Sun,* Feb. 18, 1968.
29. On differences between male and female participation rates in the strike, see Sullins, "Characteristics and Attitudes of Secondary School Teachers," 1–24.
30. My understanding of gender as a category of analysis grows from a reading of Scott, *Gender and the Politics of History.* Also see Judith Butler, *Gender Trouble: Feminism and the Subversion of Identity* (New York: Routledge, 1990); Denise Riley, *"Am I That Name?": Feminism and the Category of "Women" in History* (Minneapolis: Univ. of Minnesota Press, 1988).

    On professionalism among feminized occupations, see William J. Goode, "The Theoretical Limits of Professionalization," in *The Semi-Professions and Their Organization: Teachers, Nurses, Social Workers,* ed. Amitai Etzioni (New York: Free Press, 1969), 266–313; Alice Kessler-Harris, *A Woman's Wage:*

Historical Meanings and Social Consequences (Lexington: Univ. Press of Kentucky, 1990). On gender and librarians, see Lora Doris Garrison, "Cultural Missionaries: A Study of American Public Library Leaders, 1876–1910" (Ph.D. diss., Univ. of California, Irvine, 1973); Lora Doris Garrison, *Apostles of Culture: The Public Librarian and American Society, 1876–1920* (New York: Free Press, 1979); Anita R. Schiller, "The Disadvantaged Majority: Women Employed in Libraries," *American Libraries* 4 (Apr. 1970): 345–49; Kathleen Weibel, Kathleen Heim, and Dianne Ellsworth, *The Role of Women in Librarianship, 1876–1976: The Entry, Advancement, and Struggle for Equalization in One Profession* (Phoenix, Ariz.: Oryx Press, 1979). On gender and nursing, see Fred E. Katz, "Nurses," in Etzioni, *Semi-Professions and Their Organization,* 54–81; Barbara Melosh, *The Physician's Hand: Work, Culture, and Conflict in American Nursing* (Philadelphia: Temple Univ. Press, 1982); Susan M. Reverby, *Ordered to Care: The Dilemma of American Nursing, 1850–1945* (New York: Cambridge Univ. Press, 1987); Karen Sacks, *Caring by the Hour: Women, Work, and Organizing at Duke Medical Center* (Urbana: Univ. of Illinois Press, 1988).

31. *Gainesville Sun,* Feb. 19, 1968; Cornelia Hanna, audiotaped interview by James Sullivan, Gainesville, Fla., Mar. 31, 1989.
32. Ibid.
33. *Gainesville Sun,* Feb. 24, 1968.
34. John Dollard, *Caste and Class in a Southern Town* (New York: Harper and Brothers, 1937), 188. Also see Margaret Mead, *The School in American Culture* (Cambridge, Mass.: Harvard Univ. Press, 1951).
35. Jacob Bryan, III, chairman of the Governor's Commission for Quality Education, press release, Feb. 17, 1968, photocopy in author's possession.
36. *Miami Herald,* Feb. 19, 1968.
37. *Gainesville Sun,* Feb. 19, 1968.
38. *Tallahassee Democrat,* Feb. 23, 1968.
39. *Tallahassee Democrat,* Feb. 19, 1968; also see Mark H. Leff, "The Politics of Sacrifice on the American Home Front in World War II," *Journal of American History* 77 (Mar. 1991): 1296–1318.
40. *Tampa Tribune,* Feb. 22, 1968.
41. Ibid.
42. Ibid.
43. *Tallahassee Democrat,* Feb. 8, 1968.
44. *Gainesville Sun,* Feb. 21, 1968.
45. *Tampa Tribune,* Feb. 16, 1968.
46. *Tampa Tribune,* Feb. 18, 1968.
47. *Tallahassee Democrat,* Feb. 22, 1968.
48. *Tallahassee Democrat,* Feb. 27, 1968; *Tampa Tribune,* Feb. 20, 1968; *Gainesville Sun,* Mar. 2, 1968.
49. *Tampa Tribune,* Feb. 21, 1968.
50. Ibid.
51. *Gallup Opinion Index* 35 (Apr. 1968): 14.
52. "CBS Evening News with Walter Cronkite," Feb. 27, 1968.

53. Gilbert L. Porter and Leedell W. Neyland, *The History of the Florida State Teachers Association* (Washington, D.C.: National Education Association, 1977), 11–16, 155–67; FEA, *History of the Florida Education Association.*
54. *Miami Herald,* Feb. 19, 1968.
55. *Miami Herald,* Feb. 23, 1968. The *Herald,* like nearly every newspaper in Florida, took an editorial stance against the strike, calling the FEA "a growling menace" and demanding dismissal of teachers who stayed away from the classroom.
56. *Gainesville Sun,* Feb. 24 and 25, 1968.
57. *Tallahassee Democrat,* Feb. 22, 1968.
58. *Tallahassee Democrat,* Feb. 27 and Mar. 6, 1968.
59. FEA, press release, Mar. 4, 1968, photocopy in author's possession.
60. *Gainesville Sun,* Feb. 22, 1968. This citizen was George Kirkpatrick, later a Florida state representative and state senator.
61. Ibid.
62. Tom Raker, "Comment" (radio show), Feb. 23, 1968, photocopied transcript in author's possession.
63. *Tampa Tribune,* Feb. 20, 1968.
64. *Gainesville Sun, St. Petersburg Times,* and *Tallahassee Democrat,* all Feb. 20, 1968.
65. *Gainesville Sun,* Feb. 20, 1968.
66. *Gainesville Sun* and *Orlando Sentinel,* both Feb. 21, 1968.
67. *Orlando Sentinel* and *St. Petersburg Times,* Feb. 21, 1968; *Miami Herald,* Feb. 22, 1968.
68. *St. Petersburg Times,* Aug. 24, 1967; *Tampa Tribune,* Sept. 23, 1967; White, *Florida's Crisis,* 44; Halberstam, "Claude Kirk and the Politics of Promotion," 33–40; David R. Colburn and Richard K. Scher, *Florida's Gubernatorial Politics in the Twentieth Century* (Tallahassee: Univ. Presses of Florida, 1980), 83, 265, 284.
69. *Huntley-Brinkley Report,* National Broadcasting Corporation, Feb. 21, 1968.
70. *Miami Herald,* Feb. 19, 1968.
71. Dexter Hagman, audiotaped interview by James Sullivan, Bartow, Fla., Mar. 29, 1989; *Miami Herald,* Feb. 22, 1968.
72. *Miami Herald,* Feb. 22, 1968; Halberstam, "Claude Kirk and the Politics of Promotion," 40.
73. *Miami Herald,* Feb. 22, 1968. Tornillo's statement demanded that elected officials "call for a new session restricted to education. Pass an acceptable program and let it be enacted into law. Permit all of the principals involved to sit down in the same room at the same time and negotiate a conclusion to this crisis."
74. Ibid.
75. *Miami Herald,* Feb. 24, 1968.
76. *Gainesville Sun,* Feb. 24, 1968.
77. *Miami Herald,* Feb. 24, 1968.
78. FEA, "Facts for Area Meetings," Feb. 26, 1968, photocopy in author's possession.

79. *Tampa Tribune,* Feb. 29, 1968; *Tallahassee Democrat,* Feb. 29, 1968.
80. Kirk, press release, Feb. 29, 1968, photocopy in author's possession.
81. Ibid.
82. Ibid.
83. *St. Petersburg Times,* Mar. 2, 1968; *Gainesville Sun,* Mar. 2, 1968.
84. Kirk, press release, Feb. 29, 1968, photocopy in author's possession.
85. John C. Lee to Gov. Claude Kirk, Feb. 28, 1968, photocopy in author's possession.
86. Ibid.
87. Quotation is from Faircloth and appeared in several published accounts, including the one in *Today Cocoa,* Mar. 3, 1968.
88. *St. Petersburg Times,* Mar. 2, 1968; *Gainesville Sun,* Mar. 2, 1968.
89. *Gainesville Sun,* Feb. 29, 1968; *Today Cocoa,* Mar. 2, 1968.
90. *Gainesville Sun,* Mar. 2, 1968.
91. *Gainesville Sun,* Mar. 5, 1968; *Tallahassee Democrat,* Mar. 5, 1968.
92. *St. Petersburg Times,* Mar. 5, 1968.
93. *Tallahassee Democrat,* Mar. 6, 1968; *Gainesville Sun,* Mar. 6, 1968.
94. *Gainesville Sun,* Mar. 7, 1968.
95. *Tallahassee Democrat,* Mar. 9, 1968; *Gainesville Sun,* Mar. 9, 1968; Constans, press release, Mar. 9, 1968, photocopy in author's possession.
96. Colburn and Scher, *Florida's Gubernatorial Politics,* 201–2, is mistaken. Marjorie Murphy, *Blackboard Unions: The AFT and the NEA, 1900–1980* (Ithaca, N.Y.: Cornell Univ. Press, 1990), 229–31, also is mistaken.
97. Lee County School Board, "Lee County Reinstatement Agreement," n.d. [1968?], photocopy in author's possession.
98. FEA, "Status Report of Counties," Apr. 23, 1968, photocopy in author's possession.
99. White, *Florida's Crisis,* 78–80; Urban, "Teacher Activism," 203.
100. "FEA Action," internal memorandum, Feb. 14, 1968, photocopy in author's possession.
101. *Gainesville Sun,* Feb. 28, 1968.

Hale Boggs, Organized Labor, and the Politics of Race in South Louisiana

Patrick J. Maney

Organized labor played a major role in the career of the influential congressman Hale Boggs, who represented much of South Louisiana in the U.S. House of Representatives from the 1940s to 1972. A key southern moderate in social, economic, and even racial matters, Boggs was an ally of Presidents John F. Kennedy and Lyndon B. Johnson and a vital cog in the legislative machinery that produced the Great Society legislation of the 1960s. Louisiana labor leaders, most notably longtime AFL-CIO state president Victor Bussie, not only supported Boggs politically but also worked closely with him, especially in the sensitive area of race relations. More successfully than any congressional southerner of his generation, Boggs meshed his national ambitions with the fast-changing realities of regional politics. He owed much of his success to his alliance with organized labor, which steered him toward the moderate progressive orientation for which he still is known today.

• • •

Boggs liked to think of himself as a self-made man. He would tell labor audiences that he sympathized with working people because he, too, had had to earn everything he'd ever gotten. Boggs exaggerated—but not by much. Born in 1914, the third of six children, he grew up in Long Beach, Mississippi, and in the New Orleans area. The Great Depression hit the family hard, and his father, a bank teller, found himself out of work for long stretches of time. In the 1930s, Boggs helped put himself through

Tulane University in New Orleans by peddling chewing gum and mail-order suits to fellow students and by working the copy desk at a local newspaper. He graduated Phi Beta Kappa and earned a law degree.[1]

During his early years in politics, Boggs held trade unionists at arm's length. He first ran for Congress in 1940 as a "good government" candidate, promising to undertake the formidable task of cleaning up Louisiana politics. In those days, everyone was either pro-Long or anti-Long, depending on how they viewed the state's legendary governor and senator, Huey Long, and his successors. Boggs was decidedly anti-Long, and that pitted him against the labor movement, which had ties to the Long machine. During his maiden campaign, he drew his most enthusiastic support from prosperous lawyers and businessmen who had no sympathy with organized labor. Once in office, Boggs tried to establish his anti-radical credentials by sponsoring legislation to purge unions of "subversive" elements. He failed to gain a firm foothold in his New Orleans–area district, and in 1942 he went down to defeat. But in 1946 he regained his seat, this time for good.[2]

Mutual self-interest eventually brought Boggs and labor together. Upon reentering Congress, he realized that he needed to broaden his base of support in order to be reelected. The good government theme played well in the silk-stocking neighborhoods of his district but had limited appeal elsewhere. So, upon his return to Congress, Boggs took more of an interest in issues that mattered to ordinary working people—issues such as affordable housing and decent wages. With 20 percent of the blue-collar workers in his district belonging to unions, he also extended a hand to previously neglected labor leaders.[3] Boggs had another reason to ally himself with labor: he sought leadership in the national Democratic party. He made no secret of the fact that he wanted to be Speaker of the House, and some insiders suspected that he had set his sights on the vice presidency or even the presidency. Whatever the extent of his ambitions, he could ill afford to alienate so crucial a Democratic ally as organized labor.

The labor movement, for its part, needed all the friends it could get. After World War II, it had a larger presence in the New Orleans area than in any other city in the Deep South except Birmingham. Workers had organized themselves on the docks and wharves along the Mississippi River, in the breweries in New Orleans, in the oil fields in the Gulf of Mexico, and in the petrochemical plants that were springing up all over South Louisiana. To be sure, labor was divided—with black workers arrayed against white workers, AFL affiliates against CIO affiliates, Communist organizers against non-Communists, and racketeer-dominated locals against legitimate shops. But if factionalism prevented workers from speaking with one voice, it did infuse the labor scene with a vibrancy and excitement absent elsewhere in the South.[4]

The main threat to trade unionism was not internal conflict but a hostile political environment. As elsewhere in the South, unions in Louisiana led a precarious existence. The state legislature in Baton Rouge was always just a few votes away from enacting right-to-work legislation, and New Orleans was an anti-union town where labor held on at the sufferance of city officials and where the police served as an unofficial arm of management.[5] So labor leaders saw in the up-and-coming Hale Boggs a much-needed ally in high places.

In 1947, Boggs took the first tentative step toward collaboration by voting against the House version of the anti-union Taft-Hartley Bill. To his surprise, the response from his district was overwhelmingly negative. Close friends and key supporters denounced him for coddling corrupt labor bosses and warned him that he might lose the next election. "I am ashamed of you," wrote a prominent investment banker. "I really mean this Hale and if you keep up this kind of record I will work as hard to defeat you as I did to get you elected." "Better lean further right my friend," advised one supporter, adding, with reference to an exclusive section of New Orleans, "You come from uptown." Boggs received no comparable outpouring of support from the labor side. Soon thereafter, the House considered the final version of Taft-Hartley, which, although more moderate than the original, still was unacceptable to labor. Boggs not only voted for it but later voted to override President Truman's veto of the measure.[6]

Boggs's shift on Taft-Hartley suggested that labor remained an undeveloped force in Louisiana politics. He had wanted to forge an alliance with trade unionists to shore up his base at home and advance himself in Washington. But when he took the initiative, he found that labor was unable to reciprocate. This was symptomatic of the movement as a whole in post–World War II Louisiana. It lacked a grassroots organization of the most rudimentary sort. The CIO, which had about ten thousand members in Boggs's district, didn't even have a breakdown of them by ward and precinct, much less a mechanism for getting them to the polls on election day. "I am sorry to report," one CIO official wrote to another at the beginning of 1948, "that there has been no progress with respect to the establishment of ward and precinct organization or block workers since your visit here." Two years later, nothing had changed. After visiting the state in the summer of 1950, Tilford E. Dudley, assistant director of the CIO's Political Action Committee, reported that "none of the labor groups, including CIO and AFL, have really activated their membership. The registration is low and the activity is almost nothing."[7]

Among Louisiana labor unions, the only political activity to speak of came from a surprising quarter: African-American locals, most notably 1419 of the International Longshoremen's Association (ILA) in New Orleans, which, with thirty-five hundred members, billed itself as the largest black local in the country. Before the war, 1419 and its all-white companion, 1418, had won a brutal struggle with the CIO's International Longshoremen's and Warehousemen's Union (ILWU). Then and later, detractors considered 1419 to be little better than a company union, and, in truth, shippers had provided much of the muscle in the fight against the CIO. But after the war, 1419 became the heart and soul of a burgeoning civil rights movement in New Orleans. In 1944, the U.S. Supreme Court invalidated the white primary, which southern states had used to prevent African Americans from voting in the only election that mattered in the one-party region. In South Louisiana, newly enfranchised blacks were quick to take advantage of the court's decision. And it was Local 1419 that helped to spearhead the voter registration drive. Union leaders required their members to sign up to vote, and they conducted night classes to teach workers how to get through Louisiana's Byzantine registration process.[8] All in all, the dominant white unions in Louisiana had a lot to learn about political organizing from 1419's example.

• • •

Two events in the mid-fifties finally stirred the labor movement to action. First, in 1954, the state legislature passed a so-called right-to-work bill prohibiting compulsory union membership. Eight years earlier, the legislature had passed a nearly identical measure, but the governor, country music singer–turned-politician Jimmy H. Davis, had vetoed it. This time, however, a more conservative governor, Robert Kennon, signed the bill into law. Faced with a threat to their survival, labor officials organized as never before. The right-to-work law, reported Daniel Powell, southern director of the CIO's Political Action Committee, "has created in about 20 months more interest and activity in politics by the AFL and CIO than we could have created under normal conditions in 5 to 10 years. Nowhere in the South has there been such concentration on legislative races as there is in Louisiana—and particularly New Orleans—today."[9] In the next campaign, labor made repeal of right-to-work for nonagricultural workers a major issue. The newly merged AFL-CIO poured $70,000 into the first primary alone. The effort paid off. In 1956, the new governor, Earl Long, Huey's younger brother, pushed repeal through a pliant legislature. Agricultural workers, who were still covered by right-to-work, complained, justifiably, that their industrial brethren had sold them out. Nevertheless, repeal was an impressive demonstration of what organized labor could accomplish in a hostile environment.[10] In no other southern state did laborites manage to remove right-to-work legislation once it was on the books.

The second major development in the emergence of labor as a political force in Louisiana also occurred in 1956. That was the election of Victor Bussie to the presidency of the state AFL-CIO. Thirty-seven years old and a native of Louisiana, Bussie was the son of a railroad worker who had been fired after leading an unsuccessful strike. A firefighter by trade, Bussie was elected president of his union local the night he returned home from navy duty during World War II. Tall, balding, and bespectacled, he didn't look or act like a politician. He neither drank nor smoked, and he could be stiff and standoffish. But appearances were deceiving, for he was a natural politician who commanded respect, if not always affection, from public officials and laborites alike. He was also a quick study with a knack for sizing people up. "Before you even start talking to him," an acquaintance recalled years later, "he knows what you're going to say and how he's going to respond." In 1956, Bussie assumed command of the newly formed AFL-CIO state council.[11]

Some laborites believed that the council should maintain a low profile. Why, after all, risk being an easy target? Bussie disagreed. Upon assuming office, he moved quickly to make his presence felt in state politics. He unashamedly aligned himself with roguish Gov. Earl Long, who had helped engineer repeal of the right-to-work statute. Bussie also identified himself with the moderate wing of the national Democratic party.[12] In this latter effort, the well-connected Hale Boggs figured prominently in his plans.

By the mid-fifties, Boggs's star was ascending. A protégé of legendary

House Speaker Sam Rayburn, Boggs had worked his way into the House's inner circle. Thanks to Rayburn, he sat on the most powerful committee in Congress, Ways and Means, and thus had a major voice in a host of matters critical to labor, including tax and trade policies. He and wife Lindy, a formidable figure in her own right who was critical to her husband's success, were one of the most popular couples in Washington. "I know you do not have to be told how important Representative Boggs is to some of our principal legislative objectives," Andrew Biemiller, the AFL-CIO's legislative director, once told Bussie.[13] Bussie did not have to be told, for already he had singled Boggs out of the Louisiana delegation for special attention. He invited him to speak at state conventions and saw to it that laborites in the New Orleans area lent their full support to him at election time. Bussie also pled Boggs's case before AFL-CIO President George Meany, who, although recognizing Boggs's strategic importance, was less taken with him than Bussie was. "I had to educate Meany in the realities of Louisiana politics," Bussie later recalled. Bussie would tell the gruff labor chief that Boggs might seem conservative by New York standards, but that by New Orleans standards, he was liberal. "I had to explain to Meany that Boggs was just about the best you could get in this state," said Bussie. "He wasn't perfect. He wasn't even everything that I might have liked. But under the circumstances, he was the best you could get."[14]

• • •

The most significant area of cooperation between Boggs and Bussie was race relations. Each had a compelling reason to work with the other to mitigate racial tensions. Boggs, for his part, wanted to hold together the remarkable biracial voting coalition that he then was in the process of building. Upon returning to Congress in 1947, he had broadened his electoral base by wooing white blue-collar workers. But he had also been quietly recruiting newly enfranchised black voters, who, with the help of black unions, such as the ILA's 1419, were going to the polls in South Louisiana in numbers greater than almost anywhere else in the South. In 1946, when Boggs regained his seat in Congress, three thousand blacks were eligible to vote in his district. By 1956, nearly twenty-three thousand African Americans, comprising 16 percent of the entire electorate, had been added to the rolls.[15]

By no means was Boggs the only Louisiana politician to court black voters. But he was more adept at it than most, and he inspired trust and respect in his new constituents. He was "the first decent white politician I knew in Louisiana," recalled black civil rights activist Avery Alexander. "He was actually elected to office without calling us by that 'N' name and talking about keeping us down."[16]

For Boggs, black voters provided a political insurance policy. As a national Democrat, he would, from time to time, have to take stands that alienated white conservatives in his district. African Americans could help make up the losses.

Still, Boggs had to proceed with extreme caution, for the politics of biracialism led to uncharted and potentially treacherous territory. During the 1950s and early 1960s, for example, support for civil rights legislation was completely out of the question. When circumstances required it, Boggs could wave the Rebel flag with the best of them. He would talk about how much he loved the South and boast of his great-uncle who had been a brigadier general in the Confederacy. He would appeal to local feeling by saying that southerners didn't need outsiders telling them how to run their lives. In 1956, he joined a hundred legislators from the Deep South who signed the infamous Southern Manifesto, condemning the Supreme Court's landmark Brown decision of 1954 and implicitly encouraging the states to resist integrating their public schools.[17] For the most part, however, Boggs avoided the race issue, for it threatened to polarize his constituents and splinter his biracial coalition. Instead he tried to get voters to think about their common problems, especially their common economic problems.

Victor Bussie, meanwhile, was struggling to hold together a biracial coalition of his own. Of the AFL-CIO's 150,000 members in Louisiana, between a quarter and a third were African Americans, and almost all of them belonged to segregated locals. Immediately following World War II, the AFL and the CIO had waged a rhetorical tug-of-war for the support of black workers. Bussie's predecessor, state AFL President E. H. "Lige" Williams, had called upon white locals to admit blacks, and in 1947 he was the first labor leader in the South—AFL or CIO—to appoint an African American to the executive board of a state labor body. But these were largely symbolic gestures, and beyond them neither the AFL nor CIO was willing to go.[18]

By the 1950s, the Louisiana labor movement was rife with racial tension. "As far as I can judge," noted a close observer of the labor scene, "union men are split wide open over this problem." Sometimes, tension could lead to almost comic situations. At one state convention, black delegates from the politically active Local 1419, who were required to sit in the balcony with their black cohorts, decided to test the usual "all for one, one for all" rhetoric of white labor officials. So, at the beginning of the second day of the convention, they arrived early and took seats on the main floor of the hall, positioning themselves evenly from front to back and from side to side. Before long they looked up to see all of the white delegates crammed together in the balcony.[19]

Although Bussie earned the respect of black unionists, he believed it would be suicidal for organized labor to align itself with the civil rights movement. He did come down hard on militant segregationists, saying that their real motive was to divide workers and wreck trade unionism. And he worked behind the scenes to accommodate the demands of African-American workers. But, like Boggs, he tried to get workers to think about jobs and wages and not about race.[20]

In 1956, Boggs and Bussie joined forces to prevent racial tensions from splintering the Democratic party, as had happened in 1948, when many southerners had bolted their party for the States' Rights, or Dixiecrat, party. The incident that had sparked the southern revolt of '48 was the inclusion of a pro–civil rights plank in the Democratic platform. The ensuing presidential campaign, coinciding with Boggs's own bid for reelection, had been a political nightmare, pitting his loyalty to the national party against strong local sentiment in favor of the Dixiecrats. Boggs had survived, but never again did he want to go through anything like that. Nor did the labor movement, for the organizers of the Dixiecrat campaign in Louisiana had been, almost to a person, leaders of the right-to-work movement.[21]

A replay of 1948 seemed likely in 1956. Two years earlier, the Supreme Court had issued its school desegregation decision, and by 1956 the white South had risen up in opposition to the court's verdict. A strong civil rights plank in the Democratic platform might well lead to the formation of a third party or at least to a massive defection of white southerners from the Democratic presidential candidate in the upcoming election.

In August, when the Democratic Convention opened in Chicago, just such a plank was under serious consideration. A driving force behind it was AFL-CIO President George Meany. Backed by civil rights organizations and northern liberals such as Gov. Averell Harriman of New York, Meany urged Democratic platform writers not only to endorse the Supreme Court's Brown decision but to call upon federal authorities to enforce it. In the minds of some white southerners,

Meany's talk of enforcement conjured up images of Reconstruction, with federal troops swarming over their beloved land. Led by Mississippi Gov. J. P. Coleman, southern delegates rallied around a substitute plank that, while avoiding direct mention of the Brown decision, repudiated the use of force to carry out Supreme Court decisions.[22]

Boggs and Bussie attended the convention in hopes of keeping southern delegates from bolting the Democratic party. Joining them was New Orleans labor lawyer and former National Labor Relations Board representative, Fred Cassibry, who sat on the platform committee. Once in Chicago, the three carried out their prearranged assignments. As a key southern supporter of the Democratic presidential nominee Adlai Stevenson, Boggs used his access to Stevenson's inner circle to press for a watered-down civil rights plank. At the same time, he tried to convince fellow southerners that they would be unwise to abandon the party over one plank in the platform. Bussie, meanwhile, worked his labor connections in an effort to soften the AFL-CIO's insistence on an enforcement provision, and Cassibry tried to bring fellow members of the platform committee around to the southern point of view. In this last effort, Cassibry worked closely with George C. Wallace of Alabama.[23]

The Louisiana threesome could take satisfaction in the outcome of the platform debate. Over the objections of civil rights proponents, delegates approved a bland plank declaring that "recent Supreme Court decisions" had brought "consequences of vast importance to our nation as a whole and especially to communities directly affected." The plank went on to "reject all proposals for the use of force to interfere with the orderly determination of these matters by the country." Civil rights leaders denounced the plank as a sellout to segregationists. But Boggs and his labor cohorts got what they had come for: a platform that averted both a southern walkout at the convention and the formation of a third party.[24]

Before they left Chicago, Boggs and Bussie undertook one other joint project. They buttonholed delegates on behalf of Massachusetts Sen. John F. Kennedy, who was seeking the vice-presidential nomination. Boggs had known Kennedy since 1947, when Kennedy entered and Boggs reentered the House, and they had become good friends. But more than friendship was involved. Kennedy's religion might hurt him in much of the South, but in heavily Catholic South Louisiana, it was an asset. A Stevenson-Kennedy ticket seemed more likely to prevail there than many other combinations. Kennedy failed to get the nomination, but from then on, Boggs and Bussie were early and enthusiastic boosters of the Massachusetts senator for the presidency.[25]

• • •

During the Kennedy and Johnson presidencies, when Boggs was emerging as a prominent national leader, his ties to labor grew even stronger. As the Democratic whip or chief vote-counter for much of the sixties, he was in a position to help unions and they him. The congressional machinery of which Boggs was an integral part produced the most far-reaching legislation since the New Deal. But the New Orleans lawmaker would never have been able to exert this kind of high-profile leadership unless he had been secure in his district. Surviving Louisiana's Darwinian politics was tough enough as it was. Now national leadership meant taking many positions that angered powerful constituents. To shore up his home base, Boggs frequently turned to organized labor, as he did, for example, as the very beginning of the Kennedy administration.

No sooner had Kennedy taken office than Boggs found himself under attack at home for supporting the administration's plan to "pack" the Rules Committee of the House of Representatives. In recent years, the conservative-dominated committee, through which almost all bills had to pass before they could be considered on the floor, had become a kind of black hole into which liberal proposals entered, never to be seen again. Shortly after Kennedy's inauguration, House Speaker Sam Rayburn, inspired by FDR's effort to enlarge the Supreme Court, proposed increasing committee membership from 12 to 15.[26] For help in the ensuing fight, Rayburn turned to his top leaders, including Boggs.

If Boggs hoped that the Rules fight would go unnoticed in his district, he was disappointed. He received more mail concerning this matter—almost all of it opposed to expansion—than on any previous issue, including Taft-Hartley. Stirred up by urgent-sounding editorials in the biggest newspaper in the area, the *Times Picayune,* many of Boggs's white constituents warned that "packing" the committee would have dire consequences: Kennedy would become a dictator; the South would find itself at the mercy of a new generation of northern carpetbaggers; individual rights would be extinguished; and worst of all, a refurbished Rules Committee would throw open the doors to civil rights.[27]

Home-state labor leaders stood practically alone in defending Boggs. Taking pains to avoid any mention of civil rights, they argued that all sorts of legislation beneficial to working people, including an increase in the minimum wage, would be doomed without a change in the composition of the Rules Committee. With labor's help, Boggs survived what for a time had looked like a career-ending threat.[28]

• • •

Deflecting attention from race to economic self-interest was one key component of the mutual survival strategy adopted by Boggs and his labor cohorts. The other was Boggs's ability to bring federal jobs and other benefits to Louisiana. Few regions of the country needed government assistance as much as South Louisiana, with its fragile economy and flood- and hurricane-prone environment. Over the years, Boggs was instrumental in delivering thousands of jobs and securing generous appropriations for levee and canal projects. Federal funds flowed more freely during Democratic administrations than Republican, but Boggs always was able to get something out of Washington. "Without my vote for public works," he told a constituent, with only slight exaggeration, "we would have no tidewater channel in New Orleans, no deepening of the Mississippi River and no levee program. In other words, we would soon be under water, with no port, no commerce, no city." In 1961, the National Aeronautics and Space Administration (NASA) selected an old World War II ordinance facility in New Orleans as the site for its Saturn rocket assembly plant. The NASA contract created twelve thousand jobs and pumped over a billion dollars into the New Orleans economy.[29] Not the least of Boggs's attractions to labor leaders was his willingness to use his connections with business to ensure that most federally subsidized operations were unionized. "It didn't bother me that Boggs had close ties to big business," Victor Bussie later explained. "I thought it was an asset. He could persuade businesses to deal with our unions."[30]

The steady flow of jobs from Washington was the glue that held Boggs's and labor's biracial coalition together. As long as there was enough good work to go around, blacks and whites were less likely to turn against each other. Moreover, many of Boggs's white constituents were willing to tolerate his frequent deviations from the conservative norm because he could deliver the goods.

• • •

Because federal largesse was critical to their survival, Boggs and Bussie defended the Kennedy administration long after most white southerners had turned against it. Until late 1962, Kennedy remained popular in

Boggs's district and throughout Louisiana. In April of that year, the president received a warm reception in the Crescent City on a visit to boost Boggs's chances for reelection. In September, however, sentiment turned against Kennedy when he sent federal troops to the University of Mississippi, where white mobs had gone on a rampage to protest the admission of African-American student James Meredith. Many of Boggs's constituents reacted as though Kennedy had sent a reincarnated General Sherman on another march through the South and their criticisms of the president became increasingly more strident.[31]

On August 29, 1963, Boggs and Bussie, speaking before a raucous gathering of laborites in New Orleans, delivered their most impassioned defense of the president thus far. The occasion was the state AFL-CIO's usually uneventful Labor Day banquet. Some members of the all-white audience were in a foul mood to start with, because they were still thinking about the previous day's March on Washington, during which Martin Luther King had delivered his "I Have a Dream" speech and in which United Auto Workers President Walter Reuther and many other trade unionists had played a conspicuous role. The trouble began when Boggs predicted that Kennedy would be reelected in 1964. Several listeners jumped to their feet and booed at the mention of the president's name. As the jeering continued, Boggs listed all of the benefits Louisiana had received from the administration, everything from jobs to levees to sewage treatment plants. Even his reminder of how Kennedy had faced down Nikita Khrushchev during the Cuban missile crisis—usually a crowd-pleaser—couldn't quiet this audience. "Shut up," some shouted. "Sit down," said others. The constant heckling finally got to Boggs, who, as if to inflame the crowd even more, departed from the outline of his speech to call the March on Washington a "great exercise in Americanism." That was the first time he ever had had anything good to say about a civil rights demonstration.

Bussie followed Boggs to the podium. In a passionate, impromptu speech, the labor chieftain defended Boggs and Kennedy. Boggs, he said, was "the most distinguished citizen Louisiana has in the Halls of Congress" and Kennedy was the greatest president in his lifetime. If dissident laborites didn't like the elected officials they had in Louisiana, they should move to Mississippi or Alabama to find leaders more to their liking. "We lost the Civil War 100 years ago," the Louisiana-born Bussie concluded, "and I have no intention of fighting it again. I thank God we did lose it, because [if not,] we wouldn't have the country we have today." Bussie not only quieted the hecklers, but got most of his listeners applauding him.[32]

Bussie may have turned the crowd around momentarily, but his identification with Kennedy and later with Lyndon Johnson cost him dearly. So, too, did his opposition to efforts by Louisiana officials to shut down the state's public schools rather than comply with court-ordered integration. Bussie insisted that he was not taking a stand for or against integration. He just wanted kids to be able to go to school. In the eyes of segregationists, however, to proclaim neutrality on the issue of integration was to be for it. During the 1960s, 40 percent of AFL-CIO locals dropped their affiliation with the state council. The state AFL-CIO treasury teetered on the brink of bankruptcy. For Bussie, death threats and harassing phone calls became routine. One night while he and his wife were asleep in the back bedroom of their Baton Rouge home, a bomb exploded out front.[33] Although nothing so dramatic happened to Boggs, he did lose the support of many white voters, who now began casting their ballots for Boggs's Republican foes. In 1964, he won reelection with 55 percent of the vote, down 12 points the previous election. For the first time in his career, a majority of white voters supported his opponent.[34]

Still, Boggs and his labor allies weathered the storm better than their counterparts in most southern states, and they did so in part because of their close relationship. In 1964, Boggs owed his reelection to two factors. One was the overwhelming vote he got from African Americans, who made up for white defections from his biracial coalition. The other was organizational support from labor, particularly the state AFL-CIO. Shortly after the election, Boggs told George Meany that he never would have won the election without the leadership of Bussie and local labor leader, A. P. "Pat" Stoddard, who headed the AFL-CIO's Greater New Orleans Trades Council.[35]

• • •

In 1965, Boggs had a chance to repay his debt to labor. Thus far, he had compiled a mixed record on issues specifically related to trade unionism. He had voted for Taft-Hartley in 1947 and for the Landrum-Griffin Act of 1959, both of which unionists had vehemently opposed. His views on overseas commerce also bothered national labor leaders like George Meany. Convinced that free trade (except in Louisiana products) would boost the economy, Boggs worked to lower tariffs and to reduce the tax burden on the overseas investments of American companies.

Laborites worried that Boggs, as an influential member of the Ways and Means Committee, might succeed in making foreign investment so attractive that American firms would be tempted to relocate their operations outside the United States.[36]

Louisiana labor leaders, understanding as they did the realities of state politics, worried a lot less than their national counterparts about Boggs's transgressions. As long as he voted right on most social and economic measures and brought home the bacon, they'd continue to support him. And Bussie would continue to plead Boggs's case before Meany, explaining to the AFL-CIO head the pressures Boggs was under in his district. Still, Bussie and his colleagues didn't want to be taken for granted; so when an issue critical to labor came before Congress in 1965, they looked hopefully to Boggs for support.[37]

The issue was repeal of Section 14(b) of the Taft-Hartley Act, which enabled states to pass right-to-work laws. For nearly twenty years, organized labor had been trying to erase that section from the statute books, to no avail. Now President Lyndon Johnson put repeal on his legislative agenda. Even though Louisiana was the only southern state without right-to-work, Bussie and his colleagues would breathe easier if the open shop threat were eliminated once and for all. Boggs also had his national ambitions to consider. As majority whip, he was expected to round up the votes for passage, and it would hurt his reputation to sit this one out. Notwithstanding heavy pressure from influential businessmen back home, Boggs worked for repeal, which won House approval but fell victim to a filibuster in the Senate.[38]

• • •

The key issue in 1965 for both Boggs and labor, however, was not labor reform but civil rights. Thus far, Boggs had voted against every civil rights measure that had come before him with the sole exception of Rules Committee enlargement, which many of his white constituents had considered just as bad. Local African-American leaders, such as Avery Alexander and A. L. Davis, didn't object to Boggs's cautious approach. Like their counterparts in the labor movement, they considered themselves realists, and they knew that if Boggs went down to defeat, someone a lot worse would be likely to take his seat in Congress. If they needed any reminders on this score, they had only to look at the other congressman from New Orleans, arch-segregationist F. Edward Hebert.[39]

Following the 1964 election, however, some of Boggs's black supporters, especially the younger ones among them, began to feel that he was taking them for granted. "We wish to serve notice on you," three prominent black leaders wrote him, "that unless there are some changes of attitude as well as of practice in the future administration of your position, we shall be compelled to use any and every means at our disposal to let Negroes, as well as the entire country, know that their confidence in you is misplaced."[40] Boggs continued to enjoy overwhelming support among African Americans. But he had no way of knowing how soon it would be before this kind of critical sentiment began to spread.

In the summer of 1965, after carefully surveying the situation back home, he decided to support his first civil rights measure, the voting rights bill. He hadn't planned to speak during the floor debate, but when a home-state colleague got up and said that legislation wasn't necessary because there wasn't much discrimination in Louisiana, Boggs rose to defend the bill. He gave the speech of his life. When he finished, wave after wave of applause swept the floor and the galleries. Colleagues showered him with praise, and commentators around the country singled him out as a fresh voice among southern politicians.[41]

By 1965, African-American leaders were complaining that the labor movement was also taking them for granted. In May, for example, the New Orleans chapter of the National Association for the Advancement of Colored People (NAACP) held a conference to discuss provisions of the Civil Rights Act of 1964 that made it illegal for businesses and trade unions to discriminate in their hiring and membership practices. NAACP officials were bitterly disappointed when only a handful of white laborites showed up. Black leaders may also have been discouraged when, during the national debate over voting rights, the usually reliable Victor Bussie expressed only lukewarm support for the federal measure to guarantee the ballot. "As often happens," he reportedly said, "the cure can be just as bad as the illness."[42] But like Boggs, Bussie moved quickly to dispel black doubts. Once the Voting Rights Act became law, he called upon the U.S. Justice Department to enforce the law vigorously in Louisiana, and he worked with civil-rights organizations to register black voters.[43]

• • •

Because of increasing racial polarization, spurred in part by the Republican southern strategy, Boggs won reelection in 1968 with only 51 percent of the vote. He had little reason to rejoice. Richard Nixon had ended nearly a decade of Democratic rule in the White House, and it appeared that Boggs would face uphill reelection fights for the foreseeable future. Worse still, his prospects for advancement within the leadership suddenly looked dim. An unwritten rule holds that top congressional leaders must come from safe districts. Otherwise they would have to spend too much time campaigning for reelection to perform leadership duties. They might also become too beholden to local interests, to the neglect of a national perspective.

In 1969, labor once again helped salvage Boggs's career. The Louisiana legislature was in the process of redrawing the lines of the state's congressional districts in accordance with recent population guidelines handed down by the U.S. Supreme Court. Legislators had two proposals before them. One, supported by Boggs's foes, redrew district lines in such a way as almost to ensure his defeat in the next election. A pro-Boggs counterproposal, drafted by his top aide, Gary Hymel, restructured the district so as to guarantee future victories.[44]

A fierce lobbying campaign ensued. Boggs enlisted the support of organized labor, of course, but also of oil interests who were indebted to him for safeguarding their coveted oil-depletion allowance in the Ways and Means Committee. With Boggs's friends and foes in the legislature about evenly matched, the outcome was in doubt until the end. But the Boggs forces prevailed, and by all accounts labor was critical.[45]

Labor made one final contribution to Boggs's career. In 1971, it helped him become House majority leader. National labor leaders actually preferred James O'Hara of Michigan to Boggs. But O'Hara's close identification with labor may have hurt his candidacy, especially among southerner legislators who regarded him as a "kept man," too beholden to the union movement. On the first ballot, House Democrats eliminated O'Hara, which left Boggs and Morris Udall of Arizona as the principal contenders. AFL-CIO representative Andrew Biemiller quietly let it be known that labor's friends should go with Boggs. The deciding factor was probably each candidate's vote on the 1965 repeal of Section 14(b) of Taft-Hartley. Udall had voted against repeal, Boggs for it—thanks to pressure from Louisiana laborites.[46]

• • •

Boggs had a bumpy first year as majority leader, including a much-publicized clash with FBI Director J. Edgar Hoover and some embarrassing public incidents that most observers attributed to an excess of drink. But by 1972, his position in the leadership was so secure that most commentators were predicting that it was just a matter of time before he became Speaker of the House. By then he also had become something of a role model for a new generation of southern white moderates, including Bill Clinton, who came of age in the late sixties and early seventies.[47] What undoubtedly drew Clinton to Boggs was that the Louisiana congressman had developed a winning formula for exerting positive leadership in Washington and still getting elected back home.

The end came suddenly. In October 1972, Boggs made a campaign trip to Alaska. En route from Anchorage to Juneau, his plane disappeared without a trace. The largest search and rescue operation in American history failed to find the plane or its occupants. Boggs's wife and political partner, Lindy, succeeded him in Congress and quickly established close ties with labor. Victor Bussie stayed on as president of the state AFL-CIO, becoming a legend in labor circles for both his longevity and his political prowess.

By the 1980s, however, the structural foundations of Boggs's electoral success—a growing economy and a strong labor movement—began to crumble, undermining the biracial coalition that Boggs and his labor allies had pioneered. Plummeting oil prices devastated Louisiana. The state had gone through hard times before. But since World War II, the federal government usually had offset local losses by pumping jobs and money into Louisiana's economy. Although Lindy Boggs matched Hale's persuasiveness in pleading Louisiana's case in the halls of Congress, the attitude in Washington had changed. When the Reagan administration slashed aid to cities, New Orleans was plunged into permanent fiscal crisis.

After the jobs dried up, the state's crippled labor movement, already reeling from the effects of a recently enacted state right-to-work law, was ill-equipped to forestall racial polarization. Indeed, by the late 1980s, some of the same blue-collar communities that once had been mainstays in Boggs's biracial coalition had defected to the racist candidacy of David Duke.[48] At its pinnacle, however, the Boggs-labor partnership had helped shape the political landscape of the post–Jim Crow South.

Notes

The author wishes to express his appreciation to Lawrence Powell and Joseph Logsdon for their help in the preparation of this essay.

1. On Boggs's early life, see correspondence, clippings, and scrapbooks in boxes containing youth and early career materials, T. Hale Boggs Papers, Howard-Tilton Library, Tulane Univ., New Orleans, La. (hereafter referred to as Boggs Papers). See also Scott E. Balius, "The Courage of His Convictions: Hale Boggs and Civil Rights" (Master's thesis, Tulane Univ., 1992), 4–8.
2. On his first campaign for office and early career, see Scrapbooks 2 and 3, Boggs Papers.
3. Union membership calculated from figures in E. J. Bourg to James L. McDevitt, Aug. 23, 1957, AFL-CIO COPE Research Dept. Collection, George Meany Memorial Archives, Silver Spring, Md.
4. There is no comprehensive study of organized labor in post–World War II Louisiana. For useful background material, see Thomas Becnel, *Labor, Church, and the Sugar Establishment: Louisiana, 1887–1976* (Baton Rouge: Louisiana State Univ. Press, 1980); Bernard A. Cook and James R. Watson, *Louisiana Labor: From Slavery to "Right-to-Work"* (Lanham, Md.: Univ. Press of America, 1985); David Lee Wells, "The ILWU in New Orleans: CIO Radicalism in the Crescent City, 1937–1957" (Master's thesis, Univ. of New Orleans, 1979); Adam Fairclough, *Race and Democracy: The Civil Rights Struggle in Louisiana, 1915–1972* (Athens: Univ. of Georgia Press, 1995), 46–105; and Jack Bass and Walter DeVries, *The Transformation of Southern Politics: Social Change and Political Consequence since 1945* (New York: Basic Books, 1976), 181–85. The *Louisiana Weekly,* the largest African-American newspaper in the state and the only paper—black or white—that regularly covered the labor scene, is a rich source of information. On the time before World War II, essential works include Eric Arnesen, *Waterfront Workers of New Orleans: Race, Class, and Politics, 1863–1923* (New York: Oxford Univ. Press, 1991); and Bruce Nelson, "Class and Race in the Crescent City: The ILWU, from San Francisco to New Orleans," in *The CIO's Left-Led Unions,* ed. Steve Rosswurm (New Brunswick, N.J.: Rutgers Univ. Press, 1992), 19–45.
5. *Louisiana Weekly,* 1945–50, provides vivid accounts of police brutality against laborites. See also Nelson, "Class and Race," 32–33.
6. Edward D. Rapier to Boggs, Apr. 18, 1947; and Gervais F. Favrot to Boggs, n.d. [1947], both in Legislation File, Boggs Papers.
7. F. C. Pieper to Hoyt S. Haddock, Jan. 28, 1948, series 1; and Tilford E. Dudley to Daniel Powell, July 3, 1950, series 2; both in National PAC [Political Action Committee] Correspondence, 1945–55, in Daniel Powell Papers, Southern Historical Collection, Univ. of North Carolina Library, Chapel Hill, N.C.
8. *Louisiana Weekly,* July 12, 1947; Sept. 6, 1947; and Apr. 29, 1950.
9. Daniel Powell to Jack Kroll and James L. McDevitt, Jan. 15, 1956, COPE Papers, Box 11, File 10, in Meany Archives.
10. Becnel, *Labor, Church, and the Sugar Establishment,* 190–95; Michael L. Kurtz and Morgan D. Peoples, *Earl K. Long: The Saga of Uncle Earl and Louisiana Politics* (Baton Rouge: Louisiana State Univ. Press, 1990), 184–85.
11. Jerry Colburn, "Victor Bussie: Louisiana's Lord of Labor," *New Orleans Magazine* 11 (Aug. 1977): 62–67; Bass and DeVries, *Transformation of Southern Politics,* 181–85. The quotation is from Eamon Kelly, interview by Patrick J.

Maney, Apr. 1994, New Orleans, La. As of this writing, Kelly is president of Tulane Univ.

12. Kurtz and Peoples, *Earl K. Long,* 184–85; Victor Bussie, audiotaped interview by Patrick J. Maney, Aug. 18, 1995, New Orleans, La., tape and notes in author's possession.
13. Andrew Biemiller to Bussie, Dec. 18, 1959, in Papers of the Dept. of Legislative State and Local Central Bodies, 82–28, Meany Archives.
14. Bussie, interview by Maney, Aug. 18, 1995.
15. "Number of Registered Voters by Congressional Districts," enclosed in Clarence K. Jones, Jr., to Boggs, Apr. 2, 1965, in Campaign Files, Boggs Papers. For background on voting by African Americans, see Fairclough, *Race and Democracy,* 106–34; and James H. Fenton and Kenneth N. Vines, "Negro Registration in Louisiana," *American Political Science Review* 51 (1957): 704–13.
16. Avery Alexander, interview by Patrick J. Maney, Dec. 1994, New Orleans, La., tapes and notes in the author's possession. See also Arnold R. Hirsch, "Simply a Matter of Black and White: The Transformation of Race and Politics in Twentieth-Century New Orleans," in *Creole New Orleans: Race and Americanization,* ed. Arnold R. Hirsch and Joseph Logsdon (Baton Rouge: Louisiana State Univ. Press, 1992), 273.
17. "Ike Criticized in Louisiana," *New Orleans Times-Picayune,* n.d. [1957], in Scrapbook 16; Boggs to Robert M. Stewart, Oct. 23, 1957, in Subject File; "Boggs Assails Civil Rights Legislation," n.d. [1957], in Scrapbook 16; all, Boggs Papers.
18. *Louisiana Weekly,* Jan. 25 and Apr. 26, 1947. Black labor leaders like Avery Alexander, a member of Local 1419, scorned the first black member of the council, Dr. George W. Snowden, because he was an academic who had not risen through the ranks of labor. Alexander, interview by Maney, Dec. 1994.
19. Louis J. Twomey to James C. Gildea, Oct. 29, 1957, Box 16, File 8, Papers of Louis J. Twomey, Special Collections and Archives, Loyola Univ., New Orleans, La. (hereafter referred to as Twomey Papers); Alexander, interview by Maney, Dec. 1994.
20. Louis J. Twomey to Benjamin D. Segal, Apr. 4, 1957, Box 16, File 6, in Twomey Papers. Bussie, interview by Maney, Aug. 18, 1995.
21. Campaign Files, 1948, Boggs Papers.
22. *Times Picayune,* Aug. 12, 1956; *New Orleans Item,* Aug. 10, 1956; Herbert S. Parmet, *The Democrats* (New York: Oxford Univ. Press, 1976), 136–40.
23. Bussie, interview by Maney, Aug. 18, 1995; Fred Cassibry, audiotaped interviews by Patrick J. Maney, Feb. 20 and July 6, 1995, New Orleans, La., tapes and notes in author's possession; Bill Monroe, interview by Patrick J. Maney, Dec. 2, 1994, Alexandria, Va., notes in author's possession. Monroe was a New Orleans newsman who covered the convention.
24. Text of the civil rights plank, quoted in *New Orleans States,* Aug. 15, 1956.
25. Bussie, interview by Maney, Aug. 18, 1995.
26. For background on the Rules Committee fight, see Neil MacNeil, *Forge of Democracy: The House of Representatives* (New York: David McKay, 1963), 410–

48; and Milton C. Cummings, Jr., and Robert L. Peabody, "The Decision to Enlarge the Committee on Rules: An Analysis of the 1961 Vote," in *New Perspectives on the House of Representatives,* ed. Robert L. Peabody and Nelson W. Polsby (Chicago: Rand McNally, 1963), 167–94.

27. Legislative File, 1961–65, Boggs Papers.
28. "Rules Committee," File 101-3, Papers of the Greater New Orleans AFL-CIO, Earl K. Long Library, Univ. of New Orleans.
29. Boggs to Cecil M. Shilstone, Jan. 30, 1962, Campaign File, Box 6, Boggs Papers.
30. Bussie, interview by Maney, Aug. 18, 1995.
31. Both the tone and the volume of the letters Boggs received from constituents suggest that the crisis at the Univ. of Mississippi was a turning point in the way people in his district viewed Kennedy.
32. Audiotaped recording of labor meeting, Aug. 29, 1963, in Boggs Papers.
33. *New Orleans Times-Picayune,* Sept. 7, 1961, sec. 2, p. 5. Colburn, "Victor Bussie," 64; Alan Draper, *Conflict of Interest: Organized Labor and the Civil Rights Movement in the South, 1954–1968* (Ithaca, N.Y.: ILR Press, 1994), 92; Bussie, interview by Maney, Aug. 18, 1995. The first reports of the bombing incident, which occurred in 1967, suggested that it might be tied to Bussie's support for the creation of a state board to investigate labor racketeering. Bussie, however, blamed the Ku Klux Klan. The fact that a bomb of the same type went off at about the same time at the home of a retired African-American school principal and civil rights activist suggests that the incident was racially motivated. See *Times-Picayune,* July 19–23, 1967, and *New York Times,* July 20, 1967.
34. Colburn, "Victor Bussie," 64; Draper, *Conflict of Interest,* 92; Bussie, interview by Maney, Aug. 18, 1995; Balius, "Courage of His Convictions," 80, 103.
35. Boggs to Meany, Nov. 23, 1964, Dept. of Legislation, Congressional Correspondence, Box 65, Folder 36, Meany Archives.
36. For Boggs's views on Landrum Griffin, see Legislative Files, 1958–59, Boggs Papers; MacNeil, *Forge of Democracy,* 335–36.
37. Bussie, interview by Maney, Aug. 18, 1995.
38. Legislation Files, 1965, Boggs Papers; Bussie to Affiliated Local Unions and Councils, Aug. 9, 1965, File 101–9 in Papers Greater New Orleans AFL-CIO.
39. Avery Alexander, interview by Maney, Dec. 1994; Lindy Boggs, audiotaped interview by Patrick J. Maney, May 24, 1994, New Orleans, La., tapes and notes in author's possession.
40. Robert F. Collins, R. Douglas Nils, and Lolis E. Elie to Boggs, Nov. 11, 1964, in Campaign Files, Box 7, Boggs Papers.
41. "A Profile in Courage," *Sheboygan (Wisc.) Press,* July 14, 1965, clipping; Sam T. Morrison to Boggs, July 19, 1965; and Revius O. Ortique, Jr., to Boggs, July 14, 1965; all in Legislation File, Boggs Papers.
42. Horace C. Bynum to Pat Stoddard, June 23, 1965, and reply, June 28, 1965, File101–8 in Papers Greater New Orleans AFL-CIO; *Times-Picayune,* May 11, 1965; Bussie to Biemiller, May 14, 1965, and enclosure, "Report of Legislation, State and Local," pp. 82–89; both in Meany Archives.

43. Draper, *Conflict of Interest,* 105.
44. Bussie, interview by Maney, Aug. 18, 1995; Gary Hymel, audiotaped interviews by Patrick J. Maney, July 7 and Dec. 6, 1994, Washington, D.C., tapes and notes in author's possession; David Treen, audiotaped interview by Patrick J. Maney, Apr. 19, 1995, New Orleans, La., tapes and notes in author's possession. Hymel was Boggs's top aide and directed the legislative fight for Boggs. Treen was the GOP candidate who had almost defeated Boggs in 1968; he led the effort to change Boggs's district in such a way that he could be defeated. See also Richard L. Engstrom, "The Hale Boggs Gerrymander: Congressional Redistricting, 1969," *Louisiana History* 21 (Winter 1980): 59–66.
45. Bussie, interview by Maney, Aug. 18, 1995; Hymel, interviews by Maney, July 7 and Dec. 6, 1994.
46. Robert L. Peabody, *Leadership in Congress: Stability, Succession, and Change* (Boston: Little, Brown, 1976), 170, 189, 192, 200, 212–13.
47. Bill Clinton talked about Boggs at length during a campaign appearance in New Orleans in 1992; Patrick J. Maney was in the audience. Clinton's admiration for Boggs is also noted in an unsigned memo, Oct. 10, 1972, Boggs Papers.
48. On the collapse of Louisiana's economy and the rise of David Duke, see Lawrence N. Powell, "Slouching toward Baton Rouge: The 1989 Legislative Election of David Duke," in *The Emergence of David Duke and the Politics of Race,* ed. Douglas. D. Rose (Chapel Hill: Univ. of North Carolina Press), 12–40. See also Lawrence N. Powell, "Read My Liposuction," *New Republic* 203 (Oct. 15, 1990): 18–22.

10

The Real Norma Rae

James A. Hodges

Norma Rae, the most popular and positive labor film in Hollywood history, has become a staple of late night television movie channels and is still shown at labor gatherings.[1] Nevertheless, despite its commercial success and its continuing popularity, most viewers had in 1979, and still have, no understanding that the film was loosely based on the life of a real person, Crystal Lee Jordan, and on her role in the protracted campaign of the Textile Workers Union of America (TWUA) to organize southern textile mills. In the mid-1970s, Jordan, who usually is known by her maiden name, Sutton, was a worker at a J. P. Stevens towel mill complex in Roanoke Rapids, North Carolina. A careful investigation of Sutton's life and her views on textile workers and their lot in the South during the 1960s and 1970s enriches our understanding of those who decided to go the union way. Moreover, it helps to bring to life one of that rarest of historiographical phenomena, an authentic and multi-dimensional working-class figure. As she told it in her own words in many interviews, her story was a central feature of the union's effort to organize J. P. Stevens. In addition, it speaks more generally to the hopes and struggles of thousands of southern textile workers in the post–World War II South.[2]

Sutton spoke with intelligence, force, and clarity. She had a confident and vivid personality. Though an "ordinary" working-class woman, she exhibited many of the qualities supposedly characteristic only of "liberal feminists"—assertiveness, individualism, self-reliance, and a strong desire for autonomy at home and in the workplace.[3] At the same time, Sutton's impatience, passion for justice, and openness to change are reminiscent of other, more specifically working-class, southern heroines, such as Ola Delight Smith, an organizer and publicist of the World War I era, and the young women of the famous 1929 Elizabethton, Tennessee, rayon strike.[4]

The fictional Norma Rae as a liberated woman played by Sally Field, who won an Oscar for best actress for the role, made an enormous impression on film reviewers. Indeed, critics generally stressed the theme of the heroine as a liberated woman in preference to depicting her as a southern textile worker. To be sure, before its premier, critic Lyn Garofola said that *Norma Rae* would be "unique"; its protagonist was a working class woman of intelligence, drive, self-reliance, and courage. Labor, she predicted, would be proud of *Norma Rae* as a truer portrayal of unions and working women than previous Hollywood efforts.[5] But Hollywood publicists, historically no friends of organized labor, had other priorities, and *Norma Rae*'s theme of a woman's liberation often obscured the southern labor dimension of the picture.[6]

Set in an unnamed southern town, the movie centers around a National Labor Relations Board (NLRB) election in the fictional O. P. Henley textile mill where Norma Rae and her mother and father work. Norma Rae, widowed and with two young children, is depicted as living without order or direction, and in an early scene in the movie, she is just ending an affair with a married man. The central action of the film involves the efforts of a young, fast-talking, Jewish labor organizer from New York, Reuben Warshovsky, to organize the mill workers. Norma Rae initially greets Warshovsky with apathy and hostility. But after she becomes a time-checker of production rates on the looms, she realizes that this "promotion" serves to separate her from her fellow workers. Moving back to the looms, she overcomes her early indifference to Reuben's efforts and becomes devoted to his efforts to create a TWUA local.

Simultaneously, Norma Rae meets Sonny Webster, recently parted from an unfaithful wife and left with a child. They soon marry. Norma Rae's increasingly energetic union activities alienate Sonny, and he is angry and disturbed when black workers come to their home to discuss the union. He is suspicious of the relationship between Reuben and Norma Rae. By the end of the movie, however, he has become supportive and understanding. Thus, in both her union role and her new marriage, Norma Rae develops self-reliance and self-worth. Interwoven is her friendship with

Reuben, leavened by Reuben's intellectuality and Norma Rae's awakening to the broadening horizons and self-realization that it encourages.

The most memorable scene of the movie has Norma Rae singlehandedly stopping the powerful, clattering weaving machines. This occurs when, after detection of her efforts to copy off the bulletin board a company antiunion statement which is intended to alienate white workers from black workers, she is fired and ordered out of the plant. Amid the roaring of the machines, she mounts a table and silently displays a crudely lettered sign, which reads "UNION." Slowly, one by one, the workers stop their machines to acknowledge her protest. Though she and the union suffer many subsequent setbacks, the movie ends triumphantly. Prounion workers win the election. As Norma Rae listens outside the plant, the triumphant workers set up a loud victory chant. In the final scene, Reuben leaves town.

Reviewers were enchanted that Norma Rae, a working-class woman of the South, had achieved a form of feminist liberation. A pre-release article, based on an interview with director Martin Ritt, informed readers that Norma Rae, "an uneducated young woman whose underarms stink of mill sweat and who will unzip her pants in return for a steak dinner," was, in the movie, "transformed into a superior human being . . . a working-class 'Joan of Arc.'" David Ansen in *Newsweek* concentrated on the "tough/tender friendship" between Reuben and Norma Rae. "He's a stranger to the South. She's never met a Jew," wrote Ansen. "He's all intellect, she's pure instinct." To Ansen, Norma Rae was "a lovable, red-neck saint." Richard Schickel of *Time* saw the movie as "the story of a trashy white woman . . . who discovers that she has a social conscience" under the tutelage of Reuben, "a rainmaker figure." Robert Hatch of *The Nation* argued that Norma Rae's liberation as a working woman "with one legitimate and one bastard child, a provocative body, sharp mind and short temper" was the "substance of the film." Penelope Gilliatt of the *New Yorker* even more clearly concentrated on Norma Rae the woman: "It is Norma Rae with her frustrations and her tenacity who gives . . . body to the film," she contended. Although Vincent Canby's two reviews in the *New York Times* emphasized the union theme and the working-class content of the film, his second review stressed that it was Norma Rae, "a woman of grit and guts, of humor and compassion," who steals the show. Even Stanley Kaufman, whose review essay in the *New Republic* stuck resolutely to the theme of trade unionism, could not resist a tip of the hat to the engaging Norma Rae. "We watch the sassy, but dispirited, dissatisfied, but resigned beer-swilling, backseat-humping Norma Rae," he wrote, "move to a realization that what had been nagging and depressing her was the buried knowledge that she was better than her life; we watch her move to a beginning of living her life better."[7]

In fact, the reality that lay behind script writers Irving Raveth's and Harriet Frank's fictional Norma Rae and the one created by the artistic skill of the film director, Martin Ritt, is considerably more complex and sobering. It is also more inspiring and meaningful within the context of southern labor history. In August 1973, Henry P. Leifermann, a freelance journalist, first told Crystal's story in a *New York Times Magazine* article about the TWUA's J. P. Stevens campaign. Later he published a full-length biography.[8] Indeed, Ritt based his film on the biography, which he had purchased from Leifermann, who had secured movie rights from Crystal Lee Jordan. Ritt was not able to come to an agreement with Jordan for her cooperation in the making of the movie; consequently, to avoid legal action, he often referred to the film as fiction. In turn, fictionalization of the heroine had the result of obscuring in significant ways the real Crystal Lee and the real struggle in Roanoke Rapids and elsewhere between the TWUA and J. P. Stevens. Clearly, most moviegoers and reviewers had no sense that the movie was based on a "true story."[9]

Crystal Lee Pulley was born on the last day of 1940 in a textile worker's family in Roanoke Rapids, and her life had many more twists and turns than that of Norma Rae, although the movie and the reality have a rough similarity. When she was in her early teens, her father, a loom fixer, moved the family to Burlington, North Carolina. In 1959, she graduated from high school there, while working the night shift in a local cotton mill. She married Omar "Junior" Wood in 1959 and had one child, Mark, before Wood's death in a February 1961 automobile accident ended their troubled marriage. As Crystal Lee acknowledged to Leifermann, after her husband's death she had a brief love affair with a college student that resulted in the birth of a second child, Jay.

After returning in 1962 to Roanoke Rapids, she soon married Larry Jordan, Jr., better known as "Cookie," the son of a ne'er-do-well father and a hardworking mother who labored in the textile mills of Roanoke Rapids to support seven children. After a four-year stint in the Air Force, Cookie had drifted back to town; when Crystal Lee married him, he had just left a disastrous marriage which left him with custody of his young daughter, Renee (who later returned to live with her mother). Cookie worked as a unionized production worker at a local pulp and paper plant at considerable higher wages than those earned at the textile plants. In 1965, Crystal and Cookie had a daughter, Elizabeth; but soon afterward, bored with childcare and homemaking, Crystal embarked upon a love affair with an older man that lasted three years until she ended it, later informing Cookie about the relationship. At this point, in 1969, she began working outside the home as a waitress and nightclub hostess. Her marriage had not been happy, and Crystal enjoyed the work and the opportunity to become more independent. As her biographer wrote, "It seemed to Crystal Lee that what little romance she and Cookie had before the wedding evaporated after it."[10] After three years working as a waitress and now looking for better pay, Crystal Lee, on Feb. 2, 1972, signed on at the J. P. Stevens Company at Delta Number Four plant, working on the second shift, folding terry-cloth towels into gift set boxes.

This tangled personal past, transferred in part to the fictional Norma Rae, infused the movie and made for its moving scene in which Norma Rae informs the children of her past and their parentage. Indeed, after J. P. Stevens had fired her, Crystal *did* tell her children about her past. Crystal herself saw it as a cleansing act: "I told my children—just like everyone else, 'I'm not perfect and I made these mistakes,'" mistakes she hoped would lead them to realize that "there is a moral reason for why you should do this and why you shouldn't do this." "It set me free, it really did," she said.[11]

But after the film came out, Crystal Lee quickly deplored its emphasis on her personal life. Her objections centered less on the complaint that the film invaded her privacy—which, after all, her interviews with Leifermann already had compromised—than on her belief that the movie "should have been more about the union, about what we went through. In the movie," she charged, "they make like it is only me that's important, and there were so many others."[12]

In 1979, Ritt rather bitterly attacked Crystal Lee for her criticism of the movie. "She's obviously no longer the free spirit [portrayed] in my movie," Ritt said, adding that "she's turned into a middle-class bourgeois woman who doesn't want anyone to know about her life."[13] Nevertheless, Crystal's objections have some merit. From her point of view, her personal life had little to do with the labor dispute in which she was involved. She disliked intensely the sexual tension the movie created between her and Reuben, the union organizer. "When I heard about them making a movie, the author [Leifermann] called me about it and I wanted script rights, because you can see sex and violence anytime you cut the TV on," she told one interviewer. "I said it had to be about the union. I said that rinky-dink stuff wasn't important." The movie, for example, has a skinny-dipping scene in a rural creek on a hot summer day. Crystal thought the scene amusing. "Isn't it a shame," she said, with tongue in cheek, "that we never had that much fun."[14]

Crystal's involvement with the union began in April 1973, when she saw on the bulletin board at her plant a notice of a union meeting at a small local African-American church, the Chockoyotte Baptist Church. The TWUA was in the midst of a major organizing campaign, one that had begun officially in 1963 and was aimed at bringing unionism to the largely unorganized southern textile workers. Although comprising only a fifth of Stevens's Roanoke Rapids labor force of thirty-seven hundred, blacks were more union-conscious than their white counterparts. Indeed, at the Chockoyotte Church meeting, Crystal and another woman found themselves the only two whites among the seventy or so workers there. Right after that meeting, Crystal Lee, now afire with unionism, joined the TWUA.

From its inception in 1939, TWUA had known mostly failure in its efforts to organize the southern textile workers. Despite heartening gains during World War II, the union was unable in the 1950s and 1960s to expand its small numbers. The parent CIO's Southern Organizing Campaign, the so-called "Operation Dixie," launched amid much fanfare in 1946, had made little headway by the time of its demise in 1953. Despite enormous expenditures and initially high hopes, the TWUA gained only 10,805 new members in the South beyond the 70,200 covered under contract there in 1946.[15] Through the 1950s, internal conflict, disastrous strikes, and ruthless employers left the union battered and demoralized.

Nevertheless, in 1962, determined to organize the South, the TWUA began discussion with the Industrial Union Department (IUD) of the AFL-CIO to join the IUD's strategy of multi-union drives in particular places. On January 23, 1963, a TWUA committee picked J. P. Stevens as the target for a joint TWUA-IUD campaign. The union targeted Stevens—which, with fifty-three plants and 36,000 workers, then was the second largest textile company in the country—because it was a profitable company that concentrated large numbers of workers in three centers of operation: Rock Hill, South Carolina (eleven plants and 6,500 workers); Greenville-Spartanburg, South Carolina (fourteen plants and

12,650 workers); and the much smaller center in Roanoke Rapids, North Carolina (six plants and 3,700 workers).[16]

Despite its carefully thought out strategies, the TWUA-IUD campaign failed. Stevens fought back ferociously. The company fired, coerced, and intimidated prounion workers. In speeches to captive audiences, individual letters to employees, and pamphlets, Stevens argued that the union threatened jobs—indeed, the plants' very existence—because the union would bring "friction, terrorism, and fear."[17] The widespread dismissal of prounion workers in the companies' plants resulted in a historic legal struggle before the National Labor Relations Board between the company and the TWUA. Reed Johnston, the NLRB's regional director at Winston-Salem, North Carolina, said, "It was like nothing we ever had at the Board. Every day the union was filing a new charge of unfair practices—you know, discriminatory firings—against Stevens. Hell, the company was firing people the same day they signed the union card. Doing it blatantly."[18] During 1963 and 1964, Johnston began to put together the individual cases, rather arbitrarily labeling the first group "Stevens I." Before the final settlement of the conflict in 1983, the NLRB had gotten up to Stevens XXVI. The time, money, and effort that the legal cases took sapped the union's organizing efforts before the company's gates and in the mill communities. By the time Crystal Lee went to that union meeting at the church, the TWUA never had won an election at a J. P. Stevens plant, and the campaign she joined was mired in a legal struggle that defined "victory" as access to some company bulletin boards, direct union access to workers in the plants, and back pay and reinstatement for illegal firings. Union recognition, collective bargaining, and union contracts were remote goals. Indeed, by the mid-1970s, the union in the entire South represented only 33,227 workers in fifty-eight plants, half the number covered forty years earlier.[19]

In March 1973, one of the periodic leafleting efforts by the TWUA organizers in Roanoke Rapids elicited an unexpected response. An unprecedented 10 percent returned a mail-in card expressing interest in the union. The TWUA-IUD campaign then sent newly hired Eli Zivkovich, a fifty-five-year-old former United Mine Workers' organizer, to Roanoke Rapids, although he never before had organized textile workers in a southern town. Another organizer, Margaret Banks, soon joined him. The burly, straightforward, and conservatively dressed Zivkovich later took exception to how Hollywood actor Ron Leibman, dressed in jeans and open shirt and toting a shoulder bag, played him.

In 1979, after *Norma Rae* became a hit, Zivkovich appeared on Tom Snyder's CBS television program "Prime Time" and complained about his movie alter-ego: "Sneakers I didn't wear," he snorted. "I don't happen to own a pair of jeans. I've never worn what they call a shoulder bag in my life and I stay away from people who wear shoulder bags."[20]

Zivkovich and Banks set up shop in the Motel Dixie, close by one of the Stevens plants. It was Zivkovich who chaired the meeting at the black church, and it was Zivkovich who sought Crystal out in hope of gaining a convert among the white workers in Roanoke Rapids. He chose well. Crystal, with her usual dash and energy, threw herself into union work and became one of several key workers in Zivkovich's efforts to gain enough pledge cards for an NLRB bargaining-rights election. "By the end of May," wrote Leifermann, "no other union sympathizer in town, no one Eli had seen in twenty years of union work, seemed to have the zeal Crystal Lee had."[21]

Crystal's commitment to the union cause made her a major figure in the Roanoke Rapids campaign and changed her life. On Memorial Day, May 30, 1973, the famous scene with the union sign actually occurred. The company had posted notices implying that black workers, some seven hundred of the thirty-seven hundred Stevens workers in Roanoke Rapids, would dominate a union and take control of white jobs. Zivkovich, hearing about the notice, wanted Crystal to ascertain the exact wording. After management thwarted her first attempt, Crystal resolved to succeed during the next shift. That night she told a friend "that I was going to go to the bulletin board and copy that letter and they had better not try to stop me because if they touch[ed] me I was going to start swiping the clipboard. I said that I was going to blow this place sky high tonight."[22] During her break, after attempting unsuccessfully to memorize the notice, Crystal was seen by her supervisor deliberately copying the notice and was ordered to stop. She refused; in the ensuing argument, which resulted in her being taken to jail, she did stand on the folding table with her sign. As she remembered, "I attended my first union meeting on Mother's Day in 1973 and May 30th I was fired. Less than a month since I had attended my first union meeting."[23]

The company later dropped disorderly conduct charges but fired her for insubordination. Zivkovich thought that her firing would be a turning point in the campaign. After the incident, his weekly report noted that "white members of the Stevens work force loosened up," though "fear still prevails in the middle and older age groups." "The jailing," he told his supervisors, "should be followed through and will bear fruit." "Crystal," Zivkovich affirmed, "is honest and minus normal frailties can well spark the actions necessary to erase fear from those who perhaps can only be moved by real human interests."[24]

Zivkovich, now joined by a third TWUA organizer, Peter Gallaudet, hoped to use Crystal to break into the white workers' world in Roanoke Rapids. In June 1973, he managed to convince Harold McIver, his superior in the Stevens drive, secretly to put her on the TWUA payroll at $110 per week. And Zivkovich was right: she did prove valuable in introducing him to many white workers, as well as proving to be a tireless activist.[25]

The Leifermann article in the *New York Times Magazine* caught the attention of feminist leader Gloria Steinem. Steinem edited *MS* magazine and produced a television program called "Women Alive" for PBS. She put together a sixteen-minute segment about Crystal's work in the Stevens campaign, and on June 19, 1974, it was shown on Carolina public television. Steinem saw Crystal's story as that of "a move by blue collar women to involvement in the women's movement."[26] The program shows her participating in the union work in Roanoke Rapids. She passes out leaflets, talks union to fellow workers, and makes costumes for a young girls' union cheerleading squad. Crystal talks directly to the camera about her belief in the need for textile-worker unionism. The program's domestic shots reveal a kitchen more modern and middle-class than that of the fictional Norma Rae. After all, Cookie was a unionized paper-mill worker making twelve dollars an hour. Cookie appears in the kitchen actually cooking and talking about how proud he is of Crystal. "She couldn't be any other way," he says.[27]

This television film segment caught what Crystal Lee wanted to say about her struggle to unionize J. P. Stevens. "I don't feel that a woman's place is in the home," Crystal tells the reporter. "We are proud to be a part of the union." At the end she says, "I really got involved with the union because I feel like it really gave me the opportunity to be the woman I have always wanted to be and I can stand up and fight and I know I can win this fight."[28]

Crystal's spirited work created dissension in the ranks, as other workers resented her star status and her dominant personality. Even before the television show, Peter Gallaudet summed up the controversy. Near the end of 1973, he reported that organizers had asked Crystal to play a "less dominant role" because of "rumors" about her past sexual conduct spread by another woman worker. Gallaudet wrote that "the two women hate each other." The other woman, he claimed, had become jealous about the attention Jordan had received in the August *New York Times Magazine* article about the struggle going on in Roanoke Rapids, and Jordan disliked her in turn because of what Gallaudet called her spreading of "libelous" rumors about Crystal's sexual conduct.[29]

As Crystal worked full-time for the union, the controversy about her took its toll. The rumors concerned her relationship with Eli Zivkovich, as well as her past. Both denied wrongdoing, and even Cookie Jordan, often suspicious and jealous over Crystal, accepted the denials. Much later, Crystal explained that her relationship to Zivkovich resembled that of a daughter to father or an apprentice to a master. "Eli," she said "was a good man, a fighter and a survivor. . . . He was available when you needed him."[30]

By the fall of 1973, several workers had signed a petition asking Zivkovich to leave the campaign, and three workers had asked that Crystal Lee stay away from the office in order to encourage more participation by others. Organizer Gallaudet believed that, by fall, the rumors about an affair between Zivkovich and Crystal Lee had "evaporated," but that Jordan's hard-driving personality and a "scuffle" between another worker volunteer and Cookie Jordan had renewed some ill-will toward Crystal. At one point Crystal had argued with Gallaudet and Zivkovich, and, as in a scene in the movie, had been ordered out of the office for a week. But in his summary report of the campaign through 1973, Gallaudet in no way diminished Crystal's contribution, although the "feud," as he called it, between Jordan and the other woman had divided the white workers. But he reported that, by December 1973, the "factionalism" had waned, and the "anti-Jordan wing" had "diminished in strength."[31]

As Crystal Lee weathered the attacks on her in the campaign, she faced problems at home. The Steinem film depicted Cookie Jordan as defending her union work. In fact, Cookie was not always a supportive husband, and in late 1973 and in early 1974, her marriage grew shaky. Increasingly, Cookie resented the time and effort she gave to the union. Even though he did some of the housework, he would, Crystal later said, "throw my union work up to me." "I just didn't need that kind of crap," she said. "Cookie was afraid I had finally freed myself, that he was going to lose me."[32] Finally Cookie told her, "That union ain't done nothing for you, and it ain't done nothing for us, and I want you out of it starting now or you can get out of this house."[33] In mid-March 1974, she left, and after briefly moving in with her sister, she moved with her children to her other childhood home, Burlington, North Carolina. Although apparently she came back to Roanoke Rapids for a while, she and Cookie did not divorce until 1976.

In May 1974, Zivkovich himself left the TWUA and the struggle in Roanoke Rapids. The campaign, of course, never had been solely the work of Zivkovich, as the movie's depiction of Reuben Warshovsky so dramatically indicates. Sensing victory, the TWUA throughout 1974, both before and after Zivkovich's departure, strongly supported the Roanoke Rapids drive by assigning as many as four additional organizers. On August 23, 1974, in a stunning victory, the union won the NLRB election 1,685 to 1,448, thus gaining bargaining rights for the Stevens workers in the company's six plants in the North Carolina town.

Victory celebrations were short-lived, however. As expected, Stevens refused to bargain, and the Roanoke Rapids victory became just another Stevens unfair labor practice case for the NLRB. In 1976, the 140,000 members of the TWUA merged with the 260,000 members of the Amalgamated Clothing Workers of America to create the Amalgamated Clothing and Textile Workers Union of America (ACTWU), which in 1995 in turn merged with the International Ladies' Garment Workers' Union to form a new clothing and textile workers' union, UNITE. In the next few years, the new union, still committed to the Stevens strategy, vigorously pursued the legal battle with Stevens, one in which Crystal Sutton (the name she took after her divorce from Cookie Jordan) again played a role. In one of the union's many courtroom victories over Stevens, Crystal Lee Sutton received $13,436 in back pay for her illegal firing. On April 3, 1978, she went back to work at Roanoke Rapids, where she put in two days to make the point before returning to her home in Burlington.

Slowly the company's legal problems began to accumulate. The refusal to bargain at Roanoke Rapids after the 1974 election became a contested labor violation; on December 21, 1977, NLRB administrative law judge Bernard Reiss found that, in Roanoke Rapids and elsewhere, "Stevens had been engaged in a massive multi-state campaign to prevent unionization of its southern plants," using "corporate designed lawlessness." The company, Reiss said, had "approached the negotiations with all the tractability and open-mindedness of Sherman at the outskirts of Atlanta."[34] The Roanoke Rapids case merely added to Stevens's reputation as the "number one labor outlaw" in the nation, as Sol Stetin, president of the old TWUA and executive vice-president of the new ACTWU, repeatedly branded the company. In March 1978, Stevens was before the NLRB for 275 separate labor law violations at twenty-nine of its plants; and, for the first time in its history, the NLRB was considering a request for a national injunction against the company.

After its creation in 1976, the ACTWU added new weapons—an innovative "corporate campaign" and a widely publicized boycott—in its struggle with Stevens, which its operatives by then were calling "The War." In the "corporate campaign," unionists identified outside members of the Stevens board of directors and identified other boards they belonged to or, even more effective, other corporations they headed. ACTWU leaders wanted to focus attention on the implicit participation of these respected corporate leaders in Stevens's notoriously illegal antiunion policy. Such exposure would embarrass them in their own plants and communities. Moreover, ACTWU purchased shares of Stevens stock and had its agents picket shareholders' meetings and insert prounion resolutions on the agendas, thus further harassing Stevens's management and attracting press coverage.

In addition, the union poured enormous resources into a national boycott campaign against Stevens's products. "Don't sleep with J. P. Stevens," the union advised housewives. By the time *Norma Rae* hit the theaters in 1979, both campaigns successfully had created a nationwide awareness of the union's struggle to organize Stevens.[35]

Uninvolved in the final phases of the successful campaign in Roanoke Rapids, Crystal reconstructed her domestic life. After her divorce from Cookie, she married textile worker Preston Sutton, and they forged a lasting marriage. Wage-earning was more difficult, however, and she drifted from job to job. After leaving Roanoke Rapids, she first worked in a fried-chicken restaurant, but she hated fast-food work and turned again to the mills. She subsequently worked in Burlington hosiery mills and found other textile jobs as well, but none of these positions lasted long. She became convinced that she had been blacklisted because of her part in the J. P. Stevens campaign.[36]

When the movie came out, an enterprising reporter found Crystal working as a maid in a Hilton Inn in Burlington. She told him of her frustrated attempt to gain rights to the script, which in fact Leifermann controlled through his agreement with Ritt. She spoke of her disappointment with the movie, which she thought trivialized unionism. "I wanted a movie made of my life," she said. "They made it into a Hollywood movie, playing up sex and violence. They didn't tell my story, they used it."[37] In April 1979, another reporter, Chip Visci, writing in the *Detroit Free Press,* relied on this interview and the Leifermann book to write of the reality behind the purportedly fictional movie. "Unlike the Hollywood ending," he wrote, "Crystal Lee's story doesn't have a happy ending." Five years after the election, the Roanoke Rapids workers still had no contract. Crystal, moving from job to job, had failed to realize any money from the film. "So," Visci wrote, "Crystal Lee, the real Norma Rae, no longer works for a union, the textile workers don't have a contract and the hero union organizer is selling insurance. But then Roanoke Rapids is not exactly Hollywood."[38]

Elizabeth Stone's review of the movie in *MS* bitterly stressed the difference between the movie and the more complex realities playing out in Roanoke Rapids. She regretted that the film highlighted the romantic Norma Rae rather than the real Crystal Lee. The film's focus on Norma Rae's sexual attraction to the diffident Reuben trivialized Crystal Lee's union convictions. Stone argued that Ritt's illusions about Crystal as a working-class Joan of Arc and his desire to portray "a kind of Pygmalion relationship" overcame him. Stone wanted a real union movie about Crystal Lee, not Norma Rae. "The problem," she wrote, "is that Ritt and Company want to *use* Jordan's story rather than *tell* it. It is a pity that Ritt didn't trust Jordan's story more. In [its] fullness, it is an illumination of the lives of many thousands of textile workers." Thus, Stone wrote, Jordan's unionism, according to Leifermann, grew out of "restlessness *and* union conviction; Norma Rae's motives are trivialized [as] stemming from sexual attraction that the noble Reuben resisted and channeled into unionism."[39]

Crystal Lee's increasing public exposure, as well as the popularity of *Norma Rae,* renewed the interest of ACTWU leaders in her. True, in 1974, union officials had parted ways with her, and they disliked the movie's concentration on Crystal Lee's personal life and its glib characterization of the decidedly unglamorous former organizer, Zivkovich. "Eli Zivkovich," said union official Howard Brown, "has been transformed into a poetry-reading New York Jewish intellectual with an abrasive, if appealing, personality. He sports Yiddishisms, wears a denim jumpsuit unbuttoned to the waist, orders seltzer in a beer joint, and complains that the local hot dogs are not as good as northerner's [*sic*]." The film, Brown advised ACTWU president Sol Stetin, "perpetrates the image of the union as a bunch of New York Jews come to organize the naive mill workers." Nevertheless, Brown urged Stetin to consider the film as "useful" to the union. It might help to alter popular misperceptions of the union and reveal it as a moral force for change. It had a positive portrait of union textile workers, and it showed "individual harassment by supervisors and a general scene of injustice in the workplace."[40]

Stetin then made the decision to tie the movie and the real Norma Rae, Crystal Lee, to the ongoing Stevens campaign. On March 26, 1979, the union announced that the film was "loosely based" on the life of Crystal Lee Jordan, "a former J. P. Stevens worker active in the union organizing drive in Roanoke Rapids, N.C." An ACTWU release declared that the film accurately "outlined step by step the difficulties faced by union organizers in a hostile southern textile town." It added, "The film is realistic, the mill scenes are authentic, the acting is superlative and the characters are believable."[41] An article in the April issue of the union's monthly newspaper, *Labor Unity,* announced to its membership the relationship between the film and the campaign at Roanoke Rapids. Even so, while it praised the film, the article noted that in "real life" the workers continued to face "endless delaying tactics to avoid signing a contract." "The film," said the union, "does not show their [the company's] tactics; it leaves the impression that the workers' troubles are over."[42]

The union moved cautiously in reestablishing a relationship with Crystal Lee Sutton and using her in its organizing campaign. Crystal Lee's August 1979 appearance on the popular television show "Prime Time" disturbed some unionists, because they thought her description of events in Roanoke Rapids was "heavily slanted against the union" and made it appear that Crystal Lee was mistrusted by the union and that the Roanoke Rapids "win" was not important, given the company's delays.[43] But by now, Crystal herself had begun to embrace her role as the real Norma Rae, staunch unionist. For example, in mid-September 1979, at the invitation of the local union movement, which paid for her expenses, she spoke at the Women's Festival Day at Muskegon Community College in Muskegon, Michigan. Her talk extolled what the local reporter called "union feminism."[44]

Around this time, Crystal Lee told the union that she had come to the conclusion that the news media were manipulating her in ways not favorable to the Stevens campaign. She told a union staff member that recent interviews had made her appear to be "a tool of the company." Thus, when union leaders asked for her help, Crystal signaled her interest in being "useful" to the union. During October and November, the union put together a plan to employ Crystal at $295 a week in a public-relations capacity in the Stevens campaign. Under the direction of Gail Jeffords, a professional publicity agent, Crystal was to tour the country as "the real Norma Rae." She would attend special showings of *Norma Rae* to invited audiences and give a short talk and answer questions afterward. In each city, Crystal was to be available for television, radio, and newspaper interviews, during which she was to discuss her own experiences and those of other southern textile workers.[45]

The union approached the venture with some trepidation and put together a trial outing before the nationwide tour. On November 24–27, 1979, Crystal Lee as the real Norma Rae visited Toronto, Canada, and succeeded smashingly. She appeared on three Canadian television network shows, totaling twenty-four minutes of air time and reaching an audience of seven million viewers. She talked with reporters from three newspapers, and her interview with a *Toronto Star* syndicated columnist reached a potential of at least five million readers. In addition, she had a fifteen-minute appearance on a top local radio show.

This general publicity was excellent. But most important, reported Jeffords, "Crystal never missed an opportunity to beg listeners to *support the boycott* or to write to their or our government officials to crack down on the law-breaking Stevens. She used personal anecdotes of Stevens abuse, from being blacklisted to her aunt's treatment by the company [her aunt claimed that, after forty-nine years of working for Stevens, she had received a monthly pension of a mere twenty-seven dollars]. Wherever she went, people listened and were moved." Furthermore, Jeffords argued, "Potentially she has the talent, drive, and charisma to sway the public to her side." Jeffords praised Crystal Lee's "willingness to learn, eagerness to build support, cooperativeness and extraordinary personal magnetism and charm."[46] The *Toronto Star* article headlined her appearance at the New Democratic Party's convention, at which she received two standing ovations. Throughout her Canadian appearances, reporters concentrated on Crystal's union story and not on the movie and Sally Field.[47]

The Toronto experiment had succeeded beyond ACTWU expectations, and, beginning in January 1980, the union kicked off a nineteen-city U.S. tour featuring Crystal as the real Norma Rae. The press release emphasized that *Norma Rae,* the film, had grown out of the real life of Crystal and the struggle of the union at Roanoke Rapids. "In her own colorful way," said the release, Crystal would be "at last telling the far more dramatic true story behind the film," and it called Crystal "one of the most exciting and charismatic figures to emerge from the southern labor movement." A brief biographical sketch, to be distributed to the audiences, accompanied the press release. It emphasized her life as a worker, reporting that "in attempts to break out of the hopeless pattern of mill work, she's supported her family—starting at 16 with jobs as a waitress, barmaid, secretary, manager of a nightclub, saleslady in a dress shop, restaurant manager and fried chicken cooker, and hotel maid—she's sewn garments in an apparel factory, taken in home sewing, had a paper route, cut grass, taken in ironing and looked after the children of other working mothers." The sketch described the work at the folding table as work amid "horrible" conditions—"the noise, the heat, the dust, the disrespect of the owners—and the work was grinding, hope-killing drudgery, day after day." The sketch quoted Crystal as saying that "the union is my life—I guess it always will be." "In an area [the South] in which the prevailing attitude is anti-union, where workers are called 'Lint heads' or 'Trash,' where women are consistently paid less, and where all workers are paid the lowest wages in the nation," the publicity handout said, "Crystal Lee Sutton, heartened by recent ACTWU victories at J. P. Stevens, has found her life work: fighting for the future of her children and for that of all southern workers."[48]

In addition to the biographical sketch, ACTWU prepared a leaflet, one of the many it distributed throughout the country in its Stevens campaign, entitled "The *Real* 'Norma Rae' Was Fighting J. P. Stevens." The leaflet tied the movie and its union election to the "16-year battle for justice against J. P. Stevens and Co.—the nation's largest textile firm and one of the worst unionbusters and labor scofflaws in history." The leaflet noted that the "Hollywood happy ending in a film as realistic as was *Norma Rae* was only an encouraging episode in the lives of real Southern textile workers. J. P. Stevens has been found guilty of failure to bargain in good faith in Roanoke Rapids—workers still do not have a contract almost five years after the election."[49]

The whole purpose of the real Norma Rae tour was to balance the fictional nature of the film and to make it serve the union's purposes. At a celebrity-filled Los Angeles gathering, a photographer took a picture of Crystal and Sally Field together, their hands clasped together over their heads, fact and fiction joined. At her appearances after the movie, she spoke about the realities that lay behind *Norma Rae*. She emphasized that the movie could not adequately convey the factory environment—the lung-damaging cotton dust, the unrelenting noise, the unsafe conditions, the stretch-out to which loom workers were subjected, the presence of dangerous chemicals, and the poor medical treatment. She insisted that a union would bring decent wages, better working conditions, adequate medical insurance, and a decent pension plan. "This is the reason we organize," declared her written statement. "This is the reason I took those risks to bring a union to Roanoke Rapids. This is the real story behind 'Norma Rae.'"[50] In a prepared speech on March 8, 1980, for International Women's Day, she urged women to join the union and gain individual and worker's rights. The election victory in Roanoke Rapids, she insisted, "wasn't just done by the organizer and me as it looks like in the movie. It took a lot of people pulling together to make it work—the workers realized that sticking together—being a union—was the only way."[51]

Sly humor and intense conviction peppered her interviews. In Little Rock, Arkansas, she assured her audience that "mill workers aren't trash. We're not lint heads. We are important workers and our labor is valuable. What people have to realize is that in our world[,] without textile[s] we'd all have to shake ourselves dry."[52] In Philadelphia, she told a reporter that she was no Sally Field—she was tougher. She wanted to bring "dignity and protection to southern mill workers."[53]

Her appearances and media interviews, beginning in Boston in January and ending in Miami, brought the thirty-nine-year-old Crystal's story of the Stevens struggle to a potential audience of over seventy-five million people. There were fifteen national stories, fifty-seven newspaper feature stories, sixty-three local television appearances (including the national ABC "Good Morning America" program), and thirty-nine radio appearances. By the end of the tour, Crystal had been interviewed on television for a total of 13.5 hours and on radio for 22 hours.[54]

As a result of its decision to go public with the real Norma Rae, ACTWU gained enormous publicity for its campaign against Stevens. Of all the interviewers, perhaps Megan Rosenfeld, a *Washington Post* writer, best caught the difference between Hollywood's Norma Rae and the real Norma Rae, Crystal. *"Norma Rae,"* wrote Rosenfeld, "is probably one of the most powerful tools the labor movement will ever have. Its moving saga of simple good and bad, of plain people winning against the bad-guy establishment has inspired thousands—but of course, real life isn't that simple. Crystal Lee Sutton doesn't have a 22-inch waist—

Crystal Lee is just a woman—feistier and more plain spoken than most, but possessed of no mythical powers . . . —Her gifts are conviction and a willingness to be heard."[55]

After the tour ended, the union no longer needed Crystal. Beginning in the summer of 1980, ACTWU and Stevens took steps to end the historic confrontation. In October 1980, with the boycott and corporate campaign hurting the company's image if not its sales, and with cascading legal problems with the NLRB, the company agreed to bargain in good faith and sign a union contract at Roanoke Rapids. In return, the union ended its boycott and corporate campaign. Three years later, the company, the union, and the NLRB settled all pending complaints in an agreement that netted ACTWU $1.2 million and scores of Stevens workers back pay awards. In addition, CEO Whitney Stevens pledged that the company no longer would resort to unfair practices in its fight against the union.[56] "The War" was over. ACTWU's militant, well-conceived, and well-executed organizing drive had won for it at least a foothold in the Stevens system. But before it could exploit its new advantage, technological change, international competition, and an increasingly hostile political climate combined to impose sharp limits on ACTWU success. In the mid-1980s, Stevens downsized to only forty plants with twenty-three thousand workers. Indeed, early in 1988, the firm disappeared as a corporate entity, when it was bought and broken into three separate textile companies.

After the grand tour of 1980, Crystal's life settled back into the pattern of the late 1970s before the movie came out. A short stint working for ACTWU as an organizer in 1981 evidently did not work out well, and she permanently severed her connection with ACTWU. Finding steady work in the Burlington mills still proved difficult. For a while, she sometimes spoke at colleges in conjunction with showings of *Norma Rae,* but these appearances were rare. In those days before videocassettes and VCRs, her inability to obtain a sixteen-millimeter copy of the film from its Hollywood owner, Twentieth-Century Fox, limited even this modest opportunity to benefit from her experiences. At some point in the 1980s, she began operating a day care center in her home. She still occasionally speaks out publicly in support of unions, although sometimes she expresses bitterness about union leaders.[57] In 1993, for example, she went to Hendersonville, North Carolina, to lend support to a United Food and Commercial Workers' effort to organize a local nursing home.[58] A year later she visited Nashville, Tennessee, to encourage airline workers who were on strike.[59]

Public appearances are sporadic, however. For the most part, Crystal lives a private life in a comfortable brick home in the shade of a Burlington industrial plant, looking after her grandchildren and the children of other working women. In the 1970s, as the real Norma Rae, she provided a rare inner glimpse at the struggling efforts of some southern textile workers, particularly women, to become unionized. She never has lost faith in working people's causes. In 1985, she summed up that perseverance when she told a reporter that "with the Lord's help I'll always survive . . . —Unions are the only thing the working people have now."[60]

Notes

1. For accounts of Hollywood's distorted treatment of unions, see Francis R. Walsh, "The Films We Never Saw: American Movies View Organized Labor, 1934–1954," *Labor History* 27 (Fall 1986): 564–80; Steven J. Ross, "Struggles for the Screen: Workers, Radicals, and the Political Uses of Silent Film," *American Historical Review* 96, no. 2 (Apr. 1991): 333–67; Gay P. Zieger and Robert H. Zieger, "Unions on the Silver Screen: A Review Essay," *Labor History* 23, no. 1 (Winter 1982): 67–78; Edward Benson and Sharon Hartman Strom, "Crystal Lee, Norma Rae, and All Their Sisters: Working Women on Film," *Film Library Quarterly* 12 (1979): 18–23; and Daniel Leab, "Confronting a Myth: Films about Work and Workers," *Film Library Quarterly* 12 (1979): 8–16. For a recent article about the making of *Norma Rae,* see Robert Brent Toplin, "Norma Rae: Unionism in an Age of Feminism," *Labor History* 36 (Spring 1995): 282–98.
2. For a recent account of the literature on southern women textile workers, see Bess Beatty, "Gender Relations in Southern Textiles: A Historical Overview," in *Race, Class, and Community in Southern Labor History,* ed. Gary M. Fink and Merl E. Reed (Tuscaloosa: Univ. of Alabama Press, 1994), 9–16, 232. See also Douglas Flamming, *Creating the Modern South: Millhands and Managers in Dalton, Georgia, 1884–1984* (Chapel Hill: Univ. of North Carolina Press, 1992), 233–335. Flamming's account of unionism and the workers in the Crown Mills provides the best treatment of the changing character of the South's textile workers.
3. Susan Ware, *Still Missing: Amelia Earhart and the Search for Modern Feminism* (New York: Norton, 1993), 129.
4. Jacquelyn Dowd Hall, "Disorderly Women: Gender and Labor Militancy in the Appalachian South," *Journal of American History* 73 (Sept. 1986): 354–82; Jacquelyn Dowd Hall, "Private Eyes, Public Women: Images of Class and Sex in the Urban South, Atlanta, Georgia, 1913–1915," in *Work Engendered: Toward a New History of Men, Women, and Work,* ed. Eva Baron, (Ithaca, N.Y.: Cornell Univ. Press, 1991), 243–72. See also Mary E. Frederickson, "Heroines and Girl Strikers: Gender Issues and Organized Labor in the Twentieth-Century South," in *Organized Labor in the Twentieth-*

Century South, ed. Robert H. Zieger (Knoxville: Univ. of Tennessee Press, 1991), 84–112.

5. Lyn Garofola, "Let Us Now Praise Working Women," *In These Times,* Mar. 28–Apr. 3, 1979.
6. The commentary that most clearly evaluates the contribution of *Norma Rae* to labor history is found in Gay Zieger and Robert H. Zieger, "Unions on the Silver Screen," 69–73.
7. Aljean Hametz, "Martin Ritt Focuses on Labor Strife," *New York Times,* Feb. 25, 1979; David Anson, "True Grits," *Newsweek,* Mar. 5, 1979, p. 105; Richard Schickel, "Strike Busting," *Time,* Mar. 12, 1979, p. 176; *Nation,* Mar. 17, 1979, p. 314; Penelope Gilliatt, "Current Cinema," *New Yorker,* Mar. 19, 1979, p. 128; Stanley Kaufman, "Well Organized Labor," *New Republic,* Mar. 17, 1979, pp. 124–25; *New York Times,* Mar. 2 and Mar. 11, 1979.
8. Henry P. Leifermann, "The Unions Are Coming," *New York Times Magazine,* Aug. 5, 1973; Henry P. Leifermann, *Crystal Lee: A Woman of Inheritance* (New York: Macmillan, 1975). See also Lelia Carson Albrecht, "The Real 'Norma Rae' Is Anguished by the Hollywood Replay of Her Life and Battles," *People,* Apr. 1979, 43–44; and Mary Bishop, "The Diary of a Union Organizer," *Charlotte (N.C.) Observer,* May 7, 1978. Crystal also recounted some aspects of her life to Victoria Byerly; see "Crystal Lee Sutton," in *Hard Times Cotton Mill Girls: Personal Histories of Womanhood and Poverty in the South,* ed. Victoria Byerly (Ithaca, N.Y.: ILR Press, 1986), 201–18.
9. For a short account of the 17-year struggle between the union and the company, see James A. Hodges, "J. P. Stevens and the Union: Struggle for the South," in Fink and Reed, *Race, Class, and Community,* 53–71, 246–49.
10. Leifermann, *Crystal Lee,* 79. Here we use the names "Crystal" and "Crystal Lee" interchangeably, just as she seems to have done.
11. Ibid., 161 –63; Byerly, "Crystal Lee Sutton," 212.
12. Albrecht, "Real Norma Rae," 43.
13. Ibid.
14. Byerly, "Crystal Lee Sutton," 217; Crystal Lee Sutton, telephone interview by James Hodges, June 5, 1985, notes in author's possession.
15. Barbara Griffith, *The Crisis of American Labor: Operation Dixie and the Defeat of the CIO* (Philadelphia: Temple Univ. Press, 1988), 162.
16. Hodges, "J. P. Stevens and the Union," 56. The campaign lasted from 1963 to 1980. In addition to the Hodges account, see Barry E. Truchil, *Capital-Labor Relations in the U.S. Textile Industry* (New York: Praeger, 1988), 139–42; Phillip J. Wood, *Southern Capitalism: The Political Economy of North Carolina, 1880–1980* (Durham, N.C.: Duke Univ. Press, 1986), 182–86; and Richard Rowan and Robert E. Barr, *Employee Relations Trends and Practices in the Textile Industry* (Philadelphia: Univ. of Pennsylvania Press, 1987), 79–82. For an authoritative account of the NLRB's role, see James A. Gross, *Broken Promise: The Subversion of U.S. Labor Relations Policy, 1947–1994* (Philadelphia: Temple Univ. Press, 1995), 176–81. For the union's summary account, see *Labor Unity,* Dec 1980. The *New York Times* covered the conflict extensively, and the contemporary magazine press had numerous articles. Representative of the periodi-

cal coverage are Gloria Emerson, "The Union vs. J. P. Stevens: Organizing the Plantation," *Village Voice,* July 16, 1979; A. H. Raskin, "J. P. Stevens: Labor's Big Domino," *New York Times,* Aug. 15, 1976; and Ed McConville, "The Southern Textile War," *Nation,* Oct. 2, 1976, pp. 294–99. A particularly good historical and journalistic account that concentrates on Roanoke Rapids is William M. Adler and Earl Dotter, "A New Day in Dixie," *Southern Exposure* 22 (Spring 1994): 16–27. For an oral history of the union struggle in Roanoke Rapids in the late 1970s, see Mimi Conway, *Rise Gonna Rise: A Portrait of Southern Textile Workers* (New York: Anchor/Doubleday, 1979).

17. "Speech by G. G. to Employees, Wallace, N.C.," Feb. 17, 1975, Amalgamated Clothing and Textile Workers Union Papers, Labor-Management Documentation Center, Cornell Univ., Ithaca, N.Y. (hereafter cited as ACTWU Papers).
18. Stephen Brill, "Labor Outlaws," *American Lawyer,* Apr. 1980, 16.
19. "Survey of Bargaining Units under TWUA Agreement by Region, State and Industry—February, 1976," in Textile Workers Union of America (TWUA) Papers, State Historical Society of Wisconsin, Madison, Wisc. (hereafter cited as TWUA Papers).
20. "Prime Time" (television program), Tom Snyder host, CBS Television, 1979, undated transcript in TWUA Papers.
21. Leifermann, *Crystal Lee,* 132.
22. "Affidavit [by Crystal Lee Jordan] to Field Examiner Jack Bradshaw of the NLRB," June 21, 1973, TWUA Papers.
23. Byerly, "Crystal Lee Sutton," 205.
24. "Zivkovich Weekly Reports," June 1973, TWUA Papers.
25. Leifermann, *Crystal Lee,* 164–71.
26. Review of the program and interview with Gloria Steinem, *Durham (N.C.) Morning Herald,* June 19, 1974.
27. "Women Alive," television program produced by KERA-TV, Dallas, Tex. Rental available at the Audio-Visual Center, Indiana Univ., Bloomington, Ind.
28. Ibid.
29. Peter Gallaudet, "Progress Report on the J. P. Stevens Campaign at Roanoke Rapids, N. Carolina, 1973–1974," ca. Dec. 1973–early 1974, TWUA Papers.
30. Leifermann, *Crystal Lee,* 131, 180; Byerly, "Crystal Lee Sutton," 206–7.
31. Leifermann, *Crystal Lee,* 176–77; Gallaudet, "Progress Report."
32. Byerly, "Crystal Lee Sutton," 216.
33. Leifermann, *Crystal Lee,* 179–80.
34. U.S. National Labor Relations Board, *Decisions and Orders of the National Labor Relations Board 239* (Washington, D.C.: USGPO, 1979). Quoted in Conway, *Rise Gonna Rise,* 11.
35. Hodges, "J. P. Stevens and the Union," 61–62.
36. Crystal Lee Sutton, telephone interview by James Hodges, June 5, 1985, notes in author's possession.
37. Jim Doddon, "Crystal Lee," *Atlanta Journal and Constitution Magazine,* June 10, 1979.

38. Chip Visci, "No Happy Ending for the Real Life Norma Rae," *Detroit Free Press,* Apr. 13, 1979.
39. Elizabeth Stone, "Norma Rae: The Story They Could Have Told," *MS* Magazine, May 1979, pp. 30–32.
40. Harold Brown to Sol Stetin, Feb. 14, 1979, ACTWU Papers.
41. ACTWU press release prepared by Anne Rivera, Mar. 26, 1979, ACTWU Papers.
42. *Labor Unity,* Mar. 1979.
43. Burt Beck to ACTWU Officers, Memorandum, Aug. 14, 1979, ACTWU Papers.
44. *Muskegon Chronicle,* Sept. 14, 1979.
45. Del Mileski to Sol Stetin, Sept. 9, 1979; Sol Stetin to Del Mileski, Sept. 9, 1979; Del Mileski to Jack Sheinkman and Sol Stetin, Sept. 14, 1979; Pam Woywod to Crystal Lee Sutton, Oct. 22, 1979; all in ACTWU Papers.
46. Gail Jeffords to Murray Finley (President of ACTWU), Jack Sheinkman, Sol Stetin, and Scott Hoyman, Dec. 3, 1979, ACTWU Papers.
47. *Toronto Star,* Nov. 26, 1979. Two videos of Crystal's television appearances can be found in audiovisual collection, ACTWU Papers.
48. Press release for Jan. 30, 1980, for Philadelphia visit (releases were much the same for all cities toured) and "Fact Sheet—Background," prepared by Gail Jeffords, in ACTWU Papers.
49. "The Real 'Norma Rae' Was Fighting J. P. Stevens," Leaflet in ACTWU Papers, located in several of the officers' files.
50. "Screening Talk" for 1980 tour by Crystal Lee Sutton, in ACTWU Papers. Interview articles indicate that Crystal often deviated from her "script."
51. Speech by Crystal Lee Sutton, prepared for International Women's Day, dated Mar. 8, 1980, in ACTWU Papers.
52. *Arkansas Democrat,* June 22, 1980.
53. *Philadelphia Daily News,* Jan. 30, 1980.
54. Gail Jeffords to Murray Finley, Jack Sheinkman, Sol Stetin, Scott Hoyman, Del Mileski, and Pam Woywod, "Final Media Report on Media Coverage for Crystal Lee Sutton," June 30, 1980, in ACTWU Papers.
55. *Washington Post,* June 11, 1980.
56. Hodges, "J. P. Stevens and the Union," 62–63.
57. For an example of her disaffection with union leaders, see James Hunter, "Union Activist of Norma Rae Fame Now Weaves a Sad Tale," *Atlanta Journal-Constitution,* Jan. 9, 1985.
58. *Hendersonville Times-News,* Dec. 5, 1993.
59. Michael Folk, "Looking for Norma Rae," *Solidarity,* Mar. 1994, pp. 16–17.
60. *Atlanta Journal-Constitution,* June 9, 1985.

From Primordial Folk to Redundant Workers: Southern Textile Workers and Social Observers, 1920–1990

Robert H. Zieger

Throughout the twentieth century, southern cotton mill workers and their communities have attracted journalistic, academic, and polemical commentators. With the exception of coal miners and perhaps auto workers, no body of workers has received more attention than the textile operatives of the Piedmont. Employers and their defenders have sought endlessly to justify their paternalism and antiunionism. For nearly a hundred years now, reformers and activists have probed the hills and valleys of the Piedmont. Sociologists and economists have documented the distinctive character of the mill towns, the social and cultural attributes of their inhabitants, and the industry's patterns of industrial relations.[1]

Throughout this lengthy record of commentary, three primary characterizations of mill workers have emerged. These are the Primordial Folk, the Emerging Realists, and the Incipient Proletarians. Few of the many writers drawn to the villages and mills of the Piedmont have been able to resist, however subtly, the temptation to impose their own conceptual templates upon their taciturn subjects.

The term *Primordial Folk* identifies a view of southern cotton textile workers held by journalists, academics, and other observers, who depict them as denizens of the isolated rural South, toiling in a modern industry but tenacious in adhering to their traditional culture. In the eyes of these observers, mill workers exhibited the modes of dress, talk, and behavior allegedly characteristic of their ancestors, who, it was thought, had carried on folkways initially brought to the isolated Appalachian regions during Elizabethan times.[2]

Employers and their spokesmen, in contrast, tended to see mill workers as *Emerging Realists*. Not the most reflective or articulate of observers, employers—often through academic surrogates—acknowledged the backwardness and traditionalism of their hired hands. At the same time, they saw mill work and village life as means by which southern whites could join the modern world, with its values of individual acquisitiveness, social mobility, and improved material standards and opportunities. Mill workers, in this view, rejected labor organization and sustained social protest, not because they were repressed or intimidated, but because identification with the employer and consistent individual effort was the rational choice. Public discourse about the qualities and attributes of mill workers often centered around questions of labor markets and unionization, but implicit in employers' defense of their labor practices and policies was the image of the Emerging Realist as the normative mill worker.[3]

Where some observers saw Primordial Folk and employers saw Emerging Realists, labor organizers and their allies often found—or at least wished to find—*Incipient Proletarians*. Many laborites, it is true, initially embraced the Primordial Folk construct, but even the least ideological among them held, as an article of faith, that modern forces of industrial production and resulting social change would strip away atavistic attributes and force workers to confront the irrationalities and injustices of capitalist production. Today's docile millhand, they believed, no doubt in time would become tomorrow's disillusioned worker and, eventually, a likely union recruit. In response to the failure to build unions among textile workers, it is true, some organizers came to believe that they would never make the transition, so steeped in ignorance, apathy, and traditionalism were the Piedmont's millhands. And after World War II, as wages began to rise and the paternalistic villages gave way to employee-owned housing, CIO organizers feared that the employers' characterization of their hands as Emerging Realists was becoming all too true. Still, throughout the middle years of this century, unionists made repeated efforts to bring the blessings of unionism to the Piedmont. These efforts generically were based upon one or another variation of the Incipient Proletarian construct.[4]

Most commentary about textile workers has invoked some version of these three paradigms. The writings and pronouncements of mill operators and their spokespersons, reformers, union activists, and journalistic and social scientific observers have adverted repeatedly to them. Over the years, observers of the Piedmont's textile workers, whether trained journalists or social scientists or self-interested employers or labor activists, thus have created not only a rich documentary record of the lives and experiences of their subjects but powerful images of them as well.[5]

Employers

Employers regularly posited the view of their charges as throwbacks to "traditional" southern culture, as Primordial Folk. At the same time—indeed, often almost literally in the same breath—they invoked the image of the Emerging Realist. "They are as a class thriftless and shortsighted," declared a reporter for *Barron's* in 1925. At the same time, he assured his readers, "they have the American idea of progress by individual effort." Yet "they are the dregs of the farmer population . . . , and are too ignorant to look after themselves and their homes properly." "'[T]hey are like children, and we have to take care of them,'" lamented one mill owner in 1924.[6]

In her 1927 account of her sojourn as welfare agent for the Saxon Mills in Spartanburg, South Carolina, social worker Marjorie Potwin made careful distinctions among the various groups of mill workers. Workers drawn from nearby farms, she reported, were sturdy, colorful, energetic, and ambitious—Emerging Realists. Recruits from the mountain areas, however, were shiftless and apathetic. Indeed, "[I]f there had been a 'Jukes' family reunion they would have sat at the head of the table." Particularly pathological, according to the northern-educated Potwin, were the families who moved from mill to mill, "always undernourished and unkempt, if not downright filthy." Overall, however, Potwin's assessment of the mill people was positive: under the stabilizing influence of enlightened mill management, textile workers were learning to become responsible citizens. Education was transforming their lives; hobbies such as book collecting, quilt making, photography, chicken raising, and doll making brought "the operatives home from work with the joyful footsteps of anticipation." Sixteen years later, President William Plumer Jacobs of Presbyterian College, introducing a volume extolling the textile companies and their mill towns, observed that both mill owner and mill worker were descended from "the same Anglo-Saxon stock." He deplored "distorted pictures of the barefoot child . . . and poorly clad people of the 'Tobacco Road' environment." In the Piedmont, white southerners, workers and operators alike, had created a "democratic, friendly, homogeneous and modern life" in the textile towns.[7]

By far the most sophisticated management-inclined observer of the Piedmont people was Glenn Gilman, a social psychologist who traveled and interviewed extensively in the textile belt in the 1950s. Although his own research methods were heavily deductive, Gilman attempted to refute stereotypical views that described mill workers as dependent, ignorant, and provincial. Mill workers, Gilman's findings suggested, combined the best of the Primordial Folk with the best of the Emerging Realist.

He posited the categories *folkways* and *massways*. Even in the 1950s, he insisted, mill workers valued face-to-face relationships; and mill operators, traditionally drawn from the same population pool, naturally practiced these in an idiom that their workers intuitively understood. To be sure, by the end of World War II, more impersonal massways had come to the mills; indeed, according to Gilman, the bitter labor upheavals of the late 1920s and early 1930s had stemmed directly from the introduction of impersonal managerial techniques by a new breed of college-trained managers and engineers. But enlightened managers soon realized that the abrupt imposition of the new regime had strained the unique bonds of loyalty that the mills' folkways had sustained. After World War II, they moved promptly to rebuild the old intimacy. As a result, southern mill operators once again could count on a contented labor force. Workers responded to "the attempts of organizers to split the hourly-rated group away from management" with either resentment or amusement, so inappropriate were the organizing tactics characteristic of "massways" to the textile trade.[8]

Management-oriented observers believed that labor unions had no legitimate role in southern textiles. In the early days, employer-supplied housing and welfare work had made the union irrelevant to the Piedmont. Moreover, northern-based unions sent outsiders and even foreigners to disrupt the communal relations that characterized the southern mills. The southern textile industry was fiercely competitive, with labor accounting for a high percentage of the cost of production. Sheer economic common sense, combined with the distinctive character of the southern mill workers and their unique bonding with their employers, made organized labor irrelevant and disruptive. Employers and their spokespersons believe that, as the Emerging Realist gradually replaced the Primordial Folk, the mill worker would find no reason to abandon her or his sensible hostility toward unions. Over the years, predominant themes were the contentedness of the mill workers and the positive role that textile communities—whether employer-owned villages or, more recently, simply single-industry towns—played in bringing the advantages of industrial life to the upcountry South. Although making continual advances, the Emerging Realist never quite supplanted the Primordial Folk completely.

Activists and Organizers

Labor unionists and their allies were convinced that the world of the Primordial Folk must give way to that of the Incipient Proletarian. Of course, labor organizers and their liberal sympathizers despised the antiunionism associated with mill life. However, unionists did not always dismiss the employers' characterizations of the mill workers and their communities. Thus, union sympathizer Paul Blanshard, surveying the Piedmont for the *New Republic* in the early 1920s, declared that "the mill workers seem to show less virility and ambition than other factory workers. They look and act 'washed out.' . . . I did not meet a mill worker who expressed determination or pugnacity or a conviction powerfully held." In 1924, the liberal academician Frank Tannenbaum, deploring the effects of mill-owner paternalism and hoping for mill-worker empowerment, nonetheless concluded that "they *are* like children . . . , unhappy children . . . long, emaciated figures, wan and sleepy-looking and without any vividness or interest."[9]

Leaders of national textile unions regarded the southern mill workers as exotic and problematic. Reflecting the urban and immigrant character of the northern mills, union leaders saw the southern mills primarily as a problem to be dealt with, rather than as an opportunity for expanding labor's influence. Indeed, organized labor's perception of the problem of the South is revealingly summed up in the complaint of the CIO textile workers union in 1939 that "the South. . . seems like a bottomless pit to us and no doubt will continue to be that for some time to come."[10]

For over two decades, Textile Workers' research director Solomon Barkin struggled to understand the southern mill operative's psyche. In a 1939 report, he argued that mill hands combined chronic apathy with spasms of undisciplined militancy. They failed to grasp the fact that the technological changes that led to the hated stretchout were inevitable. Thus, instead of building sober trade unions that would give workers a voice in regulating and extracting material benefits from these changes—the sensible course that an Incipient Proletarian or even an Emerging Realist would take—southern workers lashed out in protest, only to lapse back into quiescence upon defeat. Barkin conducted surveys, commissioned public opinion polls, and subsidized academic studies in an effort to find the key to the textile workers' mysterious worldview.[11]

For some labor activists who were less tied to the existing labor movement, however, the social psyche of mill workers represented an opportunity rather than an obstacle. Thus Tom Tippett, a worker intellectual associated with the Brookwood Labor College in the 1920s and 1930s, combined the themes of Primordial Folk and Incipient Proletarians. As witness to the remarkable surge of textile worker militancy in the late 1920s, Tippett viewed the mixture of traditionalist endurance and mutuality on the one hand, and growing recognition of class position on the other, as heralding the emergence of a genuine mass movement.

His book, *When Southern Labor Stirs,* published in 1931, vividly captures the militancy the rebellious textile workers. Wherever Tippett went in the Piedmont, textile workers "look and act in almost the same way." They ran to type: tall and lean, inarticulate, undernourished. Tippett, too, saw mill people as physically weakened. "Vitality was always at a low ebb. They all seemed as tired in the early morning as when the long day was over."

But initial appearances deceived. One summer he lived with a mill family and recorded the grueling physical regimen, which began at 5 A.M. Not only did they put in twelve-hour days at the mill; each family member also had exhausting domestic chores. No wonder family members appeared listless. If this daunting schedule sapped strength, however, it integrated work and family life and thereby provided the basis for unique forms of protest, as the Primordial Folk and the Incipient Proletarian fused.

Thus strikes protesting the stretchout transformed the mill workers. Where Barkin and other trade union veterans saw irresponsible adventurism, Tippett saw courageous mass activism. The hopes engendered by the stretch-out strikes transformed the Piedmont workers. "The color of their skin changed, they took on weight," he reported. At the Marion, North Carolina, strike of 1929, "The air was thick with the perfume of magnolia trees. . . . The people . . . were expressing the sensation of industrial freedom for the first time in their lives." In the open-air meetings, workers stood in the rain, listening to speeches that translated religious messages into the language of temporal struggle. "Everybody would envisage a new kind of religion" and speak their "zeal for the brotherhood of unionism."[12]

In the end, however, the great textile uprising of the late 1920s and early 1930s failed. Subsequent efforts by the CIO, despite some successes in the World War II era, likewise bore stunted fruit. CIO organizers in the great Southern Organizing Campaign of 1946 ran into the Primordial Folk once again, although by now they detected the Emerging Realist. Mill workers proved just responsive enough to the union appeal to cause employers to meet union wage rates and to continue paternalistic largess. In the 1950s, after decades of frustration and failure, Barkin, still trying to find the key, engaged the outpatient psychiatric department of the University of North Carolina hospital to conduct an inquiry into the psyche of the mill worker. He wrote up the findings in an article entitled "The Personality Profile of the Textile Worker," which claimed that textile workers suffered from unusually high incidence of neurotic disorders.[13] Thus, this union intellectual turned to Freud, not Marx, in an effort to understand the behavior of the still-Primordial Folk of the Piedmont.

Contemporary Social Scientists

From the 1920s onward, sociologists, social psychologists, economists, and other academic observers have regarded the Piedmont as an ideal laboratory for social observation. Accounts of their findings provide historians with one of the richest bodies of social reporting available for any group of twentieth-century American workers. Most observers have fallen back on variations of the Primordial Folk, Incipient Proletarian, and Emerging Realist typologies.

In the 1920s, the Piedmont mills provided grist for several Ph.D. dissertations and other academic inquiries. Indeed, remarked one of the most active investigators, Harriet L. Herring, "The cotton mill is getting to be a favorite subject for philosophizing."[14] The most prolific of the mills' academic observers were the brothers Broadus Mitchell and George Mitchell, economists and close students of the industry and its workforce. Broadus Mitchell's 1921 dissertation, "The Rise of Cotton

Mills in the South," was the first sustained scholarly study of the Piedmont. It paid homage to the southern entrepreneurs who had created the region's modern textile industry. Acting out of a combination of altruistic and commercial motives, they had rescued the upcountry peasantry from its post–Civil War penury and enabled the southern rural underclass to gain entry into the modern world. Mill workers, in return, proved loyal and productive workers, gradually learning the ways of modern life. Thus, the Primordial Folk gradually gave way to the Emerging Realist.[15]

Through the middle and later 1920s, however, Broadus and his economist brother George Mitchell developed more critical perspectives on the employers and greater awareness of the mill workers' problems. Paternalism now had reached its limits. In a July 1927 article, the Mitchells described the Piedmont operatives as Incipient Proletarians, "300,000 Rip Van Winkles" who only now were recognizing that their interests could diverge from those of their employers. Northern observers, they charged, distorted the true situation among the millhands, "looking upon the Southern Poor Whites only as picturesque natives." The Mitchells viewed the spasmodic uprisings of textile workers in the late twenties as a sign that the mill workers were coming of age, and the brothers regarded the entry of conservative AFL unionism as a positive development. Unions would bring textile workers to the next and highest stage of industrial citizenship; through labor organization, "another industrial swamp will be gradually drained." Gone forever would be the Primordial Folk; in their place, a healthily Calculating Proletarian was emerging.[16]

Other academics focused more directly on the mill villages and their inhabitants. Thus, in a poignant 1928 volume, Lois MacDonald, a young economist employed by the YWCA, reported on findings and observations based on several years of living and working in the Carolina mill communities. Impatient with the limitations of the available statistical material, MacDonald spent much of her time talking and visiting with her subjects. Years later, she recalled her method of inquiry: "I would interview and talk to two or three people, visit in two or three houses, and then I'd go off in the bushes someplace and write up the notes before I forgot them."[17]

She painted a grim picture. In the 1920s, the Primordial Folk continued to hold sway. In the three villages she investigated, workers combined highly negative self-assessments, unhappiness with their lot, and narrow-minded provincialism with seemingly heartfelt expressions of loyalty and gratitude toward their employers. True, workers griped that wages were low and job security nonexistent, but, MacDonald reported with a hint of exasperation, "no connection was made between the [supposedly] good policies of the company and these conditions." When asked how conditions in the villages might be improved, workers usually spoke in terms of bettering their neighbors' morals or the need to practice Christian living and almost never in terms of collective civic or workplace action. "The one thing on which there is almost unanimous agreement is that the boss is the best friend a man has," she lamented.

Evidence of poverty, blighted lives, and constricted horizons abounded. Most of the women "complain of being sick very often. Almost all of them seem to be overworked and prematurely old." Yet MacDonald was forced to conclude that the almost universal passivity, hopelessness, and enervation that gripped these "typical mill villages" precluded effective collective protest.[18]

Not every northern academic shared MacDonald's negative view of mill community life. In the early 1930s, Ben Lemert, an economics instructor at Duke University, supplemented documentary research on the statistical contours of southern textiles with a four-month motor trip through the mill country. From Lynchburg, Virginia, to Anniston, Alabama, he crisscrossed three thousand miles of mountain roads, visiting forty-three textile factories and inspecting "many mill villages." He talked with employers, townspeople, city officials, and local businessmen, as well as textile workers.

Of all the contemporary accounts of mill life produced by academics, Lemert's was the most positive. Indeed, his descriptions depart from the Folk-Realist-Proletarian triptych to create a kind of solipsistic genre of reporting that might be labeled "Capitalist Realist." The contrast with MacDonald's discouraging view could hardly be greater.

Initially Lemert had been prepared for the worst, expecting to see "dirty, ragged children, tumble-down shacks and 'Simon Legrees'" running the factories. To his mounting surprise, instead he "saw comfortable houses . . . , pretty grass plots in front . . . and many garages with cars in them." Workers' accommodations far surpassed the rundown housing characteristic of the adjacent mountain and tenant farm areas. Fresh air, access to hunting, fishing, swimming, and other wholesome recreation, and lovely mountain scenery were important fringe benefits. At Lyman, South Carolina, Lemert "watched the workmen going to their work through a pine woods . . . and thought of the workers in New York . . . in the stuffy, crowded subways."

Nor were the virtues of the Piedmont confined to the physical surroundings. Lemert's observations are filled with reports of workers joking and roughhousing and "clean, neat, bright and happy looking" children. Try as he might, he "could not find the misery for which he was looking."

True, the workers with whom he spoke in this textile-industry *wanderjahr,* which took place at the tail end of the stretchout-induced upheavals of the late twenties, seemed passive. But the young economist attributed this attitude to satisfaction with work and loyalty to employers. Indeed, "The writer received the bitterest comments concerning mill laboring conditions" not from mill workers but "from persons not connected with mill life."[19]

The most systematic and authoritative of these early social-scientific examinations of mill and village life emanated from the Institute for Research in Social Change at the University of North Carolina. In the late 1920s, two of its associates, Harriet L. Herring and Jennings J. Rhyne, conducted extensive structured surveys of life and labor in the Carolina mill communities. Of all the early investigations, these were perhaps the most authoritative and concrete, focusing on conditions observed rather than on expectations of the observers. Both combined the images of Folk, Realist, and Proletarian; each stressed the variegated nature of the mill communities and the specificity of locale in making judgments.

Rhyne conducted detailed interviews and collected other survey data on over twenty-three hundred mill workers and their families in his native Gaston County, North Carolina. Even when he cut loose from his statistical data, Rhyne went beyond the impressionism characteristic of MacDonald's, Potwin's, and Lemert's accounts and stressed the diversity of the mill villages. To be sure, Rhyne could wax eloquent in describing the lives and labors of his subjects. His account of a typical work day depicts the burdens of mill life as vividly as Tippett's less academic 1931 work. The blast of the morning whistle awakened the workers at 5 A.M. After a simple breakfast, they trudged through the village, gathering in families and neighborhood knots, then in a steady stream, heading for the hulking mill. "Five hundred, one thousand, two thousand five hundred strong they come. . . . The men come clad in overalls, or a three-dollar pair of trousers and a coat that does not match."

Women wore gingham dresses. Lint from the previous day's work clung to the hair of many of the workers, too exhausted after a ten- or twelve-hour day to groom themselves adequately. The mills shrieked with the noise of the machines, and the older factories, with their overhead belts, were dark and stifling.

Yet, for Rhyne, the village and its factory had their charms. Children of mill families routinely went to work at age fourteen, but for the doffer boys, at least, toil was punctuated with comradeship and horseplay. "Sometimes the passer-by along the street, especially in the summer, sees eight or ten of these boys outside the mill lying under the shade of the trees telling jokes and smoking cigarettes." Nor were the adults beaten down and sickly, like those observed by Lois MacDonald. Evening found mill workers on their porch rockers, down at the pool hall, attending the motion picture show, or loafing around the downtown streets. Weekends and days off permitted hunting and fishing and perhaps, for the women, light gardening.

Rhyne's was far from an idyllic picture. Few workers read anything other than the *Bible,* and many, he suspected, were illiterate. They took little interest in politics or civic improvement. While Rhyne's surveys reveal that over 43 percent of the workers expressed attitudes favorable toward unions, he detected deep suspicion of the northern organizers of the United Textile Workers who had been active in the area during the World War I period. This, in short, was an insular, provincial world, but one in which "the great bulk of the cotton mill population of the state and of the South generally has undergone in recent years marked improvement in all phases of life." Above all, Rhyne warned his readers, it was important to avoid hasty generalization, for his extensive surveys and personal observations highlighted the diversity of the mill villages.[20]

Harriet L. Herring's *Welfare Work in Mill Villages,* published in 1929, contained a similar message. For Herring, also a native of the region, the industrialization of the Piedmont offered sharply defined opportunities for the uplift of poor whites. No Lady Bountiful, Herring, during her brief career as a village social worker, saw herself as someone who could use her own education—she studied at Radcliffe and Bryn Mawr—to assist less fortunate folk to make the transition from traditional to modern life.[21]

When she shifted operations from the villages to the Institute for Research in Social Change in Chapel Hill, Herring sought to play the role of interpreter of Piedmont life and labor to the larger intellectual community. Mill folk, she believed, just now were emerging from a traditionalist past. Expanding educational opportunities, medical services, and social possibilities were making mill workers less willing to tolerate poor conditions. And the best mills *were* upgrading their housing, schools, and services. She worked closely with Luther Hodges, a leader in innovative welfare work, believing that, given the existing power relations, with unions weak or nonexistent and employers all-powerful, enlightened welfare work offered the mill workers the best possibility of improvement in their lives. The Primordial Folk, about whom Herring was the opposite of sentimental, gradually would give way to more Emerging Realists.

Herring observed the mill worker activism that erupted in 1928 cautiously. Were Incipient Proletarians, long anticipated by liberal and northern observers, surging to the fore? On the one hand, she was impressed with the new sense of vigor and self-direction that strikers in Gastonia, Marion, and other flashpoints exhibited. She always had believed, she told a liberal New York editor, "that the southern textile worker has spunk enough and get up and go to fight when he really feels himself ill-treated" and now felt vindicated. The current upheaval in the Piedmont, she reported, involved the most articulate, energetic, and intelligent workers. Were these carefully calculated protests, whose leaders could master the intricacies of modern industrial relations? Or did a combination of traditionalist blood feud and raw class grievance create the potential for catastrophe in the Piedmont?[22]

Despite her sympathies for the mill workers, Herring carefully distinguished herself from the liberals and activists who saw even in the strikers of the late 1920s Incipient Proletarians. As much as she respected Lois MacDonald, who was active in worker-centered YWCA programs, Herring thought of her more as a "missionary" than an academic, while she, Herring, "wasn't missionary-ing" but rather was seeking a sober assessment of mill village life. In the end, "it is . . . obvious that the owner can largely prevent organization if he chooses," for he knows everything that goes on in the villages. Nor could textile workers be relied upon to conduct their protests wisely and peacefully. Piedmont folk, she observed, still knew little about modern techniques of negotiating, maneuvering through the legal system, and manipulating public opinion. They did, however, know a great deal about how to use firearms; and, she later recalled, her greatest hope during the 1929 strikes—an unrealized one—was that no one would be killed.[23]

Despite the atavism of violent encounter, Herring and other observers did detect a movement of mill workers away from the traditionalism of the Primordial Folk. In one area, however—that of race—traditionalism retained full sway. Over and over, contemporary observers documented the virtual absence of immigrants or even natives of nonsouthern states among the mill workers. Workers and mill owners alike, proclaimed William Plumer Jacobs, "have the same [Anglo-Saxon] blood coursing through their veins." New Englander Marjorie Potwin admired the sturdy, Elizabethan-American heritage of her mill worker charges.[24]

Racism was ubiquitous. Mill workers repeatedly had thwarted employers' efforts to introduce black workers into the mills. The few blacks living in mill villages were tolerated only as common laborers and domestic servants. Potwin found quaint the practice of the white mill children of Spartanburg, who delighted in "rocking" black children: "It was rare sport, well-nigh irresistible, to have a frightened little 'nigger' for a moving target."[25]

MacDonald reported violent antagonism toward blacks, a pervasive attitude held with an intensity that seemed far out of proportion to the unlikely role that they might play as economic rivals. "I don't believe in stringing up the blacks . . . ," observed one of her interviewees, "but its the only way you can keep them under control." Another boasted that "I helped horse whip many a nigger. It's the only way to keep the races from gettin' mixed." In both Potwin's Spartanburg and MacDonald's anonymous Carolina villages, the Ku Klux Klan was active.[26]

Social Scientists, 1942–1985

The Piedmont's prominence as a locus for social research remained high even after these studies of mill village life were completed. Accounts of mill communities, such as Liston Pope's *Millhands and Preachers* (1942), on Gastonia, and John Morland's *The Millways of Kent* (1958), an intensive study of an anonymous textile community, are classics of social research. In *The Passing of the Mill Village* (1949), Harriet Herring investigated the transition from employer-owned housing to worker ownership. In *Spindles and Spires* (1976), a team of sociologists reported still again on Gastonia, this time stressing the emergence of racial conflict as a political and social factor. Others have sought to test whether traditional mill workers' attitudes and patterns of behavior have survived the economic, racial, and demographic changes that have swept the

South since World War II, presumably erasing the material bases of Primordial Folk culture.[27] All have continued, although usually in more modulated idioms, the traditional typologies that have characterized commentary on mill workers throughout much of the century.

Pope's *Millhands and Preachers* actually did much to fix the stereotypes of the Primordial Folk in the literature. The only sustained study of the subject between the early 1930s and the late 1950s, it invoked themes of traditionalism and paternalism at the center of the Gastonia-Loray strike of 1929. *Millhands and Preachers* depicted a Gothic world of formless protest growing out of disappointed clientage. How different the atavistic mill workers were from the purposeful and triumphant CIO industrial unionists of the 1930s and 1940s. The confused lashing out of the Primordial Folk of Gaston County had little in common with the vigorous proletarianism of the resurgent New Deal labor movement.[28]

After World War II, other, more systematic investigators returned to the Piedmont to measure the extent to which recent developments had eroded the region's traditional patterns. Morland, the authors of *Spindles and Spires,* and more recent sociological investigators carefully employed the increasingly sophisticated methodologies of advanced social research. Morland, whose study is based on material gathered in 1948–49, spent a year in "Kent," a Piedmont textile town of about forty-five hundred inhabitants. He worked with local civic and educational officials to collect systematic data, coordinated questionnaire surveys of mill workers, and followed approved field-study research methods in conducting scores of interviews. Likewise, John Earle, Dean D. Knudson, and Donald W. Shriver, Jr., subjected Gastonia of the mid-1970s to carefully structured research techniques in their study of the interaction between the North Carolina community's religious institutions and the engines of social change.[29]

Whatever the method employed, however, conclusions about the character of mill people and the prospects for trade unionism were similar. All reported on the remarkable continuing ethnic homogeneity of mill workers, although it is true that, by the time of Earle et al.'s study of Gastonia, substantial numbers of black workers had begun to toil in the mills. "The real monotony of the mill village," remarked Harriet Herring in 1949, "has been ingrained in its life rather than its houses. The people are all of the same stock, the same cultural background . . . It is homogeneity run riot."[30]

Some observers believed that drastic changes in the post–World War

II villages surely would prove decisive in the transition from the Primordial Folk into Emerging Realists and perhaps, at last, modern Proletarians. In the forties, mill operators increasingly sold off their housing, usually to current inhabitants, thus ridding themselves of unproductive, capital-immobilizing properties. Would homeownership break the paternalistic bond? On the whole, Herring believed that the breakup of the mill villages would liberate textile workers by removing the paternalistic system's "limitations to personal initiative, to social freedom, and to political independence," and she looked forward to "a new experiment in democracy in the South."[31]

John Morland's "Kent," many years before, had ceased being a mill village, but he too detected the likelihood of change in mill workers' attitudes in the postwar world. True, at present, in 1948–49, paternalism continued to exert a powerful hold, with the operators of the town's two large mills actively fostering the traditional "family-like relationship" so as to insure a steady supply of "cooperative, docile, loyal worker[s]." And it was equally true that Kent's mill workers remained passive and resigned, believing that "there is little the individual can do." Attitudes toward the union remained skeptical and fearful. Indeed, Textile Workers' officials believed that it was the workers' diffidence and lack of confidence, rather than overt employer intimidation, that figured most significantly in the union's lack of progress. Thus, many indicators pointed to the continuance of the mindset of the Primordial Folk.

Still, Morland detected signs of change. Modern-day paternalism consisted largely of doing special "favors" for workers, such as distributing holiday foods, holding Christmas parties, and contributing to church building funds. Workers now exhibited a more instrumental view of employers' largess. "Kent mill people," Morland concluded, "seem generally to approve of this paternalistic care if the benefits are great enough." Workers remained chary of unions, but many believed that a nearby union presence encouraged company officials to match some union conditions as a preventive measure. Indeed, in a judgment that might serve to warn social scientists about the dangers of prognostication, Morland concluded that "it appears safe to say that unionization of Southern textile plants will eventually supplant the prevailing paternalistic system," as the mentality of the Emerging Realist seemed to be supplanting that of the Primordial Folk.[32]

The 1976 Earle, Knudson, Shriver study of Gastonia demonstrated how poor a forecaster Morland, for all his astute observation of prevailing conditions, was. Mill owners still dominated the community. Workers remained passive and, on the whole, antiunion, as a series of discouraging organizing drives since the end of World War II had demonstrated. Declared a TWUA regional director in the 1970s, "White southern textile workers tended passively to accept their surroundings and looked at themselves as people to whom things happen rather than who could join together and exercise control over their own destinies through union organization." Like Morland's Kent mill workers of the late 1940s, Gastonia's in the 1970s behaved like rational-choice theorists rather than like union stalwarts, for many Gastonia workers reasoned that, once they actually *joined* the union, organization would lose its useful function as a threat. In any event, when the authors asked workers who had their best interests at heart, their employers or the union, "The Gastonia textile worker's answer . . . in the postwar years was relatively clear: management."

The story was similar politically. Any candidate "who could prove that he was *against* unions could still convince many local workers that he was their friend." Whether workers with such attitudes were still Primordial Folk or Emerging Realists, they clearly were not Proletarians, incipient or otherwise.[33]

In a particularly shrewd 1964 study of Roanoke Rapids, North Carolina, Patricia Levenstein compared unionized paper workers and nonunion textile workers in this frequently embattled community.[34] Levenstein administered questionnaires to samples of textile and paper workers. On a superficial level, she found that, as a group, textile workers scored higher on Gilman's "folkways" scale than did unionized paper workers, suggesting that a folkish mentality remained prevalent. Further analysis, however, revealed that the specifically "folkish" responses related primarily to questions dealing with religious values and interpersonal relations and were highly correlated with lack of educational attainment. In questions relating to unions, political action, and civic engagement, Levenstein's Roanoke Rapids mill workers of the early 1960s differed little from their 1920s counterparts. Textile giant J. P. Stevens dominated the town's news media, churches, and public bodies, meeting little resistance from workers in the company's successful efforts to discourage unionism. Unionized paper workers sought to encourage their textile counterparts to organize, but to no avail. Far from being Gilman's cheerful communal loyalists, Roanoke Rapids textile workers in the early 1960s were poorly educated, resentful, powerless victims.[35]

Recent studies have added to and complicated the more current depiction of white textile workers. In the 1960s and 1970s, the changing racial composition of the Piedmont labor force provided unique opportunities for comparative analysis of textile workers along ethnic lines. Several careful studies cited the freedom of black workers from the constraints of traditional paternalism. More likely than white workers to have traveled and even resided outside the Piedmont prior to beginning work in the mills, blacks brought more cosmopolitan experiences and expectations to the workplace. Involvement with the civil rights movement left black workers with positive views of the efficacy of collective action. "It is plain," observe the authors of *Spindles and Spires,* "that Gastonia blacks strongly favor labor unions." Moreover, black ministers and other community leaders were much more likely than their white counterparts to support organization and to view the union as a legitimate agent of defense and progress. Two sociologists reporting on a detailed examination of another North Carolina mill community in the early 1980s found blacks sharply more class conscious, less deferential, and more committed to forging instruments of collective action. Indeed, the authors remarked, "It is almost as if the data were based on two totally different samples of textile workers."[36]

Thus, through the 1970s, it appeared to unionists and their sympathizers that blacks might be the textile industry's missing proletarians. White workers continued to exhibit the patterns of deference, antiunionism, and passivity associated with the Primordial Folk, at best adopting a certain narrow brand of Emerging Realism.[37] But black workers, it seemed for a historic moment, finally might provide the shock troops for southern textiles' coming of age.

Alas for these hopes, no sooner had a burst of activism—spearheaded by black workers and including victims of brown-lung disease—emerged in the 1970s than the industry plunged into its most severe economic crisis. In the 1980s, dozens of plants closed, and tens of thousands of mill jobs disappeared. Since 1980, the apparel and textile industries have lost half a million jobs. The North American Free Trade Agreement, approved in 1993, provided for the gradual elimination of tariff and quota protections. Declared one union official, "The government is saying, 'We don't want this labor-intensive industry here.' We're being told, 'You guys are done.'"[38]

Even if southern textiles might revive, some industry experts believed, they would employ only a fraction of the workforce of the traditional mills.

Moreover, a recent analyst has suggested that "the incompatibility of the existing, poorly educated, and unskilled labor force with the new high technology" will help to destroy the entire basis of the Piedmont worker culture.[39] Thus the Primordial Folk will have been displaced not by the Emerging Realists or the Incipient Proletarians but, in the end, by the Redundant Worker, long a staple in Britain's industrial North but a frightening figure indeed in the hardworking mill towns of the Piedmont.

Notes

I thank James Gregory for reading an earlier version of this paper and for his excellent bibliographical suggestions. Marsha Bryant also shared her knowledge of documentary expression.

1. During the past decade, there has been an explosion of historiographical interest in southern textile workers. For citations and commentary, see Robert H. Zieger, "Textile Workers and Historians," in *Organized Labor in the Twentieth-Century South,* ed. Robert H. Zieger (Knoxville: Univ. of Tennessee Press, 1991), 35–59. More recent citations in the increasingly sophisticated historiography of the southern textile workers include Bryant Simon, "'I Believed in the Strongest Kind of Religion': James Evans and Working-Class Protest in the New South," *Labor's Heritage* 4, no. 1 (Fall 1992): 60–77; Annette C. Wright, "The Aftermath of the General Textile Strike: Managers and the Workplace at Burlington Mills," *Journal of Southern History* 60, no. 1 (Feb. 1994): 81–112; Douglas Flamming, *Creating the Modern South: Millhands and Managers in Dalton, Georgia, 1884–1984* (Chapel Hill: Univ. of North Carolina Press, 1992); Gary M. Fink, *The Fulton Bag and Cotton Mills Strike of 1914–1915: Espionage, Labor Conflict, and New South Industrial Relations* (Ithaca, N.Y.: ILR Press, 1993); John A. Salmond, *Gastonia, 1929: The Story of the Loray Mill Strike* (Chapel Hill: Univ. of North Carolina Press, 1995); and the essays by Bess Beatty, David L. Carlton, Gary R. Freeze, Bryant Simon, and James A. Hodges in *Race, Class, and Community in Southern Labor History,* eds. Gary M. Fink and Merl E. Reed (Tuscaloosa: Univ. of Alabama Press, 1994).
2. For suggestive commentaries on the "primordialization" of southern whites, see James C. Klotter, "The Black South and White Appalachia," *Journal of American History* 66, no. 4 (Mar. 1980): 832–49; and Jacquelyn Dowd Hall, "Disorderly Women: Gender and Labor Militancy in the Appalachian South," *Journal of American History* 73, no. 2 (Sept. 1986): 378–80.
3. See, e.g., James C. Cobb, *The Selling of the South: The Southern Crusade for Industrial Development, 1936–1990,* 2d ed. (Urbana: Univ. of Illinois Press, 1993), 96–121; Gavin Wright, *Old South, New South: Revolutions in the Southern Economy since the Civil War* (New York: Basic Books, 1986), 64–70; and Gavin Wright, "Cheap Labor and Southern Textiles, 1880–1930," *Quarterly Journal of Economics* 96 (Nov. 1981): 605–29. Historians have not dealt extensively with employers' views of their labor force, but the rich literature

on workers' lives and culture is revealing on this subject. See, e.g., I. A. Newby, *Plain Folk in the New South: Social Change and Cultural Persistence, 1880–1915* (Baton Rouge: Louisiana State Univ. Press, 1989), 117–78; Allen Tullos, *Habits of Industry: White Culture and the Transformation of the Carolina Piedmont* (Chapel Hill: Univ. of North Carolina Press, 1989); Flamming, *Creating the Modern South*; and Jacquelyn Dowd Hall et al., *Like a Family: The Making of a Southern Cotton Mill World* (Chapel Hill: Univ. of North Carolina Press, 1987). Timothy J. Minchin, *What Do We Need a Union For: The TWUA in the South, 1945–1955* (Chapel Hill: Univ. of North Carolina Press, 1997), 48–68, 199–210, stresses postwar textile workers' cost-benefit calculations as a key factor in union failure.

4. Newby, *Plain Folk*, 519–46, is eloquent on the tendency of northern-based organizers to impose laborite constructs on mill workers. See also James A. Hodges, *New Deal Labor Policy and the Southern Cotton Textile Industry, 1933–1941* (Knoxville: Univ. of Tennessee Press, 1986), 22–42; and Barbara S. Griffith, *The Crisis of American Labor: Operation Dixie and the Defeat of the CIO* (Philadelphia: Temple Univ. Press, 1988), 46–61.
5. Historians and analysts of various modes of discourse have begun to examine the ways in which observers' training, upbringing, professional standing, and political and social expectations can shape their perceptions and representations of reality. While this paper is more an effort to *report* on characteristic images of textile workers than to probe their rhetorical and visual structures, I have found the following works valuable in gaining a sense of how documentary expression is generated: William Stott, *Documentary Expression and Thirties America* (New York: Oxford Univ. Press, 1973), 110–11, 143–257; Carol Shloss, *In Visible Light: Photography and the American Writer, 1840–1940* (New York: Oxford Univ. Press, 1987), 179–229; Paula Rabinowitz, *They Must Be Represented: The Politics of Documentary* (London: Verso, 1994), 35–74; and Bill Nichols, *Representing Reality: Issues and Concepts in Documentary* (Bloomington: Indiana Univ. Press, 1991), 32–75. Paul Fussell, *The Great War and the Modern Memory* (New York: Oxford Univ. Press, 1975), is a brilliant meditation on the relationships among memory, expectations, and "reality." On the relation between oral history and the shaping of historical memory, see John Bodnar, "Power and Memory in Oral History: Workers and Managers at Studebaker," *Journal of American History* 75, no. 4 (Mar. 1989): 1201–21.
6. Richard Woods Edmonds, *Cotton Mill Labor Conditions in the South and New England* (Baltimore, Md.: Manufacturers Record Publishing Co., 1925), 7–11; Frank Tannenbaum, *Darker Phases of the South* (New York: Putnam, 1924), 40.
7. Marjorie Potwin, *Cotton Mill People of the Piedmont: A Study in Social Change* (New York: Columbia Univ. Press, 1927), 49–52, 67–72; William Plumer Jacobs, "Introduction" to *Life in Mill Communities*, by William Hays Simpson (Clinton, S.C.: P.C. Press, 1943), 6–10.
8. Glenn Gilman, *Human Relations in the Industrial Southeast: A Study of the Textile Industry* (Chapel Hill: Univ. of North Carolina Press, 1956; reprint, Westport, Conn.: Greenwood Press, 1974), 170–73, 305–9, passim. See Mary

Lethert Wingerd, "Rethinking Paternalism: Power and Parochialism in a Southern Mill Village," *Journal of American History* 83, no. 3 (Dec. 1996): 872–902, for a thoughtful discussion of the theme of paternalism.

9. Paul Blanshard, *Labor in Southern Cotton Mills* (N.p.: *New Republic*/League for Industrial Democracy, 1922), 53; Tannenbaum, *Darker Phases of the South,* 42, 71.
10. Emil Rieve to John L. Lewis, May 25, 1939, in Textile Workers Union of America Papers, Installment 3, Box 43, John L. Lewis, Folder no. 1, State Historical Society of Wisconsin, Madison.
11. Paul David Richards, "The History of the Textile Workers Union of America, CIO, in the South, 1937 to 1945" (Ph.D. diss., Univ. of Wisconsin, 1978), 132–40.
12. Tom Tippett, *When Southern Labor Stirs* (New York: Jonathan Cape and Harrison Smith, 1931), 8–9, 31–36, 121, passim.
13. Abstract of interview with Solomon Barkin, Nov. 7, 1977, transcript in TWUA Papers, State Historical Society of Wisconsin, Madison, p. 12. For a recent account that implicitly suggests the Primordial Folk–Emerging Realist nexus, see Griffith, *Crisis of American Labor,* 46–61. Observer accounts emphasizing the calculating nature of textile workers' putative antiunionism can be found in John Kenneth Morland, *Millways of Kent* (Chapel Hill: Univ. of North Carolina Press, 1958), 43–50, 255–59; and John R. Earle, Dean D. Knudson, and Donald W. Shriver, Jr., *Spindles and Spires: A Re-Study of Religion and Social Change in Gastonia* (Atlanta, Ga.: John Knox, 1976), 187–89.
14. Herring to Howard Odum, Apr. 17, 1924, in Howard Odum Papers, Folder Apr. 16–30, 1924, Southern Historical Collection, Univ. of North Carolina Library, Chapel Hill (hereafter cited as SHC).
15. Broadus Mitchell, *The Rise of Cotton Mills in the South,* Johns Hopkins Univ. Studies in Historical and Political Science, Series 39, No. 7 (Baltimore, Md.: Johns Hopkins Univ. Press, 1921).
16. Broadus Mitchell and George Sinclair Mitchell, *The Industrial Revolution in the South* (Baltimore, Md.: Johns Hopkins Univ. Press, 1930), 159, 172, 183, and passim. This volume collects articles, published through the middle and late 1920s, that were based on the Mitchells' ongoing observations of southern mill conditions. See also George Sinclair Mitchell, *Textile Unionism and the South* (Chapel Hill: Univ. of North Carolina Press, 1931).
17. Lois MacDonald, interview by Mary Frederickson, Aug. 25, 1977, transcript in SHC, pp. 83–84.
18. Lois MacDonald, *Southern Mill Hills: A Study of Social and Economic Forces in Certain Textile Mill Villages* (New York: Alex L. Hillman, 1928), 53, 74, 105–6, 151, and passim. In her interview, MacDonald contrasted her more somber depictions of mill village life with the "rose-colored" views of Marjorie Potwin. "I thought I detected a seething sort of discontent," MacDonald recalled, although the text of her 1928 book emphasizes the passivity and lassitude of mill folk.
19. Ben F. Lemert, *The Cotton Textile Industry of the Southern Appalachian Piedmont* (Chapel Hill: Univ. of North Carolina Press, 1933), vi–viii, 62–70.

20. Jennings J. Rhyne, *Some Southern Cotton Mill Workers and Their Villages* (Chapel Hill: Univ. of North Carolina Press, 1930), 7–19, 205–6, 212, and passim.
21. Harriet L. Herring, interview by Mary Frederickson and Nevin Brown, Feb. 5, 1976, transcript in SHC.
22. Harriet L. Herring, *Welfare Work in Mill Villages: The Story of Extra-Mill Activities in North Carolina* (Chapel Hill: Univ. of North Carolina Press, 1929; reprint, Montclair, N.J.: Patterson Smith, 1968); Harriet Herring to Beulah Amidon, Apr. 13 and Aug. 20, 1929, both in Harriet L. Herring Papers, SHC. Quotations are from the Apr. 13 letter.
23. Herring, interview by Frederickson and Brown, Feb. 5, 1976; Herring to Horace Davis, June 27, 1929, in Herring Papers, SHC.
24. Tannenbaum, *Darker Phases of the South,* 55–56; Plumer, "Introduction," in Simpson, *Life in Mill Communities,* 6–7; Potwin, *Cotton Mill People,* passim.
25. George Sinclair Mitchell, *Textile Unionism,* 42–52; Lemert, *Cotton Textile Industry,* 63–69; Potwin, *Cotton Mill People,* 59–61.
26. MacDonald, *Southern Mill Hills,* 72, 108; Potwin, *Cotton Mill People,* 52.
27. In something of a special category is W. J. Cash, *The Mind of the South* (New York: Knopf, 1941), 171–85, 197–206, 209–15, 253–58, 343–57, 389–95. Cash's impressionistic observations have been influential in sustaining the historical image of the mill workers as victimized yet truculent denizens of the New South, but unlike the works covered in this essay, they were not based upon firsthand investigation.
28. Liston Pope, *Millhands and Preachers: A Study of Gastonia* (New Haven: Yale Univ. Press, 1942), 207–38, 252–64.
29. Ibid.; Harriet L. Herring, *Passing of the Mill Village: Revolution in a Southern Institution* (Chapel Hill: Univ. of North Carolina Press, 1949); Morland, *Millways of Kent;* Earle, Knudson, and Shriver, *Spindles and Spires.*
30. Herring, *Passing of the Mill Village,* 114–15.
31. Ibid., 117.
32. Morland, *Millways of Kent,* 43–45, 49–50, 255–59.
33. Earle, Knudson, and Shriver, *Spindles and Spires,* 178–94.
34. Patricia Hammond Levenstein, "The Failure of Unionization in the Southern Textile Industry" (Master's thesis, Cornell Univ., 1964), 119–24. Roanoke Rapids subsequently became the focal point of the Textile Workers' decade-long struggle against Stevens. See James Hodges, "The Real Norma Rae," ch. 10 of this volume.
35. Levenstein, "Failure of Unionization," 74–85, 142–60.
36. Earle, Knudson, and Shriver, *Spindles and Spires,* 220–21; Rhonda Zingraff and Michael D. Schulman, "Social Bases of Class Consciousness: A Study of Southern Textile Workers with a Comparison by Race," *Social Forces* 63, no. 1 (Sept. 1984): 98–116. See also Richard L. Rowan, *The Negro in the Textile Industry,* Racial Policies of American Industry, Report No. 20 (Philadelphia: Univ. of Pennsylvania Press, for the Wharton School, 1970); Mary Frederickson, "Four Decades of Change: Black Workers in Southern Textiles, 1941–1981," in *Workers' Struggles, Past and Present: A "Radical America" Reader,* ed. James Green (Philadelphia: Temple Univ. Press, 1983), 62–82; and

Dale Newman, "Work and Community Life in a Southern Textile Town," *Labor History* 19 (Spring 1978): 204–25.

37. For a relatively recent statement of this view, see Harry Boyte, "The Textile Industry: Keel of Southern Industrialization," *Radical America* 6 (Mar.–Apr. 1972): 4–49. For more positive assessments of textile workers' potential for activism, see Mimi Conway, *Rise Gonna Rise: A Portrait of Southern Textile Workers* (Garden City, N.Y.: Anchor/Doubleday, 1979); and Joseph A. McDonald and Donald A. Clelland, "Textile Workers and Union Sentiment," *Social Forces* 63, no. 2 (Dec. 1984): 502–21.
38. Christina Nifong, "U.S. Garment Industry Faces Crossroads," *Christian Science Monitor,* Nov. 13, 1995; Arthur Gundersheim of the Amalgamated Clothing and Textile Workers Union, quoted in Beth Belton, Doug Carroll, Michael Clements, James Cox, Kevin Maney, Bill Montague, and Paul Wiseman, "Who Stands to Win, Lose under Trade Treaty," *USA Today,* Dec. 1, 1994.
39. Julia C. Bonham, "Robotics, Electronics, and the American Textile Industry," in *Hanging by a Thread: Social Change in Southern Textiles,* ed. Jeffrey Leiter, Michael D. Schulman, and Rhonda Zingraff (Ithaca, N.Y.: ILR Press, 1991), 165. See also John Gaventa and Barbara Ellen Smith, "The Deindustrialization of the Textile South: A Case Study," in Leiter, Schulman, and Zingraff, *Hanging by a Thread,* 181–96; and Rhonda Zingraff, "Facing Extinction?" in Leiter, Schulman, and Zingraff, *Hanging by a Thread,* 199–216.

The Emergence and Growth of a Nonunion Sector in the Southern Paper Industry

Bruce E. Kaufman

Union density (proportion of the workforce organized) in the American economy has declined substantially since the late 1970s. A number of studies have examined the reasons for this development (Kochan, Katz and McKersie, 1986; Lawler, 1990) and the manner in which specific policies and practices of management, unions, and government have contributed to it (Foulkes, 1980; Verma and Kochan, 1985; Friedman, Hurd, Oswald, and Seeber, 1994). Largely missing from this literature, however, are case studies of the deunionization process at an industry or firm level. This chapter partially fills this gap through an examination of the southern pulp and paper industry. The paper industry was thoroughly organized after World War II; and, even in the largely nonunion states of the South, more than 95 percent of production workers were covered under collective bargaining contracts. The solid front of unionization began to crack in the mid-1970s, however, and by 1995 approximately one-fifth of production and maintenance employees in southern pulp and paper mills were nonunion. The factors responsible for this trend and their implications for the future of unionism in the industry and the nation are the subjects of this chapter.

Industry Overview

The domestic paper industry, classified by the U.S. Department of Commerce as SIC (Standard Industrial Classification) 26, had a wage and salary workforce of 685,000 in 1995 and a value of shipments of over $133 billion, making it the eighth largest manufacturing industry. At the beginning of 1996, the five largest companies in the industry by volume of sales were: International Paper, Kimberly-Clark, Stone Container, Georgia-Pacific, and James River. Although a significant degree of consolidation has occurred in recent years through mergers and acquisitions, numerous competing firms and a substantial degree of price competition nevertheless remain in most market segments, due to the commodity nature of many pulp and paper products and the growing importance of international competition. Unlike several other manufacturing industries in the United States, the domestic paper industry remains the world leader in sales, product quality, and technology.

The Production of Pulp and Paper

The paper industry typically is divided into primary and secondary sectors. The primary sector includes pulp, paper, and paperboard mills (SIC 261,262,263). Various hardwoods and softwoods provide the primary raw material in paper production, although recycled paper is increasing in importance. Most pulp and paper mills are located in rural and frequently remote areas. Employment varies by mill size. Some small specialty paper or paper board mills often may employ only one hundred to two hundred people, while large integrated mills employ several thousand. Some mills produce only pulp, while others produce only paper. "Integrated" mills produce both.

The first stage in making paper is pulping. Timber is transported by truck, rail, or water to a pulp mill where the logs are debarked, cut, and chipped. The chips then are turned into pulp through a mechanical or chemical process from which the cellulose fiber used in paper making is extracted. In the second stage, the pulp solution (possibly acquired from an external supplier) is pumped through large pipes to a building longer than most aircraft hangars. Inside are one or more paper machines. Each machine is a behemoth, measuring several football fields long and thirty or more feet wide and costing three hundred million dollars or more to purchase and install. The pulp solution enters the "wet end," where it is formed by metal screens (the "wire") and rollers into a smooth mat of fibers (the "web"). The web then enters the "dry end" of the paper machine, where additional moisture is extracted and the web is cut, smoothed, and rolled onto huge reels.

The secondary sector of the paper industry consists of a variety of "converting" operations in which the paper or paperboard (e.g., cardboard) is manufactured into an end product. Examples include shipping containers, milk cartons, envelopes, diapers, shopping bags, and business recordkeeping forms. Converting operations generally take place in smaller manufacturing plants employing fifty to two hundred people and frequently are located closer to larger metropolitan areas.

Geographical Distribution of Primary Mills

Historically, the production of pulp and paper in the United States has centered in several distinct regions. The industry developed first in the Northeast, spread to the states of the northern Midwest (and Canada), then to the Pacific Northwest, and finally to the South (Guthrie, 1950; Ohanian, 1993). In 1950, for example, 26 percent of pulp mills and 13 percent of paper mills were located in southern states (comprised of the South Atlantic, East South Central, and West South Central census regions); in 1995, these proportions had approximately doubled, reaching 46 percent and 30 percent, respectively (Lockwood-Post, 1995). These statistics significantly understate the degree to which production is concentrated in the South, since southern mills typically are larger-scale plants.

The regional shift in pulp and paper production is a product of timber depletion in other regions, lower costs of acquiring and transporting timber in the South, technological advances that made it possible to produce high-quality paper products from resinous southern pine, increasingly costly and restrictive environmental regulations that adversely affected the Pacific Northwest, and a climate and topography in the South that promote faster tree growth and regeneration of forests (Smith, 1971; Matics, 1982). Low wages were not a factor, as, on average, southern mills paid wages equal to or higher than mill wages in other regions.

Economic Characteristics

Several economic characteristics of the paper industry are important for understanding the evolution of human resource and labor relations practices (for an early but still useful discussion, see Macdonald, 1956).

First, the short-run demand for labor in the industry is highly inelastic (insensitive) to changes in labor cost. Paper production is extremely capital intensive, and a rise in wages leads to a relatively small increase in the unit cost of production, only a small rise in product price, and therefore only a small negative impact on employment. Likewise, given the relatively fixed operator requirements for major pulp and paper machines in the short run (a typical paper machine requires a crew of seven people), companies have limited ability to substitute capital for labor in reaction to a wage increase. The demand for the product also tends to be relatively unresponsive to price, further damping the effect of a wage change on employment (through changes in cost and price). In the long run, labor demand becomes more sensitive to labor cost, as firms have more time to make adjustments through automation and new labor-saving capital investment.

Second, the paper industry experiences significant volatility of prices and a recurrent boom-and-bust cycle in profitability. Prices for wood pulp and many types of paper products swing widely over the business cycle, reflecting the commodity nature of the business and changes in the underlying demand-supply balance. During recessions, the pressure of large fixed costs causes firms to cut prices quickly to maintain production volume, while in boom periods prices rise sharply once mill capacity is reached and companies begin to ration available supplies. The boom-and-bust cycle is then aggravated by a lag in the response of capital spending and new mill construction. When mill capacity tightens and profits boom in a cyclical upswing, companies typically build new mills or expand existing facilities. Not only is the total addition to capacity often excessive, but frequently it does not come on stream until the peak of the demand cycle is past. Cutthroat competition ensues, prices drop sharply, and producers experience a sea of red ink and face considerable pressure to reduce cost. Since 1980, the paper industry has experienced several of these cycles, with a severe trough in the early to mid-1980s, a boom in the late 1980s, a deep and prolonged trough during 1990–94, and an equally sharp rebound from 1994 to date.

Trends in Unionization and Deunionization

The primary sector of the pulp and paper industry is one of the most heavily unionized industries in the American economy. Since the mid-1970s, however, a modest-sized but nonetheless noticeable slippage in the unionization rate has occurred. Unfortunately, no consistent data series documents this trend. Several data sets can be pieced together, however, to give a rough idea of the magnitude of change (also see Eaton and Kriesky, 1994).

According to a government survey of establishments in the paper industry during 1968–72, 98 percent of production workers in primary pulp and paper mills (SIC 261,262) were covered by collective bargaining contracts (Freeman and Medoff, 1979). Inclusion of paperboard mills (SIC 263) reduces the figure to 89 percent. According to a 1972 wage survey of the paper industry (Bureau of Labor Statistics, 1975:3), "virtually all workers in the Southeast. . . . were in mills that had collective bargaining agreements." Similarly, Herbert Northrup (1969:27-28) states, after an in-depth case study of the industry: "The author knows of only one major southern mill which is not unionized, and which has been in existence for at least two years."

The Current Population Survey (CPS), a monthly nationwide survey of households that is used primarily to collect information on employment and unemployment, provides the only consistent time-series data on the unionization rate in the paper industry after the early 1970s. According to the CPS, 69 percent of wage and salary workers in 1974 in pulp, paper, and paperboard mills belonged to a labor union (Kokkelenberg and Sockell, 1985). In 1994, the figure is 52 percent—a drop of 17 percentage points over a two-decade period (Hirsch and MacPherson, 1995). The union density figures from the CPS are considerably lower than those from the earlier establishment surveys: some workers covered by a collective bargaining contract do not belong to a union, and the CPS compares union membership to total wage and salary employment in the industry, rather than to production workers alone.

If we assume that the establishment survey data also would have shown the same 17 percentage-point drop over time, then the percent of production workers covered by collective bargaining contracts in primary pulp and paper mills would have declined from 98 percent in 1970 to 81 percent in 1994, and from 89 percent in pulp and paper/board mills to 71 percent.

These estimates probably err on the low side. The American Forest and Paper Association (AFPA), the major employer association in the paper industry, estimates that 75 to 80 percent of production workers in southern pulp, paper, and paperboard mills are covered by collective bargaining. Thus, as a rough estimate, it appears that the rate of unionization among southern paper mills has decreased by 15 to 20 percent since the early 1970s.

Unpublished data provided by AFPA on the date of establishment and union status of individual pulp and paper/board mills in the South provides a second picture of the deunionization trend in the industry. Of the 116 mills in the data set (not all paper companies belong to AFPA, so the data set is a sample, not a census, of southern mills), 87 (75 percent) began operation prior to 1970, and 29 (25 percent) began operation since 1970. Of the 87 pre-1970 mills, 79 (91 percent) had union representation as of 1995.

Only eight of these early mills are nonunion. In nearly all cases, these nonunion mills are either small (e.g., Austell Box Board Company), specialty paper/board mills (e.g., Ahlstrom Filtration), and/or are operated by companies that have their roots in the South, began as relatively modest-sized entrepreneurial or family-run ventures, and gave high priority to maintaining union-free status (e.g., Sonoco, Carolina Paperboard). In contrast, a large majority of the organized mills are owned by "Fortune 1,000" companies, most of which originally were headquartered outside the South, had unions in their northern and western mills, and brought the unions with them to their new southern mills in the 1940s through the 1970s.

Of the twenty-nine mills built since 1970, twenty-two (76 percent), as of 1995, are nonunion. According to industry experts, the last new primary mill organized in the South was the result of a voluntary card-check recognition at the McGehee, Arkansas, mill of the Potlatch Company, built in 1977. For reasons that will become apparent shortly, it is significant that the planning and initial construction of this mill took place shortly before the industry's first nontraditional, "high performance" mill in Stevenson, Alabama, came on stream. The union organization of the Potlatch mill, therefore, effectively marks the end of two eras—the era of near-automatic recognition of unions in new mills and the era of traditional, "techno-bureaucratic" mill design (a concept to be discussed shortly).

Of the seventeen pulp and paper/board mills built in the South since the Potlatch mill began operation, none has been organized by a union. Thus, a small but growing nonunion sector has emerged, both within the primary sector of the industry as a whole and within particular firms. (This trend is considerably more pronounced in the secondary side of the industry. See Eaton and Kriesky, 1994.) In the primary sector in the

South, paper companies that have not built new mill facilities since 1977 remain, with only a few exceptions, 100 percent organized. Examples include Boise Cascade, Champion, Stone Container, and Westvaco. Major companies once fully organized but now with one or more non-union mills in the South include Georgia Pacific (one mill out of ten—the result of an acquisition), International Paper (one mill out twelve), Mead (one mill out of three), Union Camp (one mill out of four) and Weyerhauser (two mills out of five). Several other companies never have had union representation in their southern mills and have added yet additional such mills, such as Sonoco (three mills) and Fort Howard (two mills). Finally, several new firms, typically paper recyclers such as Southeastern Paper (one mill) and Newsprint South (one mill), have entered the industry and successfully kept their startup mills nonunion.

The Union Era: 1933–1975

To understand the emergence and growth of a nonunion sector in the paper industry after 1975, it is necessary briefly to explore the development of the organized labor movement in the industry over the preceding half-century, the nature of work in pulp and paper mills in this period, and the practices of the paper companies in setting up new mills that facilitated the unionization process.

The Development of Unionism

Prior to the Great Depression (1929), unionism in the paper industry was of small and declining significance. Two unions affiliated with the American Federation of Labor (AFL)—the International Brotherhood of Paper Makers (IBPM) and the International Brotherhood of Pulp, Sulphite, and Paper Mill Workers (IBPSPMW)—claimed jurisdiction over workers engaged in pulp and paper manufacturing. The former was a craft union that represented skilled paper-machine operators, while the latter was semi-industrial in structure and organized both skilled and unskilled workers in pulp production and nonmachine workers in paper making. A variety of other craft unions also had a smattering of representation in the industry, principally among the maintenance, mechanical, and powerhouse workers. Together these unions represented 8 to 10 percent of the industry workforce in the late 1920s, a figure which dropped during the Depression (Zieger, 1984; Smith, 1971).

During the 1930s and early 1940s, the paper industry was organized largely by the two paper unions. Two newly established industrial unions affiliated with the Congress of Industrial Organizations (CIO)—the United Paperworkers of America (UPA) and District 50 of the United Mine Workers (a catchall industrial unit)—offered the only significant competition. Unlike the auto, steel, and tire sectors, the paper industry was organized with relatively little violence or even concerted opposition on the part of the major companies.

The initial organization occurred almost simultaneously with passage of the National Industrial Recovery Act in June 1933 and reflected both a pent-up demand for restoration of wage cuts and a desire to aid President Roosevelt's economic recovery program, which was predicated upon restoring purchasing power though boosting wages (Kaufman, 1996). Some employers initially resisted the new unions, by either establishing nonunion employee representation plans (company unions) or practicing various forms of antiunion discrimination and refusal to bargain. By the late 1930s, however, most major paper companies had concluded that some type of union presence was inevitable, given that company unions and antiunion discrimination had been made illegal by the recently passed National Labor Relations Act (1935). Other factors entering into their conclusion were the birth and meteoric rise of a rival, militant labor federation, the CIO; and the successful unionization of the leading companies in other mass production industries. The paper companies thus made a strategic decision that their interests were best served not by fighting the unions but by cultivating bargaining relationships with the most responsible and businesslike of the unions and establishing a bargaining structure and a set of practices that promoted labor peace and business stability (Zieger, 1984).

The two AFL brotherhoods were seen as the ideal bargaining partners, since they worked cooperatively in organizing and bargaining (a "no-raid" agreement was worked out prior to the Depression, and the two unions often cooperated by dividing a newly organized mill into a "pulp" local and a "paper" local, which then bargained as a team). Moreover, the AFL brotherhoods espoused and largely practiced a conservative approach to collective bargaining that emphasized cooperation and adherence to written contracts, and both eschewed militant rhetoric and strikes. The AFL unions appeared even more attractive in comparison to the aggressive, radical-tinged unions affiliated with CIO, such as the United Paperworkers and District 50. Thus, with escape from unionization apparently blocked, and, given the considerable fear and loathing felt toward the CIO, most major paper companies tacitly cooperated with the AFL unions in the organization of their mills and the negotiation of union shop agreements. As a result, by the end of World War II, the southern branch of the paper industry was largely under union contract.

Once a high level of unionization was in place, three considerations led the companies to accept the status quo for the next three decades. The first was that the inelastic nature of product demand, together with the near 100 percent unionization of primary paper producers, meant that wage increases could be passed on to end users with relatively little adverse impact on the competitive position, profits, and employment of individual firms. Second, the labor relations climate between the companies and the unions continued to be relatively cooperative and free of intense conflict, particularly in the southern region. (Labor relations on the West Coast deteriorated in the 1960s and 1970s, due in part to the decision of a number of disaffected locals in the pulp and sulphite union to break away and form an independent union, the Association of Western Pulp and Paper Workers.) Finally, the companies considered it foolhardy to risk disrupting cooperative union-management relations at existing mills by opposing the unionization of new, "greenfield" facilities. For these reasons, as new mills were built in the South in the 1950s and 1960s, the unions were granted almost automatic recognition, either by a voluntary card check or a perfunctory representation election. The only exception to this policy was that most companies tried to prevent a proliferation of bargaining units in new mills by incorporating maintenance and powerhouse workers into millwide locals organized by the principal paper unions rather than in separate craft locals affiliated with the building trades unions. Still, some mills had five or more bargaining units.

The Nature and Organization of Work

Company fear of the CIO and of militant trade unionism helped in organizing the paper mills of the South, but this was not the only factor. Attention also must be given to the workers who labored in the mills, for it was their interest in union representation that gave credibility to the CIO threat. And to understand their receptivity to unionism, particularly when the regional culture and political establishments were strongly opposed to collective bargaining, consideration must be given to the types of jobs, working conditions, and management practices these workers encountered in the mills of that era.

For blue-collar workers, the paper mill meant a love-hate relationship. On one hand, working at the mill often was the best employment available in the local area (often some distance from a significant population center). The jobs paid very well, the employment was fairly steady, and opportunities existed to learn new skills and move up the occupational ladder. On the other hand, mill work often was monotonous and physically arduous, particularly in the less skilled jobs. Workers were exposed to a variety of health and safety hazards, such as loss of fingers and inhalation of caustic chemicals; moreover, mill jobs involved working eight to nine hours a day in temperatures of 100 degrees or more, with deafening noise levels. Finally, the nature of the industry, involving a continuous process, required shift work, with all its attendant personal inconveniences and disruptions to family life.

The organization and management of work was another source of dissatisfaction for blue-collar workers. Paper mills of the 1950s and 1960s were exemplars of what has been called the "techno-bureaucratic" system of work organization. (Trist, 1981. Also see Davis, 1966; Davis and Taylor, 1972). This system developed in the 1920s and 1930s out of Frederick Taylor's theory of scientific management, Henry Ford's model of mass production, and Max Weber's theory of organizational bureaucracy. In American industry, it reached its apex of influence in the two decades after World War II. In the techno-bureaucratic model, productivity and efficiency are maximized by a hierarchical chain of command, a detailed division of labor, and large production runs to exploit economies of scale. Two examples of this system in paper mills will illustrate both its benefits and its costs.

The first is the fine division of labor and line of progression on paper machines. A basic tenet of scientific management is that productivity is increased by dividing jobs into discrete, easily performed tasks, as this reduces skill requirements and training, promotes economy of effort and movement, and makes it easier for management to regulate the pace of work and monitor work performance. These assumptions were reflected in the division of labor and line of progression established in most mills for crews on paper machine.

A typical paper machine requires seven people or "hands" per shift. In a traditional work system, the tasks and duties associated with operating a paper machine are divided into seven distinct jobs, with the seventh-hand job at the bottom of the pay and skill hierarchy and the machine-tender job at the top of the hierarchy (see Northrup, 1969:43-44). Each job entails a specific set of tasks and responsibilities, and movement into a higher position is determined strictly by seniority. Training for a new position is acquired largely on the job, from such experiences as filling in for a crew member who is out sick or on vacation, and separate pay rates are established for each job classification.

This system has both benefits and costs. On the benefit side, specialization of function promotes efficiency and productivity, as each person quickly learns and develops proficiency at one set of tasks. It is also easier for the industrial engineering staff to analyze the work flow, determine the most efficient layout of equipment, and determine the optimal way to perform the work through time and motion study. Likewise, a formal, well-defined line of progression provides an incentive for the employees to remain with the company in order to move up to the higher-paying, more desirable positions; to work at least at a minimally acceptable level of performance; and to pick up the skills necessary to do the next higher job.

Several negative outcomes also arise from this system, however. For example, workers develop a narrow view of their jobs and responsibilities, as expressed by such statements as "It's not my job" or "It's someone else's problem." The result is lack of attention to process and quality improvement, and an increase in cost due to waste and inefficiency. A second drawback is the system's relative inflexibility and inability to adapt to frequent changes or unforeseen events. Because workers have narrow, fixed work assignments, are given only such information as is needed to do their specific jobs, and have to obtain the approval of first-line supervisors before reacting to a situation, they are hamstrung in their ability and motivation to respond to unanticipated contingencies, such as excessive wear on the paper-machine wire or problems with the chemical composition of the pulp. Another drawback is that organizational learning is retarded, as the system reserves "thinking" to the management cadre of experts, while it asks production workers to "check your brains at the door." Finally, employees correctly perceive that the organization regards them as a variable cost to be minimized in the short run and discarded when no longer needed.

The second paper mill example is the "command and control" management practices that accompany a techno-bureaucratic work system.

One of the behavioral assumptions of this model is that people will only do the bare minimum amount of work unless kept under close supervision or motivated by external control devices, such as being fired for poor work performance or rewarded with higher pay or promotion. (Chernes and Davis, 1972). In paper mills, this assumption was implemented through detailed job descriptions and a cadre of first-line supervisors and foremen. The foremen and supervisors were given the power to make unilateral decisions on production and personnel issues, such as who is assigned to particular jobs, how the paper machine is operated, and the administration of discipline and discharge.

A second assumption in the command and control method of management is that efficiency of operation and effective coordination requires a clear, hierarchical chain of command, beginning at the top with the mill manager and extending down through several layers of middle- and lower-level management and ending with the front-line supervisors at the base of the pyramid. Several staff and production support departments also are attached to this pyramid, such as plant engineering, maintenance, and personnel administration, and they serve as specialized service centers staffed with trained experts who are given control over a particular functional activity.

The benefit of command and control management system is that it establishes clear lines of authority and accountability, obtains the advantage of division of labor, simplifies decision making, and gets the work out. On the negative side, this system fosters elitism among managers and a "we-against-them" attitude on the mill floor. Moreover, it fosters unilateral "top-down" decision making, which breeds resentment and alienation among persons in the lower levels of the mill. It also retards organizational learning and productivity improvement by limiting opportunities for lower-level employees to participate in day-to-day operational decisions and contribute their knowledge and information. In addition, employees have difficulty developing a feeling of ownership over the work and a commitment to the company and come to feel that they need protection from arbitrary management actions, given the penchant of supervisors to reward their "pets" and punish their enemies (Strauss, 1974).

The nature of the work and the practice of management in traditionally structured paper mills, therefore, led to numerous dissatisfactions, resentments, and perceptions of inequity among the blue-collar employees. These dissatisfactions and perceived inequities led, in turn, to harmful or counterproductive behaviors, such as frequent absenteeism, inattention to quality improvement and cost reduction, sabotage of the machinery or product, drinking and drug use in the mills, and hostile relations between workers and their bosses. Companies often reacted to these problems by further tightening control, whether in the form of closer supervision, tougher disciplinary standards, or incentive programs.

This environment fosters a strong demand for union representation among workers, such as those employed in traditionally managed paper mills. According to industry observers, the demand for unions is related first and foremost to "treatment" issues, such as inequities in discipline or promotion, resentments against autocratic managers, unnecessary exposure to unsafe working conditions, and so on. The primary motive driving workers to unions, then, is a desire for protection against management actions and the rigors of the job. The desire of workers to advance their wages, benefits, vacation days, and other economic "terms and conditions" also is important and provides a second, complementary motivation for seeking union representation. Especially in years prior to the 1970s, the potential economic gains from collective bargaining looked particularly attractive because they entailed modest job loss, low probability of mill closing, and little time lost in strikes. After all, the paper companies were large and generally profitable, paper demand was growing year after year, and the companies seemed able to pass higher labor costs on to customers in the form of higher prices. In addition, the domestic industry was the world leader in technology and output, the unions and companies had a relatively amicable, strike-free bargaining history, and mill management did not actively oppose unionization.

New Mill Startups

The manner in which paper companies initiated new mill startups is a third characteristic that promoted unionization in the years prior to 1970. Two aspects are important.

When a company decided to construct a new paper mill, a large portion of the design work typically would be contracted to an industrial engineering firm. The company would specify the key parameters of the project (e.g., performance targets, product mix, and production volume), and the engineering firm, in consultation with the client company's operations and engineering staff, would develop a detailed layout of the mill, specification and configuration of equipment, and so on. Once the technology and capital equipment dimensions were determined, the engineering firm would determine the staffing requirements for the mill in terms of total head count and employment by department and occupation. Approximately three months before startup, the company's industrial relations or personnel department would begin the hiring and training process.

The process just described was largely taken for granted until the early 1970s and was perceived as having little bearing on whether the mill eventually became unionized. The thinking was that the existing state of technology gives rise to a unique configuration for each new mill in terms of minimum cost and maximum productivity, and that the job of the engineers is to discover this "one best way." Once determined, the social or "people" system then is adapted to fit the technical system of production. The problem is that this approach ignores the physiological and psychological needs of the people operating the system and, not surprisingly, gives rise to conditions that either prevent effective human interaction or create working conditions that are onerous or unpleasant. To protect themselves from these undesirable conditions, workers seek union representation.

The companies' practice of staffing new mills with large numbers of experienced hands from other mills also facilitated unionization. A number of the jobs in a paper mill require considerable skill and expertise; particularly in the days before computers and electronic process-control equipment, workers had to rely upon long years of experience and their bodily senses to operate the equipment efficiently and monitor production. Because skilled paper makers and maintenance and powerhouse workers generally are in short supply in the rural areas where new paper mills are located, the companies either had to invest in long and expensive training programs in order to staff a new mill or had to transfer in employees from other mills who already had the skills and experience. Most often they chose the latter option, and many workers jumped at the chance to take these new jobs, since doing so allowed them to move up to higher-paying, more desirable positions. Some workers, in fact, moved repeatedly from one mill startup to another, earning the sobriquet "hobo paper makers."

Although using experienced hands from other mills to staff jobs in a greenfield facility generally was the most cost-effective option, it also brought unionism into the mill. Since the skilled workers were among the first to be placed in a new mill, and since they nearly always were union members, the company in effect created its own in-house organizing committee. After the new union local was established, employees from several different mills could cause additional labor relations headaches for the new mill management, as it faced competing, and sometimes conflicting, demands for the benefits and work rules enjoyed at other mills.

Mead-Stevenson: The Mother Mill of the Nonunion Sector

As previously noted, only a handful of paper mills in the South prior to 1970 were unorganized. None of these mills was a large integrated mill or belonged to a major company. The first significant crack in the near-solid front of unionization occurred in 1975, when a new paperboard mill was built by the Mead Corporation in Stevenson, Alabama. This mill would prove to be the opening wedge in the development of a nonunion sector in the southern paper industry, although at the time this was neither intended by the company nor foreseen by industry or union leaders.

The events surrounding the Stevenson mill are largely unknown outside the paper industry. However, it represents a classic example of how new management methods and principles of work design, coupled with excessive union bargaining demands and resistance to more flexible ways of organizing work, have opened the door to the spread of nonunion plants and mills across the country.

Prelude to Stevenson

The story of the Stevenson mill begins in the late 1960s and involves several executives and managers in Mead's Paperboard Group. Principal among them are Greene Garner, group president; John Cleveland, group vice president of human resources; and Jack Murdoch, internal employee relations consultant.

Garner began his career in accounting. Later, he served stints as general manager of the Atlanta Paper Company and president of the Mead Packaging division—two other Mead subsidiaries—and developed an interest in participative management and quality of work life (QWL) programs. He and his division presidents assembled a small group of industrial relations staffers, such as Cleveland, Murdoch, and a young man named Gary Peters, who would become the first industrial relations (IR) manager at Stevenson. These individuals were interested in thinking "outside the box" on employee relations issues. Their first step was to organize a four-day conference in September 1972 at St. Petersburg, Florida, called "Insights into Productivity." Over fifty Mead executives and managers, including CEO James McSwiney, were invited to attend (Carr, 1989:108-14). In a significant departure from tradition, newspaper reporters, academics, consultants, union leaders (including John Tonelli, president of the newly formed United Paperworkers International Union), and government officials interested in QWL programs also were invited. Garner highlighted the need for new management and human resource methods by examining the operation of four Mead container plants. He had commissioned Gene Dalton of the Harvard Business School to conduct in-depth case studies of the organizational performance of each plant; employee attitude surveys at each plant were done by David Bowers of the University of Michigan's Institute of Social Science Research; and a West Coast consulting firm provided an engineering assessment of the plants. The presentations painted an eye-opening picture of industrial plants caught in a syndrome of low productivity and low employee morale.

After hearing the bad news, several speakers discussed alternative approaches to improving the performance of these plants. One presenter was Louis Davis, a business school professor and member of the UCLA Institute of Industrial Relations, who at the time was the nation's leading academic expert on a newly emergent but relatively unknown management concept called "socio-technical job design" (STJD). Davis explained the principles of STJD and made a persuasive case for its adoption. Shortly after the conference, Murdoch was allowed to implement the social system side of STJD at a small greenfield corrugated box plant then under construction at Covington, Georgia (the engineering work and layout of equipment already had been completed). Murdoch put in place many of the attributes of what later became known as a "high-performance" workplace (see Naidler and Gerstein, 1992): semiautonomous work teams, multiskilling and crossfunctional training, pay for knowledge, an all-salaried workforce, and a flat organizational structure that eliminated front-line supervisors and most middle management. The plant proved to be very successful and within a short time was the division's top performer.

Given the successful experience at Covington, Garner gained

McSwiney's approval to try a full-blown STJD system at a new, state-of-the art greenfield paperboard mill planned for the small town of Stevenson, Alabama. This would be the first application of STJD to a continuous process facility in the United States. Garner and his colleagues thus were rolling the dice on a new system of management and work design that at the time had been tried at only a handful of sites in the world.

Socio-Technical Job Design

Although Davis independently had come to some of the basic principles of socio-technical job design, it originated and gained prominence in the early 1950s through the work of Eric Trist, Frederick Emery, and a small group of other researchers associated with the Tavistock Institute of Human Relations in London, England (see Davis and Taylor, 1972; Emery, 1978; Trist, 1981).

The inspiration for STJD came from investigations made by Trist and colleagues of alternative work systems in British coal mining. In the early 1950s, Trist and colleagues were permitted to implement an experimental work system at the Bolsover Colliery. This system extensively utilized multiskilled, small-team craft production methods. Within a relatively short time after its introduction, coal output increased 30 percent, labor and material costs declined, and absenteeism and labor-management conflict dropped sharply.

Drawing on the lessons of the coal mining experiments and a later work-redesign project in an Indian textile mill, Trist and other Tavistock researchers formulated the "socio-technical" approach to job design. It was in many respects the direct antithesis of the techno-bureaucratic model that grew out of the principles propounded by Frederick Taylor, Henry Ford, and Max Weber. The name "socio-technical" comes from two propositions. First, every system of production is composed of two interdependent subsystems—a technical system (the technology and equipment) and a social system (the relations of people to the job and each other). Second, for maximum organizational performance, the two subsystems must be designed jointly to achieve the best possible "fit." (Cherns and Davis, 1975).

In the traditional approach, engineers use the laws of mathematics and the physical sciences to design the most efficient technical system of production, and people are fit into it with little regard for their psychological and social needs. The outcome is a fine division of labor and the command and control method of management and the host of behavioral problems that go with the techno-bureaucratic model. These problems, such as absenteeism and lack of attention to detail, adversely affect the performance of the production system. This causes management to further automate production, tighten discipline and other control mechanisms, or invest in various Band-Aid solutions, such as human relations training for supervisors or job rotation for shop-floor workers. Trist proposed that, instead, engineers work with behavioral scientists to design a production system in which technology is rearranged in ways that at first may appear less efficient but ultimately provides a productivity edge through positive effects on employee job satisfaction, learning, and control over day-to-day operations.

By the late 1960s, STJD had been instituted in a half-dozen plants and mills in Scandinavia and North America (Walton, 1975; Trist, 1981). One of the first STJD projects in America—one that received widespread publicity at the time—was a General Foods dog-food plant in Topeka, Kansas (see Ketchum, 1975). The Proctor and Gamble Company also had pioneered participative management principles at several of its plants, including a paper-converting plant in Mahoopanie, Pennsylvania. From these early experiments, an STJD "model" slowly evolved that served as the basis for the work system at the Mead mill at Stevenson. The most important of these principles are (Walton, 1974; Naidler and Gerstein, 1992):

1. *Self-managing work teams.* Division of labor into a one person–one job system is de-emphasized in favor of groups that take collective responsibility for performance of interdependent tasks.
2. *Whole tasks.* Jobs are enlarged to give each worker wider and more complex tasks, and the group is given control over those parts of the production process that directly affect their collective performance.
3. *Flexibility in work assignments.* Flexibility in work assignments among team members is promoted by a variety of devices, such as temporary reassignment from one position to another to cover for absences or vacations, taking on broader tasks in order to accommodate a change in staffing levels, movement through task clusters of ascending skill or difficulty, and periodic rotation to different jobs.
4. *Supervision.* Supervisors delegate to the teams many of their traditional functions of motivating, coordinating, and controlling. Some first-line supervisors and middle managers are made redundant, al-

lowing a reduction in head count. Those who remain shift roles and provide technical support and training to the teams, manage coordination among key "boundaries" in the production system, and work with internal and external customers.

5. *Information systems.* Information is distributed widely and made easily available to production employees on variables affecting their team operation and the plantwide production system. Periodic meetings and internal communications update employees on plant performance levels, the company's financial performance, and competitive conditions in the industry. Meeting rooms and breakout areas adjacent to the shop floor are included to facilitate team meetings and training sessions.
6. *Reward systems.* Compensation systems are changed to an all-salaried workforce. A pay-for-knowledge system is added, with workers earning additional pay for mastering new skills or tasks. Some type of gain-sharing system linked to the plant's productivity and/or financial performance also is common.
7. *Symbols of status and trust.* The status of production workers is enhanced, and status differentials between managers and workers are reduced. Management communicates trust that workers will responsibly exercise self-regulation. Examples include the elimination of time clocks, an open parking lot, and a common entrance for both managers and production employees.
8. *Training and recruitment.* Much greater expenditures are made on training of both production workers and managers. A significant share of the training is on social and problem-solving skills, such as understanding individual differences, group dynamics, and conflict resolution. Greater attention also is paid to the screening and selection of new employees in order to assure a good fit between the person and the work culture.

Implementation at Stevenson

Preliminary engineering work already had begun on the Stevenson mill when CEO McSwiney gave the go-ahead in 1973 to try a STJD system. Louis Davis was hired as an external consultant to the design team, while Cleveland and Murdoch headed the internal team of Mead people. In an unusual decision, several managers from operations and staff were added to the design team, including the mill's industrial relations manager, Gary

Peters. In other mill projects, the design work was the sole province of the production and engineering departments.

The Stevenson mill featured all eight principles (described above) of an STJD system. Other paper companies during the 1960s also had experimented with many of these principles, so teams, pay-for-knowledge, and enlarged tasks were not concepts new to the industry. Rather, the Stevenson mill was unique in that all eight principles were adopted as a package, and the mill was designed from a total systems perspective.

The practical significance of converting the mill from a traditional to nontraditional design can be illustrated by three examples. The first is the location of a hydro-pulper, which is a large machine that converts corrugated waste paper to pulp. The engineering company had located the machine in the shipping and receiving department, since the machine input (used newspapers) comes to the mill in rail cars that normally would be unloaded there. The socio-technical design team moved it to the pulping department, even though the rail siding had to be lengthened and the power plant moved. The reasoning was that, if each team is to be given responsibility for meeting the quality, on-time, and volume targets, the team needs control over the "variances" affecting these targets. Could the pulp team be held accountable for the quality of the pulp if a portion of it was produced and delivered by another unit of the mill? The answer was that they couldn't, so the change was made, albeit at considerable expense.

A second example is the redesign of the internal layout of the mill so that teams had access to an adjacent air-conditioned meeting room. In traditional mills, the team would have had to meet in a cafeteria or room in the management office complex. Likewise, the goal of sharing information was promoted by constructing air-conditioned control rooms on the production floor, where every team member could monitor not only key operating statistics in that department but the entire production process from beginning to end. Each team was empowered to stop the production process without first asking a supervisor.

Third, in an effort to reduce status differentials, the design team at Stevenson shifted the position of the management office building from a stand-alone location to one adjoining the mill. The team also successfully lobbied Mead corporate headquarters to be allowed to shift to an all-salaried workforce and provide a uniform benefits package for both production and management employees. No other mill in the Mead system had these features.

The implementation of a STJD system at Stevenson broke considerable new ground. As with any path-breaking project, numerous pitfalls and conflicts were encountered. The decision to try a STJD system at Stevenson was far from unanimous or popular within the company. Indeed, many felt that, had Garner not provided an umbrella of protection and support for the Stevenson project, it never would have gotten past the talking stage. Also crucial was the support of CEO James McSwiney, who approved the project despite personal reservations about some aspects of a STJD system (e.g., an all-salaried workforce). Other persons and groups in the company overtly opposed the Stevenson project. Executives in the company's corporate industrial relations group, for example, worried that Stevenson would disrupt union-management relations at other organized mills, particularly after the company, as we shall see, decided to oppose the union's organizing drive. Other executives thought that trying STJD was a high-risk gamble on a social-science experiment, using over one hundred million dollars of company money. Yet others were opposed on the pragmatic grounds that participative management, while fine in theory, would not work or would prove vastly inefficient. Others objected that sound business policy requires management to retain ultimate authority over the control and coordination of work. Whatever the reason, a number of Mead executives and managers were either lukewarm or openly opposed to the Stevenson project. Given McSwiney's approval, they could not stop it, but they impeded its extension to other parts of the company.

Stevenson remains the last new primary mill built by Mead. To this day, the Stevenson facility is "one of a kind" among the primary mills of the Mead Corporation, although an STJD system has been implemented in a number of smaller, converting plants. While management resistance slowed the spread of STJD, more important has been the fact that "retrofitting" existing, older mills to incorporate the technical and social changes for STJD is a difficult and lengthy process.

Another pitfall was that mill management had a more difficult time adjusting to a STJD system than anticipated. Since Stevenson was the first paper mill in the country to try STJD, the company had no mill managers experienced in participative management. In what later was recognized as a mistake, too much social-skills training was focused on the blue-collar workers and not enough on middle and upper managers. The new plant manager and staff were transferred from traditionally operated mills, given only modest training in STJD principles, and then told to manage participatively. Several could not or would not and had to be replaced. The turnover of mill managers created additional turbulence and contributed to employee morale problems.

The startup of the STJD system at Stevenson led to conflict between the company and the United Paperworkers International Union (UPIU). By all accounts, union avoidance was not the initial impetus for trying an STJD system at Stevenson. Four union leaders attended the "Insights into Productivity" conference and, according to the UPIU newspaper, the *Paperworker* (10/72:9), union president John Tonelli "committed himself to cooperate and work with the corporation" on implementing STJD. During the construction phase of the mill, Mead management met periodically with UPIU officials to keep them abreast of the project, and on at least one occasion they were given a tour of the facility. The company also continued the practice of staffing the facility with a significant number of union members from other mills, rather than hiring and training a new work force, as other companies were later to do.

The spirit of labor-management cooperation started to fray shortly after the mill's startup, however. While Tonelli supported STJD, other UPIU officials closer to the field were either opposed or skeptical. Like many of their management counterparts at Mead, they harbored serious doubts that STJD would work and that they would benefit from it. Union officials were afraid that STJD, stripped of its jargon, amounted to a traditional "speed-up," in which employees work harder and do more job tasks for the same pay. And, while a selling point of STJD to the company was greater flexibility in shifting employees among jobs, to union leaders the notion of "flexibility" was loaded with negative connotations. The union had spent years bargaining for contract language that limited management's ability unilaterally to shift workers among jobs, and STJD threatened to undermine these gains. Finally, they worried that participative management was a company strategy to weaken the loyalty of the workers to the union and dilute the power and position of local union leadership.

These fears seemed to gain substance when some workers began to complain about the new STJD system. Every mill startup has glitches, and this was doubly true at Stevenson. Some of the problems had nothing to do with STJD (e.g., technical problems in the power generation facility), but others did. For example, to promote multiskilling and work-assignment flexibility, the designers had eliminated seniority as the criterion governing movement up the line of progression on a paper machine and other such work units. A number of employees felt that the company had gone too far and wanted seniority still to regulate upward movement at certain key points on the job ladder.

Likewise, a major goal of the company was to improve integration of the maintenance function into operations. In a traditional mill, maintenance workers such as electricians, pipefitters, and millwrights have strict and narrowly defined job classifications. They operate out of a central maintenance center and have their own managers. This arrangement can be extremely time-consuming and rigid. For example, a machine breakdown necessitates working through the chain of command and summoning employees from the various maintenance crafts from different parts of the mill (or from home). The maintenance workers will not start the repairs until all have arrived, and each person will perform only the specific work covered in his job classification. In the original STJD system, narrow job classifications were eliminated in favor of multiskilling; in addition, some maintenance workers were transferred permanently to a specific operating department (a similar system is described in detail in Lorenz, 1993). All this also caused employee dissatisfaction.

The combination of initial skepticism and a growing number of complaints from employees caused the regional union leadership to shift course and adopt a hostile posture toward the STJD system at Stevenson. In their organizing campaign at the mill, they promised that the union's bargaining goal would be to restore a traditional contract. Only when faced with union opposition to STJD did the company actively oppose organization of the mill. Two representation elections were held, and the union lost both, although in one case only by eight votes.

While the company employed a union avoidance consultant during one of the union campaigns, the reasons for the union's defeat seem to lie elsewhere. The view of people on the management side is that the union fundamentally misread the situation, believing that widespread dissatisfaction with the new work system existed when in fact most employees favored it. From the perspective of the union organizers at the scene, the union eventually would have won if the Stevenson campaign been given a higher priority and more resources. The UPIU, however, had just been formed from a merger of the Pulp and Sulphite union with the United Papermakers and Paperworkers (itself a merger in the late 1950s of the IBPM and the UPA) and was still in a state of organizational flux. In addition, some union officials felt that other projects had higher priority. Also important was the decision of the company to form a second design team, openly solicit employee input on the sources of dissatisfaction with the STJD system, and then implement modifications. A final and very important consideration was that the decentralized bargaining structure in the paper industry and a strong tradition of local union autonomy prevented the UPIU from bringing enough pressure to bear at Mead's other organized mills to cause the company to abandon its opposition to the union at Stevenson.

STJD and Union Avoidance: From Serendipity to Strategy

The developments at the Mead-Stevenson mill did not go unnoticed in the rest of the paper industry. After the mill's startup problems were solved, it quickly became a world leader in its class in terms of productivity and cost. In addition, an alluring byproduct was that the workforce twice voted down union representation. Suddenly new options were available for strategic thinkers.

Soon other STJD mill projects were initiated. A new nontraditional paper mill built by Virginia Fiber was one of the first to follow Mead-Stevenson. It was followed by over a dozen others, including state-of-the-art integrated mills constructed by Union Camp, Weyerhauser, and International Paper.

People involved in the Mead-Stevenson project became "Johnny Appleseeds" spreading STJD to other new mills. The most important figure in this regard was Jack Murdoch. Murdoch, Cleveland, and Peters all left Mead in the latter part of the 1970s, partly out of frustration over the resistance encountered within the company to further STJD projects. Murdoch became a consultant and helped design eight other STJD paper mills, while Peters helped install a socio-technical production system at a new newsprint recycling mill in Dublin, Georgia (see Rooks, 1990). All of these facilities have remained nonunion.

According to industry observers, while the STJD project at Mead-Stevenson was not done for union avoidance, a number of companies soon afterward made a strategic decision to pursue the nonunion option in new mills. This decision was not taken lightly, nor at the time was it obviously the best choice. Since nearly all major-sized paper companies were thoroughly organized, the benefits from pushing a nonunion strategy at new mills had to be weighed carefully against the costs of strained and possibly even bitter labor relations with the UPIU at the other mills. Some might not have taken the nonunion route in earlier years, but a combination of events and developments in the late 1970s and early 1980s pushed the companies to take an increasingly confrontational position with the unions in organized mills and to pursue a more explicit, deliberate union-avoidance strategy in unorganized mills.

The driving force behind the companies' "get tough" policy was the need to rein in costs and boost profitability (Birecree, 1993). The industry had turned in only a mediocre profit performance in the 1960s and 1970s. During the ten-year period of 1970–79, for example, in only two years did paper companies earn a return on net worth that exceeded the average of all manufacturing firms.

The squeeze on profitability came from both revenue and cost sides. On the revenue side, companies had to contend with greater international competition, two bouts of wage-price controls, and a macroeconomic environment of stagflation. More threatening to profits were developments on the cost side. By the end of the 1970s, concern was growing that the paper companies' cost structure was becoming increasingly top-heavy and noncompetitive. The pressure on costs came from a variety of sources. Productivity growth, for example, slowed as 40 percent of capital spending was devoted to pollution abatement and environmental protection. Interest rates and the cost of capital also skyrocketed during the late 1970s, reaching the point at which new mill construction often was judged uneconomic (Arpan, et. al., 1986). Top company executives were also experiencing increased pressure from financial markets to cut costs if they wanted to keep their companies independent and avoid hostile takeovers and leveraged buyouts. Finally, in the early to mid-1980s, the dollar appreciated more than 50 percent against foreign currencies, making American pulp and paper exports noncompetitive in foreign markets, while imports from Scandinavia and South America surged.

Interest rates, the exchange rate of the dollar, and environmental regulations fall largely outside the control of individual paper companies. They do have some leverage over one type of cost, however, and that is labor cost. And labor cost during the 1970s and early 1980s grew at an unprecedented rate. The ratio of average hourly earnings in paper mills to average hourly earnings in the private nonagricultural economy stood at 1.16 in 1960, increased slightly to 1.18 in 1970, but then shot upward to 1.35 in 1980 and peaked at 1.56 in 1986. The dramatic increase in wages largely was won at the bargaining table, with a typical three-year agreement in the late 1970s calling for an annual wage increase of 9, 8, and 7 percent (with substantial improvements in benefits on top of that). The companies usually acquiesced to the union's demands. Double-digit inflation in the national economy made it difficult to negotiate wage restraint. Moreover, in addition to wanting to avoid crippling strikes, they could count on passing higher labor costs along to end users. Wage growth in other U.S. manufacturing industries slowed considerably in the early 1980s, due to two back-to-back recessions and widespread union contract concessions, but business conditions in the paper industry remained more buoyant, and wages continued their rapid advance. Only a severe cyclical downswing in the industry in the mid-1980s brought wage growth to an abrupt halt.

While direct labor cost became a matter of growing concern to paper companies and a source of conflict in collective bargaining, restrictive work rules and other productivity impediments ranked even higher as an irritant within the industry. Over the years the unions had negotiated a myriad of work rules that restricted the companies' flexibility in using labor or forced them to pay extra compensation for particular tasks or jobs. For example, rules prevented one type of craft maintenance person from doing the work of another craft. Other rules prevented shifting workers among jobs to fill in for a person sick or absent and instead required that an off-duty employee be called in and paid an overtime rate. There were restrictions on subcontracting construction work. Premium pay had to be awarded for all hours worked on Sunday. A minimum of, say, six hours at overtime rates had to be paid for changing the wires on a paper machine, even if the actual work was completed in considerably less time. Overtime also had to be paid for hours worked in excess of eight per day.

Many of these rules had some legitimate rationale or justification when originally negotiated but, from the companies' perspective, had become either obsolete or excessively liberal by the 1970s. The success of STJD at Mead-Stevenson thus occurred at a time when the industry was coming under greater competitive pressure and was searching for ways to boost profit margins and control costs. This constellation of environmental forces, rather than a staunch antiunion attitude on the part of management, caused most paper companies to adopt a much firmer labor-relations strategy vis-à-vis their unions.

This strategy was played out on two fronts. One was in new greenfield paper mills, where STJD principles were incorporated both to realize productivity and quality gains, and to keep the workforce nonunion. Implementation of this strategy was constrained significantly, however, by the modest number of new mills that could be put in place, due to huge capital costs, scarcity of available sites and accessible timber reserves, and increasingly onerous environmental regulations. Indeed, by the mid-1990s, construction of new integrated paper mills virtually had come to a halt.

Given the limited opportunities that existed to play the nonunion card, most paper companies pursued productivity gains and cost relief through a second strategic route (Eaton and Kriesky, 1994; Walton, Cutcher-Gershenfeld, and McKersie, 1994). This was at the bargaining table, where they demanded extensive concessions, took strikes, and permanently replaced workers. A minority of paper companies, such as Scott and James River, sought concessions through cooperative programs with the UPIU. Wage relief, work-rule relief, or implementation of a STJD system usually involved a *quid pro quo* on the company's part, such as a promise to protect bargaining-unit jobs and form companywide joint labor-management committees. Most other paper companies took a more confrontational approach. Champion, for example, tried a mixed strategy of confrontation and cooperation, while Georgia-Pacific adopted a relatively adversarial, get-tough strategy. The first major use of "hard bargaining" occurred in 1978–79 and led to numerous strikes in the Pacific Northwest. For the first time, a number of mills were kept open with supervisors and temporary workers. Then, in the early 1980s, several companies went the next step and permanently replaced striking workers. This strategy reached its most adversarial point in 1987, with a series of strikes and lockouts at the International Paper Company. The company brought in permanent striker replacements at mills at Jay, Maine; DePere, Wisconsin; and Lockhaven, Pennsylvania. After a bitter struggle, the strikes were settled largely on the company's terms, and the union locals were decertified. (Getman and Marshall, 1993; Birecree, 1993; Eaton and Kriesky, 1994).

After this episode, and having won many of the contract concessions they had set out in the late 1970s to obtain, most paper companies in the 1990s sought to put their relations with their UPIU on a more cooperative and constructive basis (see Walton, Cutcher-Gershenfeld, and McKersie, 1994). Part of management's motivation was to accelerate the adoption of STJD work systems in unionized mills, a goal perceived as requiring union support and collaboration if it was to be successful. Progress has been uneven, however, as some local unions have embraced cooperation and implementation of STJD work design principles, while others have stayed with the adversarial bargaining approach and traditional labor contract. The commitment of companies to STJD also has varied, partly because some companies fear that eliminating supervisors and middle management will leave the mills more vulnerable to shutdown during a strike. Where local unions and companies have embraced STJD, the evidence is that these mills can be as productive as, and in some cases more productive than, their nonunion counterparts. In the mills that have adopted a STJD system, according to local union leaders, the workers report higher job satisfaction.

Conclusion

Until the mid-1970s, the primary sector of the southern paper industry was almost completely unionized. Since then, a small but growing nonunion sector has emerged. The birthplace of the nonunion sector in the paper industry is Stevenson, Alabama, where a new paperboard mill owned by the Mead Corporation began operation in January 1975. The mill was the first in a continuous-process industry in the United States to incorporate a nontraditional or "socio-technical" work system. This system not only yielded substantially higher productivity and lower costs than traditionally designed mills, but also significantly reduced employees' desire for union representation. Although union avoidance was not a strategic goal of the Mead Corporation when the mill was built, the mounting pressure on paper companies to curb labor costs and boost profit margins in the late 1970s to early 1980s caused many of them to rethink their traditionally accommodative relationship with the United Paperworkers International Union. Part of this rethinking involved a strategic choice to try to keep new, greenfield paper mills nonunion through use of the type of nontraditional work system pioneered at Mead-Stevenson. This approach proved extremely successful, as the union has not organized a single new primary paper mill in the southern United States in the last twenty years.

Several lessons and implications can be gleaned from this study. Among the most important are the following.

First, some researchers (e.g., Kochan, Katz, and McKersie, 1986) have argued that American management has a relatively strong antipathy to unions and that this value structure is an important causative factor in the growth of a nonunion sector in American industry. This argument may be true as a generalization but the evidence does not provide strong support for it in the specific case of the southern paper industry. The industry was completely organized in the late 1930s to early 1940s with little violence or even overt management opposition. For several decades, collective bargaining proceeded with relatively few strikes, and new mills routinely were brought into the union fold. Certainly the paper companies did not initially welcome collective bargaining, frequently found specific union demands or behaviors unreasonable, and on occasion wished they were free of collective bargaining. These caveats notwithstanding, up to the mid-1970s the companies largely accepted unions in their mills as a matter of principle, believed that collective bargaining had a legitimate place in the industrial relations system, and tried to work with the unions on a "live-and-let-live" basis. This accommodative relationship has frayed noticeably since then, but the primary initiating cause is environmental change rather than management's hostility to unions per se.

Second, after the mid-1970s, the paper companies experienced a growing squeeze on profitability and greater pressure by financial markets for higher returns on capital. These trends motivated the companies deliberately to practice union avoidance in new mills and to adopt a more adversarial approach to collective bargaining in previously organized mills. Cost pressures intensified greatly in the 1970s and 1980s, due to a slowdown in productivity growth, substantial capital outlays for environmental protection, double-digit interest rates, a 50-percent appreciation of the dollar relative to foreign currencies, and growth in labor cost that gradually ratcheted upwards until it reached 10 percent or more a year. Among these cost pressures, paper companies had most leverage in terms of labor cost, and their attempts to rein in labor costs drove them to practice union avoidance and concessionary bargaining.

Third, the major union in the industry, the United Paperworkers International Union, experienced a noticeable decline in its membership and bargaining power in the paper industry during the 1980s, from which it has not yet recovered. Part of the blame rests with the union for pushing labor costs up too far in the 1970s and early 1980s, for resisting modifications in productivity-blocking work rules and work practices, and for foot-dragging on implementation of high-performance work systems. Although these failings are easy to spot in hindsight, it is difficult for a union to sell its members on the virtues of wage moderation or work-rule concessions absent an obvious, serious threat to their jobs. Unions also are unlikely enthusiastically to accept a new management program when that program has the potential to undercut the union's power base or lead to more work at lower pay for its members. The union's membership and bargaining power also were diminished by greater company resistance, in the form of striker replacement and union avoidance programs at nonunion mills; by improvements in worker job satisfaction in nonunion conditions, due to less onerous working conditions; by more enlightened and sophisticated management; by the introduction of self-managed teams and other nontraditional work practices; and by a more competitive economic environment that forced companies to downsize and cut costs.

Fourth, although hardly a panacea for all labor problems, socio-technical work design principles have delivered significantly higher productivity, quality, and flexibility in pulp and paper production. At the same time, they have led to substantial gains in employee job satisfaction and quality of work life. These new systems, however, are expensive to implement, often arouse substantial resistance from managers and first-line supervisors, and are relatively easy to damage (Walton, 1975). Substantial investment is required to train managers and production workers in higher-level technical and social skills, and additional costs are incurred to avoid layoffs during slow business periods. Opposition occurs because STJD redistributes power and control in the workplace from the people who have it (middle and upper management and local union leaders) to those who do not (shop floor employees). The systems are fragile because their success depends upon trust and shared control, which can easily be disrupted by financial pressures and economic downturns that force cost cutting and layoffs; the turnover of committed managers and union leaders and their replacement by new people who have different philosophies and agendas; and the tendency of mill managers and supervisors to revert back to more hierarchical, command-and-control methods without continuous reinforcement and support from top executives.

Fifth, the introduction and spread of socio-technical job design in the paper industry well illustrates the significant influence of the behavioral sciences (e.g., industrial psychology and sociology) on the theory and practice of management in the post–World War II period. It also highlights the contributions of academics and consultants in disseminating these new ideas to industry.

Sixth, trade unionism's position in the southern paper industry has both positive and negative aspects. On the positive side, the UPIU is in a relatively strong and secure position, because three-quarters of paper mill workers remain organized, companies are reinvesting large amounts of capital into expansion and renovation of unionized facilities, the growth of a rival nonunion sector is stymied by the almost complete cessation of new mill construction, and companies generally are reluctant to destabilize or decertify existing unions. On the negative side, the union has not successfully organized a major new pulp or paper mill in twenty years. Part of the reason for the union's dismal organizing record is that the paper companies have become more successful at the practice of union avoidance. Some companies run very aggressive anti-union campaigns with paid consultants and attorneys and use a mix of traditional hardball tactics (e.g., dismissal of union activists) and new, more sophisticated methods (e.g., slick anti-union videos) to discourage union support among the work force. Equally effective and widely used are "softer" methods of union avoidance, such as the weeding out of union sympathizers through elaborate screening procedures during the hiring process and paying union-like wages and benefits. Important as these tactics may be, they nevertheless rank as a secondary cause of the union's inability to organize new mills. The more important factor is that workers' demand for union services has substantially declined in recent years. Contributing factors are the cultural changes in the wider society that undercut worker support and sympathy for unions, increased employee job satisfaction due to improved conditions of work and more enlightened management practices, and the greater protection provided workers through government legislation in areas such as equal opportunity, safety, and pensions. Taken together, it must be concluded, the services provided by the union are no longer strongly demanded by the bulk of its prospective "customers." Thus, absent significant innovation on the union's part, or a major economic or social upheaval, the future for unionism in the paper industry is one of gradual decline, as productivity growth, foreign competition, and establishment of a modest number of new nonunion mills slowly eat away at the union's membership base and at its bargaining power.

Seventh, the union's long-range decline can be challenged by a new, proactive strategy. It may not succeed, but the alternative is not very attractive. The union's strategy shifts from primary focus on income redistribution and job control to emphasis on shared wealth creation and enhanced quality of work life (Heckscher, 1988). It also finds and uses forms of power and leverage that are less destructive to the economic viability of the organization and the culture of shared control and trust that are crucial to high-performance work systems. Socio-technical work systems in nonunion settings are characterized by an innate imbalance of power that favors the company's interests over individual workers' interests. Companies recognize this and try to build in mechanisms (e.g., heavy doses of management training and development, alternative dispute-resolution systems) that restrain or prevent the undesirable behaviors that result from unbalanced power, such as unilateral decision making, greater financial and status rewards for management, and inconsistent application of discipline and discharge. Since self-regulation, like every form of voluntary restraint, is difficult to maintain over time, a union can serve as a positive, value-adding agency to the extent that it balances power and uses this power to promote programs and practices that make high-performance work systems more successful (e.g., effective dispute resolution, continuous investment in training). Conflict is inevitable, and the union occasionally must exercise its power to protect workers' rights and keep the system in equilibrium, but it could do so in ways that are more positive than the traditional weapons of striking and working to rule. The problem is that some managements will prefer to remain nonunion, even if a union is good for the long-range financial health of their organizations. Also, it is an open question whether unions can muster the leadership and organizational restraint necessary to pursue a strategy of shared value creation rather than income redistribution. Without such a focus, however, unions are left with little in the way of tangible benefits to offer either unorganized paper workers or the paper companies, at least given the current economic and social environment.

Possibly the future lies with some type of new enterprise-based employee organization (e.g., European-style work councils) that can balance power in a less adversarial way than the traditional union. This option remains highly uncertain; thus, "more of the same" seems like the safest bet for the future course of labor relations in southern pulp and paper. The bottom line in this scenario is continued modest decline in union membership and power, and concomitant growth in the size of the nonunion workforce.

Note

Much of the material for this study was gained from a series of thirty-two personal interviews with people knowledgeable of the southern paper industry, including senior management at six companies, national and local union leaders, labor attorneys, consultants, and employer association representatives. Their cooperation is greatly appreciated. The invaluable assistance of Richard Klinzing and Marvin Waters is also gratefully acknowledged, as are the helpful suggestions of Robert McKersie and Adrienne Eaton.

References

Arpan, Jeffrey, Alan Bauerschmidt, J. Carl Clamp, Gregory Dess, Kate Gillespie, Daniel Sullivan, and J. Frederick Truitt. *The United States Pulp and Paper Industry: Global Challenges and Strategies.* Columbia: University of South Carolina Press, 1986.

Birecree, Adrienne. "Corporate Development, Structural Change and Strategic Choice: Bargaining at International Paper Company in the 1980s." *Industrial Relations* 32 (Winter 1993): 343–66.

Carr, William. *Up Another Notch: Institution Building at Mead.* New York: McGraw-Hill, 1989.

Cherns, Albert, and Louis Davis. "The State of the Art." In *The Quality of Working Life,* ed. Louis Davis and Albert Cherns, 1:12–54. New York: Free Press, 1972.

Davis, Louis. "The Design of Jobs." *Industrial Relations* 6 (Feb. 1966): 21–45.

Davis, Louis, and James Taylor, eds. *Design of Jobs: Selected Readings.* New York: Penguin, 1972.

Eaton, Adrienne, and Jill Kriesky. "Collective Bargaining in the Paper Industry: Developments Since 1979." In *Contemporary Collective Bargaining in the Private Sector,* ed. Paula Voos, 25–62. Madison, Wisc.: Industrial Relations Research Association, 1994.

Emery, Frederick. *The Emergence of a New Paradigm of Work.* Canberra, Australia: Australian National University, 1978.

Foulkes, Fred. *Personnel Policies in Large Non-Union Companies.* Englewood Cliffs, N.J.: Prentice-Hall, 1980.

Freeman, Richard, and James Medoff. "New Estimates of Private Sector Unionism in the United States." *Industrial and Labor Relations Review* 32 (Jan. 1979): 143–74.

Friedman, Sheldon, Richard Hurd, Rudolph Oswald, and Ronald Seeber, eds. *Restoring the Promise of American Labor Law.* Ithaca, N.Y.: ILR Press, 1994.

Getman, Julius, and F. Ray Marshall. "Industrial Relations in Transition: The Paper Industry Example." *Yale Law Review* 102 (June 1993): 1804–95.

Guthrie, John. *The Economics of Pulp and Paper.* Pullman, Wash.: State College of Washington Press, 1950.

Heckscher, Charles. *The New Unionism: Employee Involvement in the Changing Corporation.* New York, N.Y.: Basic Books, 1988.

Hirsch, Barry, and David MacPherson. *Union Membership and Earnings Data Book—1994.* Washington, D.C.: Bureau of National Affairs, 1995.

Kaufman, Bruce. "Why the Wagner Act?: Reestablishing Contact with Its Original Purpose." In *Advances in Industrial and Labor Relations,* vol. 7, ed. David

Lewin, Bruce Kaufman, and Donna Sockell, 15–68. Greenwich, Conn.: JAI Press, 1996.

Ketchum, Lyman. "A Case Study of Diffusion." In *The Quality of Working Life,* ed. Louis Davis and Albert Cherns, 2:138–65. New York: Free Press, 1975.

Kochan, Thomas, Harry Katz, and Robert McKersie. *The Transformation of American Industrial Relations.* New York: Basic Books, 1986.

Kokkelenberg, Edward, and Donna Sockell. "Union Membership in the United States, 1973–1981." *Industrial and Labor Relations Review* 38 (July 1985): 497–543.

Lawler, John. *Unionization and Deunionization.* Columbia: University of South Carolina Press, 1990.

Levinson, Harold. *Determining Forces in Collective Wage Bargaining.* New York: John Wiley and Sons, 1966.

Lockwood-Post's Directory of Pulp, Paper, and Allied Trades. San Francisco, Calif.: Miller-Freeman, 1995.

Lorenz, Randy. "Team Concept and Multi-Craft Trade Skills at Quinnesec." In *Proceedings of the 74th Annual Meeting of the Paper Industry Management Association,* 45–48. Arlington Heights, Ill.: PIMA, 1993.

Macdonald, Robert. "Pulp and Paper." In *The Evolution of Wage Structure,* ed. Lloyd Reynolds and Cynthia Taft, 99–166. New Haven, Conn.: Yale University Press, 1956.

Matics, Robert. "Georgia: Top International Producer in U.S. Papermaking." *Paper Trade Journal* (July 30, 1982): 35–48.

Naidler, David, and Marc Gerstein. "Designing High-Performance Work Systems: Organization, People, Work, Technology, and Information." In *Organizational Architecture,* ed. David Laidler, Marc Gerstein, and Robert Shaw, 110–32. San Francisco, Calif.: Josey-Bass, 1992.

Northrup, Herbert. *The Negro in the Paper Industry.* Philadelphia: Industrial Research Unit, University of Pennsylvania, 1969.

Ohanian, Nancy. *The American Pulp and Paper Industry, 1900–1940.* Westport, Conn.: Greenwood Press, 1993.

Rooks, Alan. "Great Timing, Training Power Southeast Paper Expansion." *PIMA Magazine* (July 1990): 36–40.

Smith, David. *The History of Papermaking in the United States (1691–1969).* New York: Lockwood Trade Journal Co., 1971.

Strauss, George. "Workers: Attitudes and Adjustments." In *The Worker and the Job: Coping with Change,* ed. Jerome Rosow, 73–98. New York: American Assembly, 1974.

Trist, Eric. *The Evolution of Socio-Technical Systems.* Occasional Paper No. 2. Toronto, Ont., Canada: Ontario Quality of Working Life Centre, 1981.

U.S. Department of Labor. Bureau of Labor Statistics. *Industry Wage Survey: Pulp, Paper, and Paperboard Mills, November 1972.* Bulletin 1844. Washington, D.C.: Government Printing Office, 1975.

Verma, Anil, and Thomas Kochan. "The Growth and Nature of the Nonunion Sector within a Firm." In *Challenges and Choices Facing American Labor,* ed. Thomas Kochan, 89–117. Cambridge, Mass.: MIT Press, 1985.

Walton, Richard. "Explaining Why Success Didn't Take." *Organizational Dynamics* 3 (Winter 1975): 3–22.

———. "Innovative Restructuring of Work." In *The Worker and the Job: Coping with Change,* ed. Jerome Rosow, 145–76. New York: American Assembly, 1974.

Walton, Richard, Joel Cutcher-Gershenfeld, and Robert McKersie. *Strategic Negotiations.* Boston, Mass.: Harvard Business School Press, 1994.

Zieger, Robert. *Rebuilding the Pulp and Paper Workers Union, 1933–1941.* Knoxville: University of Tennessee Press, 1984.

Bibliographical Note

The introductions to this volume and its predecessor volume outline key historiographical and institutional developments in southern labor history. In addition, they provide a broad sampling of relevant citations. The citations in the essays in that book and in this one—especially the early notes in most of the chapters—provide a guide to the relevant scholarship.

Since the publication of Ray Marshall's *Labor in the South* (1967), there has been no comprehensive history of southern workers and unions. In view of the fact that Marshall's still-useful book was based on material gathered in the 1950s, such a work is long overdue. Reflective of the tradition of labor historiography associated with institutional labor economics, *Labor in the South* is strong in its treatment of economic context and trade union activity. It was written, however, before the revolution in labor historiography that has transformed the field by virtue of its focus on the community, familial, and sociocultural dimensions of working-class life. Moreover, we have seen almost four decades of labor history since Marshall collected the material upon which *Labor in the South* rests.

While there is no comprehensive work to supplant Marshall, historians hardly have been inactive, as the bibliographical material in these two volumes clearly testifies. It is notable that, in recent years, several studies of southern labor have earned major scholarly prizes. Thus, Jacquelyn Dowd Hall et al., *Like a Family: The Making of a Southern Cotton Mill World* (1987; Taft Prize, 1988); Robin D. G. Kelley, *Hammer and Hoe: Alabama Communists during the Great Depression* (1990; Sydnor

Prize, 1991); Douglas Flamming, *Creating the Modern South: Millhands and Managers in Dalton, Georgia, 1884–1984* (1992; Taft Prize, 1993); Michael K. Honey, *Southern Labor and Black Civil Rights: Organizing Memphis Workers* (1993; Sydnor Prize, 1994, Rawlins Prize, 1994); and Emilio Zamora, *The World of the Mexican Worker in Texas* (1993; Mitchell Prize, 1994) testify to the coming of age of southern labor history.

If there is no single volume dealing comprehensively with southern workers, there is a richness of collected articles and conference papers. Important in this connection are the following: *Essays in Southern Labor History: Selected Papers, Southern Labor Conference, 1976* (1977), edited by Gary M. Fink and Merl E. Reed; *Southern Workers and Their Unions, 1880–1975* (1978), edited by Gary M. Fink and Merl E. Reed; *Race, Class, and Community in Southern Labor History* (1994), edited by Gary M. Fink and Merl E. Reed; *Hanging by a Thread: Social Change in Southern Textiles* (1991), edited by Jeffrey Leiter, Michael D. Schulman, and Rhonda Zingraff; and *Race and Class in the American South since 1890* (1994), edited by Melvyn Stokes and Rick Halpern; in addition to *Organized Labor in the Twentieth-Century South* (1991), edited by Robert H. Zieger.

Moreover, major scholarly journals have been devoting regular attention to southern labor history. Essays in recent years by Eric Arnesen; Alan Draper; Larry Griffin and Robert Korstad; Jacquelyn Hall; Jacquelyn Hall, Robert Korstad, and James Leloudis; Robin D. G. Kelley; Robert Korstad and Nelson Lichtenstein; Daniel Letwin; Bruce Nelson; Robert J. Norrell; and others have been featured in recent issues of the *American Historical Review*, the *Journal of American History, Social Science History, Labor History, International Labor and Working-Class History*, and other journals. Full citations to most of this work can be found in the introduction to this book.

Contributors

Cindy Hahamovitch is an assistant professor of history at the College of William and Mary in Willamsburg, Virginia. She is the author of *The Fruits of Their Labor: Atlantic Coast Migrant Workers and the Making of Migrant Poverty, 1870–1945* (1997).

Rick Halpern is lecturer in American history at University College London. He is the author of *Down on the Killing Floor: Black and White Workers in Chicago's Packinghouses, 1904–1954* (1997) and co-author (with Roger Horowitz) of *Meatpackers: An Oral History of Black Packinghouse Workers and Their Struggle for Racial and Economic Equality* (1996). Currently he is working on a study of race and labor in the southern sugar industry.

James A. Hodges is Michael O. Fisher professor of history, College of Wooster. He is the author of *New Deal Labor Policy and the Southern Cotton Textile Industry, 1933–1941* (1986).

Michael Honey is associate professor of history, labor, and ethnic studies at the University of Washington, Tacoma. He is the author of *Southern Labor and Black Civil Rights: Organizing Memphis Workers* (1993).

Bruce E. Kaufman is professor of economics and senior associate of the W. T. Beebe Institute of Personnel and Employment Relations at Georgia State University. His most recent book is *The Origins and Evolution of the Field of Industrial Relations in the United States* (1993).

Alex Lichtenstein teaches American history at Florida International University in Miami. He is the author of *Twice the Work of Free Labor: The Political Economy of Convict Labor in the New South* (1996) and has written an introduction to a reprint edition of Howard Kester's *Revolt among the Sharecroppers* (1997).

Patrick J. Maney is professor of history at Tulane University. He is the author of *"Young Bob" La Follette: A Biography of Robert M. La Follette, Jr., 1895–1953* (1978) and *The Roosevelt Presence: A Biography of Franklin Delano Roosevelt* (1993).

Bruce Nelson teaches history at Dartmouth College. He is the author of *Workers on the Waterfront* (1988) and is completing a book tentatively titled "The Logic and Limits of Solidarity: Workers, Unions, and Civil Rights, 1935–1974."

James Sullivan is completing his doctoral dissertation on Benjamin Spock at Rutgers University. He holds B.A. and M.A. degrees from the University of Florida.

Jacob Vander Meulen is associate professor of history, Dalhousie University, Nova Scotia. He is the author of *The Politics of Aircraft: Building an American Military Industry* (1991) and *Building the B-29* (1995).

Mark Wilkens earned a master's degree at the University of Florida and is a Ph.D. candidate in history at the University of Pennsylvania. His dissertation, "Working for the City," is a study of municipal employees in Philadelphia and New York City.

Robert H. Zieger is professor of history, University of Florida. He edited *Organized Labor in the Twentieth-Century South* (1991) and is the author of *The CIO, 1935–1955* (1995).

Index

Southern Labor in Transition was designed and typeset on a Macintosh computer system using PageMaker software. The text is set in Stone Serif and chapter titles are set in Officina Serif Bold. This book was designed and composed by Todd Duren and was printed and bound by Thomson-Shore, Inc. The recycled paper used in this book is designed for an effective life of at least three hundred years.